Coalition Challenges in Afghanistan

Coalition Challenges
in Afghanistan

The Politics of Alliance

Edited by Gale A. Mattox and
Stephen M. Grenier

Stanford Security Studies, An Imprint of Stanford University Press
Stanford, California

Stanford University Press
Stanford, California

Printed in the United States of America on acid-free, archival-quality paper

Library of Congress Cataloging-in-Publication Data

Coalition challenges in Afghanistan : the politics of alliance / edited by Gale A. Mattox and Stephen M. Grenier.
    pages cm
    Includes bibliographical references and index.
    ISBN 978-0-8047-9444-2 (cloth : alk. paper) — ISBN 978-0-8047-9627-9 (pbk. : alk. paper)
    1. Afghan War, 2001—Participation, Foreign—Case studies.   2. Alliances—Case studies.
3. International Security Assistance Force (Afghanistan)   I. Mattox, Gale A., editor.
II. Grenier, Stephen M., editor.
   DS371.4125.C63 2015
   958.104′73—dc23

                                2015005112

ISBN 978-0-8047-9629-3 (electronic)

Typeset by Newgen in 10/14 Minion

To our spouses and children

Contents

Preface

COALITION CHALLENGES IN AFGHANISTAN: *The Politics of Alliance* is the culmination of several years of research into the conflict in Afghanistan and its impact on the countries involved. It considers particularly the role of selected countries and aspects of the conflict that are important to assessing the commitments made in Afghanistan. The volume focuses on the motivations and operations of fourteen countries and their experiences as a part of a coalition in Afghanistan from 2001 to 2014. Major contributors in terms of force deployments to the coalition are considered as well as countries contributing more modest troop numbers. Both North Atlantic Treaty Organization (NATO) member countries and nonmember/partner countries are represented. For many of the selected countries, the deployment to Afghanistan was the longest and often the most intense that the country's armed forces had endured for several generations. There were differences as well as similarities in country deployments and participation in the conflict. The volume attempts to ferret out the differences on the ground and battlefield as well as in domestic support for the participation in the conflict. The broad spectrum of countries was chosen to show the diversity among the countries in their commitment and range of experiences.

Chapter authors addressed a number of overlapping issues across countries that revealed commonalities in country approaches to the Afghanistan conflict, while other issues revealed distinct cultural and domestic political differences in countries' priorities and approaches. These differences included perception of the terrorist threat experienced by the United States and the consequent motivation to participate usually thousands of miles from the home country and often without strong or with very low domestic support. In addition, several chapter authors provide the context within which the conflict occurred, both from the perspective of the Afghan government itself and from the warlords who played a large role. The motivations and involvement of neighbors Pakistan and Russia are considered. A chapter on NATO's role in coordinating the ISAF war effort addresses the frequent charges of obsolescence before the tragic events of 9/11. Were the combined efforts over more than a decade of fifty countries engaged in Afghanistan a success for NATO?

It is the objective of the authors to leave readers with thoughts on the lessons learned that are critical for the future of Afghanistan and for the NATO alliance, ISAF coalition, and other institutions involved in the conflict. Were there divergent missions from country to country? What should be the operational capabilities of member states for future conflicts? Are there common themes across countries that can be learned? What approaches worked and where did the coalition come up short? How can the alliance configure itself to successfully undertake similar missions?

Appreciation is due to a number of institutions in this effort. We would like to thank our contributors who endured the delays and work required for such a volume and produced chapters that will be part of the important history of this long and difficult conflict. Their research, interviews, and analyses will certainly contribute to a critical understanding of the war and the coalition that fought that war. Their individual country reviews will in many cases be the first in-depth analysis of the country's deployment, its hardships, and its successes. The lessons learned will be invaluable to the overall assessment of the conflict and to future planning for other contingencies requiring the use of force. The efforts in the humanitarian, development, and reconstruction area will need closer consideration.

Gratitude is due as well to the assistance given Professor Gale Mattox by the US Naval Academy Library and Research Council, the US Air Force National Institute for Security Studies, and the American Institute for Contemporary German Studies (AICGS) for various stages of the research and writing of this book. We both would like to thank the many officials and experts who took the time out of their schedules to meet and discuss with us a range of important issues. We would also like to thank the anonymous reviewers for their insightful comments. Geoffrey Burn and his team at Stanford University Press were extremely helpful throughout this project. Dan Caldwell suggested the excellent idea of presenting the information found in Appendix B. Both editors would like as well to thank their spouses, Dieter Dettke and Katherine Haldane Grenier, and their children, Elizabeth, Nathalie, and Erik Dettke, and Ian and Matthew Grenier, for their unwavering support and understanding as we worked on the manuscript. We dedicate this book to them, with love and affection.

Gale A. Mattox and Stephen M. Grenier

Please note: The views expressed in the following book chapters are the authors' alone and do not reflect those of any government or institution with which the authors are affiliated.

Select List of Acronyms

ABP	Afghan Border Police
ADF	Afghan Defense Force
ADF	Australian Defence Force
ALP	Afghan Local Police
AIA	Afghan Interim Authority or Afghan Interim Administration
AMF	Afghan Militia Force
ANCOP	Afghanistan National Civil Order Police or Afghan National Civil Order Police
ANA	Afghanistan National Army or Afghan National Army
ANP	Afghanistan National Police or Afghan National Police
ANSF	Afghanistan National Security Forces or Afghan National Security Forces
AT	Advisory Team
AUP	Afghan Uniform Police
CENTCOM	US Central Command
CERP	Commander's Emergency Response Program
CJSOTF-A	Combined Joint Special Operations Task Force–Afghanistan
COIN	Counterinsurgency
CSTC-A	Combined Security Transition Command–Afghanistan
DDR	Demobilization, Disarmament, and Reintegration
ETT	Embedded Training Team
EU	European Union
EUPOL	European Police Mission
HA/DR	Humanitarian Assistance/Disaster Relief

IED	Improvised Explosive Device
ISAF	International Security Assistance Force
MOFA	Ministry of Foreign Affairs
MRTF	Mentoring and Reconstruction Task Force
MTF	Mentoring Task Force
NA	Northern Alliance
NATO	North Atlantic Treaty Organization
NDN	Northern Distribution Network
NGO	Nongovernmental Organization
NTM-A	NATO Training Mission–Afghanistan
NZ	New Zealand
OEF	Operation Enduring Freedom
OIF	Operation Iraqi Freedom
OMLT	Operational Mentor and Liaison Team
PAT	Police Advisory Team
PKO	Peacekeeping Operations
POMLT	Police Operational Mentor and Liaison Team
PRC	Provincial Response Company
PRT	Provincial Reconstruction Team
RC(C)	Regional Command–Capital
RC(E)	Regional Command–East
RC(N)	Regional Command–North
RC(S)	Regional Command–South
RC(SW)	Regional Command–Southwest
RC(W)	Regional Command–West
TAAC(C)	Train, Advise and Assist Command Capital
TAAC(N)	Train, Advise and Assist Command North
TAAC(W)	Train, Advise and Assist Command West
3D strategy	Defense, Development, and Diplomacy
UAE	United Arab Emirates
UK	United Kingdom
UNAMA	United Nations Assistance Mission in Afghanistan
UNPROFOR	United Nations Protection Force
UNSC	United National Security Council
UNSCR	United National Security Council Resolution
US	United States
WWI/WWII	World War I/World War II

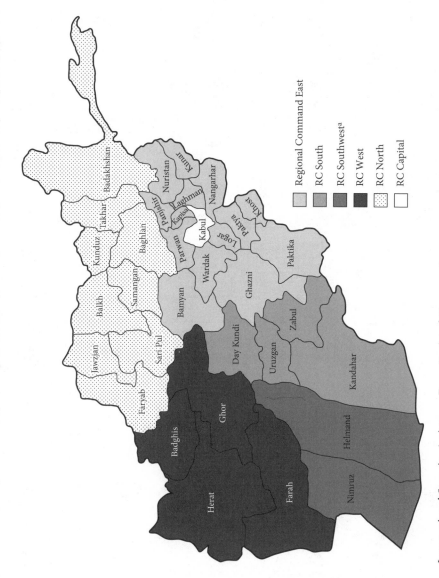

International Security Assistance Force Regional Commands, 2014

SOURCE: International Security Assistance Force.

[a]RC Southwest was created in June 2010. Prior to that, Nimruz and Helmand provinces were in RC South.

Legend:

Regional Command East

RC South

RC Southwest[a]

RC West

RC North

RC Capital

1 INTRODUCTION

Framing the War in Afghanistan

Stephen M. Grenier

FEW RECENT INTERNATIONAL events have proven more challenging than the coalition's effort to secure and stabilize Afghanistan. As of October 2014, the US and forty-nine international coalition partners have suffered almost 3,500 troops killed and more than 23,000 wounded and have spent almost $900 billion trying to establish Afghan security forces, build government ministries, and promote economic development in the troubled Asian nation.[1] More than 12,000 Afghan troops have been killed and over 37,000 wounded during that same period.[2] The coalition has invested considerable resources embracing the notion that a stable Afghanistan, with a government that can provide essential services, foster economic opportunities, and protect its citizens from organized violence, will be an inhospitable locale for terrorists. This volume, which examines events in Afghanistan from 2001 to 2014, sets out to answer two questions. First, what motivated a country to join the coalition's campaign to stabilize Afghanistan? For many nations, the September 11, 2001, terrorist attacks that killed almost 3,000 people from ninety countries served as the catalyst to take action.[3] Whether it was to demonstrate solidarity with the US or to avenge the deaths of their citizens, several countries joined the coalition to defeat al Qaeda and bring Osama bin Laden to justice. Regional security concerns, domestic politics, or the opportunity to rehabilitate international reputations also prompted states to deploy military forces or support coalition efforts in other ways.

Second, this book assesses the coalition's performance by examining how well each country employed its military, diplomatic, or economic capabilities. Some contributing nations conducted a wide range of air, ground, and naval combat operations while others focused on delivering a distinctive capability that addressed a specific operational gap or need. As the war progressed—especially after insurgent activity increased in 2006—several nations were forced to significantly augment the number of deployed troops to stabilize their assigned area of operations. When the interests of contributing members did not align, the coalition often failed to achieve its political and military objectives. For example, some governments placed limitations—commonly referred to as caveats—on their forces. Legal constraints, political considerations, and limited military capabilities prompted many leaders to restrict what type of operations their military forces could conduct. Some countries restricted their troops to performing humanitarian assistance and reconstruction efforts. Others permitted—and even encouraged—their forces to conduct combat operations, but only in areas that were generally free of insurgent activity. These types of decisions often strained bilateral relations between coalition partners and within alliances such as the North Atlantic Treaty Organization (NATO).

WHY THEY FOUGHT: MOTIVATIONS FOR GOING TO WAR

"We are all Americans" was the famous September 12, 2001, *Le Monde* newspaper headline that captured the international community's resolve as the magnitude of the terrorist attacks emerged. The 9/11 strikes represented a dramatic increase in the scale of terrorist activity, and many countries determined that they had a moral responsibility to address this amplified terrorist threat. Jack Porter recounts that less than twenty-four hours after the attacks, NATO invoked Article 5, the collective defense principle of the Washington Treaty, for the first time in the alliance's history. The US government soon confirmed that members of al Qaeda, a terrorist group led by Osama bin Laden, conducted the attacks. Bin Laden and his lieutenants planned the 9/11 attacks in Afghanistan under the protection of the Taliban, the Islamist organization governing the remote Asian nation. When Taliban leader Mullah Omar refused to turn bin Laden over to American authorities, the US and the UK planned the opening salvo of the campaign that would soon drive the Taliban from power and force bin Laden and his al Qaeda lieutenants into hiding.

The primary motivation for the UK to fight in Afghanistan was to reinforce already strong defense ties with the US. Decades of close bilateral defense and intelligence cooperation was made possible by a common language, shared culture, interconnected economic systems, and collective view of the international system. Andrew Dorman argues that exceptionally strong Anglo-American ties—commonly referred to as the "special relationship"—prompted London to immediately join the international coalition, but he also notes that London was motivated for other reasons. The UK sought to influence the conduct of the US-led war in Afghanistan, and it felt that it had a moral obligation to address the al Qaeda and Taliban threat emanating from Afghanistan with robust military force. The UK's resolve to the Afghan campaign was periodically tested, most notably in the months following the July 7, 2005, London terrorist bombings, but the UK has remained Washington's most steadfast and capable partner in Afghanistan.

Australia's motivations for deploying troops to Afghanistan also went beyond Canberra's desire to strengthen its defense ties with Washington. Maryanne Kelton and Aaron Jackson state that Australia viewed the Afghan security challenge from a regional as well as a global perspective. Canberra was concerned that al Qaeda could undermine regional stability by disrupting the tenuous peace between Pakistan and India and by financing extremist organizations in Indonesia and the Philippines. The terrorist groups operating in these island nations already possessed the ability to launch attacks that could destabilize national governments, disrupt trade, dissuade tourism, and encourage refugee movements. Additional financial support from al Qaeda could embolden them and make them even more dangerous.

Regional security considerations also prompted Jordan and the United Arab Emirates (UAE) to join the coalition despite strong domestic anti-US sentiment. Dan Brown and Ariel Ahram posit that both countries decided to address the multifaceted threat of radical Islam by deepening already strong ties with Washington. Jordan's primary security concern was countering the internal factions in Afghanistan that were being influenced by al Qaeda and other radical elements. In contrast, the UAE identified Iran and its strategy to export Islamic revolutionary ideas to the Middle East as the most dangerous threat. Both Jordan and the UAE viewed their participation in Afghanistan as an opportunity to solidify their status as moderate Islamic countries, and as a way of encouraging America's continued involvement in the Middle East.

While the horrors of the 9/11 attacks provided a legal and moral justification for action, contributing countries were also motivated by other factors. The Afghanistan mission provided Canada, the Netherlands, and Japan an opportunity to rehabilitate tarnished reputations. Canada's defense system is anchored in its close relationship with the US, and Howard Coombs argues that Canada considered the war in Afghanistan as a chance to rebuild its security credentials with the US in the wake of Canada's performance in Somalia, Rwanda, and the former Yugoslavia during the early 1990s. Canada's participation also provided an occasion to reinforce its commitment to NATO and increase its ability to influence the future of the alliance after the hostilities ended. Rem Korteweg notes that the Netherlands also wanted to rebuild its international standing and highlight the political and defense reforms it instituted after Dutch peacekeepers failed to prevent the 1995 murder of refugees in Srebrenica, a United Nations–declared "safe area" in Bosnia. Since the Netherlands was dependent on the NATO collective security umbrella, the mission in Afghanistan provided an opportunity to increase its credibility within the alliance and to strengthen the Dutch-American defense relationship. Japan also joined the coalition, in part, to repair its credibility and maintain strong ties to the US. Takamichi Takahashi states that Tokyo supported coalition naval operations in the Indian Ocean to restore its credibility after the international community criticized Japan for exercising "checkbook diplomacy" during the 1991 Persian Gulf War when it contributed $13 billion to offset coalition expenses instead of deploying military forces to the region.

Domestic politics influenced officials in Germany, El Salvador, and New Zealand to contribute forces to the coalition. Gale Mattox argues that Germany deployed troops outside Europe for the first time since World War II to fulfill its NATO commitments and to demonstrate solidarity with the US following the 9/11 attacks. In addition to military forces, Germany made significant contributions to the coalition on the diplomatic front. A large Afghan population residing in Germany coupled with a strong public support for Afghan humanitarian aid and development efforts prompted Germany to host two major international conferences on Afghanistan—Bonn I in 2001 and Bonn II a decade later. Discussion topics at both conferences included economic and social development, governance, and regional and security cooperation—areas that had strong German domestic political support and aligned perfectly with Berlin's overseas goals.

El Salvador's seemingly unlikely contribution to the coalition was due to a complex civil-military relationship in the small Western Hemisphere nation. Rebecca Bill Chavez asserts that El Salvador's President Mauricio Funes sought to improve his relationship with the Armed Forces of El Salvador (ESAF) by strengthening his country's ties with the US. The steady flow of illegal narcotics and weapons through the Central American isthmus caused an epidemic of gang-related violence, which contributed to El Salvador's having one of the highest homicide rates in the world. Funes needed the military's support to fight the gangs, but distrust between his leftist administration and the ESAF stood in the way of a coordinated response. He stunned political observers when he dismissed his own political party's concerns and joined with conservative legislators to approve the deployment of El Salvadoran troops to Afghanistan. The US responded by providing the troops with advanced training and equipment for use in Afghanistan, and against transnational criminal organizations operating in El Salvador. This strengthened El Salvadoran–American relations, improved Funes' standing with the ESAF, and helped San Salvador develop a better-coordinated government response against criminal entities.

Robert Ayson notes that New Zealand joined the international coalition to destroy al Qaeda and deny it a sanctuary to plan future attacks, not to strengthen defense ties with the US. Prime Minister Helen Clark expressed outrage and quickly condemned the perpetrators of the 9/11 attacks, but she did not commit New Zealand's military forces to joining the coalition until the military campaign was legitimized by the passage of a United Nations Security Council Resolution. New Zealand's participation in the coalition eventually contributed to stronger defense ties between Wellington and Washington, but it was an unintended consequence of the mission.

Marybeth Ulrich states that Poland, Slovakia, Hungary, and the Czech Republic viewed their contributions to the coalition through the lens of NATO and their bilateral relationship with the US. All four countries, labeled "new Europe" by former US Secretary of Defense Donald Rumsfeld, were more concerned about conventional military threats than their "Western" European counterparts. This prompted each of them to align closely with the US on a variety of defense and economic issues and to maintain a strong commitment to the collective defense principle of the NATO Washington Treaty. Poland and the Czech Republic considered al Qaeda to be a global security threat and determined that stabilizing Afghanistan and destroying the terrorist camps operating there was in their national interest. In contrast, Slovakia and Hungary deployed forces primarily to demonstrate solidarity with other NATO contributing nations.

Despite often tenuous relationships with the US and coalition forces, Pakistan and Russia provided critical support throughout the campaign. Timothy Hoyt argues that Pakistan accepted Washington's invitation to support the coalition in the days following the 9/11 attacks. US-Pakistan relations were strained in September 2001 because of ongoing disagreements over

Pakistan's nuclear program, its role in the 1999 Kargil War, the military coup that put General Musharraf in power, and Islamabad's decision to recognize the legitimacy of the Taliban regime. Islamabad viewed Washington's outreach as an opportunity to reset the US-Pakistan relationship, end economic sanctions, and restore American military assistance.

President Vladimir Putin was one of the first international leaders to call President Bush after the 9/11 attacks. Renanah Miles posits that Russia shared the coalition's goal of creating a stable Afghanistan to reduce the flow of illegal narcotics and the spread of Islamist extremism, but Moscow also embraced the contradictory policy of calling for US and International Security Assistance Force (ISAF) troops to depart Afghanistan.

HOW THEY FOUGHT: SUCCESS AND FAILURE IN AFGHANISTAN

In October 2001, US, British, and Northern Alliance (NA) forces launched the campaign to destroy al Qaeda and liberate Afghanistan from Taliban rule. The combination of ground troops and air-delivered precision-guided munitions overwhelmed the Taliban. Less than three months later, all major Afghan cities were under NA control. Those quick victories prompted other nations to join the coalition to stabilize Afghanistan and prevent al Qaeda from reestablishing safe havens west of the Durand Line. Some contributing nations conducted full-spectrum combat operations while others focused on delivering a specific, more limited capability.

Since 2001, the US deployed a staggering amount of military hardware and supplies to Afghanistan. It provided the bulk of coalition ground forces, strategic and tactical airlift, medical treatment and evacuation, cyber and communications infrastructure, and close air support to coalition troops. While each contributing country was responsible for supplying its own forces, the US actually provided most of the logistical support for the coalition. US forces conducted combat operations in every province and participated in every major operation, but they rarely fought alone. Several coalition partners also made significant contributions, which often came at a heavy cost. The UK, Australia, Canada, and the Netherlands fielded highly capable conventional and special operations forces that conducted combat and stabilization operations throughout Afghanistan. All four countries fielded Provincial Reconstruction Teams (PRTs), managed large-scale development projects, trained and advised Afghan security forces, and made substantial financial contributions at Afghanistan international donor conferences. The UK and Canada executed a series of campaigns against insurgents occupying major population areas in Helmand and Kandahar provinces respectively. The Netherlands, followed by Australia in 2010, led the coalition's effort in Uruzgan province and fought several demanding battles against insurgent forces operating there.

Others contributing nations focused on delivering a distinct capability that addressed a specific operational gap. Nicolas Fescharek notes that France deployed combat aircraft, trained three of the first six Afghan National Army (ANA) battalions, staffed the Regional Command–Capital (RC[C]) headquarters, and taught basic police skills to thousands of Afghan National Police (ANP) officers. When the security situation in eastern Afghanistan deteriorated, French troops conducted counterinsurgency operations in the volatile mountainous area surrounding Kabul and disrupted Taliban attempts to attack Afghan government ministries and assassinate senior officials. Ariel Ahram and Dan Brown state that Jordan and UAE special operations troops developed positive relationships with nearby Afghan security forces and local citizens, partly because of their shared religious beliefs. Since US law prohibited appropriated funds from being spent on religious buildings, the UAE built mosques at dozens of ANA bases. Jordanian soldiers staffed field hospitals, trained ANA Commandos, and conducted limited combat operations in Zabul province.

Coalition PRTs provided a mechanism for several nations to participate in reconstruction efforts. New Zealand, the Czech Republic, and Poland contributed forces to PRTs in Bamyan, Logar, and Ghazni respectively. In addition to fielding two PRTs in northern Afghanistan, Germany led the coalition's ANP training effort until 2005 and staffed the Regional Command–North (RC[N]) headquarters. El Salvador trained ANA mechanics and ground crews for Russian-built Mi-17 helicopters, and Japan Maritime Self-Defense Force ships replenished US and coalition vessels operating off the coast of Pakistan. Russia provided coalition forces with detailed intelligence gained during Soviet military operations in the 1980s and worked with several Central Asian nations to permit coalition nonlethal supplies to be transported through their countries along three supply routes that collectively formed the Northern Distribution Network (NDN). Pakistan permitted the US to use several air bases and provided targeting information for US air strikes and intelligence on insurgents operating along the Afghanistan-Pakistan border. Since 2002, Pakistani security forces have captured and transferred several high-ranking al Qaeda leaders to the US, most notably Khalid Sheikh Muhammad, the self-professed mastermind of the 9/11 attacks.

Despite these contributions, the coalition experienced significant problems, the most significant being the lack of a coherent strategy. Immediately following the 9/11 attacks, the coalition focused on achieving two objectives: destroy al Qaeda and remove the Taliban from power. When Afghanistan was liberated in December 2001, the coalition's strategic goals became more ambiguous. In their analysis of British, Dutch, German, and French counterinsurgency practices, John Nagl and Richard Weitz argue that the lack of a clearly understood strategy frustrated coalition efforts. Countries operating in the relatively peaceful northern and western provinces—such as Germany, Italy, and Spain—maintained that the coalition's primary missions were peacekeeping and nation-building. Nations operating in the more volatile southern and eastern provinces—Canada, the UK, Australia, the Netherlands, and the US—argued that the coalition's top priority was to defeat the insurgency and protect the population from organized violence.

The lack of an overarching strategy prior to 2009 forced military commanders and diplomatic officials to develop local strategies and focus on operational- and tactical-level issues. Counterinsurgency proponents even disagreed with each other about the most effective tactics and methods. The UK and the Netherlands criticized US counterinsurgency efforts as being too focused on killing and capturing insurgents rather than focusing on protecting civilians and developing a better understanding of their culture. These differing interpretations influenced where troops were stationed in Afghanistan, how they were equipped, and how they engaged enemy forces. Each contributing country also employed PRTs differently. US PRTs often linked humanitarian assistance to the willingness of local residents to provide information on insurgent activity. In contrast, German, British, Dutch, and New Zealand PRTs were led by civilians who took great efforts to maintain a clear separation between military operations and humanitarian assistance efforts.

Coalition forces operating in Afghanistan were often limited by national caveats dictated by national governments to comply with legal restrictions, political constraints, or a lack of military capacity. Organizational culture and military doctrine also influenced how military units conducted operations. Some countries restricted their troops to humanitarian assistance and reconstruction efforts. Other governments deployed combat troops but insisted that those forces only operate in relatively safe parts of Afghanistan. This created a rift between members engaged in heavy combat, such as Canada, the UK, Australia, the US, and the Netherlands, and members that generally avoided ground combat. For example, Germany, New Zealand, and the Central and Eastern European nations of Slovakia, Hungary, the Czech Republic, and Poland largely restricted their operations to humanitarian assistance and reconstruction efforts.

The coalition's failure to create effective Afghan security forces during the first five years of the war allowed insurgent forces to gain a foothold in key population areas in eastern and southern Afghanistan. Its overreliance on militias and other local security forces at the expense of training legitimate Afghan security forces harmed the legitimacy of the fledgling Afghan government, stifled ANA recruiting efforts until 2007, and served as a catalyst for corruption and patronage. The US eventually committed enough resources to develop Afghan security forces in 2007, but the training emphasized combat skills at the expense of critical supporting tasks such as logistics and intelligence. As a result, the nascent supply system could not support ANA and ANP units because of high rates of pilferage and waste, and inadequate stockpiles of ammunition, batteries, winter clothing, and fuel limited the ability of Afghan security forces to undertake anything beyond rudimentary operations.

External factors also influenced how the coalition fought the war in Afghanistan. The terrorist bombings in Madrid, London, and Amman reminded contributing countries that their participation could provoke al Qaeda retaliation. US commitments in Iraq prompted Washington to regard Afghanistan as an "economy of force" effort until 2009. This allowed the Pentagon to deploy more troops and equipment to Iraq but often left US and coalition units without adequate resources to fight the insurgency in Afghanistan. The security situation became so dire that in 2009, General David McKiernan, the commander of all coalition troops in Afghanistan, was relieved, and President Obama ordered a detailed review of US policy.

Tim Hoyt argues that despite cooperating with the US in a number of areas, Pakistan continued to gain leverage in its ongoing dispute with Afghanistan by supporting insurgent factions such as the Afghan Taliban, the Haqqani network, and Gulbuddin Hekmatyar. These efforts harmed Afghan civilians and contributed to the deaths of coalition troops. Tensions between the US and Pakistan have flared several times since 2001, especially when senior US officials made public claims that Pakistan's Inter-Service Intelligence Directorate (ISI) maintains close ties with several militant groups that actively fight coalition forces. Other examples of heightened US-Pakistan tensions include the shooting incident involving Central Intelligence Agency (CIA) contractor Raymond Davis, the Abbottabad raid that resulted in the death of Osama bin Laden, and the November 2011 border clash between coalition and Pakistani troops.

A strong Afghan central government could have reduced the negative impact of these issues, but that simply was not possible. S. Rebecca Zimmerman argues that the Afghan government failed to build a system capable of supporting provincial institutions, did not utilize existing subnational government structures, and refused to establish a legitimate process for channeling political opposition and dissent. In early 2002, the Afghan government desperately needed qualified public servants to staff the new government, but newly appointed ministers battled over who controlled the recruiting process to fill the positions—and the opportunity for patronage and enrichment that accompanied that responsibility. The coalition made the situation worse when it continued to negotiate with warlords and regional power brokers after the central government was being created.

Romain Malejacq posits that in October 2001, NA leaders readily accepted Washington's financial and military assistance. CIA paramilitary officers provided millions of dollars in cash, and US and coalition special operations forces coordinated allied aircraft to attack Taliban positions. Once Afghanistan was liberated in December 2001, NA and coalition interests diverged. Instead of working with coalition troops to kill and capture fleeing al Qaeda leaders, NA officials flocked to Kabul and other major Afghan cities where they could develop lucrative patronage networks and secure positions in the new government to benefit from the international aid that would soon follow. Soon thereafter, the coalition embraced an incongruous policy of working closely with regional warlords while simultaneously labeling them a threat to the legitimate Afghan government in Kabul. Warlords proved to be remarkably flexible and continuously identified opportunities to benefit from the competition between Kabul, coalition forces, and regional actors. When pressure grew, warlords "legitimized" themselves by becoming businessmen or Afghan government officials. When the pressure subsided, they resumed their competition with Kabul.

The political landscape in Afghanistan remains complex. The US-Afghanistan Bilateral Security Agreement was signed on September 30, 2014, after a contentious presidential election. The US-Afghanistan agreement permits approximately 9,800 US troops to remain in Afghanistan and provides a framework for other coalition members to begin negotiating complementary bilateral agreements with Kabul.[4] NATO and Afghanistan representatives also signed a Status of Forces Agreement on September 30, 2014. The NATO-Afghanistan agreement provides the legal foundation for a new NATO-led mission, called Resolute Support, which is scheduled to begin on January 1, 2015, the day after NATO combat operations officially end. The Resolute Support mission will permit NATO advisors to work with Afghan government ministries, institutions, and high-level military staffs.[5] But despite these recent diplomatic breakthroughs and the continued resolve of many coalition members, it will ultimately be the Afghan government and regional power brokers—not the international coalition—that will determine Afghanistan's long-term future. Thus, we begin this volume by examining how the Afghan government and regional warlords have shaped this troubled nation since the fall of the Taliban in 2001.

NOTES

The views expressed in this chapter are the author's alone.

1. All figures current as of September 30, 2014. Data concerning the number of coalition troops killed or wounded in action were compiled from multiple US Department of Defense and International Security Assistance Force (ISAF) reports. Figures regarding the financial cost of the Afghan War are based on a variety of government and nongovernment reports. For the number of ISAF contributing nations, see http://www.isaf.nato.int/isaf-placemat-archives.html.

2. Figures on the number of Afghan troops killed and wounded are based on estimates compiled from multiple government and nongovernment reports. The author would like to emphasize that these figures are only estimates. See Susan G. Chesser, "Afghanistan Casualties: Military Forces and Civilians," Congressional Research Service, December 6, 2012. Also see Chapter 2 of this volume.

3. US Department of Homeland Security, "9/11 Terrorist Attacks Fact Sheet," December 2, 2009.

4. Margherita Stancati and Nathan Hodge, "Afghanistan Signs Security Pact with U.S., NATO," *Wall Street Journal*, September 30, 2014, http://www.wsj.com/articles/u-s-afghan-bilateral-security-agreement-signed-1412076436; Sudarsan Raghavan and Karen DeYoung, "U.S., Afghanistan Sign Vital, Long-delayed Security Pact," *Washington Post*, September 30, 2014, http://www.washingtonpost.com/world/us-afghanistan-sign-security-pact-to-allow-american-forces-to-remain-in-country/2014/09/30/48f555ce-4879-11e4-a046-120a8a855cca_story.html.

5. North Atlantic Treaty Organization, "NATO Secretary General Welcomes Signing of Security Agreements with Afghanistan," last modified September 30, 2014, http://www.nato.int/cps/en/natohq/news_113393.htm; North Atlantic Treaty Organization, "NATO-led Resolute Support Mission in Afghanistan," last modified October 7, 2014, http://www.nato.int/cps/en/natohq/topics_113694.htm.

Part I
Afghan Government and Nonstate Actors

2 THE AFGHAN GOVERNMENT AT WAR

S. Rebecca Zimmerman

IN STUDIES OF THE WAR in Afghanistan, too often the Afghan state is treated as a non-entity—a set of institutions acted upon by outsiders. When the government is considered, it is often seen as no more than traditional networks of patronage, yet there is also an elusive Afghan state attempting to exert itself. Outcomes in Afghanistan are products of the interaction of these competing influences. Because the prosecution of the war necessitated rebuilding Afghanistan's security institutions and the national infrastructure to govern them, this chapter considers the recreation of the Afghan state to be an essential part of the country's war effort. International actors have often undermined state-building efforts in favor of parochial war aims, and traditional networks have subverted governance through corruption. The nascent Afghan state has been marked by indecision and duplication.

The conflicts inside the Afghan government are many-layered and opaque: center versus periphery; former *mujahideen* versus Soviet-trained; technocrats versus traditionalists; "mafia" government versus democrats; and Jamiat-i Islami or Northern Alliance versus Pashtun. In various forms, forces of tradition and modernity have been in conflict for centuries in Afghanistan and dominate the political landscape today. Those who hold power are not likely to act against their own best interests; moreover, modernization has often flouted the culture and will of rural Afghans, focusing disproportionately on desires of the urban citizenry.

Making Afghanistan a modern state would have required detailed planning from the Taliban's ouster. Instead, the international community fed both sides of the divide, supporting both warlords, such as Marshal Qasim Fahim and General Abdul Rashid Dostum, and modernizers, such as Dr. Ashraf Ghani and Ali Ahmed Jalali. These mixed messages, combined with the power of traditional authority to mobilize masses and the fledgling government's need for mass support, have given the advantage to traditional forces of authority. Today, warlords and patrons are less in favor with the international community: the cost in stability, transparency, and commitment to the coalition force goals seems too high. But the time for making such decisions is long past. The Afghan government grows ever more complex and self-absorbed, less capable and less desirous of fighting a war it did not start.

EARLY EVENTS

The Afghan government in its current incarnation began on December 5, 2001, with the signature of the Bonn Agreement, endorsed by the United Nations the following day. The country was tremendously fractured at the time of the Bonn Conference. Northern Alliance commanders of Tajik and Uzbek militant groups had de facto power, working with the US to dispel the remnants of the Taliban. The Pashtuns had seen their fortunes fall, though the ethnic group is broader and more diverse than the Taliban. The Hazara minority remained relatively powerless, but with large refugee communities in Pakistan and Iran curious about returning to a potentially less prejudiced homeland. Much of Afghanistan's intellectual class, driven abroad by the Taliban and *mujahideen*, hoped to apply their visions of modernity to a homeland they saw as backward.

Unfortunately, those selected by the US and UN to take part in the Bonn negotiations did not represent the whole Afghan polity. The international community invited the former Northern Alliance; expatriate royalist supporters of the still-living king, Zahir Shah; and technocrats such as Ashraf Ghani, then a senior official at the World Bank. Rural Pashtuns, Afghanistan's largest group, were not represented. United Nations Special Representative Lakhdar Brahimi reportedly felt that "no one would remember how unrepresentative the meeting had been if the participants managed to fashion a process that would lead to a legitimate and representative government."[1]

The Bonn process set forth an Afghan Interim Administration led by Hamid Karzai to steer the country until a transitional administration could be elected through a traditional conclave, called a Loya Jirga. The 2002 Loya Jirga undercut prospects for the creation of a representative government. While 1,051 delegates were indirectly elected, the interim authority appointed another 600 delegates, "thereby ensuring Karzai's election and keeping a lid on organized dissent."[2] The government invited several armed strongmen, even though they had been rejected by their home constituencies, further eroding the perception that the new government would be representative and free of warlord influence.[3]

The US was known to favor Hamid Karzai's continued leadership, but a majority of delegates supported a return to the deposed king, Zahir Shah. The US, led by an Afghan American, special envoy Zalmay Khalilzad, pressured the king to foreswear participation in the new government. So eager was Khalilzad that he convened a press conference to announce the king's decision several hours before the king's own announcement.[4] The entire cabinet was pushed through as a single slate, further reducing the space for negotiation about the new government.[5] Thus, political pressure, intimidation, and money outweighed public expectations for representation.[6]

BUILDING BUREAUCRACY

The central failure of the Afghan civilian government, from the perspective of its counterinsurgency, has been governing at the subnational level in a way that provides predictability for the majority of the population. As leading counterinsurgency scholar Bernard Fall wrote, "When a country is being subverted, it is not being outfought or outgunned, but it is being outadministered— particularly at the village grassroots, where it counts."[7] The Afghan government failed to capitalize on existing subnational governance structures, failed to establish a national government capable of supporting good governance in the provinces, and failed to establish constructive means for channeling opposition and dissent.

The early days of Afghan sovereignty post-Bonn were marked by conflict between modernizing, institution-driven interests and patrimonial ones. One side set about rapidly building the bureaucracy, as the other set about co-opting it. While debate raged in Kabul over what form the government should take, a very different government was already on the ground.

In the early days after the government's establishment, researchers were surprised to discover a relatively intact subnational government left from before 1978. Officials maintained a civil service structure and continued to collect taxes, though not all revenues were sent to Kabul.[8] These government structures followed the historical form of the state, fusing an ossified formal bureaucracy with a system of informal bargaining. This was far different from the system envisioned by technocrats in Kabul—a small central bureaucracy with a heavy emphasis on private-sector development and decentralized decision making. This plan required not merely the creation of a new central bureaucracy but careful transformation of the existing sub-national structure. Added to this, the emphasis on financing private-sector development presumed the existence of safeguards against corruption and co-optation.

To accomplish this ambitious agenda, the Afghan government had little human capital. For example, Ashraf Ghani, head of the Afghan Assistance Coordination Authority that devised the state-building plan, was simultaneously serving as minister of finance. When Marshal Fahim was appointed minister of defense, the staff he brought were all Northern Alliance fighters, without experience in government.[9] Ministerial positions were generally given in recognition of power and prestige already accrued, and the fortunes of ministries mirrored the power of the minister either to command patronage or to obtain assistance from the international community.

While capacity may have been lacking, the ministries rushed to fulfill the functions of the state, often overlapping or pursuing conflicting aims. A singular example of this is the National Solidarity Programme (NSP), begun in 2002 as a program of the Ministry for Rural Rehabilitation and Development (MRRD). Generally considered a high point of reconstruction efforts, the NSP created locally elected Community Development Councils, funded with small development budgets.[10]

The program's goal was to use development to build village-level governance and support for the Afghan government.[11] At that time, governance at the provincial level fell under the Ministry of the Interior (MOI), and district governance was largely in thrall to powerful provincial governors. The central government created the Independent Directorate of Local Governance (IDLG) in 2007, directly under the office of the president, to wrest control of the provinces from the MOI. The creation of the IDLG has lent needed focus to district governance and pushed for the 2010 creation of a Subnational Governance Policy.

The creation of the IDLG also brought confusion, duplication, and co-optation to both village and national levels. It is backed by the US, which has not coordinated well with the donors to the MRRD, pressing for overlapping priorities. In 2007 the IDLG, viewing the NSP as a development program only, established the Afghan Social Outreach Program (ASOP) to promote local governance.[12] Whereas the NSP's councils are locally elected and unpaid, with written mandates for representative leadership, the ASOP traditional assemblies, or *shuras,* are paid, appointed positions, with a less clear requirement for representation. Competition eroded effectiveness of the *shuras* and made the organizational chain unclear for both groups. In 2010, the Inter-Ministerial Commission on the Status of Village Councils and District Councils attempted to adjudicate the issue, but with two well-connected ministries, each with a key program on the chopping block, the commission avoided a clear decision.[13]

As in the early days of the government, Afghanistan continues to stifle dissent by blocking the formation of organized political parties. The registration process for parties is subjectively enforced and requires the Ministry of Justice to seek concurrence from the ministries of the interior, finance, and defense, as well as the National Directorate of Security and the UN Assistance Mission in Afghanistan.[14]

After pushing back parliamentary elections from 2004 until September 2005, Afghanistan held elections under a system known as the single nontransferable vote (SNTV), in which the population votes for individuals, rather than parties, and individuals with the highest vote totals win. The SNTV is among the least common electoral systems, precisely because it poorly represents a complex electorate, often splitting minority votes. Generally, it is seen as an appropriate strategy for small districts, but in Afghanistan, one third of all districts have more than nine delegates, and may have as many as thirty-three.[15] There, it creates confusion and undercuts party platforms, causing party members to run against each other, distinguished by personality or influence. Further, the Afghan government disallowed party symbols next to the names on the ballot, hampering candidates' party identification and creating confusion in a mostly illiterate country.[16]

Following the 2005 Parliamentary election, a broad coalition of political groups sought to change to a system of proportional representation.[17] While the voting system was not originally implemented to foil opposition, the Karzai cabinet had come to see it as helpful because it "envisioned a legislature divided between Pushtun MPs—most of whom, if push came to shove, would support the president—and a fragmented non-Pushtun opposition."[18]

If the Parliamentary elections of 2005 undermined possible opposition, the 2009 presidential election consolidated Karzai's hold over the government and sealed the nation in its trajectory. One international member of the Electoral

Complaints Commission in Afghanistan called the fraud "widespread and systematic" and noted:

> In 425 polling centers and 23 of Afghanistan's 365 administrative districts, more than half the presidential ballots were fraudulent. It strains credulity to think that fraud so massive could have gone on without election officials knowing about it and (at the very least) choosing to look the other way.[19]

Numerous reports showed polling stations voting 100 percent for Hamid Karzai, though there was also evidence of fraud for other candidates. Nevertheless, the international community called this election and the 2010 parliamentary elections "credible and acceptable." This is a persistent strain in Afghan intervention—the international community applauds the appearance of government, without regard for the quality of governance supplied. On the Afghan street today, a common term used to describe the Afghan government is "mafia."[20]

AFGHAN NATIONAL SECURITY FORCES

Afghan National Army

The Afghan National Army (ANA) is among the more effective Afghan institutions, capable of conducting large-scale clearing operations. However, key sustaining capabilities, such as logistics, medical, and aviation units, lag far behind combat capabilities. Perhaps more seriously, it remains unclear what portion of the force retains the will to fight on behalf of the central government, and the government, focusing on force development, has yet to articulate its long-term strategy for the military's prosecution of the war. The ANA has suffered significant losses, some 2,330 killed and 12,696 wounded from mid-2012 to mid-2014.[21]

The modern ANA began in 2002, when forces of the Northern Alliance were divided into eight corps and designated the 60,000-person Afghan Militia Force.[22] Giving these forces, overwhelmingly dominated by Tajiks of the Shura-i Nezar faction of the Jamiat-i Islami party, official status was a means of paying back war debts for powerful individuals, and by late 2002, there were 2,500 designated general officers for a force that may have numbered 200,000.[23] By comparison, in 2007, the US had 307 authorized generals for a force of 507,000.[24] The factional nature of this structure is perhaps best seen in the fact that the thirty-two divisions of the militia force varied widely in size, from 4,200 to 30,000, based on the personal power of the division commander.[25] This newfound state sponsorship further increased the power of many of these strongmen at the local level, a process helped by the fact that the first Defense Minister, Marshal Fahim, was also the Vice Chair of the Interim Administration.[26]

While these forces grabbed the reins of military power, the US took the lead in building the ANA, commencing training of the ethnically balanced units it hoped would make the core of the army in 2002. These early efforts were foiled by poor coordination in the international community in areas such as military equipment donation, as well as underfunding and overambition. By 2003, it became clear the situation could not hold:

> There is on the one hand the sort of left-over Army that's quite large and is a bit of a security problem, and there's the new army which we're training which is very different, which is multi-ethnic and disciplined and the real future of the country.[27]

In September 2003, the US decided to rebuild the army from the ground up, bringing all elements of the military into one structure, to wrest control of the military from Shura-i Nezar.[28] The US mandated a recruitment board for senior defense positions, and these followed a rigid ethnic quota system giving Pashtuns 40 percent, Tajiks 30 percent, Hazaras 15 percent, and Uzbeks 10 percent of the top 120–130 positions, with smaller ethnic groups claiming the remaining 5 percent.[29] However, the international community had viewed a political bid for control in narrow ethnic terms, allowing the existing power holders to appoint non-Tajik allies of Shura-i Nezar to many senior positions.[30] Thus Jamiat-i Islami remained firmly in control of the armed forces despite international convictions that the ethnic problem had largely been solved.

Amid these unresolved problems, development of the ANA accelerated dramatically from 2004 to 2005, with throughput increasing from one battalion to five simultaneously and rolling out all four regional commands at once, some with as few as 150 people.[31] This required the training program to be shortened and resulted in an overemphasis on infantry as opposed to logistics, medical, and other support personnel, favoring short-term gains over long-term sustainability.

As the army has matured, opinions have varied as to its sustainability. The tactical proficiency of soldiers has improved, and the army is among the more stable institutions in the country. But doubts remain as to the long-term future of the force, the most troublesome of which is the lack of initiative on the part of the army. While International Security Assistance Force (ISAF) leaders touted the Afghan authorship of Operation *Naweed*—the ANA's overarching campaign plan—in Afghan and international media outlets, ANA leaders remained silent. This raised serious doubts whether the ANA actually influenced the document's development.

Afghan National Police

The Afghan National Police (ANP) began as a warlord-dominated institution and, with its district-level chiefs and beat cops, is extremely effective at reading and manipulating local dynamics. Institutionally, the ANP is weaker than the ANA: while there have been only four acting and official ministers of defense in the last twelve years, there have been nine acting and official ministers of the interior. As a result, police training levels vary widely, and police are likely to act in service of local or familial interests above the laws and interests of the central government.

Early on, Germany had undertaken to build the Afghan police, primarily through the reestablishment of the Kabul Police Academy, believing in a top-down approach to force development.[32] While the police from the academy were well trained, by January 2005 only 41 officers and 2,583 noncommissioned officers had completed the program, too few for state security.[33] The American solution was to gradually take control of police training, but it remained an afterthought, a project of the US embassy delegated to the private contractor DynCorp.[34]

In late 2005, serious efforts at police and MOI reform were begun. In concert with international advisors, the ministry introduced rank reform, hoping to reduce its top-heavy structure from 15,000 officers to just 6,000.[35] The plan was to create an application process with an entrance exam for the top general officer positions within the police, and in the initial phase, this worked reasonably well.[36] The second phase, including provincial chiefs of police, did not go according to plan. While the Afghan selection committee recommended a slate of appointees, President Karzai chose to name his own list of generals, fourteen of whom had failed the entrance exam. Human Rights Watch alleged that others had interfered with police investigations, committed murder and torture, or engaged in bribery, and noted that Karzai's motive was to cement alliances with powerful actors.[37]

In part, reforms to the police fail because politicians, warlords, businessmen, and ordinary citizens coordinate to some degree with police for protection and profit, and this gives police information and leverage enough to resist major organizational reform. And while Kabul will intervene to manage the politics of a well-publicized tragedy, day-to-day management of departmental affairs is almost nonexistent. The imperative to reform is further challenged by the need to grow in size. At the London Conference in 2006, Afghan and international participants affirmed a prior informal commitment to a force size of 62,000 uniformed and border police by the end of 2010.[38] One year later, this number was increased to 82,000 by the end of 2008.[39] The gap between authorized strength and actual strength remained large, and a November 2006 US Inspector General report found that while there were 70,000 police, less than half were ready for duty in terms of training and equipment, and it was impossible to know how many were actually present for duty.[40] By early 2009, the international community attempted to focus on building quality over quantity, but pressure to provide security for the upcoming parliamentary election foiled those plans. That April, an international oversight board authorized a massive increase in end strength to 96,800.[41] Over the next few years force size ballooned until, by January 2011, the size was set at 157,000.[42] More ANP troops were desperately needed as the number of insurgent attacks against the ANP steadily increased. In 2013, the Ministry of the Interior estimated that six to ten police officers a day were killed in action.[43]

While this chapter focuses on the choices of the Afghan government, the pressures of the international community have frequently been conflicting, making government decisions more difficult and less consequential. As many as five organizations at one time have had major roles in coordinating police training.[44] Typically, German, Dutch, Italian, and other European forces promote the police as a civil security force, while the American forces push for offensive, paramilitary activities. Since the Afghan National Police Strategy states that the ANP is responsible for providing "internal security" for the Afghan nation, "fostering a secure environment for Afghans to conduct their religions, political, cultural, social, and economic activities," and "protecting all citizens from criminals and illegal elements," both US and European police trainers claim that they are training ANP officers in accordance with Kabul's official policy.[45]

National Directorate of Security

Perhaps the most influential security force for Afghanistan's future is the least understood: Afghanistan's National Directorate of Security (NDS) is a shadowy spy agency with the most advanced operational capabilities of any Afghan force.[46] More than the other security forces, NDS draws a direct link to its pre-2001 history. Its precursor, a robust intelligence service known as KhAD, was the centerpiece of Soviet occupation efforts in Afghanistan and fulfilled various roles as secret police, propagandists, and strike forces. It engaged in the building of militias and the reintegration of enemy combatants into those militias.[47] KhAD was the most feared organization in the Afghan government but also among the most effective and loyal to the Afghan president.

Afghan intelligence today is more transparent than under the Soviets; however, the NDS today continues to operate under national security laws from 1987 and 2004.[48] Afghanistan's National Security Council provides weak oversight; it does not play an active supervisory role, so the NDS effectively reports directly to the president.[49] The service continues to cultivate fear, as when a top official commented, "I agree that most Afghans are afraid of the NDS. But I think there is a legitimate paranoia that has to be there in order for this agency to be effective."[50] Afghan citizens often still call the NDS KhAD and international human rights organizations have reported numerous, persistent allegations of NDS torture.[51]

Over the last decade, the NDS has been overwhelmingly Tajik-dominated, led by representatives of the Shura-i Nezar inner circle such as Amrullah Saleh, with an estimated 70 percent of the organization hailing from the Tajik province of Panjshir or being part of the former Northern Alliance.[52] But in 2010, Saleh left his position in a major government shakeup and President Karzai took the agency in a very different direction, bringing it closer to him, both personally and politically, through the appointment of Rahmatullah Nabil, a man who had no background as an intelligence officer but had been chief of Karzai's personal security team.[53] Nabil's appointment changed the organization. Although he was not a personally connected, strong leader, he could shift away from Tajik dominance. During another cabinet shake-up in 2012, Nabil was replaced with a far more powerful Karzai loyalist, Asadullah Khalid, a former NDS provincial chief and governor of the powerful provinces of Ghazni and Kandahar. After Khalid was nearly assassinated, President Karzai left the organization leaderless for a year, rather than appoint a less loyal successor. In September 2013, Karzai reappointed Nabil as acting NDS chief, partially easing the leadership crisis.

The day-to-day functions of the NDS appear to be on a steady expansionary trajectory. The NDS has taken on a role as undercover policeman for other security forces, placing a number of agents in army and police uniforms

throughout the country.[54] Following the 2012 increase in so-called insider attacks, the Afghan government stepped up this role, using NDS in the police and
army recruiting process.[55]

Perhaps the fullest expression of the growing utility of the NDS for the
Afghan government is the story of its involvement in the Andar district of
Ghazni province in eastern Afghanistan. In the summer of 2012, some district
residents began a movement to overthrow the local Taliban. While this was
labeled a popular, pro-government uprising, most of the original members
appear to have been Taliban fighters who struck out on their own, though
they also appear to have been associated with Hezb-i Islami, an armed Islamist
party.[56] Just a few weeks before his appointment to the NDS, Asadullah Khalid
reinforced the rebellion with his own money and men on the government's behalf. The government augmented the effort by sending NDS officers to support
the rebels. Five months later, a reporter described the situation as extremely
factionally divided between the NDS-sponsored rebel faction and the original
Hezb-i Islami–linked faction.[57] The NDS openly defended its attempt to co-
opt the movement to protect the "clean and national uprisings."[58] This use of
NDS for combat, propaganda, and raising of militias, in addition to simple
intelligence, appears to highlight its way forward, as indicated by Khalid in a
Parliament address vowing a more robust role for NDS in the provinces.[59]

CONCLUSION

Afghanistan's national objectives in pursuing the war are murky at best. Most
glaring is the absence of a strong indigenous counter-Taliban campaign. Perhaps this attitude is abetted by America's longtime focus on the Taliban to the
exclusion of other objectives, allowing Afghans to say this is not their war. There
is little alignment between Afghan and international objectives. For foreign
combatants, defeat of the Taliban and international terrorists is the main objective, with governance and state-building as occasional instruments to achieve
this goal. Thus, there is an emphasis on short-term suppression of violence
rather than long-term resolution of political imbalances, and a willingness to
spend freely if there is a promise of quick results.

The Afghan national objective can be considered the mirror image of this:
it is a war to govern. At the collective level and among substate groups, the
quest is for control and power in the long term. Because of the effects of international funding and involvement, the Taliban are as likely to be viewed as an

opportunity as a threat. Where interests align, the international community is likely to find leadership and promise for the future, but where interests are opposed, the Afghan government is labeled as indolent and corrupt.

Afghanistan's nascent state, its ability to match the powers of the institutions to the problems of the electorate, has been all but buried under the weight of co-optation by unsavory elites and well-intentioned involvement by the international community. Afghanistan's war to govern may be lost, and with it the international community's hope of winning the war against its enemies.

NOTES

1. Barnett R. Rubin, "Crafting a Constitution for Afghanistan," *Journal of Democracy* 15, no. 3 (2004): 7.

2. Andrew Reynolds, "Constitutional Engineering and Democratic Stability: The Debate Surrounding the Crafting of Political Institutions in Afghanistan," in *Building State and Security in Afghanistan*, ed. Wolfgang F. Danspeckgruber and Robert P. Finn (Princeton, NJ: Liechtenstein Institute on Self-Determination at Princeton University, 2007), 37.

3. Rama Mani, *Ending Impunity and Building Justice in Afghanistan*, Issues Paper Series (Kabul: Afghanistan Research and Evaluation Unit, December 2003), 1.

4. "Former King Renounces Throne to Save Afghan Council," *The Guardian*, June 11, 2002.

5. Mani, 1.

6. Ali Ahmad Jalali, "The Legacy of War and the Challenge of Peace Building," in *Building a New Afghanistan*, ed. Robert I. Rotberg (Cambridge, MA: World Peace Foundation; Washington, DC: Brookings Institution Press, 2007), 31.

7. Bernard B. Fall, "Insurgency Indicators," *Military Review*, April 1966, 8.

8. Anne Evans et al., "Subnational Administration in Afghanistan Assessment and Recommendations for Action," March 2004, http://dspace.cigilibrary.org/jspui/handle/123456789/8244.

9. Barnett R. Rubin, "(Re)Building Afghanistan: The Folly of Stateless Democracy," *Current History* 103, no. 672 (April 2004): 166.

10. Sultan Barakat, *Mid-Term Evaluation Report of the National Solidarity Programme (NSP), Afghanistan* (York, UK: University of York, Post-war Reconstruction & Development Unit, May 2006), 1, http://www.york.ac.uk/media/politics/prdu/documents/publications/NSP%20Evaluation%20Summary.pdf.

11. Ministry of Rural Rehabilitation and Development, "National Solidarity Programme Phase Three (NSP III) Operational Manual Version Six ('OM VI')," 2012, 11, http://www.nspafghanistan.org/default.aspx?sel=16.

12. Douglas Saltmarshe and Abhilash Madhi, *Local Governance in Afghanistan: A View from the Ground*, Synthesis Paper Series (Kabul: Afghanistan Research and

Evaluation Unit, June 2011), 56, http://www.areu.org.af/Uploads/EditionPdfs/1114E%20 Local%20Governance%20in%20Afghanistan%20SP%202011.pdf.

13. Ibid.

14. International Crisis Group, *Political Parties in Afghanistan*, Asia Briefing No. 39 (Kabul/Brussels, June 2, 2005), 5, http://www.crisisgroup.org/~/media/Files/asia/south -asia/afghanistan/B039_political_parties_in_afghanistan.pdf.

15. Andrew Reynolds, "The Curious Case of Afghanistan," *Journal of Democracy* 17, no. 2 (2006): 105.

16. International Crisis Group, *Political Parties*, 6.

17. Reynolds, "The Curious Case of Afghanistan," 110.

18. Ibid., 111.

19. Scott Worden, "Afghanistan: An Election Gone Awry," *Journal of Democracy* 21, no. 3 (2010): 11, 22.

20. Ahmad Shah Katawazai, "Government-Mafia-Warlords Nexus and the Present Turmoil," *Khaama Press*, April 6, 2013, http://www.khaama.com/government-mafia -warlords-nexus-and-the-present-turmoil-2365; Antonio Giustozzi, "War and Peace Economies of Afghanistan's Strongmen," *International Peacekeeping* 14, no. 1 (2007): 81.

21. Special Inspector General for Afghan Reconstruction, "Quarterly Report to the United States Congress," July 30, 2014, 102, https://www.sigar.mil/pdf/quarterlyreports/ 2014-07-30qr.pdf.

22. International Crisis Group, *A Force in Fragments: Reconstituting the Afghan National Army*, Asia Report No. 190 (Brussels, May 12, 2010), 7, http://www.crisisgroup .org/~/media/Files/asia/south-asia/afghanistan/190%20A%20Force%20in%20 Fragments%20-%20Reconstituting%20the%20Afghan%20National%20Army.

23. Antonio Giustozzi, "Re-Building the Afghan Army," 2003, 12, http://eprints.lse .ac.uk/28363/1/giustozzi_LSERO_version.pdf.

24. Priscilla Offenhauer, "General and Flag Officer Authorizations for the Active and Reserve Components" (Washington, DC: Library of Congress, December 2007), 16, http://www.loc.gov/rr/frd/pdf-files/CNGR_General-Flag-Officer-Authorizations .pdf; Francis J. Harvey and Peter J. Schoomaker, *A Statement on the Posture of the United States Army*, 2007, 8, http://www.dtic.mil/cgi-bin/GetTRDoc?Location=U2&doc=Get TRDoc.pdf&AD=ADA466893.

25. Michael Vinay Bhatia and Robert Muggah, "The Politics of Demobilization in Afghanistan," in *Security and Post-Conflict Reconstruction : Dealing with Fighters in the Aftermath of War* (New York: Routledge, 2009), 156, n. 13.

26. Ibid., 129.

27. US Department of Defense, Office of the Assistant Secretary of Defense for Public Affairs, "Deputy Secretary Wolfowitz Media Availability at Bagram Air Base, Afghanistan," January 15, 2003, http://www.defense.gov/transcripts/transcript.aspx?transcriptid=1345.

28. Terrence K. Kelly, Nora Bensahel, and Olga Oliker, *Security Force Assistance in Afghanistan: Identifying Lessons for Future Efforts* (Santa Monica, CA: RAND Corporation, 2011), 27.

29. Antonio Giustozzi, "Reconstructing the Defence Sector," in *Afghanistan's Security Sector Governance Challenges: DCAF Afghanistan Working Group*, DCAF Regional Programmes Series 10 (Geneva: Geneva Centre for the Democratic Control of the Armed Forces, 2010), 3, http://www.dcaf.ch/content/download/73136/1118012/file/DCAF_RPS_Afghanistan.pdf.

30. Ibid., 4.

31. US Government Accountability Office, *Afghanistan Security: Efforts to Establish Army and Police Have Made Progress, but Future Plans Need to Be Better Defined*, Report to the Committee on International Relations, House of Representatives (Washington, DC: DIANE, 2005), 13, http://www.gao.gov/assets/250/246956.pdf.

32. Kelly et al., *Security Force Assistance*, 29.

33. US Government Accountability Office, *Afghanistan Security*, 21. Another 4,880 officers and NCOs received "short-term specialized training."

34. Ibid., 26–27.

35. Tonita Murray, "Police-Building in Afghanistan: A Case Study of Civil Security Reform," *International Peacekeeping* 14, no. 1 (2007): 113.

36. Andrew Wilder, *Cops or Robbers? The Struggle to Reform the Afghan National Police*, Issues Paper Series (Kabul: Afghanistan Research and Evaluation Unit, July 2007), 40–41, http://www.areu.org.af/Uploads/EditionPdfs/717E-Cops%20or%20Robbers-IP-print.pdf.

37. Ibid.; "Afghanistan: Reject Known Abusers as Police Chiefs" (Human Rights Watch, May 5, 2006), http://www.hrw.org/news/2006/05/03/afghanistan-reject-known-abusers-police-chiefs.

38. Government of Afghanistan and the International Community, *The Afghanistan Compact*, 2006, 6, http://www.operationspaix.net/DATA/DOCUMENT/5305~v~Quarterly_Report_to_the_United_States_Congress.pdf.

39. Joint Coordination and Monitoring Board, "JCMB Task Force on Afghan National Police Target Strength," presented at The Kabul Process, Fifth JCMB, Kabul, Afghanistan, 2007, 3, http://www.thekabulprocess.gov.af/images/JCMBdocs/5th/5.6task-Force-on-Police-Ceilings.pdf.

40. Inspectors General, US Department of State and US Department of Defense, *Interagency Assessment of Afghanistan Police Training & Readiness* (Washington, DC, November 14, 2006), 11, 15, https://oig.state.gov/system/files/76103.pdf.

41. Department of Defense, *Report on Progress Toward Security and Stability in Afghanistan* (Washington, DC, 2009), 9, http://www.defense.gov/pubs/OCTOBER_1230_FINAL.pdf; Department of Defense, *United States Plan for Sustaining the Afghanistan*

National Security Forces (Washington, DC, 2009), 8, http://www.defense.gov/pubs/pdfs/april_2009.pdf.

42. Ray Rivera, "Afghans Plan 42% Surge in Police and Army Forces; Rise to 378,000 by 2012 Reflects Improvements in Training and Retention," *International Herald Tribune*, January 18, 2011, 3.

43. Saleha Soadat, "Interior Ministry Concerned by Increase in Police Casualties," *Tolonews*, January 28, 2013, http://www.mobygroup.com/moby-media-update/602-mmu-afghanistans-security-prospects-after-nato-withdrawal-28-january-2013.

44. Peter Dahl Thruelsen, "Striking the Right Balance: How to Rebuild the Afghan National Police," *International Peacekeeping* 17, no. 1 (February 2010): 85.

45. Ministry of Interior Affairs, Islamic Republic of Afghanistan, "Afghan National Police Strategy" (March 2010), 21, http://moi.gov.af/en/page/5076.

46. Joseph A. L'Etoile, "Transforming the Conflict in Afghanistan," *PRISM* 2, no. 4 (September 2012): 5.

47. UN High Commissioner for Refugees, *Note on the Structure and Operation of the KhAD/WAD in Afghanistan 1978-1992*, May 2008, http://www.unhcr.org/refworld/pdfid/482947db2.pdf.

48. Tonita Murray, "The Security Sector in Afghanistan: Slow and Unsteady," *South Asian Survey* 16, no. 2 (February 12, 2010): 199.

49. Christian Dennys and Tom Hamilton-Baillie, *Strategic Support to Security Sector Reform in Afghanistan, 2001-2010*, Centre for International Governance Innovation, 2012, 9–13, http://www.operationspaix.net/DATA/DOCUMENT/6732~v~Strategic_Support_to_Security_Sector_Reform_in_Afghanistan_20012010.pdf.

50. Rosie DiManno, "Breakfast with Kabul's Shadowy Spy-Master; Feared Security Official Denies Using Torture While Helping to Spread 'Legitimate Paranoia,'" *Toronto Star*, June 28, 2008, AA02.

51. Jon Boone, "International: Revolutionaries within: Burqas Conceal Women's Dangerous Battle for Rights: Underground Feminist Group Has Cell Organisation to Foil Powerful Enemies," *The Guardian*, May 1, 2010, 29; Jason Burke, "The Secret War: Behind the Lines Torture, Bundles of Cash, Treachery and Spies. America May Be Carpet-Bombing Afghanistan. But the Real Battle for Power Is Being Waged by More Sinister Means," *The Observer*, November 4, 2001, 16; Kate Clark, "NDS Torture: UN Report Makes Bleak Reading," *Afghanistan Analysts Network*, October 11, 2011, http://aan-afghanistan.com/index.asp?id=2147.

52. Tom A. Peter, "Why Afghanistan's Intelligence Agency Has a Major Blind Spot," *Christian Science Monitor*, April 23, 2012; Kate Clark, "New NDS Boss—Who Is He?," *Afghanistan Analysts Network*, July 18, 2010, http://aan-afghanistan.com/index.asp?id=905.

53. Kate Clark, "New NDS Boss."

54. "Afghan MPs Criticize Lack of Coordination Among Security Bodies," *BBC Monitoring South Asia—Political Supplied by BBC Worldwide Monitoring,* May 2, 2011.

55. "Spying on Turncoats Rogue Afghan Troops Threat," *Daily Telegraph (Australia),* February 22, 2012, World sec., 17.

56. Alissa J. Rubin and Matthew Rosenberg, "Ragtag Revolts in Parts of Afghanistan Repel Taliban," *New York Times,* August 25, 2012, A6.

57. Emal Habib, "The Andar Uprising—Co-Opted, Divided and Stuck in a Dilemma," *Afghanistan Analysts Network,* October 30, 2012, http://www.aan-afghanistan.org/index.asp?id=3086.

58. "Afghan Official Says Insurgents Should Not Misuse People's Uprisings," *Tolo TV, Transcribed by BBC Monitoring South Asia* (Kabul, Afghanistan, August 27, 2012).

59. "Afghan Spy Chief-Designate Pledges Tough Action against Terror," *BBC Monitoring South Asia—Political Supplied by BBC Worldwide Monitoring,* September 15, 2012.

3 WARLORDS AND THE COALITION IN AFGHANISTAN

Romain Malejacq

THIS CHAPTER FOCUSES on the relationships between coalition forces and the so-called warlords of post-2001 Afghanistan. While the term *warlord* is frequently used in political and normative ways to evoke "brutality, racketeering and the suffering of civil communities,"[1] these actors are astute political entrepreneurs whose legitimacy rests on "the power to make war effectively"[2] and who play critical roles in people's access to the political arena and economic opportunities. They act at various times as the principal suppliers of governance to people in areas where they wield influence. As such, they cannot be, and have not been, ignored by ISAF. They have been instrumental to allied forces from the very beginning of the US-led intervention. In turn, they have exercised a surprising capacity to shape state-building and state formation processes to suit their interests by exploiting the cross-cutting agendas of external actors. While a multitude of warlords coexist with the state in post-2001 Afghanistan, this chapter focuses on two typical cases: Abdul Rashid Dostum, the ethnic Uzbek leader of northern Afghanistan, and Ismail Khan, the self-proclaimed Emir of Herat.

It is often argued that the main objective of state-building is the centralization of sovereignty, or conversely, the weakening and destruction of alternative forms of governance. Most international actors involved in Afghanistan (foreign governments, aid agencies, international organizations) therefore prefer that warlords recede into insignificance as the central state asserts its authority. While this state-building project promotes the construction of a state along the path most closely associated with the historical rise of Western states, the political survival of Afghan warlords is an indication that the process is in reality being shaped by interactions between the state, the international community, and de facto power holders (warlords in particular). State-builders have to engage in a process of hybridization—arguably the real process of state formation—as they attempt to construct institutions that at least appear to conform to Weberian ideals of bureaucratic institutional and territorial control.

Warlords are "by definition illegitimate and unrecognized."[3] It is therefore striking (and for some truly shocking) to see that coalition forces that are supposed to back and support the official democratically elected government of Afghanistan have been in business with warlords since the very beginning of the US military intervention. The growing role of regular and irregular indigenous forces in external interventions raises practical concerns about the military and political objectives of the Afghan war and the nature of state-building in Afghanistan and elsewhere. In this chapter, I show that warlords maximize their authority in permissive environments—that is, in environments with limited external pressure. They take advantage of the heterogeneity of the international community, both within and outside NATO, to maximize their interests and survive. I chose two cases of warlordism that illustrate how warlords exert diplomacy and how it allows them to survive in changing environments.

WORKING WITH THE DEVIL: AFGHAN MODEL OF WARFARE AND WARLORD STRATEGY

Coalition forces began to achieve a series of quick military victories soon after they began combat operations in October 2001. The success of the "Afghan model" of warfare—US air power working in concert with coalition special operations and Northern Alliance forces on the ground—quickly expelled Taliban forces from key cities around the country.[4] Unfortunately, the "Afghan model" did not support coalition state-building efforts. Afghan warlords took control of regional and national state institutions with the blessing of the Bush administration. Seeking short-term stability through deals with regional leaders to compensate the absence of a central state in turn empowered these illegitimate armed actors and prevented the long-term emergence of the said central state. This "warlord strategy"[5] required "living with ambiguity":[6] US special operations forces worked hand in hand with warlords in their fiefdoms in spite of their increasing stigmatization by human rights organizations.[7]

Things started to change around 2003–2004. US policy makers began at that time to impose "new rules of the game"[8] as most in the Bush administration believed the war in Afghanistan to be about to end. Michael Bhatia wrote,

[The] dominant post-Bonn discourse, particularly among external observers, has been that of the warlord challenge to the central government, which is partly a process of demythologizing the mujahideen. Practically, this is linked to advocacy for the increased pace of DDR [Demobilization, Disarmament, Reintegration], broader security-sector reforms (SSR), governance reform and the proposed creation of a war crimes tribunal.[9]

As *jihadi* credentials became "a liability,"[10] warlords were either co-opted or abandoned by the US and international organizations to favor the construction of the central state.[11] Zalmay Khalilzad, former special presidential envoy and US ambassador to Afghanistan, recalls,

> We worked with President Karzai to persuade major regional leaders to give up their arms in exchange for an opportunity to become legitimate political actors, either through appointments to new positions or though entry into electoral politics.[12]

In this context of weak international demand for proxies and the increasing role of the US State Department over strictly military considerations, Afghan warlords had no choice but to transform their bases of power. At times when the state becomes stronger, warlords transition into something else: they become businessmen, notables, ministers, and governors. They become *dormant* warlords. Because of the kind of authority that they have in their communities and their ability to conduct international relations, they can make the transition back to being warlords if the opportunity presents. They exercise a surprising ability to shape-shift. They reinvent themselves and instrumentalize what Westerners perceive as social disorder to ensure their survival in a changing political environment.

DOSTUM: THE "UNSAVORY FRIEND"[13]

In the 1990s, Abdul Rashid Dostum was the most powerful warlord of northern Afghanistan. His case illustrates both the early ties that were created between coalition forces and warlords and the long-lasting relationships that some warlords manage to initiate and maintain with regional neighbors (in this case with Turkey). It also shows how they take advantage of this.

In spite of his reputation as a violent and self-interested man, Dostum provided the US with a powerful ally on the ground. He immediately recognized that the US-led intervention would give him the opportunity to turn his situation around (both militarily and financially) and reaffirm his local authority. He thus embraced a pro-American stance and became "absolutely gaga on America."[14] He cooperated fully with CIA paramilitary officers and US Army Special Forces, with whom he and his men created what journalist Doug Stanton described as a "familial bond."[15] Together, and with the help of other Northern Alliance's commanders, they were quickly able to recapture Mazar-e Sharif.[16]

Dostum's political opponents have accused him of being sympathetic to American interests, calling him an American stooge. "Dostum is like clay, [the Americans] can shape him however they wish," said a Northern Alliance source.[17] But as subsequent events show, the Americans also were clay in Dostum's hands. The Uzbek leader used his warrior ethos—which resonates particularly well with US Army Special Forces—as a tool to increase his power. He told foreign forces what they wanted to hear to benefit from this new relationship, calling American troops his "friends."[18] General Dostum organized a farewell ceremony for them, offered them presents, and even erected a memorial to honor a deceased CIA paramilitary officer.

Dostum's collaboration with the US allowed him to re-arm and remobilize, but it was also instrumental to his power in many other ways. Like other warlords, Dostum has used foreigners as a way of legitimizing and strengthening his local authority, as his arrival in Mazar-e Sharif perfectly illustrates: "Dostum wanted to be seen riding alongside the Americans as they entered [Mazar]. . . . He suggested that they hoist an American flag on a pole attached to the buggy," wrote Stanton.[19] Like many others, Dostum also tried to instrumentalize American forces to get rid of his opponents by asking them to strike what he claimed were Taliban safe houses.[20]

An elite unit of US Army Special Forces continued advising Dostum long after the fall of Mazar-e Sharif and the signature of the Bonn Agreement. They traveled in his car, sat by his side during military briefings,[21] and became so intimate with him and his men that they reportedly "took an inaugural dip in [Dostum's] new indoor pool" almost a year after the beginning of the US-led intervention.[22] The significance of this form of diplomacy lies in the extent to which Dostum was able to personalize his relations with Americans. Warlord diplomacy is a distinctive form of diplomacy that exploits personal networks as much as formal ties and is conducted to enhance personal authority. One would imagine that the US exercise of power would occur along more formal bureaucratic lines and would be applied in support of a state-building project.

Instead, Dostum's close personal ties, right down to individual soldiers accompanying him, showed how he could manipulate this set of foreign relations to bolster his personalized form of authority.

In the past twenty years, Dostum has acquired the reputation of being "a thoroughly self-interested man"[23] who "goes where the wind blows."[24] Ahmed Rashid, a Pakistani journalist and expert on South Asia, claims that Dostum has "been on every country's payroll, receiving funds from Russia, Uzbekistan, Iran, Pakistan and lately Turkey."[25] Dostum owes his survival, above all else, to his ability to conduct his own diplomacy (toward both foreign and domestic actors) in a highly pragmatic fashion that accommodates to immediate conditions. This is nowhere better exemplified than in his relationship with Turkey, which has offered him great support over the years and has clearly been instrumental to his political and physical survival.

Dostum's relations with Turkey have been conducted along more formal channels than the ones with the US, though personal networks have also played a critical role, at least initially. Dostum managed to develop contacts with that country through Azad Beg, a Turkish nationalist who mobilized Uzbeks and Turkmens from northern Afghanistan in the fight against the Soviet Union. Through his family connections—his cousin, Mirza Aslam Beg, was Pakistan's Chief of Army Staff—Azad Beg became the chief contact between Dostum and Pakistani intelligence.[26] He then developed ties with Turkey, which started to finance Dostum's party (the Junbesh). Turkey has been supporting Dostum ever since, as illustrated by the Akbar Bai episode.[27]

Akbar Bai is an Afghan of Turkmen ethnicity, head of Afghanistan's Association of Islamic Turks, and former Junbesh representative in Kabul, who was sacked in 2004 for not being in line with the party's policy.[28] In 2007, he began to vehemently accuse Dostum of killing Turkmens and Uzbeks, of possessing arms depots, and of entertaining close links with the Inter-Service Intelligence Directorate and the Taliban.[29] A number of minor episodes followed these declarations, during which Dostum's dog was allegedly kidnapped and Akbar Bai's office was set on fire.[30] In November 2007, the Turkmen leader was arrested by a local branch of the National Directorate of Security under Dostum's control on charges of insurgency activities and masterminding an attempt on the general's life.[31]

The tensions between Dostum and Akbar Bai reached another level in the night of February 2, 2008, as the general's men reportedly beat up Akbar Bai and members of his family, kidnapped him, and brought him back to Dostum's palace in Kabul.[32] When police surrounded the tacky pink mansion, Dostum appeared on the roof, allegedly drunk. According to media reports, President Karzai refused permission to make an arrest, Dostum released Akbar Bai, and the standoff ended.[33]

While Akbar Bai demanded that Dostum be officially prosecuted,[34] the attorney general argued that bringing Dostum to court would be difficult, for it could provoke factional fighting in northern Afghanistan. "[Even] in those places where the rule of law does exist, sometimes we cannot enforce the law over some people," he said after Turkey allegedly interceded with Karzai and with the UN to protect the Uzbek leader.[35] According to Peter Tomsen, former US envoy to the Afghan resistance, the Afghan president "[worried] that arresting Dostum could destabilize the relatively stable northern provinces."[36] In fact, a spokesman for Dostum warned of unrest in seven or eight northern provinces if the police tried to arrest the general.[37] After news of the siege emerged, hundreds of protestors demonstrated in Maymana, capital of Faryab province, to support Dostum, threatening to pick up weapons against the government if the police did not leave the Uzbek leader alone.[38]

Dostum was placed under house arrest and suspended from all official positions after he refused to comply with the attorney general's summon for interrogation.[39] In December 2008, a special plane was chartered by Turkish Foreign Minister Ali Babacan, who had reached an agreement with Karzai to put an end to the Akbar Bai case. All charges would be dropped under the condition that Dostum would stay in exile indefinitely.[40] The spokesman for the Turkish Ministry of Foreign Affairs declared that his country had sent a plane for him because he was "the honorary leader of [the] Turkish community in Afghanistan."[41] Less than a year later, right before the 2009 presidential election, Dostum made a triumphant and surprising return to his northern stronghold of Shibirghan, where crowds of followers gathered as a choir sang, "Our King is coming."[42] Karzai, in need of the Uzbek vote, had decided to bring him back—a move that provoked the ire of the international community.

While it is common for leaders of a part of a country (such as Canada's Quebec, Belgium's Wallonia, and so forth) to conduct their own relations with officials in other countries, Dostum's conduct is calculated to highlight to observers the extent to which he, rather than the government, is the central authority responsible for northern Afghanistan's international affairs. This role enhances his image as a patron and as the apex of power in his region. To foreigners, working with Dostum has seemed necessary and pragmatic; to him, international connections are critical to asserting personal power against the state-building enterprise. Dostum's post-2001 authority stems directly from his ability to concentrate multiple sources of power while preventing his competitors from doing the same. What mattered to Dostum has been to remain the only Turkic leader able to combine political and military power, as well as the ability to act in the international system to receive international protection.

ISMAIL KHAN: THE EMIR OF WESTERN AFGHANISTAN

Ismail Khan is a "creature of the borderland."[43] He is the perfect illustration of the way warlords have taken advantage of the heterogeneity of the international system in post-2001 Afghanistan to increase their local autonomy. "The Lion of Herat" portrayed himself as a bulwark against terrorism to benefit from American largesse, while at the same time receiving extensive support from Iran. In October 2001, he expressed his willingness to cooperate with whoever could advance his interests: "To win, we need more money, men and weapons. We're willing to accept help from whoever has our best interest in mind."[44]

Ismail Khan's position vis-à-vis the US has been ambiguous and ambivalent from the beginning of the intervention. The Herati leader always publicly opposed the presence of foreign troops because he understood that they would limit his ability to rule western Afghanistan as he pleased. Interviewed via satellite phone in early October 2001, he said, "We have no desire to see any foreign troops on our soil. The coalition's mission is to provide assistance for the liberation of Afghanistan from terrorist occupation by the Pakistanis and the Arabs. The mission is not to impose a new type of foreign rule."[45] In other words, the US-led intervention should not aim at building a conventional Weberian state.

After he had regained control of Herat, Ismail Khan became more confrontational vis-à-vis the US: he called the deployment of American and British soldiers "a mistake,"[46] and declared that Afghanistan did not need outside help to form a representative government.[47] "[We] do not need the American expert. . . . We have gained enough experience from 23 years of war,"[48] he said. After the signing of the Bonn Agreement in December 2001, Ismail Khan stated that no international troops would be allowed to stay in his territory.[49] Since 2001, he has consistently reiterated his disapproval of foreign interference through the conduct of high-level diplomacy of a sort commonly reserved for formally recognized sovereign states.[50]

Ismail Khan has managed to portray himself as a leader able to deal on an equal footing with powerful heads of state and diplomats, which has in turn strengthened his local legitimacy. His oft-reaffirmed anti-American stance also increased his ideological power, yet it was compatible with accepting considerable resources and behind-the-scenes support from foreign forces. The main point at this stage in Ismail Khan's political evolution was that he was able to force foreigners and the government in the capital to take him seriously as an autonomous political force and realize that they needed to negotiate with him and take his interests into account in any wider political arrangement. Simply put, Ismail Khan was trying to take advantage of the international situation without paying the price—in this case formal allegiance to the state. By holding private meetings with foreign officials, Ismail Khan demonstrated to observers that he should be regarded as the leader of western Afghanistan.[51]

By February 2002, Ismail Khan seemed to have softened his tone toward the US, declaring that he would abide by the government's decision regarding foreign forces: "Whenever the center of government is recognizing that their presence in Herat is needed, we never prohibit,"[52] he said. By March 2002, Ismail Khan had allowed both a UN office to be reopened and a civil affairs unit to be stationed in Herat.[53] Approximately ten US Army Special Forces soldiers also spent several months in one of his guesthouses. They developed a close relationship with him and supported him financially.[54] "Fights were still going on. . . . Giving . . . money [to the warlords] was the normal thing to do to keep them on your side," a Western diplomat said in justification.[55]

At the same time that he developed his relationship with the US, Ismail Khan, despite being a Sunni, also received strong support from Iran.[56] Although he never officially admitted receiving weapons and ammunition, he did not conceal his good relationship with his Western neighbor. He always considered that not dealing with Iran would be "unnatural," considering their geographic and personal historical ties.[57] In early 2002, observers reported that Ismail Khan's soldiers were trained by Iranian advisors, wore Iranian fatigues, and carried Iranian-made rifles.[58] Iran even allegedly sent money to Ismail Khan to pay for his soldiers[59] and provided him with tanks captured from the Taliban.[60]

As the strongest armed actor in western Afghanistan, Ismail Khan found himself at the center of a power struggle between Iran and the US and took great advantage of this peculiar situation. Ahmed Rashid said,

> I think there is a kind of competition going on to gain the favor of the local warlord, Ismail Khan, who controls three of the western provinces that border Iran. . . . He is a master at this game. He's been playing it for the last 10, 15 years. And he frankly has been taking advantage of the Americans and the Iranians.

He's getting them both to start reconstruction in the region he controls, build-ing roads and other things. As far as he's concerned, and as far as the local Herati people are concerned, he's, you know, been playing a very wise game, which has been helping him and helping the territory under his control.[61]

In a typical Afghan ploy, the wily Ismail Khan made sure that the Iranians and the Americans spent most of the time watching each other rather than him, as he fed them with tidbits of misinformation and gossip that kept their daggers drawn.[62]

Both the US and Iran were desperately in need of a strong ally to limit each other's influence in the border region.[63] Ismail Khan's balancing act clearly al-lowed him to accumulate various sources of power, in particular military and economic ones. His military might gave him the means to control Herat and its region and, most of all, to control the borders and the economic benefits associated with them.[64] It also gave Ismail Khan the opportunity to portray himself as the city's only liberator, even though other factions were involved as well. Ismail Khan further increased his local legitimacy by providing goods and services that were in fact paid for by American and Iranian money, custom revenues, and international aid. According to a UN official,

[Ismail Khan] basically presented us with a shopping list of what he wants and stressed the urgency. . . . But it also seems pretty clear that he wants it to be rec-ognised that he is in charge in this region, not the UN, or western governments, or indeed, the government in Kabul.[65]

It is true that "[much] of the power Ismail Khan and his fellow warlords enjoy was a byproduct of U.S. anti-terrorism efforts in Afghanistan."[66]It is more accurate that Ismail Khan's survival is largely due to his ability to navi-gate between different levels, and keep pressure on the various actors involved in western Afghanistan, by never fully cooperating with nor fully defying and antagonizing the central government and its allies. His central position in mul-tiple networks enabled him to acquire military and economic power, which he could in turn use to resist Kabul's homogenizing pressure and run his own fiefdom, without much interference from the center.

CONCLUSION

In the immediate postintervention period, warlords such as Dostum and Ismail Khan developed complex marketing plans to boost their image. They used different "faces" (warrior, businessman, notable, ally against terrorism)

to instrumentalize international actors.[67] Confronted with a changing environment, warlords had to shape-shift and become "dormant," as they were no longer able to exert undisputed control over their territories. They used the heterogeneity of the international community to maintain authority and survive, both physically and politically.

With the growing influence of the Taliban insurgency and the announced departure of US troops, political dynamics have radically changed in the past few years. The tensions between Hamid Karzai and the international community indirectly led the Afghan president, in need of local power holders able to deliver votes, to bring the political brokers back into the loop prior to the 2009 presidential elections.[68] Today, the uncertainty regarding the international community's intentions in Afghanistan after 2014 creates a level of domestic uncertainty that drives the local demand for military leadership. Afghan warlords are reorganizing, remobilizing, and reuniting, and evidence shows that they have the ability to circumvent both the Afghan state and the international community to exert their own kind of diplomacy and negotiate directly with the Taliban.[69]

NOTES

This chapter draws on extensive fieldwork undertaken by the author in Herat, Kabul, Mazar-e Sharif, and the Panjshir, for which he conducted nearly two hundred interviews and spent over nine months in Afghanistan over the course of five years. This author is grateful for research support from the embassy of France in Afghanistan, the Institut des Hautes Etudes de Défense Nationale, the Fondation Pierre Leroux, Northwestern University, Sciences Po Paris, and Columbia University's Harriman Institute.

1. John MacKinlay, "Defining Warlords," in *Peacekeeping and Conflict Resolution*, ed. Tom Woodhouse and Oliver Ramsbotham (London: Cass, 2000), 48. On the normative use of the term *warlord*, see Keith Stanski, "'So These Folks Are Aggressive': An Orientalist Reading of 'Afghan Warlords,'" *Security Dialogue* 40, no. 1 (2009).

2. See Ariel Ahram and Charles King's discussion on *Kriegsherr* in "The Warlord as Arbitrageur," *Theory and Society* 41, no. 2 (March 2012): 171.

3. Robert Rotberg, "Failed States, Collapsed States, Weak States: Causes and Indicators," in *State Failure and State Weakness in a Time of Terror*, ed. Robert Rotberg (Washington, DC: Brookings Institution Press, 2003), 10.

4. For more on US policy options and the "Afghan model" of warfare, see Chapter 4 of this volume.

5. Human Rights Watch, *Afghanistan's Bonn Agreement One Year Later: A Catalog of Missed Opportunities*, December 6, 2002, http://www.hrw.org/news/2002/12/04/afghanistans-bonn-agreement-one-year-later.

6. Zalmay Khalilzad, "How to Nation-Build: Ten Lessons from Afghanistan," *National Interest* (Summer 2005): 22.

7. Michael Bhatia, "The Future of the Mujahideen: Legitimacy, Legacy and Demobilization in Post-Bonn Afghanistan," *International Peacekeeping* 14, no. 1 (January 2007): 94.

8. Khalilzad, "How to Nation-Build," 22.

9. Bhatia, "The Future of the Mujahideen," 95.

10. Interview with Afghan researcher, Kabul, March 13, 2011.

11. Olivier Roy, "Afghanistan: la difficile reconstruction d'un Etat," *Cahiers de Chaillot* 73 (2004): 37.

12. Khalilzad, "How to Nation-Build," 23.

13. Jan Cienski, "Uncle Sam's Shifty New Ally," *Chicago Sun-Times*, October 21, 2001.

14. Ann Marlowe, "'Warlords' and 'Leaders,'" *National Review*, February 18, 2002.

15. Doug Stanton, *Horse Soldiers: The Extraordinary Story of a Band of U.S. Soldiers Who Rode to Victory in Afghanistan* (New York: Scribner, 2009), 197.

16. For a detailed account, see ibid.

17. Quoted in Justin Huggler, "Campaign Against Terrorism: Strategy—American Aircraft Carry Out First Carpet Bombing Raids on Front Line," *The Independent*, November 1, 2001.

18. Jeffrey Schaeffer, "Afghan Soldiers Bid Farewell to U.S. Special Forces," Associated Press Worldstream, December 19, 2001.

19. Stanton, *Horse Soldiers*, 253.

20. Ibid., 280.

21. Quoted in Anna Badkhen, "Reports of Rape, Looting by Afghan Militiamen," *San Francisco Chronicle*, February 15, 2002.

22. Christopher Torchia, "Afghan Commander Gets Indoor Pool," Associated Press Online, September 7, 2002.

23. Cienski, "Uncle Sam's Shifty New Ally."

24. Sudarsan Raghavan, "Charismatic Uzbek Chieftain Important to Future of Afghanistan," Knight Ridder, October 14, 2001.

25. Ahmed Rashid, *Taliban: Militant Islam, Oil and Fundamentalism in Central Asia*, 2nd ed. (New Haven, CT: Yale University Press, 2001), 56.

26. Interview with Afghan researcher, Kabul, February 2, 2011.

27. Interview with Antonio Giustozzi, Kabul, October 11, 2008; interview with Afghan intellectual, February 21, 2011.

28. "Afghan Paper Warns Against Hasty Action in Dealing with Dostum's Incident," *Hasht-e Sobh*, February 6, 2008; Antonio Giustozzi, *Empires of Mud: Wars and Warlords in Afghanistan* (New York: Columbia University Press, 2009), 183.

29. "Head of Afghan Islamic Turks Body Accuses Ex-Jonbesh Leader Dostum," Ariana TV, January 5, 2007; "Afghan Politicians Accuse Gen Dostum of Establishing Links with Taleban," Ariana TV, January 14, 2007.

30. Interview with Michael Semple, former deputy to the EU special representative for Afghanistan, Cambridge, MA, October 27–28, 2011; "Afghan Paper Urges Government to Rein In Tensions in North," *Rah-e Nejat*, June 1, 2007, supplied by BBC Monitoring South Asia.

31. "Afghan Turk Council Head Arrested on Terror Charges," Afghan Aina TV, November 7, 2007.

32. "Afghan ministry Says "Drunk" Northern Leader Attacked Rival's House," Afghan Islamic Press News Agency, February 3, 2008.

33. Rosie DiManno, "Kabul's Big, Bad Warlord; Wanted by Police, Notorious Militiaman Hides Away as City Awaits His Next Move," *Toronto Star*, May 13, 2008.

34. "Battered Afghan Turk Leader Urges Official Prosecution of Dostum," Ariana TV, February 5, 2008, supplied by BBC Monitoring South Asia.

35. Quoted in "Afghanistan: Prosecutor Suggests 'Some People' Cannot Be Tried," Radio Free Europe, February 6, 2008; interview with member of Parliament, Kabul, September 4, 2008.

36. Quoted in Sara Carter, "The Art of Warlord; Flip-flopping General a Mixed Blessing to U.S. in Afghanistan," *Washington Times*, October 12, 2008.

37. Quoted in "Afghanistan: Kabul Siege Underscores Warlord Threat to Rule of Law," Radio Free Europe, February 3, 2008.

38. "Famous Afghan Warlord in Standoff with Police," Agence France Presse, February 3, 2008.

39. "Afghan Daily Says Police Plan to Arrest Northern General Dostum," *Arman-e Melli*, May 18, 2008, supplied by BBC Monitoring South Asia; "Afghan Chief of Staff Suspended as Part of Investigations into Alleged Assault," Tolo TV, February 18, 2008.

40. "Afghan Party Leader Leaves for Turkey After End of House Arrest," *Arman-e Melli*, December 3, 2008, supplied by BBC Monitoring South Asia.

41. "Foreign Ministry Confirms Afghan Warlord Dostum Is in Turkey," Anatolia News Agency, December 4, 2008.

42. Jeremy Page, "Brutal Ally Back to Boost Karzai's Flagging Campaign; 20,000 Supporters Cheer Return of Exiled Warlord," *The Times (London)*, August 18, 2009.

43. Ahram and King, "The Warlord as Arbitrageur," 170.

44. "Afghans Beginning to Rebel Against Taliban in West: Opposition," Agence France Presse, October 4, 2001.

45. "Afghan Northern Alliance Commander Says Foreign Troop Support Unnecessary," *Asharq al-Awsat*, October 11, 2001, supplied by BBC Monitoring South Asia.

46. "'Foreign Troops Should Go Home': Unwanted and Unwelcome, Say Alliance Leaders," *Edmonton Journal (Alberta)*, November 17, 2001.

47. Amy Waldman, "A Nation Challenged: Herat; The Warlord, in Charge Again, Thanks the West but Wants It Gone," *New York Times*, November 17, 2001.

48. Behrouz Mehri, "Hatred Drove Afghan People to Rise Up Against Taliban: 'Lion of Herat,'" Agence France Presse, November 16, 2001.

49. Kim Sengupta, "Campaign Against Terrorism: Last-Minute Hitch Could Stall Peace-Keeping Deal; Warlord Insists Western Soldiers Are Not Wanted," *The Independent*, December 31, 2001.

50. "Afghan Leader to Visit Iran," IPR Strategic Business Information Database, February 5, 2002; "No Evidence of Iranian Interference in Afghanistan: UN Official," Agence France Presse, January 24, 2002; "Governor of Herat, Afghanistan, Ismail Khan," National Public Radio, February 3, 2002; "Afghan Leader to Visit Iran"; Regan Morris, "U.S. Commander Seeks to Shore Up Ties to the Men Who Wield Real Power in Afghanistan," Associated Press Worldstream, July 24, 2002.

51. "Afghan Herat Governor Says Kabul Visit 'Effective and Useful,'" Herat TV, August 18, 2002; "Afghan Governor, UN Envoy Discuss Security Issues," Herat TV, August 18, 2002; Ahmed Rashid, *Descent into Chaos: How the War Against Islamic Extremism Is Being Lost in Pakistan, Afghanistan and Central Asia* (London: Allen Lane, 2008), 143; Susan Glasser, "Karzai Team Sent to Calm Unruly Area; Afghan Militia Leader Evasive About Truce," *Washington Post*, July 25, 2002.

52. "Governor of Herat, Afghanistan, Ismail Khan," National Public Radio, February 3, 2002.

53. "Afghan governor, UN Officials Agree to Reopen UN Office in West—Iranian Radio," Voice of the Islamic Republic of Iran, February 2, 2002; Morris, "U.S. Commander Seeks to Shore Up Ties."

54. Interview with Jean Malekzade, head of office (Herat), UNAMA, Kabul, March 4, 2011.

55. Interview with Western diplomat, Chicago, October 10, 2011.

56. Amy Waldman, "A Nation Challenged: Warlords; Courted by U.S. and Iran, an Afghan Governor Plays One Side Off the Other," *New York Times*, April 3, 2002.

57. "Warlords in Afghanistan, Like Ismail Khan, Reluctant to Give Up Power After Election for New Government," ABC News, June 11, 2002; Margaret Coker, "Iranian Influence, and Guns, Felt in Western Afghanistan," Cox News Service, February 1, 2002.

58. Waldman, "Courted by U.S. and Iran"; Coker, "Iranian Influence."

59. Suzanne Goldenberg, "War in Afghanistan: Global Aid for Kabul, Iranian Arms for Herat: The Warlord Ismail Khan Has Found an Eager Ally in the Fight to Keep His Regional Fiefdom," *The Guardian*, January 24, 2002.

60. Bay Fang, "The Great Game 2002," *U.S. News & World Report*, August 12, 2002. According to Giustozzi, "Iranian trucks were reported unloading weapons in Ismail Khan's armories" as late as 2004 (*Empires of Mud*, 236).

61. "Iran and US Seem to Be Competing for Favor of Afghanistan's Warlords and Ruling Government," National Public Radio, July 19, 2002.

62. Rashid, *Descent into Chaos*, 125.

63. Telephone interview with Ahmed Rashid, May 10, 2012.

64. Abdulkader Sinno, *Organizations at War in Afghanistan and Beyond* (Ithaca, NY: Cornell University Press, 2008), 264; Rashid, *Descent into Chaos*, 127.

65. Sengupta, "Campaign Against Terrorism."

66. "Afghan Warlord Brings Stability to Region, But at a Price," Voice of America News, November 22, 2002.

67. Yama Torabi, *State-, nation- et peace-building comme processus de transaction: l'interaction des intervenants et des acteurs locaux sur le théâtre de l'intervention en Afghanistan, 2001–08*, PhD dissertation, Institut d'Etudes Politiques de Paris, 2009, 214–265.

68. Interview with former aide to Massoud, Kabul, February 28, 2011.

69. "Karzai Opponents Talk with Taliban, Other Militant Group in Search of Peace Deal," Associated Press, March 18, 2013.

4 UNITED STATES
Examining America's Longest War

Stephen M. Grenier

SOON AFTER THE SEPTEMBER 11, 2001, terrorist attacks, the US government confirmed that members of al Qaeda, a terrorist group founded and led by Osama bin Laden, was responsible for the strikes that killed almost three thousand civilians from ninety different nations.[1] Bin Laden and his lieutenants planned the attacks while operating from a collection of terrorist training camps in Afghanistan under the protection of the Taliban, the Islamist organization governing the remote central Asian nation. The 9/11 attacks were not al Qaeda's first successful terrorist operation; it was also responsible for several other strikes including the 1998 US embassy bombings in Kenya and Tanzania and the 2000 attack on an American frigate anchored in the Gulf of Aden in Yemen. When Taliban leader Mullah Omar refused to turn bin Laden over to American authorities, the US led an international coalition that quickly toppled the Taliban and forced bin Laden and other al Qaeda leaders into hiding.[2]

During the subsequent thirteen years, US policy in Afghanistan underwent three phases that will also serve as the general outline for this chapter: initial liberation (2001), consolidation (2002–2006), and counterinsurgency and phased withdrawal (2007–2014). This chapter will examine why the US and its international partners have failed to bring lasting security to significant portions of Afghanistan. Despite over 2,300 American troops killed in action, almost 17,700 wounded, $750 billion spent, and an impressive influx of technologically advanced military hardware, large parts of Afghanistan remained under insurgent control in 2014.[3] Afghanistan National Security Forces (ANSF), the training of which has long been touted by US civilian and military leaders as a critical task in enabling Afghanistan to address its long-term security needs, remain largely incapable of conducting combat operations without coalition assistance. There are several reasons for these failings; resilient insurgent networks, an uncooperative Pakistani government, the illicit narcotics trade, corrupt Afghan government officials, and the Bush administration's focus on Iraq are just a few of the complex issues that have contributed to the dire security situation in Afghanistan today.[4] Because of space limitations and an effort to complement the information presented in other parts of this volume, this chapter will focus on US bureaucratic shortcomings, the most glaring of which is the absence of an overarching strategy. Immediately following the 9/11 attacks, President Bush articulated America's strategic goal in Afghanistan: to remove the Taliban from power and destroy al Qaeda as an effective terrorist organization.[5] However, when Afghanistan was liberated three months later, US strategic goals became ambiguous and public remarks by senior leaders in Washington often contradicted standing guidance to military commanders in the field. As a result, US Afghanistan policy has consistently focused on operational- and tactical-level questions such as how many American troops should be deployed, how they should be organized, and what type of missions they should undertake, instead of articulating how this mission fits into a larger regional or global strategic context.

Recognizing the operational and tactical nature of US policy, this chapter argues that the US military, through a series of intentional and unintentional actions, hindered the creation of an effective Afghan National Army (ANA). The absence of an effective ANA was a key reason the security situation steadily deteriorated, eventually becoming so dire that in 2009, Secretary of Defense Robert Gates relieved General David McKiernan, the commander of all US and coalition troops in Afghanistan, and President Obama ordered a "top-to-bottom" policy review. American military officials put parochial interests ahead of Afghanistan's security needs and harmed the nascent ANA in three ways. First, the US military's insatiable appetite to work with local militia forces stifled ANA recruiting efforts until 2007. Militia fighters enjoyed higher wages and potential ANA recruits saw little incentive in joining the fledgling army. Second, Pentagon officials transferred the responsibility of training and advising the ANA from special operations units to the US Army National Guard. Once relieved of the ANA training mission, special operations forces returned their focus to their preferred types of operations: raids, ambushes, and combat patrols.[6] Third, US special operations forces created specialized units within the

ANA. These units, such as the ANA Commando battalions, were not created to address ANA capability gaps as senior officials claimed. Rather, these units were established in response to the requirement that all US military forces conduct combat operations with "official Afghan security forces"—a category that did not include the militia fighters that special operations forces preferred to work with. When conventional coalition units refused to allow special operations troops to partner with their assigned Afghan troops, special operations forces created elite ANA units to comply with the directive. This caused bureaucratic infighting among senior ANA officials and diverted promising junior officers and sergeants away from the ranks of regular ANA units, further eroding the ANA's overall combat effectiveness.[7]

Blame for America's bureaucratic failings cannot be solely levied against the Pentagon; multiple US government agencies and departments also share responsibility. However, when the US agreed to train and advise the new ANA, Pentagon leaders acknowledged that a professional army was needed to protect the population and create a secure environment for reconstruction and international aid efforts. Their actions undermined the ANA's combat effectiveness, harmed the legitimacy of the fledgling Afghan government, and served as a catalyst for corruption and patronage.

INITIAL LIBERATION (2001)

The war in Afghanistan is in many ways America's war. The US was attacked and the nation demanded an immediate response. On September 14, 2001, Congress authorized the president to use all "necessary and appropriate force" against those who "planned, authorized, committed or aided" the 9/11 attacks.[8] Central Intelligence Agency (CIA) operatives immediately deployed to Afghanistan to reestablish their contacts within the Northern Alliance—a loose confederation of anti-Taliban forces that controlled northeast Afghanistan.

The coalition invasion of Afghanistan—named Operation Enduring Freedom—began on October 7, 2001, when US and British warships launched dozens of cruise missiles and coalition aircraft bombed al Qaeda training camps and Taliban facilities. America's strategic goal was clear: to remove the Taliban from power in Afghanistan and destroy al Qaeda as an effective terrorist organization. On October 12, 2001, US special operations forces began entering Afghanistan and linked up with Northern Alliance fighters. The initial plan called for US troops to spend three months training indigenous forces before launching an offensive against the Taliban, but Northern Alliance leaders, most notably Mohammad Fahim Khan and Abdul Rashid Dostum, objected to the plan and convinced their US counterparts that the offensive should begin immediately. A combined force of Northern Alliance militia, CIA paramilitary officers, and US Army Special Forces operators attacked Taliban positions guarding the key northern city of Mazar-e Sharif on November 9, 2001, beginning what many experts thought would be months of hard fighting. But once US Army Special Forces teams directed coalition aircraft to bomb Taliban positions, enemy resistance crumbled, and over two thousand Taliban fighters surrendered Mazar-e Sharif two days later.[9] The combination of Northern Alliance ground forces, air-delivered precision-guided munitions, and satellite communications—dubbed the "Afghanistan model" by military experts—created a potent force, which quickly tipped the military balance in favor of the coalition.[10] By the end of 2001, all major Afghan cities were under Northern Alliance control.

The coalition's failure to kill or capture bin Laden did not dampen the international community's willingness to reinforce the political and security gains made over the previous three months. Meeting in Bonn, Germany, in December 2001, Afghan representatives selected Hamid Karzai as the leader of the Afghan Interim Authority (AIA) and the United Nations authorized the creation of the International Security Assistance Force (ISAF) to secure Kabul and support the new government. Only a few months after the 9/11 attacks, the US and its British, Australian, Canadian, and other international partners had achieved President Bush's stated objective of destroying al Qaeda and driving the Taliban from power. With little fanfare, however, President Bush significantly altered America's Afghanistan policy of liberating Afghans from an oppressive government that supported transnational terrorism to undertaking long-term nation-building efforts.[11] Speaking at a White House press conference with Hamid Karzai in January 2002, President Bush stated, "The United States is committed to building a lasting partnership with Afghanistan. We will help the new Afghan government provide the security that is the foundation of peace."[12] Unfortunately for military commanders in Afghanistan, Washington provided little strategic guidance on the new policy, leaving US military and diplomatic officials to figure it out on their own.

CONSOLIDATION (2002–2006)

The coalition began to use local security forces in early 2002 when US special operations and CIA operatives consolidated numerous Northern Alliance formations. Although these groups were largely independent of each other, co-alition forces collectively referred to them as the Afghan Militia Force (AMF). Totaling almost sixty thousand fighters, the AMF were paid by the CIA and gar-risoned adjacent to American special operations outposts located throughout eastern and southern Afghanistan. The average AMF unit consisted of three hundred to five hundred fighters, which enabled local AMF commanders to guard coalition facilities while simultaneously dispatching units to accompany special operations troops on combat operations.[13] As special operations forces and their AMF partners searched for Taliban and al Qaeda stragglers, a US Army Special Forces battalion arrived in April 2002 to train the first nine bat-talions of the ANA at the Kabul Military Academy, a dilapidated, Soviet-built compound located on the outskirts of Kabul.[14] That same month, President Bush stated, "Peace will be achieved by helping Afghanistan train and develop its own national army."[15] General Tommy Franks, the commander of US Cen-tral Command, said training the Afghan national army will "certainly be one of our more important projects in the days, weeks, months ahead, because the national army of Afghanistan is going to be an essential element of their long-term security."[16] According to US Army Special Operations Command's official history, US Army Special Forces were the ideal choice for this mission: "This ANA training mission was what Special Forces units were created to do. Ex-perience from previous training missions had prepared the 1st Battalion, 3rd SFG [Special Forces Group] to operate from a 'bare-base' facility and to train a local military force. No other force in the US military has the capability and flexibility to perform such an important political mission with such global implications."[17]

Despite the endorsement of General Franks and other senior officials, the ANA training mission soon experienced serious setbacks. The number of re-cruits reporting for training in Kabul was far below initial predictions and by November 2002, seven months after training began, only four ANA battalions had been created, all of which were unable to conduct anything beyond rudi-mentary tasks.[18] Coalition leaders identified the AMF as both the cause of the ANA's woes and a potential solution to its recruiting problem. In June 2002, the average AMF fighter was paid $200 a month and served near his home in an ethnically homogenous group. In contrast, ANA recruits received a monthly salary of $30, were stationed in Kabul (often far from home), and were assigned to an ethnically diverse unit whose leaders often condoned the physical, emo-tional, and sexual abuse of ethnic minorities.[19] Afghan and coalition officials determined that a large-scale demobilization of AMF fighters was necessary if the nascent ANA had any chance of enticing fighting-age Afghans to join its ranks. Despite the objections of US special operations and CIA representatives, the number of US-funded AMF fighters was reduced by half and by the end of 2002, over four thousand AMF fighters had reported to ANA recruiting depots, enough trainees to staff six ANA battalions. This surge of new recruits quickly evaporated, however, when more than half of them deserted before they completed basic training, many opting to rejoin the AMF.

As coalition trainers and Afghan government officials struggled to retain ANA recruits, US special operations forces continued to focus on disrupting sporadic insurgent activity throughout the country. In response to concerns that insurgents were planning to launch an offensive from Pakistan, coalition forces doubled the number of heavily fortified outposts that were used to stockpile supplies and ammunition. Securing these outposts necessitated the recruitment of additional local security forces, which made it even more difficult to persuade men to join the ANA. Collectively labeled the Afghan Defense Force (ADF), these local forces represented the coalition's first attempt to create a modern version of the *arbakai*, a traditional tribal community defense force that had been largely used in southeastern Afghanistan throughout the second half of the twentieth century.[20] Whereas AMF fighters were often indebted to former Northern Alliance leaders, ADF forces would, in theory, guard their villages and answer to local leaders. In reality, few legitimate elders remained and ADF leaders routinely developed patronage relationships with local strongmen and corrupt officials.

As the Pentagon began preparations for the invasion of Iraq in early 2003, many of the same officials who earlier insisted that US Army Special Forces were the ideal troops for training and advising the new ANA now argued that conventional forces—not US Army Special Forces troops—were the appropriate entity to train the Afghans. This change of opinion was not prompted by US military commitments in Iraq, as the number of US special operations troops in Afghanistan remained relatively constant between 2002 and 2009.[21] Rather, special operations leaders changed their minds because they did not like the image of the nation's elite warriors teaching lackluster recruits how to march and do other rudimentary tasks, especially when just a year earlier the world witnessed bearded Green Berets dressed in local attire attacking Taliban positions on horseback.[22] Responsibility for training the ANA was transferred in July 2003 from US Army Special Forces to Combined Joint Task Force Phoenix, a newly established organization mostly consisting of US Army National Guard soldiers.[23] For the next three years, US special operations forces—long touted as the military's most culturally astute and effective combat advisors—had little interaction with ANA troops, instead partnering almost exclusively with local militias.[24]

As US special operations forces deepened their ties with local security forces, the number of US conventional troops slowly increased. Coalition bases in Bagram and Kandahar began to swell, and new installations such as Forward Operating Base Salerno in Khost served as launching pads for large-scale clearing operations.[25] Frustrated field commanders developed "local campaign plans" in an effort to tie their activities to nebulous US strategic goals, but the focus of these efforts varied widely between rotating units. Some plans emphasized killing and capturing insurgents while other units focused on protecting the population and assisting newly appointed district and provincial governors. The US, like several other countries mentioned in this volume, fielded Provincial Reconstruction Teams (PRTs) in an effort to win the "hearts and minds" of local residents by using the Commander's Emergency Response Program (CERP) and other funding sources to repair roads and other small-scale projects. Although the US PRT model emphasized a strong civilian-military balance, many PRTs suffered a perpetual shortage of civilian personnel, which often led to the "militarization" of reconstruction efforts. International aid workers were especially critical of US PRTs, which often linked humanitarian assistance to the willingness of local residents to provide information on insurgent activity, a practice that violated the principle of neutrality of international aid efforts.[26]

Despite growing levels of violence—most notably the frequent use of improvised explosive devices—US officials remained optimistic and consistently described the Taliban as a beaten foe throughout 2005.[27] This positive outlook prompted three major sequential changes to US policy in an effort to quicken the transition of security duties to Afghan security forces. First, in 2005 the US agreed to take over from Germany the responsibility for training and reforming the Afghan National Police (ANP). The US added trainers, extended the initial training program from eight to twelve weeks, and raised ANP salaries to retain educated recruits. Building on the lessons learned from US ANA Embedded Training Teams (ETTs), which had been advising ANA formations since 2003, US officials created advisory teams to work with Ministry of Interior staff sections and ANP units in the field. American conventional units that were not already advising the ANA were partnered with ANP formations.

Recognizing that US forces would remain in Afghanistan until the ANP and ANA were capable of fighting the Taliban without coalition assistance, Lieutenant General Karl Eikenberry, the senior American commander in Afghanistan, prompted the second major policy change in early 2006 when he ordered all tactical units to partner with their Afghan counterparts to increase host nation capacity. For the first time, American commanders would now be evaluated on the capability of their indigenous partners. The demobilization of all Afghan militias—to include AMF and ADF fighters working with special operations troops—marked the third change in US policy. Officials in Kabul and Washington agreed that warlords and local strongmen constituted a growing threat to the Afghan government by orchestrating narcotics trafficking and other nefarious activities. The coalition moved quickly and by late 2006, over fourteen thousand militia fighters were disarmed and demobilized. Many militia members participated in local award ceremonies where they received a severance package of two months' pay (on average approximately $350), a certificate of appreciation from the US government, and an Afghan service medal, the Order of the Lion.[28]

The long-term effects of these policy changes were mixed. Under American ETTs, the ANP slowly evolved from a Western-style city police organization into a paramilitary force. Although ANP attrition rates remained far above that of the ANA and significant capacity issues remained, the longer training program, better weapons, higher salaries, and additional advisors improved the combat effectiveness of some ANP units. The directive to partner with official Afghan forces and the order to demobilize militias caused a serious predicament for US special operations forces. Conventional units had already formed official partnerships with ANA and ANP units before the militias were demobilized, and this left few remaining Afghan troops for special operations forces to work with. According to one US Army Special Forces field grade officer, "The decision to give up the ANA finally caught up with us. Our desire to get into gunfights and drop a bunch of bombs got in the way of our real purpose for being here—training and advising indigenous forces in combat. Now we are stuck on the firebase while an infantry squad leads fifty ANA guys on a dismounted patrol."[29] Another Special Forces officer bluntly stated, "Our [US Army Special Forces] doctrine clearly states the twelve-man detachment is organized, trained, and equipped to advise a battalion-size indigenous force. When we finally got the opportunity to advise indigenous troops in combat for the first time since Vietnam, we trained a couple of ANA battalions and walked away."[30]

Special operations leaders considered the lack of available Afghan partners their "most critical issue," and they began to brief visiting officials and congressional delegations incessantly.[31] After their appeals were ignored or dismissed by prominent visitors as an "internal command issue," they resolved to create and partner with their own ANA units.[32]

COUNTERINSURGENCY AND PHASED WITHDRAWAL (2007–2014)

In January 2006, delegates from sixty-six nations and eleven international organizations participated in the London Conference on Afghanistan to assess the coalition's progress over the previous four years.[33] The security situation in Afghanistan was steadily deteriorating and the optimistic outlook presented by US intelligence officers just a few months earlier proved to be grossly inaccurate. American officials blamed the surge in violence on a cumbersome North Atlantic Treaty Organization (NATO) command structure and the inability of coalition partners to conduct effective counterinsurgency operations.[34] Others criticized Secretary of Defense Donald Rumsfeld's "light footprint" policy and viewed his December 2005 decision to withdraw 3,000 US troops—at a time when violence levels were rising—as evidence that Washington was preoccupied by the war in Iraq.[35] In this context, the delegates in London approved the Afghanistan Compact, which provided an overarching framework for reforming the security, governance, and economic development sectors. To address security concerns, the delegates approved a sizable expansion of both the ANA (from 18,000 to 70,000 soldiers) and the ANP (from 20,000 to 62,000 officers) over the next four years.[36] To some analysts, the ANA was nothing more than an "auxiliary force" under the control of US military forces rather than a national military organization.[37] These observations forced the US and NATO to acknowledge that their ANA and ANP training efforts had failed and that both security forces suffered from dangerously low morale, inadequate weapons, poor training, and ineffective leadership.

The Combined Security Transition Command–Afghanistan (CSTC-A)—the organization responsible for all Afghan security training—redoubled its efforts to create a highly trained military force that emphasized quality over sheer numbers. In reality, the US and NATO went even further and began to "mirror image" Afghan security forces into a Western-style defense enterprise. CSTC-A established a collection of regional training centers and technical training schools and added embedded advisors throughout the ANA and ANP, which adopted modern American weapons and equipment. ANA battalions—whose primary mode of transportation was limited to walking or using rented (or commandeered) civilian automobiles—received a complement of light tactical vehicles. Night-vision devices gave Afghan security forces the ability to operate at night, and individual body armor reduced life-threatening injuries and raised soldier confidence and morale. After a slow start, the coalition's reinvigorated ANA training effort began to show promising results and by the end of 2007, the ANA end strength reached 35,000 troops. After the authorized size of the ANA was raised even further, end strength increased to 75,000 in 2008; 95,000 in 2009; 134,000 in 2010; 171,000 in 2011; and 198,000 in 2012.[38]

As CSTC-A accelerated its ANA training efforts, special operations leaders presented their plan to create six ANA Commando battalions—one for each ANA corps—to address the need for a highly trained raid force and to serve as a "leadership incubator" for the ANA by training junior officers and sergeants who would then return to regular ANA units.[39] Afghan officials initially balked at the idea of creating elite units, but according to three senior ANA officers, they soon recognized the benefits. Commandos provided an opportunity to establish new relationships with US special operations forces, which often yielded financial rewards through the awarding of lucrative private security contracts.[40] Commando volunteers were selected from existing ANA units to attend ten weeks of additional infantry instruction modeled on US Army Ranger training. The US established the first ANA Commando battalion in July 2007 and activated subsequent units approximately every four months until a total of nine battalions were created.[41] ANA officers criticized the Commandos for spending too much time in garrison and questioned why they only conducted short-duration, helicopter-borne operations, which enabled them to avoid the biggest killer on the battlefield—improvised explosive devices—an option denied to the rest of the vehicle-borne ANA. Official Commando records for 2010–2012 validate some of this criticism. None of the nine Commando battalions conducted combat operations on more than thirteen days a month. Although the lack of available helicopters, adverse weather, evolving intelligence, and religious holidays all contributed to low utilization rates, these factors do not explain why every Commando battalion remained idle for at least seventeen days each month.[42] In addition to the Commandos, US special operations forces established other elite Afghan units such as ANA Special Forces detachments, counterimprovised explosive device units, and ANP Provincial Response Companies, which resemble police special weapons and tactics (SWAT) teams often found in Western cities. Although each of these organizations achieved inter-mittent tactical success, they also contributed to long-term problems. Elite units reinforced patronage networks by providing opportunities for senior leaders to promote well-connected officers and offer choice assignments. Pre-dictably, tensions flared when Commando units conducted raids and cordon-and-search missions near ANA garrisons, which threatened illicit trafficking networks operated by local ANA and ANP units.[43]

Despite these issues, US officials viewed the Commandos and other elite units as proof that with the proper training and equipment, effective Afghan units could be established. However, most Afghan security forces were unable to stem the violence that paralyzed large portions of Afghanistan in 2007–2008. In response, General David McKiernan, the commander of all US and ISAF troops, requested thirty thousand additional US troops to address increased in-surgent activity. McKiernan based his request on a variety of sources including the US Army counterinsurgency manual, which dismissed the "light footprint" approach the US had employed until 2007 and stressed the importance of hav-ing a high per-capita security force presence to protect the population.[44] The Obama administration seemed to agree with McKiernan's assessment when it announced its new strategy in March 2009, which established four priorities—security, governance, reconstruction, and development—and called for greater coordination between military and civilian officials. US military forces were directed to focus on two areas: secure the Afghan people and train Afghan secu-rity forces. As insurgent attacks grew more complex—buried roadside bombs and suicide attacks became common—US and coalition forces began to rely more heavily on combat aircraft and artillery to compensate for the lack of ground troops. The White House approved McKiernan's request for additional troops, but only a few arrived before the summer fighting season began in April 2009.[45] The coalition's reliance on air power and artillery prompted insurgents to adjust their tactics and engage coalition forces while positioned among the civilian population. The insurgents' goal was to entice a coalition airstrike or artillery barrage that would inadvertently cause civilian casualties. One ex-ample occurred on May 4, 2009, in Granai, a small village located south of Herat. Insurgents engaged US troops from several buildings in the village and then stealthily withdrew before aircraft dropped several bombs, killing 147 men, women, and children.[46]

Secretary of Defense Robert Gates announced during a May 12, 2009, press conference that he had requested McKiernan's resignation, making a rare decision to remove a top wartime commander.[47] General Stanley McChrystal, the former head of US Joint Special Operations Command, was selected to take over. Although incidents like the Granai bombing concerned Gates, they were not the primary reason for McKiernan's relief. Prominent insiders—to include General David Petraeus—convinced Gates that McKiernan lacked the "flexibility and understanding" needed to conduct modern counterinsurgency operations.[48] McKiernan's supporters countered that the Afghanistan campaign had been grossly underresourced since the war began, and he was the first American commander to accurately assess how the war was progressing. The Obama administration's new strategy, which incorporated most of McKiernan's earlier recommendations, seemed to support their claim that McKiernan was wrongly cashiered.[49]

McChrystal's initial assessment of the situation in Afghanistan was alarming. The Afghan government was on the brink of collapse and the US faced the real possibility of defeat. McChrystal requested an additional forty thousand US troops to support a new strategy built on three core (and familiar) principles: protect the Afghan people, partner with Afghan security forces, and build Afghan government capacity. To achieve these objectives, he issued a series of directives that dramatically changed how the coalition fought the war. For example, airstrikes would be approved only if coalition forces were in danger of being overrun. If coalition ground troops identified the presence of civilians while they were engaging insurgents, they were required to break contact and withdraw. McChrystal justified these restrictions, saying, "We will not win by simply killing insurgents. We will help the Afghan people win by securing them, by protecting them from intimidation, violence, and abuse, and by operating in a way that respects their culture and religion. That means that we must change the way we think, act, and operate."[50] An intense debate over how the US should proceed in Afghanistan began in September 2009. McChrystal's request for forty thousand additional troops, fraud allegations surrounding the August 2009 Afghan presidential election, and the growing number of US casualties prompted President Obama to conduct a "top-to-bottom" policy review. In reality, the review focused almost entirely on military operations. The "counterinsurgency" option, advocated by McChrystal, Petraeus, and several Washington insiders, stressed the importance of protecting Afghan civilians, expanding reconstruction efforts, and deploying additional US forces to achieve a high per-capita security force presence to protect the population. Ironically, this was the same argument that McKiernan made before he was fired. Vice President Joe Biden promoted the "counterterrorism" option, which would employ special operations teams and unmanned aerial vehicles (drones) to target al Qaeda cells and promote efforts to support a stable government and secure nuclear stockpiles in Pakistan.[51]

In November 2009, President Obama approved the deployment of thirty thousand additional troops with the caveat that these troops would begin to withdraw by July 2011. The additional US troops enabled McChrystal to implement a version of the "clear, hold, build" approach that was used in Iraq. Two large-scale operations in southern Afghanistan—Operation Moshtarak in Helmand and Operation Hamkari in Kandahar—served as an opportunity to coordinate security, governance, and development efforts and test McChrystal's much-publicized "government in a box" concept, which promised to provide local residents with basic government services as soon as hostilities ended.[52] In both campaigns, US and coalition forces "cleared" insurgent fighters (with considerable effort) from major population areas, but the follow-on "hold" and "build" efforts featuring Afghan police forces and government administrators were largely ineffective.[53]

On June 23, 2010, President Obama fired McChrystal after insubordinate comments directed toward Vice President Biden and other senior administration officials appeared in a *Rolling Stone* magazine article.[54] General Petraeus was quickly named as McChrystal's successor. Petraeus had little Afghanistan experience, but he was highly regarded on Capitol Hill and had authored the US military's current counterinsurgency doctrine. Soon after taking command, Petraeus convinced President Hamid Karzai to authorize the creation of the Afghan Local Police (ALP), a force of local villagers who would be trained, equipped, and advised by US special operations forces to defend their homes against the Taliban. The ALP was the fourth attempt by US special operations troops to create a viable local defense force since the demobilization of AMF and ADF fighters in 2006.[55] Supporters argued that the ALP protected residents of isolated villages neglected by Afghan security forces. Critics claimed the ALP was another poorly vetted militia that undermined the central government and preyed on local residents.[56] Unlike previous efforts to establish local defense forces, the ALP initially delivered promising results. In June 2011, media reports citing leaked intelligence documents indicated that the ALP and special operations raids—not the surge of coalition troops—were largely responsible for the security gains in central Afghanistan.[57] These reports served as a catalyst to expand the ALP program and by October 2013, over twenty-four thousand ALP troops were stationed among 119 districts across the country. While US officials promoted the effectiveness of local security forces, US and coalition units began to transfer security responsibilities to Afghan security forces such as the ALP. Once US and coalition forces withdrew from the isolated villages, dozens of ALP units quietly negotiated cease-fire agreements with local insurgent forces. Other ALP outposts became active participants in narcotics trafficking and other illicit behavior while ALP units that remained loyal to the Afghan government were routinely infiltrated by insurgents with horrifying results.[58]

NEGOTIATING THE WAY AHEAD

Osama bin Laden's death in May 2011 coupled with the phased drawdown of US troops in 2011–2012 prompted senior Afghan officials to question whether the US would continue to support Afghanistan after 2014. President Obama answered those critics when he and President Karzai signed a Strategic Partnership Agreement (SPA) in early May 2013. The agreement reaffirmed Washington's commitment to Afghan stability by pledging security and economic assistance until 2024, a decade after US combat forces are scheduled to leave the country. Although the SPA lacks many specifics, the US agreed to designate Afghanistan as a Major Non-NATO Ally (MNNA), a category that would permit Kabul to receive sophisticated military equipment and advanced training.[59] The agreement also established the framework for developing a detailed US-Afghanistan Bilateral Security Agreement (BSA), the negotiations for which were completed in October 2013 and eventually signed on September 30, 2014, the day after President Ashraf Ghani took office. The BSA permits approximately 9,800 US troops to remain in Afghanistan after 2014 to train and advise Afghan National Security Forces and conduct counterterrorism operations against al Qaeda stragglers and senior insurgent leaders.[60]

The BSA marks a significant milestone in US-Afghanistan defense relations, but it will not be enough to address many of the issues that await the Ghani administration. Invasive neighbors on Afghanistan's eastern and western borders, resilient insurgent networks, a growing illicit narcotics trade, and corrupt Afghan government officials—the same problems that challenged the new Karzai administration in early 2002—remain. Despite significant investments in American blood and treasure, most Afghan security forces, to include elite special operations forces, remain incapable of conducting and sustaining effective counterinsurgency operations because of poor logistics and corrupt leaders, many of whom participate in patronage relationships with local strongmen and corrupt government officials. Even worse, the massive Western-style defense enterprise that the US invested so much time and money building has now become a liability due to Kabul's inability to pay its security forces or maintain its equipment without significant, long-term international aid. As the fourteenth anniversary marking the beginning of America's longest war approaches, the goal of creating a stable, democratic Afghanistan appears to be more elusive than ever.

NOTES

The views expressed in this chapter are the author's alone.

1. US Department of Homeland Security, "9/11 Terrorist Attacks Fact Sheet," December 2, 2009.

2. Gary Schroen, *First In: An Insider's Account of How the CIA Spearheaded the War on Terror in Afghanistan* (New York: Ballantine, 2005).

3. All figures current as of September 15, 2014. Data concerning the number of US troops killed or wounded in action were compiled from multiple US Department of Defense reports. Figures regarding the financial cost of the Afghan War are based on a variety of government and nongovernment reports.

4. Matt Waldman, "System Failure: The Underlying Causes of US Policy-Making Errors in Afghanistan," *International Affairs* 89, no. 4 (2013): 825–843; Anatol Lieven, "The War in Afghanistan: Its Background and Future Prospects," *Conflict, Security & Development* 9, no. 3 (2009): 333–359.

5. President George W. Bush, "Statement to the Nation," October 7, 2001.

6. Stephen M. Grenier, "Local Security Forces in Afghanistan," paper presented at the Annual Conference of the International Studies Association, San Francisco, California, April 3, 2013.

7. Stephen M. Grenier, "The Failure to Create Effective Afghan National Security Forces," paper presented at the New Ways of War Conference at the William J. Clinton Institute for American Studies, University College Dublin, Dublin, Ireland, June 1, 2011.

8. Authorization for Use of Military Force in Response to the 9/11 Attacks (Public Law 107-40).

9. Charles H. Briscoe et al., *Weapon of Choice: U.S. Army Special Operations Forces in Afghanistan* (Fort Leavenworth, KS: Combat Studies Institute Press, 2003).

10. Stephen D. Biddle, "Allies, Air, and Modern Warfare: The Afghan Model in Afghanistan and Iraq," *International Security* 30, no. 3 (2005/2006): 161–162.

11. Dan Caldwell, "Military Strategy in Afghanistan and Iraq," in *US Policy in Afghanistan and Iraq: Lessons and Legacies*, ed. Seyom Brown and Robert H. Scales (London: Lynne Rienner, 2012), 57–87.

12. Remarks by President George W. Bush and Chairman of the Afghan Interim Authority Hamid Karzai, January 28, 2002, http://georgewbush-whitehouse.archives.gov/news/releases/2002/01/20020128-13.html.

13. Interview with US Army Special Forces field grade officer, January 2003; interview with Central Intelligence Agency paramilitary officer, January 2003.

14. In October 2002, the Kabul Military Academy was renamed the Kabul Military Training Center (KMTC). See also Ali A. Jalali, "Rebuilding Afghanistan's National Army," *Parameters* 32, no. 3 (2002): 72.

15. President George W. Bush, "Speech at Virginia Military Institute," April 17, 2002.

16. Laurie Goering, "Kabul Sees Army as Key to Peace," *Chicago Tribune*, May 22, 2002, http://articles.chicagotribune.com/2002-05-22/news/0205220364_1_national-army-afghanistan-al-qaeda-remnants.

17. Briscoe et al., *Weapon of Choice*, 360.

18. Interview with US Army Special Forces field grade officer, January 2003; interview with US Army Special Forces company grade officer, January 2003.

19. ANA monthly pay records for June–August 2002.

20. Mohammed Osman Tariq, "Tribal Security System (Arbakai) in Southeast Afghanistan," Crisis States Occasional Paper No. 7, December 2008.

21. "State of the Regiment," US Army Special Forces Command briefing slides, January 2012.

22. Interview with US Army General Officer, January 2004; interview with US Army General Officer, April 2007.

23. Office of Military Cooperation–Afghanistan briefing slides, December 2003.

24. This analysis is based on interviews of 117 special operations troops conducted in 2002–2010, multiple surveys of special operations troops, and the examination of unclassified data from operational plans—commonly referred to as "Concept of Operations" or CONOPS—that were conducted in Afghanistan between 2002 and 2006.

25. Donald P. Wright et al., *A Different Kind of War: The United States Army in Operation Enduring Freedom (OEF) October 2001–September 2005* (Fort Leavenworth, KS: Combat Studies Institute Press, 2009), 212–216.

26. Sean M. Maloney, "Conceptualizing the War in Afghanistan: Perceptions from the Front, 2001–2006," *Small Wars and Insurgencies* 18, no. 1 (2007): 32; interview with US Army field grade officer previously assigned to a US PRT, January 2014; James Russell, "Into the Great Wadi: The United States and the War in Afghanistan," in *Military Adaptation in Afghanistan*, ed. Theo Farrell, Frans Osinga, and James Russell (Stanford, CA: Stanford University Press, 2013), 54.

27. Tim Bird and Alex Marshall, *Afghanistan: How the West Lost Its Way* (New Haven, CT: Yale University Press, 2011), 147–151.

28. Interview with US Army Special Forces field grade officer, June 2006.

29. Interview with US Army Special Forces field grade officer, December 2006.

30. Interview with US Army Special Forces field grade officer, January 2007.

31. Interview with Senate professional staff member, July 2010; interview with member of the US Department of Defense Senior Executive Service, August 2010.

32. Interview with US Army Special Forces field grade officer, September 2009; interview with US Army Special Forces field grade officer, August 2010.

33. Interview with member of the US Department of Defense Senior Executive Service, December 2013.

34. Interview with senior US defense official, January 2014; Bird and Marshall, *Afghanistan*, 149–150.

35. Craig Smith, "NATO Runs Short of Troops to Expand Afghan Peacekeeping," *New York Times*, September 18, 2004, http://www.nytimes.com/2004/09/18/international/asia/18kabul.html; Bird and Marshall, *Afghanistan*, 156.

36. Afghanistan Compact, London Conference on Afghanistan, January 31–February 1, 2006, 6.

37. Antonio Giustozzi, "Auxiliary Force or National Army? Afghanistan's 'ANA' and the Counter-Insurgency Effort, 2002–2006," *Small Wars and Insurgencies* 18, no. 1 (2007): 45–67.

38. "Status of the ANA," International Security Assistance Force briefing slides, January 2013.

39. Interview with House Armed Services professional staff member, July 2008; interview with member of the US Department of Defense Senior Executive Service, July 2008.

40. Interview with ANA General Officer, December 2010; interview with ANA field grade officer, December 2010; interview with ANA field grade officer, January 2011.

41. "History of the Afghan National Army Commandos," International Security Assistance Force briefing slides, July 2013.

42. ANA Commando Monthly Utilization Records, September 2010–June 2012.

43. Interview with ANA Commando field grade officer, January 2011.

44. Bird and Marshall, *Afghanistan*, 285.

45. The Afghanistan fighting season normally runs from April through September.

46. Carlotta Gall, *The Wrong Enemy: America in Afghanistan, 2001–2014* (Boston: Houghton Mifflin Harcourt, 2014), 104–105; Dexter Filkins, "U.S. Tightens Airstrike Policy in Afghanistan," *New York Times*, June 21, 2009, A1.

47. Ann Scott Tyson, "General David McKiernan Ousted as Top U.S. Commander in Afghanistan," *Washington Post*, May 12, 2009, http://www.washingtonpost.com/wp-dyn/content/article/2009/05/11/AR2009051101864.html.

48. See Robert M. Gates, *Duty: Memoirs of a Secretary at War* (New York: Knopf, 2014), 344–345.

49. Interview with US Army General Officer, January 2014.

50. International Security Assistance Force, "ISAF Commander's Counterinsurgency Guidance," August 2009; Hy Rothstein, "America's Longest War," in *Afghan Endgames: Strategy and Policy Choices for America's Longest War*, ed. Hy Rothstein and John Arquilla (Washington, DC: Georgetown University Press, 2012), 66.

51. Bird and Marshall, *Afghanistan*, 231–235.

52. Ibid., 240–242; International Security Assistance Force, "ISAF Counterinsurgency Training Guidance," November 10, 2009.

53. Russell, "Into the Great Wadi," 71–72.

54. Michael Hastings, "The Runaway General," *Rolling Stone*, July 8, 2010, http://www.rollingstone.com/politics/news/the-runaway-general-20100622.

55. Stephen M. Grenier, "The Strategic Impact of Village Stability Operations in Afghanistan," paper presented at the Biannual Conference of the Inter-University Seminar Canada, Queen's University, Kingston, Ontario, Canada, November 3, 2012.

56. Michael Stevens, "Afghan Local Police in Helmand: Calculated Risk or Last Gamble?" *RUSI Journal* 158, no. 1 (2013): 64–70; Stephen M. Grenier, "The Afghan Local Police in a Strategic Context," paper presented at the Joint Annual Conference of the International Security Studies Section of the International Studies Association and the International Security and Arms Control Section of the American Political Science Association, Irvine, California, October 14, 2011.

57. Kimberly Dozier, "Petraeus Says He'll Leave Army Behind as CIA Chief," *Seattle Times*, June 23, 2011, http://www.seattletimes.com/politics/petraeus-says-hell-leave-army-behind-as-cia-chief/.

58. For example, see Rod Nordland, "Betrayed While Asleep, Afghan Police Die at Hands of Their Countrymen," *New York Times*, December 27, 2012, A4; Tom A. Peter, "Afghan Policeman Attacks Colleagues, Undermining Cornerstone of US Strategy," *Christian Science Monitor*, March 30, 2012, http://www.csmonitor.com/World/Asia-South-Central/2012/0330/Afghan-policeman-attacks-colleagues-undermining-cornerstone-of-US-strategy.

59. "Enduring Strategic Partnership Between the United States of America and the Islamic Republic of Afghanistan," May 2, 2012, http://www.whitehouse.gov/sites/default/files/2012.06.01u.s.-afghanistanspasignedtext.pdf.

60. Sudarsan Raghavan and Karen DeYoung, "U.S., Afghanistan Sign Vital, Long-delayed Security Pact," *Washington Post*, September 30, 2014, http://www.washingtonpost.com/world/us-afghanistan-sign-security-pact-to-allow-american-forces-to-remain-in-country/2014/09/30/48f555ce-4879-11e4-a046-120a8a855cca_story.html; Margherita Stancati and Nathan Hodge, "Afghanistan Signs Security Pact With U.S., NATO," *Wall Street Journal*, September 30, 2014, http://www.wsj.com/articles/u-s-afghan-bilateral-security-agreement-signed-1412076436.

5 CANADA

The Evolution of a New Canadian Way of War

Howard G. Coombs

CANADIAN COMMITMENT TO a brief combat mission in 2002 was followed by participation in a 2003–2004 stabilization intervention. This involvement was, in turn, trailed by provincial reconstruction and then in 2006 to a deadly low-intensity conflict that would eventually cost Canada 162 lives.[1] In 2011, Canada's role transitioned from fighting in southern Afghanistan, primarily Kandahar, to providing advice and assistance within the North Atlantic Treaty Organization Training Mission–Afghan with Canadian troops located in Kabul. That advisory mission ended in March 2014, and Canadian troops have since departed Afghanistan.

A CANADIAN WAY OF WAR

Upon reflection, this "slippery slope" is inescapably part of a Canadian way of war that is characterized by Canada's experiences of conflict and relationships with major allies. Since World War II, Canada has aligned its interests with its closest partner—the US. As a result, a number of facets of this national behavior seem to form a discursive package descriptive of Canada and its use of military power. First, national policy is at times predicated by alliances, and the linking of national interests to military objectives is not always clear. Second, military force is not always deployed based on martial considerations but is determined by political interests. Consequently, force deployments are normally incremental over time in response to political deliberations. Third, there is a requirement, seldom adhered to but constantly reinforced, for maintaining a standing expeditionary force to meet the national requirements. Fourth,

Canada commits tactical forces as a result of alliance strategy and sometimes has little input into operational decisions, which dictate how the tactical forces will be employed. As a result, strategic ends, operational ways, and tactical ends are not always a smooth linear progression but often disjointed. Finally, there is an initial lack of adaptation and innovation with a rearward focus on the last conflict that involved Canada.[2]

While these threads were present throughout Canada's experience in Afghanistan, this war was different from previous conflicts in one significant fashion—national implementation of an integrated governmental approach to military operations. This "whole of government" (WoG) approach has come to define Canada's involvement in Afghanistan, particularly between 2006 and 2011 in the southern province of Kandahar. An examination of the development of this WoG methodology provides a perspective on evolving Canadian approaches to the use of its instruments of national power in the twenty-first century.

The absence of strong overarching security policy during the Cold War combined with the desire to achieve saliency as a middle power[3] within existing alliances permitted the Canadian military to become focused on its own geostrategic commitments. All three services developed close affiliations with corresponding American military forces and viewed military strategy through the prism of their support for a *Pax Americana* that took the form of the North Atlantic Treaty Organization (NATO), the North America Aerospace Defense Command, and the United Nations. Accordingly, without a national focus Canadian defense policy remained diffuse.

Canadian deployments to Somalia in 1993 and Rwanda during 1993–1994 and disclosure of incidents at Bacovici in the former Yugoslavia in 1993–1994 created a great deal of public and private introspection regarding the nature of the profession of arms in Canada.[4] The 9/11 terrorist attacks provided the Canadian government the impetus to reestablish defense and security credentials with the Americans, which took form in a military contribution to Operation Enduring Freedom in Afghanistan.[5] With the commitment of these forces in the context of its alliances with the US, Canada, whether knowingly or not, became bound to a commitment that inexorably grew with time.

Canada's military commitment initially lacked clear strategic objectives or a vision of what mission success would look like beyond stabilizing the security environment. Consequently, an initial lack of comprehension by Canadian politicians resulted in an approach to the military mission that demonstrated a lack of understanding of the Afghanistan conflict. That miscomprehension did not change until casualties started to mount in 2006 after the move from Kabul to Kandahar.[6] This relocation was part of the larger strategy of establishing Provincial Reconstruction Teams (PRTs), which initially were coordinating mechanisms that incorporated military and civil affairs, bringing together government departments to ensure that development and reconstruction efforts were aligned with the demands of the mission. The PRTs later became more involved with supporting local governance and priorities.

This absence of clear strategic goals resulted in unfocused military objectives and, from 2006 until the surge of 2009, piecemeal force employments. Despite some early success, notably Operation Medusa—a large-scale combat operation that destroyed organized Taliban units in Kandahar—Canadians were primarily used as a "fire brigade" rushing around the south to reinforce other NATO forces or to fight. Some Canadian officers dryly referred to these activities as "whack-a-mole" when discussing the constant shifting of tactical deployments in response to or attempting to preempt insurgent activities. Also, this lack of tactical coherency sometimes resulted in criticism regarding Canada's commitment. To address the lack of a national campaign plan that explained—to the Canadian military, government and public—the use of tactical force, the Canadian Expeditionary Forces Command (CEFCOM) created a document that integrated a number of international and national civilian policy documents, as well as military plans and directives. The resultant document, which wove together these sometimes conflicting plans, was described by the former commander of CEFCOM, retired Lieutenant-General Michel (Mike) Gauthier as presenting a "challenge."[7]

The lack of standing expeditionary force capabilities and key functions such as intelligence, special operations, armor, artillery, aviation, air transport, and upgraded equipment and precision weaponry created unanticipated costs and an impetus to continue structural transformation of the Canadian Forces. These initiatives began in earnest with the appointment of General Rick Hillier as the Canadian Chief of Defence Staff in 2005.[8]

EVOLVING WOG OPERATIONS

As Canada became enmeshed in the evolving counterinsurgency in Afghanistan, its military campaign became integrated to a large degree with civilian efforts. Gauthier described its development and impact accordingly: "In late 2008/early 2009, just as the full weight of US leadership and ownership of the mission was beginning to emerge, Canadian WoG planning was beginning to coalesce and the Canadian civilian presence was increasing dramatically." Along with this engagement, "an explicit government policy framework had been developed, with clearly articulated set of objectives . . . which continue to guide Canada's broader engagement."[9] This policy framework was articulated within the recommendations of the Manley Report,[10] which critically examined the Afghan mission. The report recommended a comprehensive focus on Afghan capacity building and specifically stated, "We believe that Canada's role in Afghanistan should give greater emphasis to diplomacy, reconstruction and governance and that the military mission should shift increasingly towards the training of the Afghan National Security Forces."[11] This methodology was something that had only existed in a nascent form during the peacekeeping and enforcement operations of the late twentieth century. In the crucible of the violence of Afghanistan, the WoG approach emerged as a distinctly different nuance in the way that Canadians conducted conflict. This was also reinforced by Hillier, who noted in 2006 that "rebuilding failed states was not a security, governance or economic problem; it was all three, and had to be approached with that in mind."[12]

The WoG construct evolved as part of an overall Western response to the small wars of the twenty-first century. The US used the term *interagency* to describe its methods, while the UK developed the *joined-up* approach. Canada at first coined the sobriquet *3D* to describe combined diplomacy, defense, and development efforts in order to stabilize conflict or postconflict situations. From a Canadian perspective, this integration built upon hard-won knowledge during peacekeeping and peace enforcement operations that Canada participated in during the late twentieth century. During the first few years of this century, NATO adopted a "comprehensive" approach that Canada built upon by creating the WoG paradigm in order to more accurately capture the nuances of the multifaceted effort that was needed to deal with the complicated problems of the modern security environment.

The context of the Afghan mission required the Canadian government to put together organizations that did not normally work with each other on such a scale so as to provide a coherent Canadian effort in conjunction with that of the international community. This meant that the occasionally conflicting imperatives of national policy, practices, and international partners, primarily that of the US but additionally partners within the NATO alliance, had to be all taken into account. All this was in the context of a fragile Afghan government and security apparatus: an insurgency whose strength had been consistently underestimated by the international community, which had shifting views of both counterinsurgency and nation-building.[13]

Simultaneously, the US had become more preoccupied with achieving military success in Iraq, which resulted in Washington diverting its focus from Afghanistan. However, with the success of the 2007 American military surge in Iraq as well as the 2008 election of President Barack Obama, the US became reinvested in the dilemmas of the ongoing conflict in Afghanistan. Consequently, this provided a strategic vision and the resources necessary to create a multinational counterinsurgency campaign in Afghanistan. This improved strategic coherence, as an addition to the flow of American personnel and material, renewed international interest in Afghanistan and gave fresh impetus to NATO efforts to resolve the expanding violence.

The absence of a consistent and clearly articulated international strategy for Afghanistan between 2006 and 2009 gave rise to what has been described by critics as a series of "locally designed" national campaigns across the Afghan area of operations such as those conducted by Canadians in Kandahar, the British in Helmand, and the US in the eastern provinces. With an influx of tens of thousands of American troops, along with more clearly defined international campaign leadership in late 2009, these national campaigns became more fully integrated into broader international counterinsurgency and nation-building campaigns. Within this context, a relatively robust Canadian WoG campaign was able to evolve in Kandahar province.

Canada's involvement in southern Afghanistan resulted from the enlargement of the International Security Assistance Force (ISAF) in that region in 2006. During that time, the NATO mission took over from US-led coalition forces in the region. During this period of transition, Canadian military units that had been supporting ISAF in the area of Kabul were withdrawn and moved to Kandahar. Brigadier General Dave Fraser and his staff formed Multi-National Brigade (South) (MNB (S)) with units from 1 Canadian Mechanized Brigade Group on July 31, 2006. Subsequently, the command of Regional Command (South) (RC(S)) rotated among a number of NATO nations, including Canada, until changing from British to American leadership in July 2010.

While Canadian troops were being deployed to southern Afghanistan in 2006, Canada implemented the intergovernmental approach to addressing the complex dilemmas of the contemporary environment through the application of the PRT concept. Although initially ill-defined by Ottawa, the WoG effort became much more coherent and well understood with the integration of high-level Canadian governmental officials into Canadian military operations. It also included Privy Council Office and Cabinet interest in, plus coordination of, a comprehensive governmental approach with quarterly assessment of activities at the national level.

Over the course of Canada's involvement in Afghanistan, there have been two significant parliamentary votes—May 2006 and March 2008—concerning the extension of the mission and its essential character. Considerable attention was also paid to the convening of an independent panel to make recommendations on the future course of the mission in 2007—the Manley Report—and a highly politicized public discourse over the government's detainee transfer policy, which began in 2007 and continued throughout Canada's involvement.[14] A positive effect of this public political debate was recognition of the breadth and complexity of the Afghan challenge, which contributed to a substantial evolution in both the strategic WoG coordination framework in Ottawa and the corresponding mission structure and civilian resourcing in Afghanistan. After early 2008, Canadian efforts were overseen by a Cabinet Committee on Afghanistan, supported by the Afghanistan Task Force in the Privy Council Office and an ad hoc committee of deputy ministers that met on a weekly basis. By 2009 there were more than 100 Canadian civilians and police in Afghanistan, with a robust civilian leadership cadre at the embassy in Kabul and Kandahar.

Following the Manley Report and the parliamentary vote of March 2008, the Canadian government unveiled a detailed set of policy objectives for the mission, and soon thereafter developed benchmarks to measure and report on the progress achieved in each of its six key policy priorities. In Kandahar the objectives were to (1) provide a secure environment and the rule of law through building capacity in security forces, justice, and corrections, (2) encourage employment and provide critical services, such as water, (3) deliver humanitarian aid where needed, and (4) increase the security of the Afghanistan-Pakistan border. From a broader, national perspective, Canada would support (5) Afghan institutions that would assist Canadian initiatives in Kandahar and (6) Afghan-led reconciliation initiatives meant to eliminate violence and foster a sustainable peace.[15]

Only one of these priorities involves security, and it focused on building the capacity of Afghan National Security Forces (ANSF) to sustain a more secure environment and to promote law and order. Also, with significant increases of American military personnel in the region after 2009, the Canadian Forces, the Department of Foreign Affairs and International Trade (DFAIT), the Canadian

International Development Agency (CIDA), and Afghans were able to focus their efforts and resources to support security operations in an increasingly smaller area in southern Afghanistan—in 2010–2011 the districts of Panjwaii, Dand, and Daman within the province of Kandahar. Concomitantly DFAIT and CIDA remained engaged across the province.

Furthermore, with the purpose of facilitating Canadian efforts toward development and governance in Afghanistan through security assistance, the Manley Report recommended prolonging the Canadian military commitment beyond 2009. Parliamentary approval was given to extending the Canadian Forces involvement in Kandahar until 2011 and, later, the training mission in Kabul until 2014. Consequently, the Canadian military strategy included training the ANSF, providing security for reconstruction and development efforts in Kandahar, continuing Canada's responsibility for the Kandahar Provincial Reconstruction Team (KPRT), and preparing for changeover of the security mission in southern Afghanistan to American or other allies in 2011. It was a comprehensive focus that involved all departments of government.

INCREASING AFGHAN CAPABILITY

Ultimately the hallmark of the Canadian mission was the overarching effort on building Afghan capacity. As much as the international community collectively underestimated the strength of the insurgency, it overestimated the capacity of Afghan leadership, in governance and security efforts, to assume full responsibility to the challenges in Kandahar province. Under these circumstances, Canadian activities revolved around balancing its efforts to enable Afghan authorities and security forces while keeping the insurgents at bay with a single battle group, or an augmented infantry battalion, in an area of operations that required a much larger military commitment. By 2010–2011, the levels of Afghan and international security were considered sufficient, thus enabling more efficient WoG activities.

Also by 2010–2011, the KPRT,[16] by then a combined Canadian-American effort, was a mission that included sixty-two Canadian civilians. This group worked closely with local Afghan officials to support the implementation of priority Afghan-determined projects throughout the province. First, the KPRT worked intimately with the appointed provincial executive officer, Governor Tooryali Wesa, and his office. Governor Wesa's direction and leadership was important to Canada's efforts, and the KPRT worked closely with him to assist with the planning, budgeting, and coordination of major projects. Although attempts had been made to establish working relationships with previous incumbents, members of the Canadian mission would argue that it was not until the 2008 appointment of Wesa—an Afghan Canadian—that this relationship reached its apogee.

Second, the KPRT partnered with the attorney general's office and the provincial court on justice issues, with the Afghan National Police (ANP), the Afghan National Army (ANA), and the Central Prison Directorate. In all projects and initiatives, the KPRT affiliated with provincial ministries to support them in their efforts to deliver projects and outcomes that were in line with government plans, as well as to encourage better financial linkages with ministerial budgets. Third, the KPRT had a strong relationship with the Provincial Council. As a body of elected representatives, the council promoted participation of the people and governance of civil society. The Provincial Council was best known as a place that Kandaharis could come to seek help with their problems. The work of the council in listening to the people, mediating disputes, and finding common ground was important. Consequently, the council's oversight of government and service delivery, as established by policy, remained important and supported by the KPRT.

Lastly, District Stabilization Teams (DSTs) composed of small groups of American and Canadian governmental advisors, with military assistance—in the form of regular military security personnel, liaison officers, and staff— worked closely with their Afghan counterparts in the district line ministries and district governors to increase local capacity. The measurable growth of district governance over time was in no small part due to the efforts of these teams of dedicated professionals.

When Canadian troops arrived in Kandahar in 2006, they focused on clearing insurgent forces that controlled many of the key districts. To confront these destructive forces in a holistic fashion and support the government of Kandahar, Canada decided to expand WoG contributions in Kandahar through its KPRT. At the same time the need for continuing military capabilities in this security environment were imbued within the 2008 Canada First Defence Strategy.[17]

Subsequently in 2008, Canada promised to move 50 percent of the aid budget for Afghanistan to Kandahar and defined six priorities, plus three signature projects, which served as overarching terms of reference for the civilian mission, an effort to aid the local authorities in addressing their identified priorities. At the same time, Canada created a new, unique, and larger WoG civilian operational capacity for Kandahar, which enabled a more robust partnership with the provincial government, supported by programs financed by DFAIT and CIDA. To measure progress, the benchmarks mentioned earlier were established and progress was reported to the Canadian Parliament every three months. In all of Canada's major initiatives, close partnership with the Government of the Islamic Republic of Afghanistan (GIRoA) in planning and delivery ensured that the benefits of Canadian projects were sustainable by Afghan authorities. These initiatives included (1) the Arghandab irrigation rehabilitation program, including revitalization of the Dahla Dam, (2) fifty signature schools, (3) polio eradication, (4) improvement of Sarpoza Prison, (5) police training, and (6) secure governance infrastructure.

Canada worked to improve the Dahla Dam and the irrigation canals in order to bring water to farmers. The KPRT worked closely with the Ministry of Energy and Water on this project, particularly to improve the technical requirements of the water system. While the Canadian portion of this project was completed in 2012, GIRoA has continued putting in place the regional water management aspects of this project, and the US government is funding work on the dam itself to allow its capacity to be fully utilized.[18]

Canada also collaborated with the provincial Department of Education (DoE) to build, expand, and repair fifty schools in Kandahar and to improve the quality of education across the province. While this project was not without setbacks, from insurgent opposition and a fragmented subnational education system, there were local successes as the provincial government assumed more responsibility for the newly opened schools and the security environment improved. This partnership in education continues at a national level through Canadian representatives in Kabul.

Working with the Department of Public Health (DoPH), Canada supported the immunization of children across Afghanistan in an effort to eradicate polio. Unfortunately, while the country is very close to eliminating polio, there are still cases in eastern Afghanistan due to cross-border transmission from Pakistan.[19] This program will continue through the UN and the DoPH until polio is eradicated entirely in Afghanistan. Furthermore, Canada in partnership with the DoPH built, expanded, and/or repaired a significant number of health clinics, particularly in the south. Many had been destroyed or severely damaged because of prolonged insecurity.

Additionally, the KPRT worked very closely with the Central Prison Directorate (CPD) to make Sarpoza Prison, in Kandahar city, a model facility that operates in accordance with international standards and Afghan law. While there have been challenges in the form of two significant prison breakouts in 2008 and 2011, progress within the correction system was discernible. Canada also assisted the ANP at the Police Training Center by building and operating a facility located at Camp Nathan Smith, home of the KPRT in Kandahar city. Training was developed and delivered by Canadian civilian police in conjunction with ANP trainers. In 2011 the facility was formally and effectively transferred to the ANP, which is currently supported by the NATO Training Mission–Afghanistan.

Over several years, the KPRT cooperated with the ANP to improve or build most police substations throughout Kandahar city. These stations allow for police representation across the city. The KPRT supported projects that assisted with strengthening provincial government—a state-of-the-art media facility providing a venue for press conferences, releases, and statements and a project to build safe housing for government officials in Kandahar city in order to help improve security for senior officials. Also constructed was a provincial council building, home of the only elected government body in Kandahar. As these projects were completed, the GIRoA took responsibility for their operation. In addition to buildings, Canada also played a significant role in the construction and repair of roads, culverts, and bridges.

Canada's civilian commitment to Afghanistan continues beyond 2014. Canada and Afghanistan have entered a new phase of partnership and cooperation in a national program that is based out of Kabul. This program focuses on four areas: (1) investing in the future of Afghan children and youth through projects in education and health; (2) advancing security, the rule of law, and human rights; (3) promoting regional diplomacy, and (4) delivering humanitarian assistance. This national program will build on Canada's experience in Kandahar while working together on priorities identified by the GIRoA. At the same time, Canada's objectives remain the same: to support Afghans in building a country that is well governed, stable, and secure.

"TIPPING POINTS"

Simultaneously, throughout 2010–2011 the Canadian and American military forces that composed Task Force Kandahar[20] implemented initiatives to ensure that all military activities were coordinated within a WoG framework—with its Canadian and American field partners. These could be grouped in the areas of security, governance, and development. First, security initiatives supported increasing capability in the army and police while directly combating the insurgency. Second, governance-related work attempted to strengthen district and subnational institutions, as well as build a capable civil service. Lastly, development work was aimed at determining local development priorities and sustainable solutions, in addition to increasing economic growth.

This meant that Task Force Kandahar worked toward a number of "tipping points" in its WoG approach. Within the area of security, it was necessary to ensure adequate numbers of capable Afghan police addressing village requirements and protecting, not preying on the people. Along with that, ANSF led combined and single-service operations in addition to integrated ANSF command and control responsive to the district governor and village elders, called *maliks*. When examining support to governance, it was necessary to reinforce and assist with creating responsible and responsive district governors and staff, representative and functioning district and village *shuras* and subnational processes, and line ministry representatives from primary ministries working at the district center and reactive to village requirements. Support to development led to functioning District Development Committees. These were part of the formal processes of subnational government and were designed to assist with the prioritization and disbursement of centrally controlled funds against district development needs. With village development representation, this process ensured that all development that was coordinated through district governors met priorities set by the district, in conjunction with villages and a working rural/urban interface—markets, agricultural warehousing, transportation and other related services.

The net effect was that Task Force Kandahar made a major difference in extending stability by unifying the actions of involved agencies within an overarching security context. This approach addressed the disintegrating influences affecting the Canadian portion of southern Afghanistan in a regional and coordinated manner that, from a military perspective, enabled the prioritization and allocation of resources. Furthermore, this approach provided sufficient resources in the villages and village clusters, to demonstrate directly to the Afghan people the commitment of the GIRoA and the international community vis-à-vis national reconstruction and state-building.

This method of negating the insurgency was local and sought to create functioning districts through an integrated effort targeting specific villages and groupings of villages for substantial governmental and developmental intervention. These locations were connected to national and provincial programs; urban, market, transportation, and trade development packages; and local security sector reform activity. This prioritization also permitted security forces to allocate their resources in the best manner in order to create a secure environment for those involved with these activities.

Consequently, Task Force Kandahar and its WoG collaborators fought the insurgency in a number of ways. Canadian military efforts were oriented toward removing destabilizing influences by establishing and maintaining community-centric security. This created the conditions for an integrated interagency approach that generated and promoted local governance and development, mostly from the bottom up. As part of this, the WoG effort, wherever possible, established or reinforced partnerships that put Afghan officials and security forces in the forefront and the population's interests first. Once appropriate conditions were established—such as responsible and functioning governance, burgeoning local economies with a rural/urban interface, and a capable ANSF—those districts were transferred to complete Afghan control. Even though Canada's combat mission ended in July 2011, its military contribution continued through its security capacity-building efforts as part of the NATO Training Mission–Afghanistan. Despite its departure from the area, Canada has left a legacy in Kandahar province. That legacy is rooted in the service and sacrifices of military and civilian personnel who have created conditions for a more stable and secure Kandahar. The impact of these efforts on the people of this troubled region will far outlast Canada's presence and will contribute to the ultimate goal of securing Afghanistan's future as a functioning member of the international community.

MOVING FORWARD

The amalgamation of these various interdepartmental perspectives, objectives, programs, plans, and activities directly underpinned the creation of a Canadian WoG approach in Afghanistan over the last several years.[21] A United States Army officer, Major-General Michael Flynn, expressed it best when describing contemporary warfare:

> The most effective organizations on today's battlefields are those that have integrated capabilities. Teams and networks of people leveraging their parent organizations have demonstrated a high degree of success. . . . There is little question that when you put people from multiple agencies and coalition partner nations with the right skills together, they will be more effective.[22]

Twenty-first-century interventions require teams of people familiar with each other and their capabilities. This suggests the establishment of integrated professional development systems and the wider use of interdepartment assignments to increase operating familiarity between the various departments dealing with defense and security, international relations, and development. Creation of a common understanding among major actors is crucial to any success. Moreover, the Canadian government needs to increase its pool of deployable capabilities. This is in addition to developing WoG structures that contain a cross-spectrum of skills and attributes that can deploy quickly to conflict or postconflict areas. Some experts argue that the Canadian government should create a "hybrid" organization consisting of "soldiers, development workers, diplomats and others who can protect themselves." This organization needs to be funded and resourced sufficiently to deploy quickly and commence working effectively wherever required, regardless of security concerns to produce integrated effects.[23] The ability to create, deploy, and sustain such a structure over the duration of the mission would permit Canada to maintain the skills and relationships so arduously gained over the duration of the Afghanistan experience. In order to do this, capability and capacity must be improved, likely within existent funding. This effort will be somewhat painful, to be sure, but the cost of not doing so far outweighs any budgetary constraints that will result from current strategic reviews. Canadian development specialist Andy Tamas aptly captures this sentiment with the pithy comment that "unstable regions affect us all,"[24] and in a global community of nations this is more accurate now than ever before—a situation that will not change for the foreseeable future.

Canadian efforts to build coordinated interdepartment activities in Afghanistan evolved in conjunction with the growth of the NATO mission, national debate, and the end of the combat mission in 2011. As the Canadian government looks toward involvement with other war-torn environments, it needs to heed the lessons identified as the result of its contribution in southern Afghanistan, particularly over the period of the combat mission, and ensure that the observations that were captured are addressed in order to strengthen and increase the effectiveness of future WoG activities and also address the exigencies of a new strand in the Canadian way of war.

NOTES

I am indebted to the review and comments of General Walt Natynczyk (Retired), CMM, MSC, CD, Canadian Chief of Defence Staff from July 2008 to December 2012; Matt Fischer, long-serving Postmedia war correspondent; Colonel Dr. Randy Wakelam (Retired), professor of history and war studies at the Royal Military College of Canada; and

Colonel Pat Kelly, MSM, CD, Canadian Armed Forces, Director Land Reserves and senior advisor to the Afghan vice chief of the General Staff from October 2010 to July 2011; and to the editing of my daughter Lindsay Coombs in the construction of this chapter. Any errors or omissions in the final writing should be attributed to my understanding of the information and research that was accessed or provided.

1. Janice Gross Stein and Eugene Lang, *The Unexpected War: Canada in Kandahar* (Toronto: Penguin Group (Canada), 2007; reprint 2008), 244–245; "Afghanistan: In the Line of Duty: Canada's Casualties," CBC News, http://www.cbc.ca/news2/interactives/canada-afghanistan-casualties/.

2. See Howard G. Coombs with Richard E. Goette, "Canada and the Cold War," in *The Canadian Way of War: Serving the National Interest*, ed. Bernd Horn (Toronto: Dundurn Press, 2006), 265–289.

3. See Christopher Thorne, *Allies of a Kind: The United States, Britain, and the War Against Japan, 1941–1945* (New York: Oxford University Press, 1979).

4. See Donna Winslow, "Misplaced Loyalties: The Role of Military Culture in the Breakdown of Discipline in Two Peace Operations," *Journal of Military and Strategic Studies* 6, no. 3 (2004): 345–367.

5. Stein and Lang, *The Unexpected War*, 13.

6. General Rick Hillier, *A Soldier First: Bullets, Bureaucrats and the Politics of War* (Toronto: HarperCollins, 2009), 343–344.

7. Email from Lieutenant General Michel Gauthier, October 10, 2010.

8. Hillier, *A Soldier First*, 322–323.

9. Email from Lieutenant General Michel Gauthier, October 10, 2010.

10. See Canada, "Independent Panel on Canada's Future Role in Afghanistan" (Ottawa: Minister of Public Works and Government Services, 2008).

11. Ibid., 37.

12. Hillier, *A Soldier First*, 389.

13. See Andy Tamas, *Warriors and Nation Builders: Development and the Military in Afghanistan* (Kingston, Ontario: Canadian Defence Academy Press, 2009).

14. See Canada, "Independent Panel on Canada's Future Role in Afghanistan"; Canada, House of Commons of Canada, *39th Parliament, 2nd Session Journals*, no. 53 (February 25, 2008).

15. Canada, "Backgrounder: Canada's Six Priorities in Afghanistan," http://www.afghanistan.gc.ca/canada-afghanistan/news-nouvelles/2009/2009_05_07b.aspx?view=d.

16. The discussion of KPRT activities is derived from a speech by ambassador Tim Martin to the Kandahar Provincial Council, Kandahar, Afghanistan, March 6, 2011. Martin was the representative of Canada in Kandahar from August 2010 to July 2011.

17. Hillier, *A Soldier First*, 481; Stephen Harper, "PM unveils Canada First Defence Strategy," May 12, 2008, http://www.pm.gc.ca/eng/media.asp?id=2095.

18. David Pugliese, "Out of Afghanistan: A Legacy Under Construction," *Ottawa Citizen*, February 16, 2014, http://www.ottawacitizen.com/news/Afghanistan+legacy+under+construction/9517124/story.html.

19. Global Polio Eradication Initiative, "Afghanistan," http://www.polioeradication.org/Infectedcountries/Afghanistan.aspx.

20. Information concerning activities of Task Force Kandahar is taken from a previously noted presentation by Brigadier General Dean Milner, OMM, CD, Commander Joint Task Force Afghanistan 5-10, to the Conference of Defence Associations, Ottawa, Ontario, June 18, 2010, and a presentation by Dr. Howard G. Coombs, Assistant Professor, Royal Military College of Canada, to the Conference of Defence Associations, Ottawa, Ontario, November 3, 2011.

21. See Canada, Department of National Defence, "3350-1 (JLLO) Report on Kandahar Whole of Government Lessons Learned Workshop," June 2, 2011; Canada, "Kandahar Lessons Learned Workshop, Task Force Kandahar and Kandahar Provincial Reconstruction Team," February 24, 2011. Report published by TFK and the KPRT in Kandahar to capture lessons learned.

22. Major General Michael T. Flynn, "Sandals and Robes to Business Suits and Gulf Streams," *Small Wars Journal* (April 20, 2011): 5–6.

23. Tamas, *Warriors and Nation Builders*, 219.

24. Ibid., 223.

6 EL SALVADOR

Exporting Security in the National Interest

Rebecca Bill Chavez

WHEN ONE THINKS of contributors to coalition efforts in Afghanistan and Iraq, the small Central American nation of El Salvador is not typically among the countries that come to mind. However, because of its close relationship with the US, El Salvador deployed over 3,400 troops to Iraq and was the only Latin American nation to send troops to Afghanistan. In the case of Iraq, the deployments took place during the conservative governments of President Francisco Flores Pérez and President Antonio Saca. In contrast, it was the leftist Frente Martí para la Liberación Nacional (FMLN) administration of Mauricio Funes that sent troops to Afghanistan. The leftist administration's decision to support US efforts in the Middle East came as a surprise to many and caused friction between the president and more radical members of the FMLN. Despite opposition from his own party, the pragmatic President Funes maintained close ties with the US, and both nations continue to enjoy the benefits of partnership. The Afghanistan deployment strengthened El Salvador's bilateral relationship with the US and provided President Funes an opportunity to improve relations with his country's armed forces.

SECURITY BENEFITS OF STRENGTHENING
THE US–EL SALVADOR PARTNERSHIP

Although at first glance the Funes administration's support for coalition efforts in Afghanistan seems to counter political logic, it makes sense given the importance of continued US security and economic assistance. El Salvador relies heavily on US support in its fight against organized crime and violence. Like his conservative predecessors, Funes faced a daunting public security crisis, which placed exacting pressure on El Salvador's security forces. The 1992 peace accords that ended El Salvador's twelve-year civil war sparked optimism that the country would break from its violent past. The optimism was short-lived, however, as crime and insecurity remain a fact of everyday life. Illicit trafficking organizations increasingly move drugs, humans, and weapons through the Central American isthmus, and like much of Central America, El Salvador suffers from an epidemic of gang-related violence. With a homicide rate of 69 per 100,000 inhabitants, El Salvador has one of the highest rates in the world. Although widespread violence in Mexico captures headlines in the US, Mexico's homicide rate is 24 per 100,000 citizens. As another point of comparison, the rate in the US is 5 per 100,000.[1]

El Salvador is a major recipient of US Foreign Military Financing (FMF), which contributes directly to the fight against transnational criminal organizations in an effort to improve citizen security. FMF funding has provided the Salvadoran navy with communications equipment, training, and maintenance support, all of which have improved the navy's interdiction capabilities. In 2012, the US donated three helicopters, valued at $9.7 million, plus a maintenance and spare parts package to the Salvadoran air force for surveillance flights.[2] Other 2012 donations include a $1 million package of pickup trucks and spare parts and a $600,000 package that included six Zodiac patrol boats and vehicles to transport the boats.[3] In addition to funding, the US military participates in and helps coordinate the effort to stem illicit trafficking of narcotics, precursor chemicals, and weapons in Central American coastal waters as part of the multinational Operation Martillo. US Navy and Coast Guard vessels and US federal law enforcement aircraft work in conjunction with Salvadoran security forces in detection and monitoring operations along El Salvador's coast.

El Salvador is also home to Comalapa, the only US Cooperative Security Location (CSL) in Central America. Since 2000, the US has used the Comalapa Air Base for aerial detection and monitoring activities in the eastern Pacific Ocean and the Caribbean Sea. The US aircraft offer surveillance capabilities that complement the counternarcotics efforts of Salvadoran security forces. Comalapa's importance to the US increased with the 2009 closure of Manta in Ecuador, the only CSL in South America. In 2009, Funes supported a five-year renewal of the CSL agreement, another indication that the FMLN victory did not trigger a cooling of relations with the US.[4]

US and Salvadoran defense establishments have prioritized open lines of communication and frequent high-level meetings. In 2007, the two countries approved a long-term Status of Forces Agreement and a General Security of Military Information Agreement that facilitates the sharing of classified defense information and military intelligence. Since 2008, the US Defense Department and the Salvadoran Ministry of Defense have conducted regular defense talks. The US Army, Navy, and Air Force also participate in regular discussions with their Salvadoran counterparts.[5]

The Obama administration's decision to select El Salvador as one of only four countries along with Ghana, the Philippines, and Tanzania to participate in the Partnership for Growth Initiative is another result of the close ties. The Obama and Funes administrations worked together to identify and mitigate constraints to economic growth in El Salvador. They concluded that public insecurity has been a major obstacle to sustained growth. Thus, US aid provided through the Partnership for Growth targets enhancing the capabilities of El Salvador's security forces as they confront criminal organizations.

THE AFGHANISTAN DEPLOYMENT AS THE IMPETUS
FOR A NEW ERA IN FMLN–ESAF RELATIONS

In addition to strengthening relations with the US, the Afghanistan deployment allowed Funes to offer an olive branch to the Salvadoran military by showing his support for its engagement with the US military, which is highly valued by the Armed Forces of El Salvador (ESAF). President Funes prioritized improving his party's relationship with the military, which has been fraught with conflict and distrust since height of the Cold War. Like his conservative predecessors, President Funes depended on the ESAF to contain the epidemic of drug- and gang-related violence that paralyzed significant portions of El Salvador.[6]

Until the end of the Salvadoran civil war in 1992, President Funes' FMLN was a guerrilla movement that fought a conservative military- and US-backed government that represented the Salvadoran elite. Extreme socioeconomic inequality fueled the bloody twelve-year struggle between ESAF and the FMLN that claimed the lives of an estimated seventy-five thousand people. During the conflict, ESAF committed human rights abuses, including torture and extrajudicial killings. The United Nations Truth Commission attributed 85 percent of the acts of violence to state agents. When the FMLN laid down its arms and entered mainstream politics as a legitimate political party with the signing of the

1992 UN-brokered Chapultepec Peace Accords, it sought to reduce the size, autonomy, and authority of the armed forces, which stoked the historic tensions between the FMLN and ESAF. Thus, it is remarkable that an FMLN president deployed the Salvadoran armed forces to Afghanistan.

Not surprising, when Funes sent the Afghanistan proposal to the unicameral Salvadoran National Assembly in 2011, his FMLN bloc voted against it. The president depended on the three conservative parties in Congress for support. FMLN leaders were vocal in their opposition to the measure. For instance, one FMLN deputy declared that Salvadoran participation would legitimize the US invasion, which the FMLN bloc argued was the result of the US pursuit of natural resources. The FMLN deputy echoed the feelings of many Salvadorans when he declared that the soldiers would be put to better use in their own country.[7]

The Salvadoran military has actively sought to improve its reputation after the country's civil war. Partnering with US and North Atlantic Treaty Organization (NATO) forces in Afghanistan provided ESAF with an opportunity to showcase its evolution into a professional and apolitical institution since the 1992 conclusion of the civil war. During legislative debate, supporters of deployment argued that that Salvadoran participation would enhance ESAF's prestige and recognition in the international community.[8] Indeed, El Salvador gained an opportunity to demonstrate its expanded global role and its ability to operate with coalition partners from across the world. Working alongside NATO forces enhanced ESAF's reputation as an effective and professional military. ESAF took great pride in its international role, which also included participation in UN humanitarian and peacekeeping missions in Haiti, Lebanon, Western Sahara, Liberia, Ivory Coast, and Sudan.

The Afghanistan deployment also provided the ESAF with operational experience and important training. Like their Iraq veteran counterparts, Salvadorans who served in Afghanistan gained valuable joint and US planning experience. According to defense officials at the US embassy in San Salvador, Salvadoran soldiers sought to serve in Afghanistan, and many volunteered for multiple rotations in Iraq. The chief of El Salvador's air force, Colonel Carlos Mena, observed that "the airmen that went [to Iraq] wanted to be there, they wanted to receive the training, and they wanted to be a part of the mission."[9] Indeed, Iraq and Afghanistan combat experience soon became an unspoken prerequisite for senior command positions. One indicator of the importance that ESAF placed on the Afghanistan mission was the decision to deploy a colonel to command the Salvadoran contingent in Afghanistan.[10]

EL SALVADOR IN IRAQ

El Salvador's deployments to Iraq set the stage for the country's contribution to NATO efforts in Afghanistan. Popular opposition to the war in Iraq was strong across Latin America, including El Salvador. Latin American regard for the US declined as a result of the incursion, and approximately 70 percent of Salvadorans opposed the US invasion of Iraq.[11] Nevertheless, El Salvador was the last and the longest-serving Latin American nation in Iraq. More than 3,400 Salvadoran troops were deployed to Iraq during eleven consecutive rotations beginning in August 2003. During five and a half years of involvement, five Salvadoran soldiers from the Cuscatlán Battalion were killed in action and another twenty were wounded. In acknowledgment of their support and sacrifice, former Secretary of Defense Donald Rumsfeld awarded six Salvadoran soldiers the Bronze Star for their heroic actions that saved the lives of six Coalition Provisional Authority workers.[12] Former Secretary of Defense Robert Gates praised ESAF's participation in Iraq, calling El Salvador "one of the most faithful coalition partners."[13]

Despite increasing pressure and intermittent protests from the opposition in El Salvador, the conservative pro-US National Republican Alliance (ARENA) governments of Presidents Saca and Flores did not withdraw Salvadoran troops until January 2009. El Salvador's Cuscatlán Battalion was stationed in Najaf in south-central Iraq, Al Hillah in southern Iraq, and the southeastern Shiite city of Al Kut. In addition, El Salvador maintained staff officers at Coalition Force headquarters in Baghdad. Salvadoran troops participated in checkpoint security, guarded convoys, and conducted explosive ordnance disposal operations. They also helped secure Coalition Provisional Authority facilities in Najaf, trained Iraqi civil defense forces, and built clinics, schools, water treatment facilities, bridges, and roads.[14]

EL SALVADOR IN AFGHANISTAN

ESAF troops first deployed to Afghanistan in August 2011. The first twenty-two troops served as trainers within NATO Training Mission–Afghanistan. Of the twenty-two soldiers, nine Air Force trainers worked with Afghan forces in Herat in western Afghanistan, three military police trainers worked with the Afghan Police Academy in Kabul, and ten counterinsurgency instructors were part of six mobile training teams that worked with military and police units.[15] In later rotations, Salvadorans served as NATO and ISAF liaison officers in positions such as intelligence and logistics. ESAF committed to further expanding its role by contributing a Police Advisory Team (PAT) in 2013. At the time, Major David Schulz, Deputy U.S. Army Section Chief of the Military Group in El Salvador, explained, "As the US administration begins its withdrawal from Afghanistan, US service members will have to be replaced with partner nations. Historically, El Salvador is one of the strongest partners in Central America and the missions that they're doing now in Afghanistan are ones that had been done by US counterparts in the past."[16]

Salvadoran air force trainers provided the Afghan forces with valuable expertise on the Mi-17 helicopter, the mainstay of the Afghan air force's helicopter fleet. The Salvadoran commanding officer declared, "When I see my soldiers working with the Americans and Afghans I feel very proud because we are representing El Salvador. The American and Salvadoran armed forces have a very strong, long lasting relationship. We've gained a lot from that relationship and now our hope is to leave here, having worked with our American friends to help build a better, strong Afghan air force."[17]

Like other coalition members, El Salvador restricted its troops to noncombat operations in Kabul and western Afghanistan rather than in more volatile parts of the country. The Funes administration feared that if the Salvadoran contingent were to suffer casualties in Afghanistan as they did in Iraq, domestic pressure to withdraw would likely end the mission. Moreover, any move to another region of Afghanistan would depend on US logistical support. In addition to safety considerations, Regional Command–West was under Italian and Spanish command and control, which mitigated the language obstacles faced by the Salvadoran soldiers.

El Salvador demonstrated its willingness to take on more responsibility in Afghanistan by contributing to a nineteen-member Police Advisory Team (PAT), which deployed to Herat in July 2013. The PAT comprised thirteen Salvadorans, two US Special Operations troops, and four New Hampshire National Guard soldiers. By contributing to a PAT that partnered directly with an Afghan police battalion, the Salvadorans placed themselves in greater danger. The decision to operate beyond the confines of a camp or base requires a higher level of force protection training, and US Special Operations Command South played an important role in equipping and training the Salvadoran advisors. New Hampshire National Guard and US special operations personnel trained with the Salvadoran PAT members at the Joint Readiness Training Center at Fort

Polk, Louisiana, and the Salvadoran police advisors had the same equipment as their US counterparts. In order to qualify for the mission, the Salvadoran troops underwent a battery of medical and psychological evaluations.[18]

PATs like the Salvadoran-led team played a critical role in maintaining progress in Afghanistan as the US brings its troops home. PATs facilitated the transfer of responsibility to Afghan forces and are essential to peacekeeping efforts and long-term success. The members of the Salvadoran PAT lived alongside their Afghan counterparts in the western region of Herat. After seeing the advances that NATO troops were making in the less volatile regions during his July 2012 visit to Afghanistan, Salvadoran Defense Minister Benítez Parada advised Funes to participate in the police advisory mission.[19]

In addition to the intensive PAT training at Fort Polk, ESAF troops received specialized training through the State Partnership Program (SPP). The New Hampshire National Guard–El Salvador partnership has been an effective tool for the exchange of military expertise since its creation in 2000. Multiple SPP exchanges each year have contributed to the professionalization of ESAF and its ability to operate effectively in the Middle East.[20] US Ambassador to El Salvador Mari Carmen Aponte commented on the value of the robust relationship: "The fact that the New Hampshire National Guard has taken a special interest in El Salvador has been wonderful for our bilateral relationship. Regular visits of New Hampshire National Guard personnel to the country—often to the same locations year after year—provide a sense of continuity in terms of people-to-people relations."[21] New Hampshire's Adjutant General stated: "I truly believe that one of the reasons why El Salvador went to Iraq . . . was because of [the New Hampshire Guard]."[22] As a result of the close partnership, three members of the New Hampshire National Guard who had trained alongside their Salvadoran counterparts at Fort Polk were deployed to Afghanistan to support the Salvadoran-led PAT.[23]

EL SALVADOR AS A SECURITY EXPORTER

In the context of limited resources, the US has encouraged its partners to become security exporters. By deploying troops to the Middle East, El Salvador demonstrated its willingness and ability to assume that role by contributing to global security. According to the 2012 Department of Defense Western Hemisphere Defense Policy Statement, the Defense Department "will seek to build partnership capacity elsewhere in the world to share the costs and responsibilities required to ensure global peace and security." The document focuses on El Salvador as one of two Latin American countries (along with Colombia) that has become a security exporter: "Salvadoran trainers are supporting the Afghan National Security Forces and deployed 11 rotations of personnel to support the Government of Iraq."[24]

El Salvador's participation in Iraq and Afghanistan demonstrates the value of robust US engagement with Latin America. The Obama administration has prioritized promoting the US as a partner of choice in the Western Hemisphere. In the case of El Salvador, the US has successfully accomplished this goal by rewarding a reliable partner with security and economic assistance. By demonstrating its commitment to El Salvador, the US gained an important partner in Afghanistan.

NOTES

1. United Nations Office on Drugs and Crime, "Homicide Statistics 2012," http://www.unodc.org/unodc/en/data-and-analysis/homicide.html.

2. "General Atilio Benítez, Ministro de Defensa de El Salvador: Recibimos los helicópteros serie MD500 en septiembre," August 7, 2012, http://www.infodefensa.com/?noticia=general-atilio-benitez-ministro-de-defensa-de-el-salvador-recibimos-los-helicopteros-serie-md500-en-septiembre.

3. "El Salvador: 2013 Defense Budget Approved," Defence Market Intelligence, January 1, 2012, http://www.dmilt.com/index.php?option=com_content&view=article&id=5260:el-salvador-2013-defense-budget-approved&catid=35:latin-america&Itemid=58. See also US Embassy in El Salvador website.

4. President Funes also pledged to maintain the US dollar as El Salvador's currency and to support the Dominican Republic–Central America–United States Free Trade Agreement.

5. "Fact Sheet: U.S.–El Salvador Defense Cooperation," http://www.defense.gov/news/FACT_Sheet_SLV.pdf.

6. See Rebecca Bill Chavez, "Integrating Human Rights and Public Security: The Challenges Posed by the Militarization of Law Enforcement." *Joint Forces Quarterly* 64 (2012): 67–74.

7. Patricia Carías, "Funes decide enviar tropas a Afganistán," *El Faro* (online newspaper), August 18, 2011, http://www.elfaro.net/es/201108/noticias/5364/.

8. Ibid. Forty-five of the eighty-four deputies voted in favor of deployment.

9. Shanda L. De Anda, "U.S., El Salvador Partnership Leads to Mission Success in Afghanistan," http://www.socso.southcom.mil/news.aspx.

10. "Ministro salvadoreño supervisa tropas en Afganistán," *Revista Estrategia y Negocios*, July 9, 2012, http://www.estrategiaynegocios.net/2012/07/09/ministro-salvadoreno-supervisa-tropas-en-afganistan.

11. Jimena Aguilar and Gabriel Labrador, "Desde 2009 Funes se comprometió con EUA a enviar tropas a Afganistán," *El Faro*, September 12, 2011.

12. Donna Miles, "Rumsfeld Presents Bronze Star to Salvadoran Heroes," American Forces Press Service, November 12, 2004, http://www.defense.gov/News/NewsArticle.aspx?ID=24843.

13. Fred W. Baker, "Gates Praises El Salvador for Iraq Efforts," American Forces Press Service, October 7, 2007, http://www.defense.gov/News/NewsArticle.aspx?ID=47656.

14. Barbara Fick, "Integrating Partner Nations into Coalition Operations," *Joint Force Quarterly* 41 (2006): 21.

15. "Salvadoran Troops Deploy to Afghanistan," August 26, 2011, http://sansalvador.usembassy.gov/news/2011/08/26.html; "El Salvador irá a nuevas misiones de paz de ON," *La Prensa* (Nicaragua), February 2, 2012, http://www.laprensa.com.ni/2013/02/02/planeta/133173-salvador-a-a-nuevas.

16. De Anda, "U.S., El Salvador Partnership."

17. Patrick McKenna, "U.S. and Salvadoran Airmen Team Up to Mentor Afghans," *Air Force Print News Today*, November 22, 2011, http://www.centaf.af.mil/news/story.asp?id=123280449.

18. De Anda, "U.S., El Salvador Partnership."

19. "Ministro salvadoreño supervisa tropas en Afganistán."

20. *New Hampshire National Guard Legislative Plan Fiscal Year 2013*, 16, http://nganh.org/Docs/LL_Brochure_FY_2013.pdf.

21. Thomas Johnson, "American Ambassador to El Salvador Comments on New Hampshire's State Partnership Program," March 1, 2013, http://www.ang.af.mil/news/story.asp?id=123337894.

22. Jon Soucy, "Partnership Benefits New Hampshire Guard, El Salvador," February 10, 2012, http://www.southcom.mil/newsroom/Pages/Partnership-Benefits-New-Hampshire-Guard,-El-Salvador.aspx.

23. "Deployment Ceremony for NH soldiers," New England Cable News, April 21, 2013, http://www.necn.com/04/21/13/Deployment-ceremony-for-NH-soldiers/landing.html?&apID=de93cc34b1714d4dbd29c150393a148d.

24. US Department of Defense, "Western Hemisphere Defense Policy Statement," October 2012, 1–2, http://www.defense.gov/news/WHDPS-English.pdf.

7 GERMANY

The Legacy of the War in Afghanistan

Gale A. Mattox

A MEMBER OF THE COALITION against the 9/11 Afghan terrorist threat and the International Security Assistance Force (ISAF), Germany has been the third largest contributor to the Afghan mission for over a decade and has committed the largest force second only to the US for the Resolute Support postconflict phase. For Germany this commitment to the North Atlantic Treaty Organization (NATO) mission marks a significant milestone in its responsibilities as an alliance member. Given its past decisions with respect to participation in conflict, the longer-term implications of this role are less certain. The leadership, training, and operational experience during the Afghanistan mission have been unprecedented for the country and its readiness for future deployments has significantly increased. But while its role in Afghanistan has given the Bundeswehr the operational experience, it remains unclear if this means a more forward leaning international role for Germany in the future.

To determine the impact of the Afghanistan mission on the German future alliance and international role, this chapter will consider the historic and legal framework on which the mission was based for over thirteen years and the political and military challenges posed for the Bundeswehr and police as they deployed, first, to Kabul and, second, to assume leadership of the Regional Command–North. The perceived primacy of humanitarian aid and development for the German public, particularly in the initial years of deployment before 2009 and the Kunduz tragedy when German troops directed an airstrike that accidentally killed Afghan civilians that year, changed the perception of the German public about participation in Afghanistan. While its commitment has remained steadfast, the German deployment continues to pose a challenge to Berlin policy makers with respect to future Bundeswehr commitments and the use of force more broadly. Will the German participation have been a catalyst for a more active international role or have sobered the country about military involvements?

THE GERMAN MILITARY TAKES ON A NEW ROLE:
THE 1994 KARLSRUHE DECISION

The Federal Republic of Germany did not engage the Bundeswehr into an area of conflict until after a Karlsruhe Constitutional Court ruling in 1994 with the possible self-defense exception of the German special forces rescue of eighty-six passengers from terrorists on Lufthansa Flight 181 in Mogadishu, Somalia, in 1977. Striking was the German decision not to take part in the 1990 Gulf War when there was a blatant abrogation of international law by Iraq's invasion of Kuwait. In this case Germany and Japan did not send troops but rather financed the UN coalition led by the US. This is not to say that there had been no German international missions. German commitment to emergency relief efforts dated as far back as 1960, when Bonn provided humanitarian/disaster assistance to Angola and earthquake assistance to Morocco, later including aid in over 120 incidences focused on the Middle East and Africa in nonconflict situations. In 1992 the Bundeswehr went beyond the constraints of the earlier forays, according to a Bundeswehr officer involved, and flew 150 medical personnel to Cambodia on a civilian mission, but into an area still embroiled in conflict (part of the UN Transitional Authority). It proved challenging, as the Bundeswehr had to stop at least five times along the way to refuel.

In 1994 the Karlsruhe Constitutional Court lifted the limitations that had restricted German use of force in conflict and ruled that "out of area" deployments were permitted,[1] albeit under strict limitations, including explicit approval by the Bundestag on length of time, conditions and other requirements, as necessary.[2] Since the decision, the Bundestag has held over 240 debates dealing with overseas deployments, which far exceeds the procedures governing other NATO countries. This has led to the German army being dubbed a "Parliamentary Army." The Bundestag defines any mission in detail, including size, political/military objectives, and budget. The Afghanistan deployment has accordingly faced annual mandates that specifically outlined caveats such as troop stationing and other deployment details. There have been infrequent exceptions to the annual mandate, as in the 2009 election when the political parties agreed to delay the debate by a few months to avoid it becoming an election issue.

In accord with the 1994 ruling, the Bundeswehr sent limited ground forces in support of German air force aircraft (Panavia Tornado) in 1995 for reconnaissance to Bosnia. In 1999, in the case of what Foreign Minister Joschka Fischer (Green coalition partner to the Social Democratic Party [SPD]) termed a genocide that Germans of all people could not ignore, Berlin sent Tornados into the Kosovo conflict, the first German combat mission undertaken in the post-WWII era and the first outside NATO territory, albeit still in Europe. After the September 12, 2001, invocation of Article 5 of the NATO Treaty, Chancellor Gerhard Schroeder laid his chancellorship on the line to request parliamentary approval to send troops to Afghanistan with an emphasis in the debate on humanitarian assistance. It was a vote of confidence (*Vertrauensfrage*) with clear support by the governing coalition (336–326, with four members of Schroeder's 341-member coalition not voting), albeit with an opposition vote against the wider issue of Schroeder's leadership. The Afghan deployment became the first incidence of ground forces sent out of Europe into a conflict zone, initially to Kabul in 2002 and in 2003 as ISAF lead with the Dutch, and, finally, to assume command of Regional Command–North (RC[N]) in 2005. In political terms, it was also important that the SPD/Green Coalition took this critical decision, which was then further extended by the Grand Coalition CDU/CSU/SPD (Christian Democratic Union/Christian Social Union) after 2005 and by the CDU/CSU/FDP (Free Democratic Party) after 2008, avoiding potentially contentious debate over the annual mandate. The 2013 Grand Coalition Agreement continued support. Only the Left Party has consistently opposed the mandates.

GERMANY VENTURES OUT OF EUROPE

In addition to NATO Article 5 support, United Nations Security Council (UNSC) resolution 1386 passed December 2001 in support of "international efforts to root out terrorism, in keeping with the Charter of the UN." In an often overlooked response to 9/11, multinational NATO crews flew Airborne Warning and Control System aircraft (AWACS) along the US East and West Coasts from October 2001 to May 2002 in support of the US. Despite this support, the US did not turn to NATO when it entered Afghanistan in October 2001 but instead deployed its special operations forces together with the UK and the Northern Alliance against the Taliban regime, with German special forces joining later. But as its attention and, critically, its resources had to be used for operations in Iraq in

2003, the US reached out through the NATO ISAF for a greater role by coalition allies. This included German and Dutch ISAF command in February 2003. In August 2003 NATO assumed command of ISAF initially (from August 11, 2003, to February 9, 2004) by German Lieutenant General Goetz Gliemeroth.

Restricted under rules of engagement (ROE) agreed to in the Bundestag, the Germans took on oversight of the initially quiet RC(N) with a focus on development assistance. In an interesting incident that underscores the German approach to the Afghanistan deployment, German soldiers initially donned baseball caps on arrival—within days, they had changed to helmets. At first purportedly over twenty caveats on German combat forces restricted operations for the Parliamentary Army. The Bundestag only gradually modified the ROE to permit combat roles beyond self-defense. Even as the German contribution remained the third largest, the attention on development activities underscored the public perception and government description of Germany's role in Afghanistan, at least until the 2009 Kunduz incident led to Afghan civilian deaths. In fact, as the US and other countries moved forces in and out of the area for home leave or restationing, sometimes over or under the projected force sizes, the Bundeswehr assiduously remained under the Bundestag-approved force numbers just to ensure that there was no time at which they exceeded the mandate. In addition, as former Member of Parliament (MP) Hans-Ulrich Klose noted, the Bundeswehr self-imposed many of the so-called caveats, in anticipation of parliamentary concerns.[3]

An ongoing issue mentioned frequently between the allies albeit without great detail were other caveats imposed on the German forces. These *Vorbehalte* (*limitations* became the preferred term, as *caveats* took on a negative connotation) varied over the deployment and with the political atmosphere, making the exact number difficult to pin down. A critical caveat related by a former intelligence officer and team chief was the strictly enforced limitation on the collection of intelligence on potential threats (using signal, human, and technical intelligence) to German or allied forces. Although Germans sat on committees to evaluate their reliability, the Bundeswehr's use of the information was strictly for potential capture, with no participation in so-called kill lists of insurgents posing a threat to ISAF forces under the German RC(N). Unlike with other allied forces, no payments were permitted for intelligence beyond cost of transportation and expenses. Further *Vorbehalte* regulated the use of drones for intelligence and situational awareness and also imposed restrictions on use of air support for forces. While restrictions on nighttime ops early in the deployment were reported, the author was unable to substantiate that this was more than lack of equipment which, by at least 2007, was available—at minimum—to special forces.

THE BONN CONFERENCES: UNDERSCORING HUMANITARIAN ASSISTANCE

With the public focus initially on humanitarian aid and development, it is not surprising that the Germans hosted the first major international conference on Afghanistan and a follow-on ten years later. In at least part, the decision was influenced by a high number of Afghans residing in Germany—more than eighty thousand. At one point, at least a third of Afghan cabinet members purportedly spoke a degree of German; many had attended Kabul German School and studied in Germany. In fact, Dr. Rangin Spanta, former foreign minister (2006–2010) and Karzai's national security advisor (2010–2014) moved to Germany in 1982, received his doctorate, and taught at Aachen University, returning to Kabul to teach in 2005. He holds Afghan and German citizenship.[4] In 2000 Germany had also been a member of the Geneva Contact Group (Germany, the US, Italy, and Iran) to address issues with respect to Afghanistan. The Bonn Conferences of 2001 and 2011 reflected the importance of the humanitarian assistance aspect to the deployment as well as the security aspects. The first sentence of the Bonn I agreement declares the determination to "promote national reconciliation, lasting peace, stability and respect for human rights in the country . . . the independence, national sovereignty and territorial integrity of Afghanistan . . . toward the establishment of broad-based, gender-sensitive, multi-ethnic and fully representative government."[5] It addressed the legal framework and judicial system as well as institutional needs. Annex 1 addresses ISAF and training of the Afghan security/armed forces.

While setting a framework for the intervention and encouraging a broader coalition, Bonn I was modest at best in its achievements.[6] Bonn II preceded the 2012 Tokyo Conference with its emphasis on international economic assistance for the transition period, such as "sustainable development, including aid effectiveness and regional economic cooperation," all priorities for Berlin. The conclusions to Bonn II focused on governance, economic and social development, regional cooperation, and security,[7] persistent goals throughout the German deployment, often more so than among many of the allies.

RECONCILING STATE/FEDERAL RESPONSIBILITIES:
THE POLICE

The rebuilding of an Afghan police force had been assigned to the Germans (the UK was assigned the drug issue; the US, the army; Italy, judicial issues; and Japan, demining). One of the German negotiators commented that it was an understandable assignment for the Germans with their preference for limited use of force. But progress was slow because of a number of structural and cultural issues. Although German police deployment outside its borders is not subject to a Bundestag vote or mandate and therefore parliamentary caveats, there are organizational cultural differences, as argued by Cornelius Friesendorf[8]— which impact the deployment of German police on national as well as local levels. Foremost, the WWII experience and the Holocaust underlie a national culture of pacifism and aversion to violence. At the state level, even without mandates, this aversion to violence is present. Likewise, a second component of the police deployment has been, on a smaller scale, the Grenzschutzgruppe 9 (GSG 9, the Border Protection Group 9 of the Federal Police for counterterrorism and special ops), a special-ops group of the Border Patrol under the jurisdiction of the Ministry of the Interior. While these forces are typically more forward leaning, inherent limitations remain, based on both German history and its culture against use of force developed since WWII.

On a local level, where two thirds of foreign deployments are drawn, the police are affected by the recruiting states' culture as well. Even in conservative Bavaria, it is difficult to persuade police to leave the communities where they expected to serve when joining the police force. Local police unions often step in to reinforce these expectations. This aversion to use of force carries over to the foreign region to which they are sent, even in operational decisions. In contrast to US/allied focus on counterinsurgency, the German police are not trained for nor have they adopted counterinsurgency. As Friesendorf points out, "the German police force is dominated by a civilian policing approach that puts a premium on close, positive interaction with the population, and more specifically, the avoidance of deaths of and by police."[9] Once in country, the focus has been more on training and less on foot patrols. The numbers of German police remained low, and accordingly the impact on the Afghan National Police (ANP) was limited. Within a year the responsibility for ANP training shifted initially to the US State Department and by 2005 nationally to the Pentagon, which greatly increased spending and trainers.[10]

In 2007 the European Union also stood up a police mission (EUPOL—European Union Police Mission) drawn from European states, including a limited German role but lifting the German responsibility while also responding to US complaints that the Europeans were not contributing. In sum, the German police effort in RC(N) adopted a more civilian Provincial Reconstruction Team (PRT) integrated approach than that of other allies, particularly the US, which pursued distinctly more militarized police training.[11] As a UK officer commented, the German police appeared to spend more time training at the National Police Academy than in teaching the ANP to patrol and encounter the enemy.[12]

A TURNING POINT: KUNDUZ

In September 2009 the German self-perception of a civilian power in Afghanistan, both for its police and for combat forces, received a jolt when an RC(N) commander observed two fuel trucks one evening parked by suspected terrorists outside Kunduz. Colonel Georg Klein requested US air support. In the meantime, the villagers were alerted by insurgents and enticed by free fuel. Unbeknownst to the German military, families carrying pails headed for the trucks alongside a riverbed outside town. Two F-15e Strike Eagle jets bombed the tanker site, causing 90 to 150 casualties or more, with between 24 and 100 civilians wounded, according to contradictory media reporting. The bombing clearly shook Germany and confronted the public with the fact that Bundeswehr forces were not in Afghanistan only for development assistance—the deployment was also a military mission. A poll before Kunduz by the German Marshall Fund in 2009 on optimism about stabilizing Afghanistan garnered 23 percent of those polled, which then sank to 10 percent in 2010.[13] The controversy led to the eventual resignation of Defense Minister Franz Josef Jung and subsequent events undermined the incoming Defense Mminister Karl-Theodor zu Guttenberg as well.[14]

The incident also ignited a discussion over whether Germany could be said to be in a war. Previous defense ministers had avoided the term, reflecting public unease over involvement in war. As Constanze Stelzenmueller commented, the Kunduz episode "undermine[d] one of Germany's cherished ideas about itself; that, whatever the state of its military, it is at all times morally a superpower."[15] Former Defense Minister zu Guttenberg encouraged a more realistic acceptance of German involvement by shifting the rhetoric to describe

Afghanistan as "*kriegsaehnliche Zustaende*" (warlike conditions) and colloquially a war[16] rather than a "*kriegsaehnliches Szenario*" (a warlike scenario)[17]—a major shift for the German public.

In a further indication of German public discomfort with the use of the Bundeswehr, President Horst Koehler abruptly resigned the presidency in 2010 after broad criticism of his remarks to a reporter on the use of German forces "[it could be that] now and again, in an emergency, military operations could become necessary to safeguard our interests, for example free trade routes, . . . to prevent instability in entire regions that would surely hurt our chances."[18] The comments were viewed as a justification for wars fought for economic reasons. An opposition leader commented that Koehler was "endangering acceptance of Germany's foreign missions," and a constitutional law specialist called it "an imperialist turn of phrase."[19] This sharp reaction reflected a Germany that has clearly not yet come to terms with its role either within the country's elite or in the public and reflects the German difficulty in defining its national security challenges and role in the world.

Only through a slow evolution of public comfort with its Bundeswehr will future agreement be struck on the appropriate use of force and the involvement of Germany in a conflict situation. As recently as July 2011, Berlin suspended a mandatory draft and shifted focus from the constraints of a force not permitted to deploy in conflict areas except as volunteers. It is not only on personnel that Germany has been slow to adapt to the demands of the post–Cold War world and international expectations, but also in equipment and restructuring of its force, not to mention its defense budget, which has consistently been below the NATO 2 percent target of gross domestic product (GDP) reinforced at the 2014 Wales Summit.[20]

The concept that German security will be defended at the Hindu Kush—"*Deutschlands Sicherheit wird auch am Hindukusch verteidigt*"—was declared by Peter Struck, who served as minister of defense from 2002 to 2005, during the time that the guidelines for an evolving new Bundeswehr in 2003 were released.[21] He led the Bundeswehr into Afghanistan and experienced the first casualties: fifty-four military and three police killed in combat since World War II. The German opposition to merging Operation Enduring Freedom and ISAF stemmed from their determination to be "good" allies while avoiding the perception that they were part of "bad"/less acceptable allies who did not carry their weight.

The use of force continues to be uncomfortable for Germans. Even a multi-lateral involvement is not always accepted by Berlin, as the 2011 UNSC abstention on the no-fly zone vote over Libya (Russia and China against US, UK, and French allied support) and the subsequent decision not to participate with its NATO allies demonstrated. The acceptance of participation in Afghanistan for the public depended heavily on the perception of German humanitarian assistance. This perception came increasingly into doubt over the years of German ISAF participation, particularly in light of worsening incidents such as the May 11, 2013, killing of engineers on a project, presumably by the Taliban, before the Afghan police could control the situation in Shakh Moghlan.[22] With approximately 110 aid workers and potential nongovernmental organizations (NGOs) in RC(N) dependent on the military for security, it was feared that the cost of their continued presence could spiral and require further intervention if under attack.[23]

FIRST COMBAT ENGAGEMENT

While Kunduz prompted a political turning point in German perception of the Afghanistan conflict, in another event the Germans confronted an enemy on the ground and engaged in combat for the first time since WWII. When this event was coupled with Kunduz, the impact for Berlin security experts was significant, albeit certainly less so for a public that in 2009 began to confront a fiscal crisis of huge proportions in Europe—one in which Europe looked to Germany to resolve the crisis—and required substantial leadership, not to mention financial resources.

By the end of 2009 the Germans had reached a point where the insurgency had grown in size and in impact in RC(N). Whereas Germany had not had to confront the more strident Taliban in the south, a point of contention and not just a small amount of anger from the other allies, the pressure in the north had increased. The focus on stabilization, not to mention development, no longer appeared sufficient. At the beginning of 2010, the Kunduz incident had shaken Berlin, and two Specialized Forces units had been formed in Kunduz and Baghlan to address the increasing challenges from the insurgents. Quick Reaction Force 5 (QRF5), which then–Lieutenant Colonel Jared Sembritzki took over in Mazar-Scharif (battalion size by this point), moved forces out of the compound, at which point they encountered insurgents and were fired upon. In April four German soldiers became casualties in the fighting termed

Taohid II. This confrontation in Baghlan marked the first time Germans had fought outside their protected compound/camp and exchanged ground fire since WWII. Also in a first, Defense Minister zu Guttenberg was visiting RC(N) to see the QRF5 with Lieutenant Colonel Sembritzki when his helicopter had to turn back because of word that the German unit had come under fire, thus placing the minister in the general zone of combat.[24]

It was not widely reported that the driving force was a sense that the Germans needed to regain initiative, which could not be done within the confining camps and without mobility or good intelligence about the area outside (situational awareness). Based on the operational requirements, concerns had grown among Berlin decision makers and in the Bundestag that another Kunduz incident could be devastating to the German participation in Afghanistan. Leaders decided that a German contingent would fight outside the German compound, a decision that found resonance among the US and other allies. In reaction, the US brought in both combat and aviation helicopters in mid-2010 as well as ten thousand US forces. Eventually the German QRF5 unit worked with locals to reintegrate insurgents and build fortifications around Shahabudin homes whose inhabitants previously had lived in a general climate reminiscent of the "Wild West,"[25] joining the US in efforts at "Partnering . . . Winning Hearts and Minds."

Whether deployment outside camps in RC(N) under German command could have stemmed the increasing insurgent hostilities earlier is difficult to gauge, but there was a clear sense that the Bundeswehr had reached a turning point in its operational abilities within its political mandate. The subsequent vote on the Afghan mandate reinforced a Bundestag comfortable with the enhanced mission of the Bundeswehr. The military leadership decorated Lieutenant Colonel Sembritzki after the deployment. The international community supported the expanded mission, and General David Petraeus praised Sembritzki in an interview with *Bild-Zeitung*, a widely read German newspaper.

PROVINCIAL RECONSTRUCTION TEAMS (PRTS)

The concept of PRTs clearly reflected the German approach to the war in Afghanistan as one to support women, provide wider access to education, improve governance, and address abuses of human rights.[26] Whereas the generally adopted alliance concept was a merger between security and reconstruction and, for the US, reflected its stabilization operations, the German emphasis was reconstruction under secure conditions. Germany undertook these challenges through a collaboration of military/civilian personnel while reaching out to the provincial government and ministers. The Bundeswehr would provide force protection and cooperate with NGOs and German development agencies on humanitarian-focused efforts. Over time the efforts included not only training of teachers, but also the building of schools, streets, irrigation projects, and government buildings, including a hospital. As J. D. Bindenagel has pointed out on German peace building and the soft power approach, Chancellor Angela Merkel articulated the German approach to deployment at the UN: "No development without security and no security without development—mutual dependence."[27]

This civilian face of efforts in Afghanistan was vital for the public as well as for the annual parliamentary mandates beginning in 2001. Although PRT activities included security, the civilian nature of the reconstruction efforts fell within what had historically been part of the German self-image or civilian paradigm articulated by Professor Hanns Maull.[28] The government established two PRTs beginning in 2002 located in Feyzabad and Kunduz and also what some have termed a half PRT. In 2012 Berlin replaced the PRT military-civilian joint leadership with civilian head Helmut Landes, a Foreign Office diplomat initially in Feyzabad and finally in Kunduz. The switch to a civilian head also reflected the planned 2014 withdrawal of German combat forces. At the same time, Berlin announced the continuation of 430 million in annual financial aid for 2014–2024, specifically allocated to development.

While assessments of the PRTs established throughout the ISAF commands were mixed,[29] the concept generally received good marks in RC(N). In part this was due to the German focus on development. Also, unlike US PRTs, civilian participation was less problematic until later in the deployment, as conflict in the northern region was less than in other commands, although by October 2014 substantially increased conflict had made it a more challenging region. Enthusiasm for the PRTs waned throughout ISAF in the years leading up to the 2014 force withdrawals, including in Germany. The shift to PRT civilian leadership by the Germans may or may not change the overall skeptical assessment of the PRT ability to make a difference in the long term.

COLLABORATION ACROSS GERMAN MINISTRIES

For Afghanistan, German documents underscored the need for *vernetzte Sicherheit* (interconnected security), an effort to link various government departments structurally to work together. When Bundeswehr cooperation with the ministry of development became difficult, a restructuring was undertaken. The restructuring assigned the Gesellschaft fuer Internationale Zusammenarbeit (GIZ) to focus on development issues, not solely for Afghanistan but spurred by the experience there. The attempts to connect the Bundeswehr, the Ministry for Economic Cooperation and Development, the Intelligence Agency, the German Security Council, and others such as the police were slow and often quite poor. Despite the rhetoric of networked security, the results were mixed over more than ten years of involvement in South Asia in terms of consultation and coordination in Berlin. While the Ministry for Economic Cooperation and Development worked in country and with both NGOs and the Bundeswehr, experts noted that coordination in Berlin often fell short in operation. Based on the Afghan experience, the German Security Council began to reach out beyond its traditional discussions of arms sales to more collaboration at the highest levels on other issues,[30] later bringing the foreign, defense, and development ministries together at the table.

CONCLUSIONS

Given the high priority of reconstruction for the German public in its involvement in Afghanistan, the importance of the post-2014 era is significant. Unlike many of the other allies, Berlin not only made clear its intention to remain committed—assuming a continued US presence—but also assumed the position of Resolute Support Deputy Command after the 2014 pullout and announced plans to commit a residual force of 600–800 troops. This was an operational advance for the Germans and also a symbolic gesture of commitment.

The decision to come to the defense of its closest ally since WWII within the responsibilities of its multilateral alliance NATO was natural, even to a region outside Europe. But the challenges of the German commitment of over thirteen years, over fifty casualties, and growing public dissatisfaction with the war cannot be underestimated. In April 2002, when there were few German forces in Afghanistan, 61 percent of Germans approved of the "U.S. led military campaign against the Taliban and Al Qaeda in Afghanistan."[31] By 2011, German support of the war in Afghanistan fell to 40 percent,[32] and 58 percent of Germans polled wanted to remove troops. Interestingly, even after Kunduz, there were no substantial public street demonstrations against the deployment as casualties became known and parliamentary support remained astonishingly supportive. Indicative of the caution—the so-called culture of restraint with respect to use of force—with which elected officials approached the Afghanistan deployment is the lack of attention at the highest level. By 2010, Chancellor Angela Merkel had visited Afghanistan only three times (her defense ministers were there frequently) after her 2005 election. As the opposition SPD/Greens had made the initial decision to deploy and the government CDU/CSU/FDP had maintained the German commitment, the parliamentary mandate was handled in the legislature with minimal debate and among the political elite, a traditional German approach to security issues.

The Common Approach

At the alliance level, the common approach touted by ISAF for its allies did not always meet expectations. For the Germans, there were often structural, institutional, and even bureaucratic issues for a country first attempting a deployment outside its experience level or historical tradition. At other times, the political nature of the parliamentary requirements set cautionary limitations other allies did not experience. Cross-alliance problems also caused difficulties that affected the Germans and others, such as the Five Eyes (US, UK, Canada, New Zealand, Australia) policy on intelligence or operational sharing to a different degree across allies, which was particularly difficult for the Germans, who were providing the third largest force consistently during ISAF. While informal collegiality often informed those outside the native-English-speaking briefs after a military operation, the process led an American pilot to complain about required differences in debriefings where at least three different briefs were required for the US, Five Eyes, and other allies when all would have benefited from the information, leading some allies to complain about a lack of sufficient information for their operations. Generally the sense was that the process improved over time, but could/should be improved further in the future.

Working with Coalition Members

Working with allies often posed its own issues, particularly given the German *Vorbehalte*, or caveats/limitations. The most striking example occurred in 2006, when Canadians in the Kandahar region were denied their requests for assistance based on the German parliamentary restrictions. As the weekly *Spiegel* reported after the German government had denied the request for helicopter assistance: "The gulf that separates the *Bundeswehr* and its NATO allies holding the south is a wide, tangled mess of legal caveats and domestic politics that no chopper can traverse."[33]

The reaction from allies was swift and damning, and Germans felt the fallout at all levels, including quite personally. At one point the Dutch turned their

backs to the Germans in Kabul at a meeting. At a gathering of allied parlia-
mentarians in Quebec City, Canada, the *Frankfurter Allgemeine Zeitung* quoted
a Green Party defense expert Winfried Nachtwey as hearing a Brit comment:
"there are soldiers in Afghanistan who drink beer or tea, and there are soldiers
who risk their lives." At that point the countries in the region—the US with
350 casualties, the UK with 41, and Canada with 42—accounted for 90 percent
of total coalition casualties.[34] (See the Coalition Fatalities chart in Appendix B.)

But this has been the exception; allied coordination in the north was
marked by purportedly excellent collaboration with other coalition members, including NATO nations Albania, Belgium, Croatia, Hungary, Latvia, the
Netherlands, Norway, the US, and Turkey and non-NATO nations Armenia,
Bosnia and Herzegovina, Finland, the former Yugoslav Republic of Macedonia,
Mongolia, Montenegro, and Sweden. The general experience in RC(N) and its
follow-on Train, Advise and Assist Command North (TAAC[N]) represented
a large step forward in terms of coalition building and cooperative efforts for
future conflicts.

The Hungarian PRT was one example, as well as a PRT that included the
Norwegians and Swedes. But while the PRTs were an important element in the
German public acceptance of the deployments, they were not without problems. The PRT civilian contingent was initially small and its head had little staff
support and depended on the military. As one commented, it was a "great idea"
but the concept never really produced as designed. The post-2014 reconstruction effort remains an unwritten page. To date the focus on development in
2001–2002 has been replaced by an appreciation for the necessary cooperation
between security and development if reconstruction is to be successful. With a
residual force after 2014, the PRT efforts—led by a civilian—will confront difficulties in ensuring adequate security. Should this fail and relations with the
Afghan government deteriorate to the point of total withdrawal, the assessment
of the German deployment of more than thirteen years may undermine future
deployments.

Germany's Future International Role?

What of the larger issues of German leadership? What kind of leadership should
Germany exert in the future? On the one hand, there are those like Henry Kiss-
inger who have argued that Germany is "too big for Europe and too small for
the world."[35] On the other hand, at the Brandenburg Gate in 2011, Polish Foreign Minister Radosław Sikorski lamented that Germany did not sufficiently
exercise leadership with respect to the financial crisis, but the implication

extended as well to broader leadership: "I fear German power less than I am beginning to fear German inactivity. You have become Europe's indispensable nation. You *may not* fail to lead."[36] Where do the Germans themselves stand in this respect? There are clearly differing views. At the 2014 Munich Security Conference, President Joachim Gauck warned that Germans should not "turn a blind eye, not run from threats, but instead stand firm, let us not forget, neglect, or, worse, betray universal values, but instead uphold them together with our friends and partners. Let us be seen to be living by them, let us defend them."[37] The euro crisis has seen Chancellor Merkel take the lead on a geo-economic level, but in the geopolitical and security arena, the Germans have not yet made that choice and will continue their unique path. But President Gauck's vision presages the evolution of a more substantial international role in the future and, should Germany assume that role, the Afghanistan deployment will have prepared the Bundeswehr.

NOTES

The views expressed reflect solely those of the author and do not in any way reflect the views of the US government or any other institute or affiliation. Appreciation goes to the Institute for National Security Studies (INSS) for its travel support of this chapter and to the US Naval Academy Research Council as well as the Nimitz Library for their support.

1. The opinion resulted from a Christian Social Union/Free Democratic Party (CSU/FDP) query in 1992 with respect to use of force in Bosnia-Herzegovina and Somalia.

2. See Dieter Dettke, *Germany Says 'No': The Iraq War and the Future of German Foreign and Security Policy* (Baltimore: Johns Hopkins University Press, 2009). in 1992 the SPD/FDP asked the Constitutional Court for clarification on two resolutions dealing with use of German AWACS over Bosnia-Herzegovina and a Bundeswehr transport battalion in Somalia. Georg Nolte, "Bundeswehreinsaetze in kollektiven/Sicherheits systemen—Zum Urteil des Bundesverfassungsgerichts vom 12. Juli 1994," *Zeitschrift fuer Auslaendisches Oeffentliches Recht und Voelkerrecht* 54: 652, 673 (1994). BVerfGE 90: 286, 383–384.

3. Interview with Hans-Ulrich Klose, June 5, 2014.

4. Dr. Rangin Spanta was affiliated with the Green Party while in Germany. See http://www.afghan-web.com/bios/spanta.html.

5. *Agreement on Provisional Arrangements in Afghanistan Pending the Re-establishment of Permanent Government Institutions*, Bonn Conference, December 2001, http://www.un.org/News/dh/latest/afghan/afghan-agree.htm.

6. A more optimistic assessment, albeit with a focus on negotiations and diplomacy is Mark Fields and Ramsha Ahmed, *A Review of the 2001 Bonn Conference and*

Application to the Road Ahead in Afghanistan, Institute for National Strategic Studies, Strategic Perspectives, No. 8 Paperback, July 6, 2012.

7. See *International Afghanistan Conference in Bonn, 5 December 2011: Afghanistan and the International Community: From Transition to the Transformation Decade,* http://eeas.europa.eu/afghanistan/docs/2011_11_conclusions_bonn_en.pdf.

8. Cornelius Friesendorf, "Insurgency and Civilian Policing: Organizational Culture and German Police Assistance in Afghanistan," *Contemporary Security Policy,* June 18, 2013, 332. He makes a strong argument for organizational culture, although I would argue a case of broader cultural impact. See his article for an excellent discussion.

9. Ibid., 333.

10. Ibid., 338.

11. Ibid., 339–343, discusses the German civilianized approach and its characteristics.

12. Ibid.

13. German Marshall Fund of the United States, *Transatlantic Trends: Key Findings 2010,* 15, http://trends.gmfus.org/files/archived/doc/2010_English_Key.pdf.

14. Zu Guttenberg eventually resigned from office in the face of plagiarism charges, but the Kunduz incident had undermined his administration.

15. Constanze Stelzenmueller, "Germany Shoots First and Thinks Again," *Financial Times,* September 9, 2009, 8.

16. Ibid.

17. Ibid.

18. Lutz Lichtenberger, "Highest Office in the Land," *Atlantic Times,* July/August 2010, 5. See also Gale A. Mattox, "German National Security Policy in the post–Cold War," in *Providing for National Security: A Comparative Analysis,* ed. Andrew M. Dorman and Joyce P. Kaufman (Stanford, CA: Stanford University Press, 2014), 53–73.

19. Lichtenberger, "Highest Office in the Land," 5.

20. North Atlantic Treaty Organization, *Wales Summit Declaration* (September 5, 2014), para. 14, also calls for 20 percent over ten years for capability shortfalls, as discovered in the case of its Sea Lynx helicopters grounded for maintenance in October 2014. http://www.theguardian.com/world/2014/oct/07/germany-military-hardware-disrepair-exposure.

21. Ministry of Defense, *Verteidigungspolitischen Leitlinien 2003.* These guidelines were issued in a cabinet resolution and then were followed by the ministry's *White Book 2006* under Struck's successor, Franz Josef Jung, to lay out the Bundeswehr framework.

22. Ralf Beste et al., "*Schuesse in der Nacht* (Shots in the Night)," *Spiegel,* July 29, 2013, 29.

23. Ibid., p. 30.

24. Ulrike Demmer, "Afghanistan-Besuch: Guttenberg in der Gefechtszone," *Spiegel Online,* August 29, 2010, http://www.spiegel.de/politik/ausland/afghanistan-besuch-guttenberg-in-der-gefechtszone-a-714459.html. Minister zu Guttenberg's first visit co-

incided with news of fire by QF5. He turned back and a month later returned to view the Highway Triangle taken by the German unit.

25. Interview with Jared Sembritzki, July 31, 2013.

26. The US deployed the first of eventually approximately twenty-five unique PRTs in Afghanistan.

27. Speech by Angela Merkel, Chancellor of the Federal Republic of Germany, to the High-Level Plenary Meeting of the UN General Assembly on the Millennium Goals, New York, September 21, 2010, http://www.un.org/enmdg/summit2010/debate/ DE_en.pdf. See also J. D. Bindenagel, "Peacebuilding: Germany's Military Mission, The Soft Power Approach and Civilian-Military Teaming," 2014, 1.

28. Hanns W. Maull, "Zivilmacht Bundesrepublik. Vierzehn Thesen fuer eine neue deutsche Aussenpolitik," *Europa Archiv* 47, no. 10 (1992): 269–278.

29. Lawrence Vasquez, "Time to Reevaluate the Role of Provincial Reconstruction Teams in Afghanistan?" Brookings Up Front, November 4, 2010, http://www.brookings .edu/blogs/up-front/posts/2010/11/04-afghanistan-vasquez. Vasquez, commander of PRT Farah in 2010, discusses the need for US PRTs to move from their focus on smaller projects with local governments to work at the district/provincial levels.

30. The US has similar issues, particularly in collaboration between US Agency for International Development (USAID) and US Department of State (within the same ministry), not even to mention US Department of Defense (DOD) and USAID.

31. Pew Research Center for the People and the Press, *International Herald Tribune*, and the Council on Foreign Relations, "Bush International Poll II," April 2002, http:// www.pewglobal.org/files/2002/04/Pew-Bush-Euro-Poll-Topline.pdf.

32. Pew Research Center, "Views of the U.S. and American Foreign Policy," June 17, 2010, http://www.pewglobal.org/2010/06/17/chapter-1-views-of-the-u-s-and-american -foreign-policy-3/.

33. "Allies Have It Out in Canada: Afghanistan Testing NATO Alliance," *Spiegel On-line*, November 17, 2006, http://spiegel.ivwbox.de/cgi-bin/ivw/CP/1182;/international/ c-676/r-3675/p-druckversion/a-449183/be-PB64-aW50ZXJuYXRpb25hbC9hcnRpa2Vs/ szwprofil-1182?d=69537481.

34. Ibid.

35. Zanny Minton Beddoes, "Europe's Reluctant Hegemon," Special Report for the *Economist*, June 15, 2013, 3. This report is primarily about German economic strength but discusses Germany's political/military role as well.

36. Speech by Polish Foreign Minister Radosław Sikorski at the Brandenburg Gate, November 27, 2011, German Marshall Fund, http://www.economist.com/node/21540683/ print.

37. German President Joachim Gauck, "Germany's Role in the World: Reflections on Responsibility, Norms, and Alliances," Munich Security Conference, January 31, 2014, 8.

8 THE UNITED KINGDOM

Innocence Lost in the War in Afghanistan?

Andrew M. Dorman

THE UK HAS ENGAGED in combat operations in and over Afghanistan from the start of the conflict. This has not been without controversy.[1] As one of the largest troop providers, surpassed only by the US and the Afghan government, and consistently based in some of the most dangerous parts of the country, successive British governments have remained committed to the NATO mission. And, although the UK plans to withdraw the majority of its forces and end its combat role alongside the US in 2014, it has promised to remain committed to the Afghan government, principally by developing the Afghan's initial officer training capability from 2013 onwards—the so-called Sandhurst in the Sun.[2]

The price of Britain's commitment to the Afghan war has been far higher than initially planned. By the end of 2013 the number of British war dead had reached 447.[3] The price has not been paid by just service personnel and their families. The terrorist attacks on the London transport system on July 7, 2005, and various other failed plots have been directly linked to the deployment of British military personnel in Iraq and Afghanistan, as has the tragic 2013 murder of Drummer Lee Rigby, Royal Regiment of Fusiliers, in London. Thus British public opinion feels generally less safe as a result of the deployment of its forces to Afghanistan. Partly this is because public opinion has conflated the Iraq and Afghan wars with the result that domestic support for the Afghan commitment continues to fall, with some within society fighting against British involvement. As a result, while support for Britain's armed forces remains generally high, they are now viewed by many as victims of "Blair's illegal wars."[4] Moreover, the credibility of Britain's armed forces has been questioned, particularly from a US perspective, and there is a question whether the failures of British forces in Iraq and Afghanistan mark a watershed moment in their use.[5]

This chapter examines why a military campaign for which the British government had such high hopes, and which domestic public opinion initially supported, has led to major divisions within the UK and questions over its worth. The first part examines the first phase of Britain's Afghan War. It looks at the reasoning behind the government's decision to engage in combat in Afghanistan and then analyzes the initial campaign from 2001 to 2005. The second part reviews the second phase of the war. It considers the government's decision to make the case for the North Atlantic Treaty Organization (NATO) to escalate its involvement to southern and eastern Afghanistan and the subsequent deployment of British forces principally to Helmand. The third part then reflects on the wider impact of the Afghan War on the UK. Finally, the last part draws a series of conclusions.

PHASE ONE OF BRITAIN'S AFGHAN WAR (2001–2005)

During the days of empire, Britain engaged in a series of Afghan wars with varying degrees of success, but this history was ignored. Instead, Britain was drawn into Afghanistan by the events of 9/11. The attacks on the World Trade Center represented the largest loss of British life in a single terrorist incident since the bombing of the King David hotel in 1946. For Prime Minister Tony Blair the 9/11 attacks represented a step change in the scale of terrorist atrocity,[6] and the British government believed it had a duty to react to the attack. The British Parliament was united in its call for a response.[7] Moreover, during the Kosovo conflict Blair had articulated the Doctrine of the International Community,[8] which argued that at times the international community had a moral responsibility to intervene using force, and the case for Afghanistan was built on this previous experience.[9]

Other factors reinforced this view. The US has been a key ally, with the two countries developing what has become known as the "special relationship." The US remains a key ally both formally, through such bodies as NATO, and informally, through intelligence, nuclear, and general defense links. However, the ties are deeper. The US is a major trading partner, with the interconnectedness of the banking system most evident in the 2008 financial collapse. There are also strong cultural, historical, and linguistic links.

In committing itself to military action, the government formally set two objectives: to root out those responsible for the attacks and to ensure that they and their associates were prevented from committing further acts of terror, and to bring about a step change in the international community's ability to defeat terrorism. A third objective was left unstated—to influence the American conduct of the so-called Global War on Terrorism in a manner that was consistent with Britain's interests. To achieve this, the British government set three formal military objectives: first, "to destroy the terrorist camps"; second, "to pressurize the Taliban regime to end its support of Osama bin Laden"; and finally, "to allow us to mount future operations in Afghanistan."[10]

For the UK, the projection of military power into Afghanistan presented new challenges. The 1998 Strategic Defence Review had been predicated around a large-scale deployment, similar to that in the 1991 Gulf War, in the Middle East or North Africa. It had not been envisaged that British forces would have to deploy in force beyond this "Arc of Concern" or to such a remote and difficult a place as Afghanistan. Britain simply did not have any aircraft comparable to the US Air Force's long-range bombers.[11] The Vulcan long-range bomber force had left service in 1982 and been replaced by the much shorter-range Tornado. At sea the single-engine Harrier force could not be used over such long distances, so the UK had few options. The navy had a limited Tomahawk Land Attack Missile (TLAM) capability that could be covertly deployed to within striking range of Afghanistan, but it could only be used against fixed targets and required overflight rights. These were negotiated and a force of three submarines, two carrying TLAMs, was deployed to within striking distance of Afghanistan. On the ground neither the UK nor the US could deploy significant ground forces quickly.

Initially the British military contribution focused on the provision of special forces and key enablers to support the US air strikes. These included a force of air-to-air refueling tankers to support the US Navy, Canberra reconnaissance aircraft capable of providing high-level aerial photography, and Nimrod maritime patrol and reconnaissance aircraft capable of tracking ground units and acting as communication relay stations. The ensuing campaign was assisted by the deep unpopularity of the Taliban regime in Afghanistan. Gaining the support of the Afghan people was identified as a key goal to prevent the return of al Qaeda. Here the British government saw its role as promoting a wider nation-building strategy in Afghanistan, in contrast to that envisaged by the Americans in order to prevent al Qaeda from returning. This difference in view would have a profound impact on the conflict as the British government pushed the US administration toward expanding its remit and not simply leaving Afghanistan once the Taliban and al Qaeda had been ejected.

The conflict formally began with a combined US-UK TLAM strike. The timing was dictated in part by the need for moonlight to provide light for the insertion of special forces teams to support the Northern Alliance. The main British force movements were masked by exercise Saif Sareea II in Oman. The forces deployed on the exercise provided a readily available pool, relatively close to Afghanistan, available to take advantage of changing events. As the campaign continued and the exercise came to an end, the government had to make a number of decisions about which forces to retain close to Afghanistan. This marked a significant increase in the British deployment with the allocation of an Amphibious Task Group to provide a forward operating base while also providing the potential for a ground contribution if required.[12]

Throughout this period small groups of British special forces sought to provide appropriate support to the Northern Alliance and also engaged in some individual operations. Not surprisingly this operation, like many others, received little public attention. In early November, Northern Alliance forces began advancing southward.[13] Mazar-e Sharif was identified as the first major city likely to fall to the Northern Alliance, and it was seen as a litmus test for the future. A small British party undertook a reconnaissance of the city to consider the possibility of deploying a brigade force to secure and stabilize the situation. However, the Northern Alliance was able to impose order in Mazar-e Sharif, and the British government's offer of a brigade headquarters plus two infantry battalions was not required. Instead it was replaced by a much smaller combined American/French/Jordanian force.

In mid-November 2001, reports were received of the Taliban fleeing the capital, Kabul. Kabul was the epicenter of Afghanistan, and the British government was keen to offer a military contribution for the security of the city to maintain its independence from any particular faction. It was thought that if the Northern Alliance forces secured the city, then they would have an undue influence over how the follow-on government would develop. A special forces team was therefore flown to the nearest operational airfield at Bagram to secure an entry point for coalition forces into Kabul.[14] The assumption was that a brigade headquarters and a light battalion would follow on. The speed of changing events meant that not all of the formalities had been completed, and an apology had to be made to the Northern Alliance's foreign minister about the unannounced deployment. Nevertheless, the force remained in control of the airfield and would provide the basis for the later deployment of the International Security Assistance Force (ISAF).

As mentioned earlier, the Blair government sought to emphasize the nation-building role and pushed the agenda forward despite the skepticism within the Bush administration. The subsequent Bonn Agreement called for the creation of an Interim Authority on December 22, 2001, and the holding of a Loya Jirga within six months to decide on a Transitional Authority for Afghanistan.[15] With the Interim Authority to be based at Kabul, an international force was needed to ensure that no single group would dominate subsequent proceedings. Blair indicated on December 11, 2001, that Britain was willing to provide the initial lead for such a force. Although the American administration was initially less convinced, they were won over by Blair who argued that a narrower focus on defeating the Taliban and al Qaeda in Afghanistan in the short term would not provide for the longer-term security of Afghanistan that the coalition obviously required. The Chief of the Defence Staff, Admiral Sir Michael Boyce, openly criticized the US for pursuing the Afghan campaign in only one dimension. He pointed out that winning the "hearts and minds" campaign across the Arab world was also needed if the supply of personnel to al Qaeda was to be stopped.[16] This was the first example of what would become a common theme in Iraq and Afghanistan—a British claim to a form of exceptionalism when it came to a counterinsurgency campaign born of their colonial history and their experiences in decolonization and Northern Ireland. There appeared to be an inbuilt assumption that British forces were born with the ability to conduct such operations in a superior way to anyone else, particularly the Americans, and the fallacy of this would unfortunately be revealed in both Iraq and Afghanistan where underresourced British forces failed.

The final decision about makeup and mandate was the subject of intense discussion among allied military forces and the United Nations.[17] One of the main unresolved issues at Bonn was the remit under which the international force would operate. The UK dispatched a reconnaissance team under Major General Jon McColl to begin planning for the deployment of the force. After a series of bilateral negotiations, the force was pared down to around 5,000, with the United Kingdom initially contributing 1,500 personnel. It was planned that Britain's contribution would be reduced after two months to approximately 900 as a Canadian infantry battalion replaced 2nd Battalion, The Parachute Regiment (2 PARA) as the second battalion in the force (the other battalion was provided by Germany, with a Dutch contingent included). ISAF was established by United Nations Security Council Resolution 1386 on December 20, 2001, for six months and achieved an initial operating capability a month later.[18] With these positive developments the UK then faced the problem of the handover of command of the ISAF force. From the beginning the Turkish government indicated its interest in taking over from the British, and the Canadians indicated that they would provide a replacement infantry battalion. This plan did not work out as intended. Instead, the Canadians decided to deploy their battalion in support of American forces operating in the south of Afghanistan as part of Operation Enduring Freedom.[19] The Turkish government also delayed their agreement to replace the British headquarters until a number of concerns were addressed. This meant that the British force was deployed for closer to six months.

At the same time, US-led military operations continued in the south and southeast of the country against remnants of the Taliban and al Qaeda. After the fall of Kabul, the focus of attention was the southern city of Kandahar, traditionally a stronghold of the Taliban. Like Kabul, the city fell without much resistance, and the Taliban and al Qaeda forces fled to the south and east toward Pakistan. In the spring of 2002 the American administration formally requested British assistance in the continuing clearance of southern and eastern Afghanistan. A Royal Marine Commando unit, code-named Operation Veritas, amounting to some 1,700 personnel, was sent.[20] The Americans assured the British that the planning envisaged British forces being deployed as part of an American operation in a serious war-fighting role.[21] In fact, no further large groups of Taliban or al Qaeda forces were located, and the Royal Marines instead conducted "sweep and clear" operations in southeastern Afghanistan in which only small parties of Taliban and al Qaeda were seen.[22] Nevertheless, these operations involved destroying some twenty-eight bunkers and caves, flying more than a thousand helicopters, finding and destroying forty-five thousand rounds of munitions, and conducting significant humanitarian assistance work.[23] In June 2002 the Royal Marines withdrew and British attention focused almost exclusively on ISAF and nation-building. In part this was because there was the belief that the Afghanistan mission had been successful and there was merely a need to consolidate the situation and support the fledgling government. Moreover, much of the attention of the British government, including the key policy makers, had already moved toward the buildup to subsequent war in Iraq. Thus the British military presence, apart from a few personnel in the Provincial Reconstruction Teams (PRTs), was almost exclusively confined to a special forces contingent that was tasked with tackling the remnants of al Qaeda and the Taliban as part of the US Operation Enduring Freedom.

Thus, in the north of the country the British government supported the development of PRTs, initially setting one up at Mazar-e Sharif. At the same time the British government sought to expand the ISAF mission and get it placed under NATO auspices, thus bringing in more partners to share the burden. In August 2003 NATO assumed command of ISAF, and by December 2003 it had agreed to enlarge the ISAF mission to northern Afghanistan as part of a phased expansion that incorporated western Afghanistan in early 2005.

PHASE TWO OF BRITAIN'S AFGHAN WAR (2006–2014)

The British government's attention began to return to Afghanistan in 2005.[24] After the reelection of Labour in 2005, Blair felt he was at last able to begin to confront a series of issues. The first was the problem of the continuing commitment of British forces to Iraq at a level far higher than originally envisaged and with no clear end in sight.[25] The second was the future direction of ISAF's mission: in particular, should it be expanded to include the remainder of the country in the south and east? The third challenge was the loss of public support for the Iraq War, which was exacerbated after the attacks on the London transport network on July 7, 2005, and a failed attack a fortnight later.

Here the interests of a number of domestic constituencies came together to advocate the expansion of the NATO mission to the south and east and the deployment of an initial British force of some 3,300 personnel. For the Blair government the unpopularity of the Iraq War together with internal dissent from the Chancellor of the Exchequer, Gordon Brown, was proving to be deeply burdensome. For Blair and his inner circle, an expansion of the mission not only supported its nation-building agenda but also offered a potential avenue for the government to extract British forces from Iraq by deploying to Afghanistan instead. For the new Defense Secretary, John Reid, the deployment of British forces to southern Afghanistan would be a commitment that he had not inherited from his predecessor, Geoff Hoon, and thus would help establish him within the cabinet. Reid's view was encouraged by the Defence Academy's Advanced Research Assessment Group (ARAG), which had successfully displaced the Policy Planning Division within the Ministry of Defence (MoD), albeit temporarily, as the principal source of policy advice to the defense secretary. ARAG's agenda was to make itself indispensable to the defense minister, and this was achieved by advocating increasing commitments, which it promised to support through the provision of appropriate advisors.

For the army, and in particular members of the Parachute Regiment, the need to deploy all or part of the 16 Air Assault Brigade on an active operation was viewed as necessary not only to help preserve the regiment's current strength but also to boost the careers of its officers and thus maintain its relative influence within the upper echelons of the British Army. The 2004 army reorganization had resulted in the army's losing three of its forty infantry battalions, with one of the Parachute battalions given to the director of special forces to create a new Ranger force. The politics of which battalions to cut had led to calls for the Parachute Regiment to lose one of its battalions, and the regiment's senior cadre were very concerned about the regiment's vulnerability should further cuts be made to the army.[26] Moreover, Afghanistan offered the army as a whole the prospect of leaving Iraq without being seen to abandon the Americans. Britain's planning for Iraq had assumed that the commitment would rapidly diminish after the convention phase as its troops were replaced by other allies who had not been previously involved. This was compounded by the 2003–2004 defense review, which assumed that Britain's future wars would be quick, high-intensity operations and had therefore reconfigured the armed forces to support this, removing the army's ability to sustain long-term operations.[27] The subsequent failure to find other nations to share the burden and the politicians' unwillingness to increase the level size of the British commitment to Iraq meant that the whole operation was underresourced, and while initially the British sector looked to be far calmer, the bubbling discontent subsequently erupted and British forces began to take a steady stream of casualties while their grip on the region began to loosen.[28]

Thus there was a coming together of interests for a deployment of British forces to southern Afghanistan in place of the Iraq commitment. The main problem was that an initial reconnaissance undertaken in 2005 by British special forces advised against such a deployment, suggesting there were no Taliban to fight and deployment would most likely create a war. Nevertheless, the British government announced that it would support the extension of the NATO ISAF mission to southern and eastern Afghanistan, with the UK deploying a force of some 3,300 personnel that comprised the major part of NATO's Allied Rapid Reaction Corps headquarters to take command of all NATO's forces, including the US Operation Enduring Freedom element plus parts of the 16 Air Assault Brigade, which would deploy to Helmand province under Canadian command (see Chapter 5 of this volume).[29] It was envisaged that the deployment would be to a largely compliant area, and although southern Afghanistan had historically been where the Taliban had been strongest, John Reid expressed his hope that not a single shot be fired.[30] At the same time it was hoped that the British force level in Iraq could be reduced and replaced by the Americans. The reality was somewhat different, with British forces surrounded in a series of platoon houses in Afghanistan as hundreds of Taliban attempted to overrun the various British bases. The British were fortunate that none of their bases were overrun, and given the ferocity of the fighting, the number of casualties they suffered was remarkably light. This still meant that the news at home was regularly filled with details of British casualties. At the same time, the planned reduction in Britain's presence in Iraq was much slower than planned and the army became stretched to support both operations.

After six months, the 16 Air Assault Brigade was replaced by the 3 Commando Brigade, Royal Marines, which in turn was replaced some six months later. The result was a succession of six-month campaigns each fought differently depending on the culture of the brigade taking over and the philosophy of its brigade commander.[31] This disjointed approach was worsened by the lack of cross-governmental coordination. Initially the Department for International Development (DFID) sought to avoid becoming embroiled in the Afghanistan campaign and instead remain focused on its existing African projects in order to achieve its millennium goals. When it did start to become involved in Afghanistan, its initial engagement was a disaster reflecting a lack of cultural awareness and its unpreparedness to send staff into a hostile environment. Partly this was because Afghanistan proved different from what it was accustomed to. The department had traditionally used its resources to pay other organizations such as the United Nations, charities, and aid agencies to provide the capacities that DFID had identified as those it wished to build in a country. In southern Afghanistan this was impractical because of the dangerous security environment. Moreover, bureaucratic politics played a big part. DFID, the Ministry of Defence, and the Foreign and Commonwealth Office (FCO) all thought they should be in charge, and the failure to appoint a higher representative to Afghanistan, as had occurred in the Balkans, meant there was no one to force the departments to work together. The initial lack of DFID and FCO engagement and the steadily increasing violence resulted in an exponential increase in British troop numbers that reached ten thousand within a few years, a figure lower than the services wanted but the highest the government was prepared to accept. Even with this force, Helmand remained uncontrolled. Only until the US decided to undertake a surge of forces into Afghanistan, including the deployment of some twenty thousand US Marines, did the force-to-space ratios in Helmand mean that security could start to be provided.

Thus for the second time in a decade the British armed forces have repeated many of the same mistakes made in Iraq. The main difference was that Britain's armed forces did not plan to abandon the situation to the US but instead drew down their forces roughly in line with those of the US. The goals of Afghanistan have been replaced by the goals of getting out while retaining some degree of credibility with their US partner. Thus just before Christmas 2012, David Cameron, the new Prime Minister, announced the first phase of the drawdown and planned reduction of forces by 40 percent in 2013, thus placating public opinion. Unfortunately for the British relationship with its US partner, this was a month too early and out of line with the subsequent US announcement of a 50 percent reduction in early 2013.

AFGHANISTAN'S WIDER IMPACT ON THE UK

The wars in Afghanistan and Iraq have raised the fundamental question of whether successive British governments have been able to think strategically.[32] The failure of the government to coordinate its different elements was quite surprising. The Ministry of Defence response was to produce a Discussion Note on the Comprehensive Approach, which argued for far greater central control of resources.[33] Both the FCO and the DFID looked at this and ignored it, stating that this was a defense document that did not apply to them. Only in 2010 when the Conservative–Liberal Democrat government came to power was this revisited. A new National Security Council (NSC) has been set up, chaired by the prime minister, with the major departments of state represented by their ministers together with the chief of the defense staff and the intelligence services heads. The aim of the NSC is to ensure a properly coordinated government response, and there does appear to be greater cohesion. The main problem is that the cabinet office supporting the NSC lacks the requisite capacity to support it appropriately.

The reaction of Britain's public to Britain's wars in Iraq and Afghanistan has raised a number of issues. First, the two wars have almost uniformly become conflated, and thus the alleged illegality that surrounded the Iraq War has been passed on to the Afghanistan War despite successive governments' attempts to separate them and highlight the justification for the war in Afghanistan. There

have been two consequences of this. First, within part of the British population the opposition to both wars has led to violence against the British state, its
armed forces, and its citizens.[34] The attacks on London's transport network in
2005 brought home to the country that there was "an enemy within," and this
has challenged the whole multicultural agenda that governments have emphasized and raised the issues of identity and values.[35] More recently, the murder
of Drummer Rigby has heightened these divisions and led to a rise in support
for far-right groups such as the English Defence League.

Following the failings of Britain's armed forces in Afghanistan and Iraq, a
number of analysts have suggested that the decade of "liberal interventionism"
begun with Kosovo is over and future British governments would be unlikely
to partake in such risky operations. This seemed to be supported by the 2010
Strategic Defence and Security Review (SDSR), which suggested that in the
so-called Age of Austerity there would be no wars of choice, only of national
necessity. The logic behind their argument appeared compelling until the current government was presented with the first opportunity to play a leading role
in the NATO campaign over Libya. Thus while public opinion may well have
lost its appetite for the use of Britain's armed forces overseas, the government
appears to have retained its penchant for overseas adventures despite the arguments articulated in recent National Security Strategy and the SDSR.

The Afghanistan experience has continued to divide the three armed
services—the British Army, the Royal Navy (RN), and the Royal Air Force
(RAF)—about the Future Character of Conflict (FCOC), the approach in
2010 that represented a classic bureaucratic compromise embracing every-
one and everything.[36] For the British Army, an emphasis on Afghanistan-type
wars provides a basis for preserving its current strength, although elements
within it, notably the armored corps, would like to shift the focus back toward traditional warfare. The RN and the RAF have been more reluctant to
embrace Afghanistan as the template for the future. Partly this is about bureaucratic politics. Afghanistan does not favor them in the bureaucratic battle
for resources. Both, therefore, have articulated a more air-sea focus for FCOC,
with the ability to project military power over long distances for a limited
period of time. It is also about how the UK sees its armed forces being used
in the future.

For all the failings of the British government and its armed forces, the
Afghan War follows on from the Kosovo conflict in highlighting the weaknesses in Europe's armed forces. Since the Kosovo conflict, the British and

French governments sought to improve Europe's ability to deploy and sustain military forces initially through the Helsinki Accord. This was subsequently re-shaped after the first phase of the Afghan War, with the recognition that Europe struggled to deploy even a smaller force such as a battle group of 1,500 with any degree of speed and over any distance. Again Europe has responded poorly to this, and successive governments have begun to look toward other partnerships. Thus, despite the fact that much of Britain's Afghanistan War was undertaken as part of NATO, the war has reminded the British government of its favored, traditional partners. The ABCA relationship of Australia, Britain, Canada and America, with New Zealand also playing a part, remains the default partnership in the absence of NATO. This is most evident in the continuing intelligence relationship between the five nations and a series of bilateral treaties signed between them. This initially caused some problems in Afghanistan, where the British and Australian armies, including their special forces communities, had to relearn how to work together despite the embedding of personnel in each other's training establishments. To this grouping have been added particular European allies, namely Norway, Denmark, and the Netherlands, who have been accepted as de facto Anglo-Saxon nations. This is in spite of the rhetoric surrounding the new Anglo-French Treaty and the continued public emphasis on NATO.

CONCLUSION

In drawing some conclusions, it is at times difficult to separate the Afghanistan War from the Iraq War because they have become conflated in the eyes of British public opinion and those hostile to the UK. Both are generally viewed as illegal wars, notwithstanding the differences between them. There is now a question mark over the government's legitimacy in its use of the armed forces, and there have been steps toward giving Parliament greater involvement in approving the use of armed forces. This has so far failed to go ahead as questions remain over operational secrecy and the need to allow government to make rapid decisions in areas such as noncombatant evacuation operations. Even if the issue is resolved, the level of trust between citizen and state has been shaken and there is a reluctance to believe anything the government says. In a sense Iraq and Afghanistan saw the British people lose an element of innocence.

The second point is that the average citizen now feels more rather than less vulnerable as a result of Britain's Afghanistan involvement. There is some evidence to suggest that British public opinion now views 9/11 as an attack on the US and tends to forget the scale of British lives lost. Here the 7/7 attacks on London have played a big part in shifting the focus from keeping potential enemies away to one of encouraging "the enemy within." The problem with this argument is that it is difficult to prove one way or another.

The third conclusion that emerges is that the credibility of Britain's armed forces, in the eyes of both potential opponents and allies, has been damaged. Too much was promised with too few forces committed and, perhaps more substantially, an inability to adopt a long-term strategy and adapt. This should not be seen to belittle the sacrifices made and the price in terms of the need to provide long-term care for large numbers of wounded, both physically and psychologically. Afghanistan and Iraq revealed opponents who were far more agile in adapting to the British than the British were to their opponents.

NOTES

1. See Paddy Ashdown, "This Awful Mistake Mustn't Claim More Lives," *The Times (London)*, November 16, 2012, 34; Richard Shirreff, "Stand Firm in Afghanistan. We Are Winning," *The Times*, November 26, 2012, 24; Warren Chin, "Colonial Warfare in a Post-Colonial State: British Military Operations in Helmand Province," *Defence Studies Journal* 10, no. 1–2 (2010): 215–247; Frank Ledwidge, *Losing Small Wars: British Military Failure in Iraq and Afghanistan* (New Haven, CT: Yale University Press, 2011).

2. Ben Farmer, "Afghanistan 'Sandhurst in the Sand' Academy Announced by Philip Hammond," *Daily Telegraph (London)*, March 29, 2012, http://www.telegraph.co.uk/news/uknews/defence/9173032/Afghanistan-Sandhurst-in-the-sand-academy-announced-by-Philip-Hammond.html.

3. For full details, see http://www.bbc.co.uk/news/uk-10629358.

4. See Helen McCartney, "The Military Covenant and the Civil-Military Contract in Britain," *International Affairs* 86, no. 2 (2010): 411–428.

5. Peter Mansoor, "The British Army and the Lessons of the Iraq War," *British Army Review* 147 (2009): 11–15; David Ucko, "Lessons from Basra: The Future of British Counter-Insurgency," *Survival*, 52, no. 4 (2010): 131–158.

6. Geoff Hoon, "One Year On—A UK Perspective," speech given at the University of Louisiana, September 9, 2002, http://news.mod.uk/news/press/news_press_notice.asp?newsItem_id=1982.

7. See Tony Blair, *A Journey* (London: Hutchinson, 2010).

8. Tony Blair, "Doctrine of the International Community," speech given at the Chicago Economic Club, April 22, 1999, http://webarchive.nationalarchives.gov.uk/20061004085342/number10.gov.uk/page1297.

9. See Andrew M. Dorman, *Blair's Successful War: British Military Intervention in Sierra Leone* (Farnham, UK: Ashgate, 2009).

10. Admiral Sir Michael Boyce, "Defence Secretary and Chief of the Defence Staff: Press Conference—11 October 2001," Commons, October 11, 2001, http://www.opera tions.mod.uk/veritas/statements/press_brief_11oct.htm.

11. US Air Force, "US Air Force White Paper on Long Range Bombers," March 1, 1999, http://www.fas.ord/nuke/guide/usa/bomber/bmap99.pdf.

12. Hoon, "One Year On—A UK Perspective."

13. General Tommy Franks, *American Soldier* (New York: HarperCollins, 2004), 314.

14. Geoff Hoon, radio interview, *Radio Four The World at One*, BBC, November 16, 2001.

15. "Agreement on Provisional Arrangements in Afghanistan Pending the Re-Establishment of Permanent Government Institutions," UN Security Council, S/2001/1154, December 5, 2001.

16. Admiral Sir Michael Boyce, "UK Strategic Choices Following SDR and the 11th September," *RUSI Journal*, December 10, 2001, http://news.mod.uk/news/press/news_ press_notice.asp?newsItem_id=1262.

17. Patrick E. Tyler, "Britain Ready to Lead for the UN After the War," *New York Times*, December 12, 2001, http://www.nytimes.com/2001/12/12/world/nation-challenged -coalition-britain-ready-lead-force-for-un-after-war.html.

18. United Nations Security Council Resolution 1386 (2001), S/RES/1386/(2001), http:// ods-dds-ny.un.org/doc/UNDOC/GEN/No1/708/55/PDF/No170855pdf?OpenElement.

19. Geoff Hoon, "International Security Assistance Force for Kabul," Statement to the House of Commons, January 10, 2002, http://news.mod.uk/news/press/news_press_ notice.asp?newsItem_id=1336.

20. "The Secretary of State for Defence's Statement in the Commons—18 March 2002," http://www.operations.mod.uk/veritas/statements/statement_18mar.htm.

21. For example, see http://www.operations.mod.uk/veritas/index.htm.

22. "CinC CENTCOM and the Chief of the Defence Staff: Press Conference—26 April 2002," http://www.operations.mod.uk/veritas/statements/press_brief_26apr.htm.

23. "The Secretary of State for Defence's statement in the Commons—20 June 2002," http://www.operations.mod.uk/veritas/statements/statement_20jun.htm.

24. Blair argues that the British never took their eye off Afghanistan, it just received more attention from 2005. Blair, *A Journey*, 610.

25. See Jack Fairweather, *A War of Choice: The British in Iraq 2003–09* (London: Cape, 2011).

26. See Andrew M. Dorman, "Reorganising the Infantry: Drivers of Change and What This Tells Us About the State of the Defence Debate Today," *British Journal of Politics and International Relations* 8, no. 4 (2006): 489–502.

27. See "Delivering Security in a Changing World: Defence White Paper," *Cm.6,041* (London: MOD, 2003); "Delivering Security in a Changing World: Future Capabilities," *Cm.6,269* (London: MOD, 2004).

28. Richard North, *Ministry of Defeat: The British War in Iraq, 2003–9* (London: Continuum, 2009).

29. See Stuart Tootal, *Danger Close: Commanding 3 Para in Afghanistan* (London: Murray, 2009).

30. See James Fergusson, *A Million Bullets: The Real Story of the British Army in Afghanistan* (London: Corgi Books, 2008).

31. See, for example, Toby Harnden, *Dead Men Risen: The Welsh Guards and the Real Story of Britain's war in Afghanistan* (London: Quercus, 2011); Ewen Southby-Tailyour, *3 Commando Brigade, Helmand, Afghanistan: Sometimes the Best Form of Defence Is Attack* (London: Ebury Press, 2008); Sam Kiley, *Desperate Glory: At War in Helmand with Britain's 16 Air Assault Brigade* (London: Bloomsbury, 2009).

32. This debate started with Paul N. Cornish and Andrew M. Dorman, "Blair's Wars and Brown's Budgets: From Strategic Defence Review to Strategic Decay in Less than a Decade," *International Affairs* 85, no. 2 (2009): 247–261; http://www.chathamhouse.org/sites/default/files/public/International%20Affairs/2009/85_2cornish_dorman.pdf; Hew Strachan, "The Strategic Gap in British Defence Policy," *Survival* 51, no. 4 (2009): 49–70; Paul Newton, Paul Colley, and Andrew Sharpe, "Reclaiming the Art of British Strategic Thinking," *RUSI Journal* 155, no. 1 (2010): 44–50.

33. "The Comprehensive Approach," *Joint Discussion Note 04/05* (Swindon, UK: Defence Concepts and Doctrine Centre, 2006).

34. For example, consider the attacks on the homecoming parade of 1st Battalion The Royal Anglian Regiment in Luton. See Jenny Percival, "Two Arrested After Protest at Soldiers' Homecoming Parade in Luton," *Guardian Online*, March 11, 2009, http://www.guardian.co.uk/uk/2009/mar/10/two-arrested-army-protest-luton.

35. See Stuart Croft, *Securitizing Islam: Identity and the Search for Security* (Cambridge: Cambridge University Press, 2012).

36. *Future Character of Conflict* (London: Defence Concepts and Doctrine Centre, 2010), https://www.gov.uk/government/uploads/system/uploads/attachment_data/file/33685/FCOCReadactedFinalWeb.pdf.

9 FRANCE

Vigilant Pragmatism in Afghanistan

Nicolas Fescharek

AFGHANISTAN, BARNETT RUBIN famously wrote, can be seen as a "mirror of the world."[1] It served as a buffer state for imperial interests between Russia and Great Britain in the nineteenth century, and became the archetypical rentier state under Zahir Shah when Soviet money absolved Afghan political elites from forging strong bonds of accountability to a largely rural population. It became the major battlefield for the showdown of the Cold War in the 1980s, epitomized post-1989 optimism about the "dividends of peace" when the US withdrew from the region, and came back to center stage as a "failed state" with 9/11. In each of these phases, Afghanistan in one way or another shed light on international power structures. Similarly, the nations that have contributed troops in Afghanistan in one way or another have illustrated the nature of their relationship to the US—and France is no exception.

Given that the Afghan campaign has often put great strain on US-European relations, it is of particular interest to consider the French example, traditionally the most unruly European North Atlantic Treaty Organization (NATO) ally. After a historical overview and looking at French contributions to Afghan National Army (ANA) training, counterinsurgency (COIN), and "civ-mil" policies, this chapter examines how the relationship between France and NATO has changed as a result of its thirteen-year engagement in Afghanistan. In a nutshell, it argues that instead of driving France and the US further apart (as might have been expected during the crises in 2006–2007), the campaign has reinforced many ties and contributed to a normalization of sorts, even though a great deal of ambiguity still characterizes the relationship.

France's relations with NATO have always been ambiguous. On March 7, 1966, Charles de Gaulle announced in a handwritten letter to President Lyndon Johnson that France was ceasing "her participation in the integrated commands" and no longer intended to "place her forces at the disposal of NATO."[2] However, even while leaving NATO's integrated military command, de Gaulle decided not to withdraw fully from the alliance and to maintain France's seat in the North Atlantic Council. Despite a certain Gaullo-Mitterrandian-Chiracian "consensus" on the diplomatic advantages that this decision conferred to the French,[3] numerous scholars have long pointed out that the symbolic nature of this move always outweighed the actual consequences on cooperation in ongoing international military affairs. For instance, this is illustrated by the Ailleret-Lemnitzer and Valentin-Ferber agreements in the late 1960s and early 1970s, which allowed for cooperation between allied regional commands and French forces.[4] Joint maneuvers were organized, and in case of war in Europe, French forces would be placed under NATO's operational control.[5] "In other words, despite Gaullist rhetoric, France remained militarily much more closely linked to its allies than has been imagined, even if this *ersatz* 'integration' could hardly be advertised by decision-makers in Paris."[6] With the fall of the Berlin Wall, the question of full reintegration surfaced again, but both François Mitterrand's and Jacques Chirac's initiatives to strike a comprehensive deal for France to join NATO fully in return for a strengthened European pillar outside NATO failed. In the absence of a grand bargain, Jeremy Ghez and Stephen Larrabee argued that the 1990s saw a process of behind-the-scenes or "creeping" reintegration.[7] Throughout the 1990s, France deployed soldiers for US-led missions in Bosnia and Kosovo and later in Afghanistan. In 2004–2005, with the US and UK embroiled in Iraq, France even briefly became the largest troop contributor to NATO, whereas in 2006 more than a third of its eleven thousand troops deployed abroad were engaged under NATO rather than under the European Union's banner.[8] Thus, Michel Fortmann and colleagues point out that President Nicolas Sarkozy's 2008 decision to join the strategic command "really should be interpreted as marking not the beginning but the closing chapter in a lengthy process of 'normalization.'"[9] In 2011, the French contributed 247.3 million euros to the NATO budget, making France the fourth largest financial contributor.[10]

THE FRENCH MILITARY ENGAGEMENT IN AFGHANISTAN

On September 11, 2001, like the US and others, France rediscovered Afghanistan.[11] The subsequent events opened an opportunity for the two countries to collaborate closely, as the *Le Monde* headline "We are all Americans" garnered wide play in the US.[12]

Following formal requests from the George W. Bush administration during the first days of Operation Enduring Freedom (OEF), the French military contributed to the elaboration of the combat plan. In addition to French naval forces in the Pakistani coastal region, combat planes started their first missions in October (even though the first flights by the French over Afghanistan itself would occur only on December 19). The Chirac government decided not to station French planes inside Afghanistan despite the fact that the US had already set up important bases in Mazar-e Sharif, Bagram, and Kabul. As Jean Dominique Merchet notes, militarily speaking this made things more complicated, but it served a clear political purpose, which was Chirac's desire to retain a small footprint.[13] For Paris, autonomy came before control over the mission's goals and outcomes. Thus, the French air force moved into military bases in Dushanbe, Tajikistan, and Manas, Kyrgyzstan. From those outside bases, the French air force participated in the air strikes on the Gardez sector, where al Qaeda fighters were thought to be hiding. Differences with the US surfaced quickly, notably when it became clear to the US military that French airplanes were almost never authorized to actually drop bombs, preferring "show of force" sorties.[14] Thus, a high degree of wait-and-see tactics and cautious contributions marked the first years.

With the exception of the Iraq crisis, nothing would bring Chirac to engage more ground troops than the five hundred initially sent to Kabul in 2001 as part of the Kabul Multinational Brigade (KMNB). And even then, support remained lukewarm—and secret: in 2003, Chirac met with Bush at the Evian Summit and agreed to a top secret special forces mission (*Arès*) to Spin Boldak on the Pakistani border region. But the political success of the operation only lasted until the Afghan insurgency gained full speed. When NATO decided to spread out and cover the whole country, France clung to its Regional Command–Capital (i.e., Kabul) and declined any further engagement.[15] Chirac also pulled back the two hundred special forces operating in the dangerous east in February 2007, shortly before elections. When the British encountered difficulties in Kandahar, Helmand, and Uruzgan provinces, he refused flatly to commit more troops,[16] contributing to what has been described as the greatest crisis since the establishment of NATO.[17]

Relations changed with the 2007 election. Despite some critical campaign remarks about the necessity of the Afghan war, President Sarkozy quickly made it clear that he would seek full reintegration to NATO's strategic command.

Pundits heavily criticized his decision, not only from the left-wing opposition, but also from heavyweights within his political family. Former French Foreign Minister Dominique de Villepin commented that "not only does France's return to NATO not serve the interests of our country, but I believe it is also dangerous . . . we run the risk of being perceived as taking part in the confrontation with the Muslim world, something we have sought to avoid with our engagement against the war in Iraq."[18] Alain Juppé, later Minister of Foreign Affairs, was "worried" about reintegration, publicly asking himself whether France had not been duped by entering under such unclear conditions.[19] Criticism notwithstanding, in the 2008 *White Book on Defense*, Sarkozy argued, "it is difficult to continue to proclaim the necessity of a fundamental difference in our position vis-à-vis NATO, given the fact that with our European partners we recognize the Alliance as a key to our collective security."[20]

Hence, despite 55 percent disapproval by the French of the surge,[21] President Sarkozy announced at the 2008 Bucharest Summit that an additional 700 men would be deployed to Kapisa province,[22] bringing the overall number of French troops physically present in Afghanistan to 2,800 (about 5 percent of overall military presence). In close cooperation with the US, about 60 of these troops operated under OEF. The core of French forces headed the Regional Command–Capital (Kabul), while roughly 190 were stationed on the Kandahar air base and about 355 in six Operational Mentor and Liaison Teams (OMLTs), in addition to 230 airmen in Dushanbe and 40 in Manas. In May 2011, French forces peaked at about 4,000 (including French military on outside bases), placing France on the fourth rank of troop commitments.

The French surge naturally increased French fatalities, which have totaled 89 to date. The curb reflected a growing military exposure and engagement after 2007, a peak in 2010, and a slight decrease since then.[23] Incidentally, both fatalities in 2011 and 2012 include "green on blue" attacks and are thus not strictly combat-related.[24] After 2012, President Sarkozy, who was facing a tough reelection campaign, issued strict orders that continued to restrict engagement even after his election defeat. He speeded up the planned 2012 withdrawal from 600 to 1,000 soldiers and announced that the French would hand over responsibility of Kapisa to the Afghan Army four months earlier than originally planned. With this move he tried to avoid giving an opportunity to François Hollande—his contender and a critic of French engagement in the war—to challenge him on this issue.[25] Following Sarkozy's defeat, Hollande assumed office (after a campaign in which neither Afghanistan nor NATO played an important role) and fulfilled his campaign promise to speed up the withdrawal one more year.[26] It must be said that this decision, which has triggered speculations about deterioration in France's relationship with NATO, was more symbolic and much less significant in actuality. Hollande's campaign promise for complete troop withdrawal at the end of 2012 was always impossible from a logistical viewpoint.[27] Thus, despite the 2000 combat troops withdrawn by December 15, 2012,[28] in April 2013 the troop presence remained at about 1,500. Roughly 1,000 soldiers left in the summer of 2013, and the last 150 French troops, stationed at Kabul airport to train Afghan security personnel, left Kabul on December 31, 2014.[29]

TRAINING: ANCOP AND ANA

Pulling back troops from Afghanistan only to replace them with noncombatant military trainers has been a recurrent pattern for the Allies, be they Canadian, Dutch, or French. However, the French have been involved in the training of the ANA since 2001 and of the Afghan National Civil Order Police (ANCOP) since 2008. Hence, it would be too simplistic to depict French training as a mere exit strategy, especially since they have been involved in training missions in the Balkans and Africa for years. Moreover, the French currently seem to be willing to deploy more military trainers to African theaters, which converges with general "nation-building fatigue" and points to a future role for France.

Training of the ANA has occurred in close collaboration with the US.[30] After training three of the first six ANA battalions in 2002, Operation Epidote started focusing on higher-ranking officers. French training has undergone the same transformation as all Afghan training and mentoring missions: What used to be a direct training mission subsequently focused more on training *trainers*, who would themselves carry out the training under French oversight.

Alongside the US, the French have also played a role in the Kabul Commando School. They deployed the first of ultimately seven French OMLTs to Afghanistan in 2006 to supervise the 1st brigade of the 201st ANA corps in Wardak and Logar.[31] Initially, French OMLTs worked only in Kabul, but in 2008 one OMLT went to Uruzgan, a more volatile southern region (since April 2012, OMLTs are called Advisory Teams [ATs]). One hundred thirty French senior military personnel were stationed at ANA schools. According to the Ministry of Defense, by 2012 French forces had helped instruct about sixteen thousand men.[32] At the height of their engagement in Kapisa province and the Surobi district, the French had armed five Police Operational Mentor and Liaison Teams (POMLTs) in Kapisa and Surobi, working with Task Force Lafayette in Tagab,

Nijrab, Memouderaki, Tora, and Kapisa. POMLTs were concerned not so much with training but with on-the-job mentoring. In the training center in Wardak (which the French left in March 2013), mentoring also spread out from police savoir faire to wider management tasks on how to run a camp, take care of logistics, and so on.[33] In October 2011, 120 of 200 French gendarmes were part of a POMLT, while approximately 80 worked with the NATO Training Mission–Afghanistan (NTM-A) in two major training centers (Regional Training Center Mazar-e Sharif and the National Police Training Center Wardak, with total capacity of 3,000 and for which France temporarily accepted lead-nation status).

A second major training role concerns ANCOP, a hybrid police force combining civilian order control and counterinsurgency, in the European tradition of state-controlled police forces with military status. It is one of the three major police forces that make up the Afghan National Police (ANP), the other two being the Afghan Border Police (ABP) and the Afghan Uniform Police (AUP). In 2009, France took over the direction of an ANCOP training center in Mazar-e Sharif (since abandoned). In 2010, 60 gendarmes were stationed there, and later 200 in 2011. In 2012, according to official numbers, 7,000 from a total 15,600 to-be-trained Afghans had received the twenty-two-week training necessary to serve in ANCOP.[34]

A colonel interviewed in October 2011 describes the French attitude vis-à-vis the US:

> The way we try to have an impact [on the NATO mission] is two-fold: First, we try to convince through quality by deploying high-ranking gendarmes. The US does not have such an instrument as the Gendarmerie and they appreciate it. So while we have to acknowledge that we are small, what we do bring to Afghanistan, and to the US mission, is a "civilian police" vision ("*le regard policier*"). The US has many excellent COIN experts and advisers. But there are not enough policemen capable of coming up with a coherent security scheme for the time once combat ends.[35]

As not only this interview shows, the French strategy was to avoid being confrontational with the US, Canada, and the UK and, rather, complement those allied forces while trying to improve ISAF.

Importantly, some French ANSF training is bound to continue after 2014. A friendship treaty between France and Afghanistan states that cooperation "shall consist in training and counseling carried out by the French side" as well as a "support for the creation of a national Afghan Gendarmerie force."[36]

KAPISA AND SUROBI

When President Sarkozy decided to send an additional seven hundred troops, the army took responsibility for Kapisa province and the Surobi district. Situated east of Kabul, Kapisa province is the smallest with 1,842 square kilometers (only 2 percent of the territory of Afghanistan) and an estimated population of 350,000.[37] The northern part, mostly Tadjik, has been more inclined to support the French and US forces, whereas the Pashtun south has more often than not given "French forces a tough time, mostly through supporting the Hizb-I Islami Gulbuddin insurgency."[38] Notwithstanding its small size, the region is strategically important, especially for insurgent attacks against Kabul.[39] Interestingly, US forces running the local Provincial Reconstruction Team (PRT) would occasionally call in French fire support when engaged in combat—a unique partnering which reveals a degree of pragmatism.[40]

On the operational level, the French approach to fighting has undergone several phases. In early 2008, a large-scale operation was set into motion in collaboration with the US to clear insurgents from Alasay Valley. At this time, the French "left their bases very often, be it to go look for weapons caches or to conduct larger operations in the lower parts of the valley."[41] This was the first phase in a broader stabilization effort, relying on the ANP and the ANA to hold the area after combat and develop "governance." However, as the US experienced many times, there was almost no competent ANP to secure the site, and shortly after, the ANA was reassigned to other areas.[42]

At the end of 2008, Colonel Nicolas Le Nen took over the command of the French forces in Kapisa province; his approach consisted of securing roads and pursuing rebels in surrounding areas. During Operation Dinner Out (March 2009), he had several outposts established in populated areas, following a so-called oil-spot model.[43] The military approach soon changed and in fact evolved into something very similar to the US COIN approach. Indeed, a later task force under French battalion commander Colonel Francis Chanson (by the name of Task Force Korrigan) "changed the military stance toward Kapisa—rather than a policy of direct and intentional physical confrontation, it instead built relationships with locals to establish individual areas of security through controlling roads."[44]

It would be erroneous to assume that the French somehow adopted the US COIN model.[45] Often overlooked is that many of the French missions in Africa have pursued this tactic in quite similar, although not as intense, circumstances. Moreover, General David Petraeus' counterinsurgency manual draws heavily on French COIN thinker David Galula. Indeed, ground facts have shaped French adaptation more than alliance pressure.

UZBIN AMBUSH

Notably, one incident accelerated the change from classic peacekeeping to COIN: the Uzbin ambush in August 2008, which killed ten French soldiers and had several consequences. First, politically speaking, Uzbin became a lightning rod in French politics, attracting the attention of the wider French public. Opinion polls before and after the incident indicate that French support or disapproval of Afghanistan was related to this loss—while a majority supported the French engagement in Afghanistan before Uzbin, a majority was opposed to the French fighting in Afghanistan thereafter.[46] Second, President Sarkozy took decisions that improved the French army's ability to fight insurgents. As Jean de Ponton d'Amécourt, French ambassador in Kabul (2008–2011) recalls, Sarkozy visited him right after the attack and stated that he did not want a repeat.[47] In the wake of the attack, French ground forces were granted the helicopters and drones they requested, and the necessary decisions were made to order laser-guided César cannons able to kill enemies at thirty kilometers. Importantly, French armored vanguard vehicles (VABs) were equipped with automatic gun turrets, allowing the soldier to remain inside during combat. In other words, the post-Uzbin level of force protection for the individual soldier increased manyfold. A third decision, and one that was relatively innovative at the time according to Ambassador de Ponton d'Amécourt, consisted of ensuring that Afghan forces be on the front lines as much as possible. Militarily speaking, this made perfect sense, as ANA troops were more familiar with the terrain. All in all, although President Sarkozy did not officially modify the caveats after Uzbin, the incident played an important role in forging a less confrontational approach.

Moreover, although military cooperation with the US initially posed some logistical problems (US and French forces occasionally encountered each other on patrols, without having been informed both were running operations at the same place and time),[48] most of these problems seem to have been resolved over time. This indicates that there is no insurmountable ideological element in the relationship. Eventually, a burden sharing of sorts emerged. Throughout 2010, the US PRT focused on the northern half of Kapisa, while the French focused on the Tagab. According to the French colonel quoted earlier:

I do not believe that there are essential differences with the US approach. . . . Simply put, we do not situate our support at the same spot on the time line. That means that the Americans have elections coming up and they want to leave in 2014, so they want to see immediate results. They need to secure big parts of the country before they can go further conceptually [toward less COIN-oriented approaches to ANSF and police training].

In summary, it is not so much Sarkozy's decision to join the Strategic Command, but on-the-ground cooperation, the deployment of seven hundred additional troops (freeing US troops to help the hard-pressed Canadian troops in the Afghan south),[49] and their engagement in real combat that made France become a trusted ally again. French transformation of weaponry and conceptual convergence toward Afghan-style counterinsurgency provided a clear signal to the NATO alliance that France was there to fight the Taliban. Five years after its serious clash with its US ally over Iraq, France was able to demonstrate that not only had it taken on real responsibility—it was also capable of conceptual adaptation to a "new" kind of war.

"CIVILIAN" APPROACHES

The debate about the relation between civilian and military tools may seem tangential at first sight, but a deeper analysis reveals that the issue not only goes to the heart of the French commitment to the Afghan campaign but also reveals its wider stance vis-à-vis its German and US allies, its position toward the EU and the role France wants it to play eventually.

In 2003 and 2004, when the US developed its PRT concept, France adopted a very skeptical position, denouncing the PRTs as the Bush administration's attempt to avoid a heavier footprint.[50] Thus, France's reaction to early proposals from Washington to fuse OEF and ISAF was outright resistance. The Iraq War changed the situation, as President Chirac wanted to mend fences with the US after his fallout with Bush. He not only agreed to send more special forces to the south, but also gave in to the alliance's decision to merge ISAF with OEF. As Sten Rynning notes, the underlying idea of the French refusal had been to strengthen EU defense and avoid NATO taking on the civilian state-building tasks it felt the EU was best equipped to manage.[51] NATO was to remain a purely military alliance. Thus, when the PRTs started to be rolled out across Afghanistan, France refused. France was fearful that "a PRT effort of this sort would bolster NATO's strategic role in civil-military affairs and thus turn the EU into NATO's handmaiden. . . . where Germany sought an expanded ISAF based on PRTs to bolster NATO's role in a transatlantic division of labor, France sought a purely military mission that would boost Europe's foreign policy credentials, not NATO."[52] France was unable to block Germany and the allies from moving ahead, but it maintained its position.

However, the French never seized the opportunity to prove their point and increase visibility of French civilian projects and the French savoir faire: After France took over Kapisa and Surobi, the budget for civilian cooperation doubled, but only from 20 million to 40 million euros. In 2009, Paris made available 15 million euros for development projects via a so-called Pôle de Stabilité, focusing on agricultural development, education, and health. These projects were carried out under the interministerial AfPak Cell and the embassy in Afghanistan. Despite good intentions, these projects were small-scale and piecemeal. Upon termination of France's military mission in Kapisa and Surobi, considerable frustration remained among the local population. The French "decision to limit most of their activity to the completion of a single road project alienated large segments of the population of Kapisa, which felt abandoned."[53] Either way, even with 40 million euros, French insistence on separating civilian and military contributions to the war was more a conceptual debate than the foundation of a real alternative French civilian role in Afghanistan.[54] When it comes to civilian aid, France makes up only 1 percent of the total. This led Serge Michailof to conclude: "France is more generous with the blood of its soldiers than with its development money."[55]

The other possible platform to promote civilian state-building tools could have been the EU and especially the European Union Police Mission (EUPOL). The French never invested much money and personnel in what was essentially perceived as a "German—but not our—baby."[56] According to a high-ranking French diplomat, "EUPOL was a logistical failure. Europe is simply not prepared yet for such a theater."[57] In other words, despite much rhetoric to the contrary, in Afghanistan France has always preferred its contributions to NATO/NTM-A over its EU commitment. Afghanistan has forced France to be pragmatic about the EU taking on large-scale state-building missions. Incidentally, even in Libya, one can observe that civilian reconstruction and governance efforts are not carried out by NATO or the EU; the Libyans assumed responsibility. This does not mean that France has given up on the idea of handing the EU wider civilian state-building tasks. But even if it approved the 2010 NATO

Strategic Concept (which states that NATO must establish a "modest civilian crisis management capability" that can be used "to plan, employ and coordinate civilian activities until conditions allow for the transfer of those responsibilities and tasks to other actors"),[58] it still does not like the idea that NATO should entirely evict the Europeans from this sector.

THE VÉDRINE REPORT

On July 18, 2012, freshly elected French President François Hollande asked former Socialist Foreign Minister Hubert Védrine to produce a report reflecting France's place in NATO and the consequences of Sarkozy's decision to rejoin the Strategic Command of the alliance. Védrine had been an outspoken critic of Sarkozy's 2008 decision, but his conclusion was somewhat contradictory. On the one hand, he lamented Sarkozy's decision as an unfortunate abandonment of a "politically comfortable" situation,[59] which had become the "political symbol"[60] of an autonomous France. On the other hand, Védrine left no doubt that France should from now on accept the status quo, since "a new situation has been created." It must realize that a renewed "French exit from the Joint Strategic Command is no option. Neither the USA nor the Europeans would understand this, and it would give France no new leverage. . . . To the contrary, this would ruin her options of action or influence with any other European partner and in every imaginable area. Moreover, between 1966 and 2008, i.e. in more than 40 years, no other European country has ever aligned itself on the French position of autonomy [from the US]."[61]

Védrine was uncompromising on certain redlines and repeatedly used the word *vigilance* to describe the right attitude vis-à-vis NATO. "The inconveniences of France's return to the Joint Strategic Command would outweigh the positive effects if this was to lead to a normalization of France in NATO, or even render its membership commonplace. Hence, France needs to assert herself much more in the Alliance, exert accrued influence and be vigilant and demanding."[62] Importantly, France must work to "ensure that the Alliance remains a *military* alliance, focused on collective defense, and the least possible political-military in its actions."[63] Moreover, "it is obvious that threats can come from outside" of the transatlantic zone. Therefore, decisions will be taken on a "case by case basis."[64] From a historic perspective, this is significant. In 1999, just two years prior to the entry into Afghanistan, the Europeans—not only France—had prevented NATO's 1999 Strategic Concept from suggesting involvement in military operations reaching out beyond Europe's borders.[65] Now

France is ready to consider it, albeit on a case-by-case basis. When it comes to France's European ambitions, which can always be a threat to NATO, the report was careful. It did not rule out the possibility and stated that France was in favor, but avoided sweeping declarations.

CONCLUSION

The Afghan mirror shows that France remains a valuable partner in NATO. After the troubled Iraq episode, France successfully repositioned itself as a credible ally thanks to its commitment. After Chirac's initial unresponsiveness, Sarkozy's decision to rejoin the Strategic Command and to organize a "surge" (even before the Obama administration) was the crucial game changer. Hollande's early withdrawal cannot fundamentally change the fact that Afghanistan has profiled France as a trustworthy ally, especially since other allies (such as the Netherlands and Canada) withdrew earlier.

Militarily speaking, France has learned valuable lessons in Afghanistan; it has endured heavy combat and suffered significant, tragic casualties. It willingly agreed to take over the Kapisa/Surobi region, thus signaling that France was a *fighting* ally. Even though force protection became more important after Uzbin, the incident did not stop the engagement, despite domestic hostility. A comprehensive reflection on counterinsurgency and the necessary equipment and weaponry has been undertaken. Also, the French military has cooperated closely with the US and operated quite pragmatically under a US-dominated structure.

Joining the Strategic Command gave France an expanded role in the alliance and has allowed France to shape some of the conceptual and strategic debates in Afghanistan and NATO (especially with respect to nuclear deterrence, but also regarding civilian affairs). However, Afghanistan has no major strategic relevance for France, and it has fought this war as a duty but with no stakes of its own in the conflict. Those who favor a "Global NATO" should remember this. Today, all indications are that French membership in NATO has been largely accepted. As early as 2009, polls showed that a solid 52 percent of French public opinion was in favor of full reintegration into NATO.[66] This support level rose to 70 percent among eighteen- to twenty-five-year-olds. Events like Uzbin do lead the French to question the sense or degree of realism of a particular campaign. But what used to be a heated debate about NATO membership has made space for a more pragmatic attitude among the wider French public.

Védrine's report, which mentions Afghanistan only on the margin, continues this trend: full membership in NATO is no longer a political problem. To the contrary, one can argue that today, this position increases French leverage, as France is able to use both the EU and the NATO platform to advance its agenda, be it on "smart defense" or on a "civilian EU." Conceptually speaking, France remains rather hostile to NATO taking on civilian tasks, but it has not formulated a clear alternative either. The most important redline concerns NATO's global outreach. On a case-by-case basis, NATO might be used in out-of-area missions, but for France, NATO's primary domain remains Europe, and its main task is territorial defense. In this respect, Védrine rightfully points to an increased US "demand" for more involvement in defense matters. Given German reservations and British defense cuts, France will probably remain the most valuable European military partner for the US. Moreover, on matters like Syria or Iran, French mediation remains essential.

One quote from a senior French diplomat in Kabul in 2011 is indicative with respect to the way the French perceive their role in the alliance: "The fact that we have no real interests of our own in this [Afghan] conflict gives us a high credit of sympathy among the Afghans. Despite all they have done, the Americans are not liked. We haven't spent the same money, but we also aren't responsible for the corruption of the elites."[67] In other words, and in the same vein as a recent scholarly debate about "more being less,"[68] the modesty of the French approach, France's limited resources and restrained global ambitions, are thought to be an asset.

As the Védrine report has shown, traditional reticence to what is often perceived as US dominance is likely to continue. The French military remains a competent war force, but the French political elites see benefit in not being perceived as too reliable. In Hubert Védrine's famous words: France is an "*ami, allié mais non aligné*" (friend, ally but not aligned).

NOTES

1. Barnett Rubin, *The Fragmentation of Afghanistan: State Formation and Collapse in the International System* (New Haven, CT: Yale University Press, 2002).

2. Letter from French President Charles de Gaulle to US President Lyndon B. Johnson, March 7, 1966, http://www.cvce.eu/viewer/-/content/d97bf195-34e1-4862-b5e7-87577a8c1632/en.

3. Hubert Védrine, *Rapport pour le Président de la République Française sur les conséquences du retour de la France dans le commandement intégré de l'OTAN, sur l'avenir*

de la relation transatlantique et les perspectives de l'Europe de la Défense, November 14, 2012, 4. See also Frédéric Bozo, "France and NATO Under Sarkozy: End of the French Exception?" Fondation pour l'Innovation Politique, Working Paper, Paris, 2008; Anand Menon, "Continuing Politics by Other Means: Defence Policy Under the French Fifth Republic," *West European Politics* 17 (October 1994): 74–96.

    4. Jolyon Howorth, "Prodigal Son or Trojan Horse: What's in It for France?" *European Security* 19, no. 1 (2010): 11–28.

    5. Michel Fortmann, David Haglund, and Stéfanie von Hlatky, "Introduction: France's 'Return' to NATO: Implications for Transatlantic Relations," *European Security* 19, no. 1 (2010): 1–10.

    6. Ibid.

    7. Jeremy Ghez and Stephen Larrabee, "France and NATO," *Survival* 51, no. 2 (April–May 2009): 78.

    8. Pierre Lellouche, *L'allié indocile. La France et l'OTAN, de la Guerre Froide à l'Afghanistan* (Paris: Editions du Moment, 2009).

    9. Fortman et al., "Introduction: France's 'Return' to NATO," 3.

    10. Védrine, *Rapport pour le Président de la République Française*, 11.

    11. Afghanistan had lost so much strategic significance that the Ministry of Defense had decided to hand over the Afghanistan file to the German liaison officer in Paris. Jean Dominique Merchet, *Mourir pour l'Afghanistan—Pourquoi nos soldats tombent-ils là-bas?* (Paris: Editions Jacob-Duvernet, 2008), 104.

    12. Jean-Marie Colombani, "Nous sommes tous Américains," *Le Monde*, September 13, 2001, http://www.lemonde.fr/idees/article/2007/05/23/nous-sommes-tous-ameri cains_913706_3232.html.

    13. Merchet, *Mourir pour l'Afghanistan*, 108.

    14. Ibid., 107.

    15. Ibid., 112.

    16. Ibid.

    17. Sten Rynning, *NATO and Afghanistan: The Liberal Disconnect* (Stanford, CA: Stanford University Press, 2012).

    18. Ibid., 243.

    19. Ibid., 243–244.

    20. Livre Blanc sur la Sécurité et la Défense 2008, 110, http://www.defense.gouv.fr/ portail-defense/enjeux2/politique-de-defense/livre-blanc-2008.

    21. "55% des Français contre l'envoi de renforts en Afghanistan," http://tempsreel .nouvelobs.com/societe/20080405.OBS8345/55-des-francais-contre-l-envoi-de-ren forts-en-afghanistan.html.

    22. "Afghanistan: Un battalion français en renfort," *L'Express*, April 3, 2008, http:// www.lexpress.fr/actualite/monde/afghanistan-un-bataillon-francais-en-renfort_ 471722.html.

23. Fatalities were 3 in 2004; 2 in 2005; 6 in 2006; 3 in 2007; 11 in 2008; 11 in 2009; 16 in 2010; 26 in 2011; 10 in 2012. http://www.defense.gouv.fr/operations/afghanistan/in-memoriam/in-memoriam.

24. "France, Breaking With NATO, Will Speed Afghan Exit," *New York Times*, January 27, 2012, http://www.nytimes.com/2012/01/21/world/europe/sarkozy-weighs-afghan-withdrawal-after-4-french-troops-killed.html.

25. Ibid. Hollande called the French mission a "finished" one.

26. See "Il n'y a plus de soldats français combattant en Afghanistan," *Le Monde*, February 15, 2012, http://www.lemonde.fr/asie-pacifique/article/2012/12/15/il-n-y-a-plus-de-soldats-francais-combattant-en-afghanistan_1807005_3216.html?xtmc=vedrine_otan&xtcr=7.

27. Régis Gente, "Le casse-tête du retrait afghan," *Les dossiers de Grotius International*, May 6, 2012, http://www.grotius.fr/le-casse-tete-du-retrait-d%E2%80%99afghanistan/2012.

28. Jocelyn Mawdsley, "Hollande's Pledge to Withdraw French Troops from Afghanistan Is Not as Significant as It May Seem," *European Politics and Policy*, June 11, 2012, http://blogs.lse.ac.uk/europpblog/2012/06/11/hollande-troops-afghanistan/.

29. "Les derniers soldats français quittent l'Afghanistan," December 31, 2014, http://www.france24.com/fr/20141231-afghanistan-soldats-france-otan-kaboul-taliban-isaf-soutien-resolu. See also "Il n'y a plus de soldats français combattant en Afghanistan," *Le Monde*, December 15, 2012, http://www.lemonde.fr/asie-pacifique/article/2012/12/15/il-n-y-a-plus-de-soldats-francais-combattant-en-afghanistan_1807005_3216.html. See also "Le dispositif français pour l'Afghanistan," http://www.defense.gouv.fr/operations/afghanistan/dossier/le-dispositif-francais-pour-l-afghanistan.

30. Oriane Barat-Ginies, *L'engagement militaire français en Afghanistan de 2001 à 2011. Quels engagement militaires pour quelles ambitions politiques?* (Paris: L'Harmattan, 2011), 46.

31. "Le dispositif français pour l'Afghanistan."

32. Ibid.

33. Interview with French colonel, Kabul, October 10, 2011.

34. "Afghanistan: les gendarmes français participent à la formation des policiers afghans de l'ANCOP," http://www.defense.gouv.fr/actualites/operations/afghanistan-les-gendarmes-francais-participent-a-la-formation-des-policiers-afghans-de-l-ancop-video.

35. Interview with French colonel, Kabul, October 2011.

36. "Projet de loi autorisant la ratification du traité d'amitié et de coopération entre la République française et la République islamique d'Afghanistan," 5, http://www.assemblee-nationale.fr/14/dossiers/traite_cooperation_Afghanistan.asp.

37. Amaury de Féligonde, "La Coopération civile en Afghanistan. Une coûteuse illusion?" *Focus stratégique* 24 (August 2010): 8.

38. Interview with French diplomat, Kabul, October 2011.

39. Interview with gendarmerie colonel, Kabul, September 2011.

40. Joshua Foust, "France in Kapisa," in *Statebuilding in Afghanistan, Multinational Contributions to Reconstruction*, ed. Nik Hynek and Péter Marton (New York: Routledge), 92.

41. Interview with senior French diplomat stationed in Kabul in 2008, Paris, 2012.

42. Foust, "France in Kapisa," 91.

43. Stéphane Taillat, "National Traditions and International Context: French Adaptation to Counterinsurgency in the 21st Century," *Security Challenges* 6, no. 1 (Autumn 2010): 85–96.

44. Foust, "France in Kapisa," 93.

45. Stéphane Taillat, "Moral Conquest Rather Than Physical Conquest: Stabilization and Counterinsurgency in French Practices and Doctrine in Afghanistan," http://coinenirak.files.wordpress.com/2009/11/taillat-paper-rmas-esrc-seminar-091119.pdf.

46. "Les français disent non," *L'Humanité*, http://www.humanite.fr/node/431828.

47. Interview with Jean de Ponton d'Amécourt, Paris, November 12, 2012.

48. Foust, "France in Kapisa," 93.

49. Andrew Hoehn and Sarah Harting, *Risking NATO: Testing the Limits of the Alliance in Afghanistan* (Santa Monica, CA: RAND Corporation, 2010), 70.

50. Sten Rynning contests this view. Rynning, *NATO and Afghanistan*, 87ff.

51. Ibid., 100.

52. Ibid.

53. Foust, "France in Kapisa," 100.

54. Most interviews were done in November 2011 with French field workers directly. Implied in the "Pôle de Stabilité" show French "civilian approach" tended to be seen as "*cache-sexe*" or a fig leaf.

55. Serge Michailof, "L'échec de l'aide internationale en Afghanistan," *Commentaire* 122 (Summer 2008): 449.

56. Interview with French diplomat, Quai d'Orsay, Paris, 2012.

57. Interview with senior French diplomat, Paris, 2012.

58. "Active Engagement, Modern Defence: Strategic Concept for the Defence and Security of the Members of the North Atlantic Treaty Organisation Adopted by Heads of State and Government in Lisbon," November 19, 2010, http://www.nato.int/cps/en/natolive/official_texts_68580.htm.

59. Védrine, *Rapport pour le Président de la République Française*, 19.

60. Ibid., 9.

61. Ibid., 10. Author's translation.

62. Ibid., 19.

63. Ibid. Emphasis added.

64. Ibid., 20.

65. Stanley Sloan, *NATO and the Transatlantic Bargain from Truman to Obama* (New York: Continuum, 2010), 189.

66. "L'approbation des Français concernant l'intervention militaire en Afghanistan," August 22, 2011, http://www.sondages-en-france.fr/sondages/Actualit%C3%A9/Politique%20%C3%A9trang%C3%A8re.

67. Interview with French diplomat, Kabul, October 2011.

68. Astri Suhrke, *When More Is Less: The International Project in Afghanistan* (London: Hurst, 2011).

10 THE NETHERLANDS

To Fight, or Not to Fight? The Rise and Fall
of a Smaller Power

Rem Korteweg

TWENTY-FIVE SERVICEMEN lost their lives during the deployment of the
Royal Netherlands Armed Forces to Afghanistan. Since the Korean War no
other military mission has led to so many Dutch fatalities. In no other operation in recent years did the Netherlands engage in combat operations as
intensively as in Afghanistan. Aside from the human toll, the expected total
financial costs of the deployments approach 3 billion euros, nearly half of the
annual defense budget. For over a decade the commitment to the International
Security Assistance Force (ISAF) was the defining mission for the Netherlands'
military and security policy. From 2001 the military deployed to various parts
of Afghanistan, but it was the strenuous campaign in Uruzgan province that
proved politically contentious. The mission was controversial because of the
combat involved, which ultimately became the pretext for the collapse of the
government in 2010. This chapter highlights how a smaller power struggled
with the political, military, and financial pressures of sustained expeditionary
operations and the dissonance that emerges as domestic political considerations clash with the military-operational reality.

THE PRIMACY OF URUZGAN

The Dutch contribution to ISAF started in December 2001 and ended in early
2014. The Netherlands twice shifted the focus of its commitment. It scaled its
commitment up, and later down again, reaching a peak during the Uruzgan
effort. The Netherlands undertook increasingly demanding and risky missions, from deploying small-scale contingents to patrol Kabul and a Provincial

Reconstruction Team (PRT) in northern Baghlan province under overall German command, to counterinsurgency operations in Uruzgan where it operated alongside Australian forces and with the British, Canadian, and US militaries. When the Dutch government collapsed over the question whether to extend the mission in 2010, it was one of the first NATO member states to withdraw forces. In 2011, the Netherlands returned to northern Afghanistan to participate in a German-run police training mission in Kunduz province and contribute to the European Union's (EU's) civilian policing mission (EUPOL) as well. But it never reached the scope of the Uruzgan effort. Separately, from 2002 to 2014, an F-16 detachment provided close-air support to ISAF missions, first from Kyrgyzstan, later from Kandahar and Mazar-e Sharif.

Since the Cold War, the Dutch military had gone through a process of strategic transformation, changing its orientation from territorial defense to expeditionary operations, including combat at the high-end of the conflict spectrum. This process of military reform culminated in the mission in southern Afghanistan in 2006–2010. At the political level, participation in Uruzgan reflected the desire to play a prominent role in NATO operations, contribute to international stability, and demonstrate relevance within the alliance and to the US, its preeminent ally. For the military, the mission was the defining operation that determined procurement decisions and improved the skill set of the Dutch military. By 2008 the Ministry of Defense confirmed that the "cornerstone of Dutch security policy is the mission in Afghanistan." Not only was the Uruzgan mission the climax for its ISAF contribution, it was the high-water mark for expeditionary crisis management operations and a benchmark for future military commitments.

THE BURDEN OF SREBRENICA

The impact of Srebrenica is essential to understand the main military and political factors that shaped the Dutch commitment to Afghanistan. In 1995, as part of the United Nations Protection Force (UNPROFOR) peacekeeping mission in Bosnia-Herzegovina, a Dutch contingent was responsible for the "safe haven" of Srebrenica. The Serbian military overran the enclave, taking Bosnian Muslim refugees prisoner and killing roughly seven hundred men and boys. The lightly armed Dutch blue helmets were not equipped to withstand the heavily armed Serbian forces, and other UN member states did not provide military support.

The experience traumatized the Dutch military and the political establishment in The Hague. At the political level, Srebrenica led to the formulation of the Toetsingskader, a parliamentary framework for evaluating expeditionary military operations: upon the decision to undertake a crisis-management operation, the government would send parliament a so-called Article 100 letter—referring to the relevant article in the constitution—detailing how the government took Toetsingskader criteria into account. While the Dutch constitution provides that the government is solely responsible for the use of military force and need only inform Parliament of its decision, it was now required to seek implicit approval of a parliamentary majority. Parliament thereby gained a greater voice in decision making on non–article V missions. It made the deployments to Afghanistan subject to continuous political negotiations. At the international level, Srebrenica substantially reduced the Dutch appetite to participate in UN operations, giving preference to the more trusted North Atlantic Treaty Organization (NATO) framework and its robust military capabilities.

On the military front, the Netherlands concluded that during crisis management operations it could not rely on other powers for protection. As a result, The Hague approved continued investment in high-spectrum capabilities such as next-generation fighter aircraft, heavy artillery, and attack helicopters. From then on, Dutch troops would only be deployed with robust military capabilities able to provide escalation dominance. Such happened in the peacekeeping mission in Eritrea and Ethiopia (UNMEE), the stabilization mission in Iraq (SFIR), and ISAF.

THE MISSION IN URUZGAN

On December 22, 2005, Parliament was officially informed along the contours of the Toetsingskader that a battalion-sized contingent would deploy to southern Afghanistan. The Article 100 letter said the objective was to support the Afghan authorities and guarantee security and stability in Afghanistan. Minister of Defense Henk Kamp wrote, "the stabilisation and reconstruction of Afghanistan, particularly in the south where the Taliban's roots lie, is of great importance to improve the international rule of law and combat international terrorism which also threatens Europe."[1]

Why did the Netherlands opt for Uruzgan? Until 2005 the military had operated in Kabul and northern Afghanistan rather successfully. From an operational perspective it made sense that because of this experience, it should expand its commitment there. In theory, the Dutch could also free-ride on contributions by larger states. While ISAF was branching out to the east, south, and west of Afghanistan, there was no pressing reason why a smaller NATO power should engage in Uruzgan. Or was there? The mission to Uruzgan was a so-called war of choice, while for the US, following 9/11, the war was a necessity and the US did not have the luxury of introducing caveats or preferring operations in less risky areas. But for a smaller ally with limited military resources, the decision to deploy to a demanding environment was a deliberate choice and shaped by domestic political trade-offs.

THE REASONS FOR GOING TO URUZGAN

Domestic politics strongly impacted the Dutch path into Uruzgan. Parliamentary support, although constitutionally not necessary but desirable, was not guaranteed. During the parliamentary debate in February 2006, three arguments were made: the Netherlands had a responsibility to support NATO solidarity; it wanted to contribute to international stability, international rule of law, and avoid the creation of a terrorist sanctuary; and finally, it had a unique "Dutch approach," making the mission qualitatively different from previous US efforts in Uruzgan. These reasons reflected important tenets of Dutch strategic culture. Their interaction would shape the Dutch discussion over Uruzgan.[2]

Solidarity

The most straightforward reason for the Uruzgan mission was that the Netherlands was capable, and solidarity in the alliance required its contribution. Now was the time to use the capabilities it had been developing since the end of the Cold War. On June 13, 2006, Foreign Minister Ben Bot wondered out loud what the use of the military was if it was not used. He echoed a similar question that US Secretary of State Madeleine Albright had raised in the Clinton administration a decade earlier. Bot implied that the existence of Dutch expeditionary forces provided ample justification to go to Uruzgan. It was connected with the argument of NATO solidarity. Pressure to participate came from Brussels. Two days before the crucial debate in Parliament, solidarity within the alliance became a central theme. NATO's Dutch Secretary-General Jaap de Hoop Scheffer pressured the Netherlands with a similar "use it or lose it" argument.[3] NATO Supreme Allied Commander General James Jones said that the Dutch contribution would fill important shortfalls.[4] Besides, not participating would negatively impact ISAF planning and hurt the Dutch image. Diplomatic pressure especially came from those allies with whom the Dutch would operate in southern Afghanistan: the UK, the US, Canada, and Australia. For the Netherlands, these were among the most important military partners.[5] Dutch credibility in NATO was used as a diplomatic instrument to influence decision making.

Solidarity in the alliance and the willingness to bandwagon with the US superpower is not sufficient to explain why the Netherlands would want to be at the front line of a demanding counterinsurgency mission. This requires a more nuanced argument. The relevance of a smaller power in a period of coalition-based warfare is measured in terms of its willingness to participate in operations alongside major allies, to engage in high-intensity or initial-entry operations, and to develop the necessary military capabilities. By being a good ally and making relevant contributions, the Netherlands could increase its political credit and get a seat at the table. In turn, a healthy relationship with the US would keep Washington committed to NATO and reduce the risk that the US would exclusively rely on London, Paris, and Berlin as European interlocutors. It would improve the Netherlands' ability to protect its security interests. A close transatlantic relationship would give provide greater leverage with the powers in Europe. By proving itself a relevant ally, The Hague could make its voice heard, a central tenet of its security policy since WWII.[6] The Netherlands was proud that in 2007 it was the only non-English-speaking country able to credibly contribute forces to Afghanistan's most demanding areas. This offered a means to differentiate internationally and demonstrate its membership of the "A-team," a term coined in 1999 by then Minister of Defense Frank de Grave to describe a group of countries willing and able to undertake high-intensity expeditionary operations. Uruzgan allowed the Dutch government to distinguish itself from others, most notably Germany, which was facing criticism from NATO allies regarding its reluctance to participate in counterinsurgency operations. It was solidarity with a dose of self-interest.

Stability

The second argument was based on the understanding that the Uruzgan mission would be a stability operation focused on promoting the international rule of law. According to the constitution (Article 97), the Netherlands has a military to defend and protect the interests of the kingdom and "to maintain and promote the international legal order." It offers a constitutional mandate to use the military for stability operations.

In 2006, the largest member of the governing coalition, the Christian Democrat Appèl (CDA) Party, said it supported the Uruzgan mission because it had the "obligation to improve the international rule of law."[7] The second-largest party, the social-Democratic Labour Party (Partij van de Arbeid; PvdA), indicated their support "in principle" because the mission was a UN operation executed by NATO at the request of President Hamid Karzai and thereby contributed to the international rule of law.

Critics, however, said that the mission would be different; instead of stabilization and reconstruction, the mission would involve fighting the Taliban and al Qaeda operatives. The smallest party of the governing coalition, the Liberal-Democratic D66 Party, was vehemently opposed. This jeopardized a parliamentary majority for the mission and cohesion in the governing coalition. D66 leader Boris Dittrich referred to the situation prior to Srebrenica, warning that the Netherlands should not "stumble into another war."[8] Was a stabilization operation possible in a war zone?

Criticism of the US and the "Dutch Approach"

The third argument was that the Netherlands would operate differently from the US. The Dutch, and others, perceived the US as focused on pacifying Afghanistan by removing the threat of al Qaeda and the Taliban, instead of pursuing institution building and reconstruction. Critics were pointing to America's overly "kinetic approach."[9] The government complained that the US had taken an enemy-centric rather than a population-centric approach, focusing on targeting terrorists at the expense of promoting stability. The Article 100 letter said the US military had antagonized the local population, and an operation "explicitly focused on winning the hearts and minds of the population, is therefore necessary."[10] Both countries participated in the same campaign, but the US was fighting a war, while the Netherlands wanted to wage a stabilization campaign.

The parliamentary debate echoed this criticism. D66 leader Boris Dittrich declared that the Americans were partially to blame for the level of resistance they had encountered: "Over the past period, Uruzgan has become more unsafe, in spite of, but also due to the actions of the Americans." The leader of the CDA, Maxime Verhagen, argued that the Dutch would be more effective than American forces because of greater consideration for the local population. He said, "[if you] do not kick in the doors but hang them up again, it implies a very different military operation."[11] The political elite went to great lengths to underline military differences with the US. The greatest risk to Dutch troops seemed not to be the Taliban but rather whether they were considered American. The irony was that the Netherlands deployed to Uruzgan stressing how different it was from the same ally whose credit it was seeking by participating. A key element in this reasoning was the belief in a successful "Dutch approach."

The letter to Parliament plainly referred to Uruzgan's security situation as "bad."[12] Such a bleak assessment had not appeared in previous deployments. Corruption and weak local governance were part of the problem. A telling example was that in 2006 more people were scared of the police than of the Taliban.[13] The province was a black hole, lacking effective local governance but with warlords, guns, drugs, rebel activity, and difficult terrain. The government recognized that the mission had "real military risks," adding that "offensive actions may be necessary to create a safe environment."[14] This was an important departure from previous missions. But the risks were deemed acceptable. The letter stated that the Netherlands had the necessary experience to perform high-risk operations successfully, alluding to Iraq and northern Afghanistan.[15] Although the Uruzgan mission would be very different from these earlier, less risky stabilization operations, they had led to the emergence of the "Dutch approach."

During the 2003 mission in Iraq the Dutch military focused on reconstruction efforts. The mission was population-centric, not enemy-centric. This appealed to the Dutch preference to be a stabilizing power and not an occupier or warfighter. More importantly, the military believed it improved force protection. The *New York Times* published an article that described the approach as "part neighborhood police officer, part social worker," and the Dutch commander in Iraq suggested this approach might be suitable for US operations in lawless Baghdad as well.[16] Thus, the self-serving narrative of a unique Dutch approach to counterinsurgency was born.[17] The highest-ranking officer in the Dutch armed forces, General Dick Berlijn, gave further support: "the Dutch Approach is based on respect and understanding for the cultural context, but one that neither closes its eyes to the risks, and gives our soldiers the protection and rules of engagement that are necessary to act adequately."[18]

Of course, this was hardly new thinking, let alone unique to the Dutch. It borrowed from UK and US experiences in Iraq and built on classic counterinsurgency doctrine. Yet the fact that the Netherlands was able to operate in Iraq in an open manner, engage with the population, and leave the province after two years relatively unscathed boosted Dutch confidence. In northern Afghanistan, the "Dutch approach" would mature, and the question was whether "stabilization with a light touch" could hold in a high-intensity environment like Uruzgan. Politicians embraced the narrative of the "Dutch approach." It appealed to a strategic-cultural preference to promote the international rule of law in a nonconfrontational manner through stability and reconstruction efforts. PvdA support was crucial to get a parliamentary majority in favor of the mission. While acknowledging the complexity of Uruzgan's environment, PvdA leader Wouter Bos stated that if there was one approach that had a chance of success, it was the "Dutch approach."[19] At the final tally, 126 of the 150 members of Parliament voted in support of the mission.

The idea that the Netherlands could achieve success in Uruzgan without fighting the Taliban was utopian. The distinction between war and reconstruction is wholly artificial in a counterinsurgency, which requires both. Alongside winning hearts and minds, it is necessary to engage in direct action against insurgents.[20] This idea plagued the Dutch debate.[21] Before the parliamentary vote, the prospect of combat was hardly emphasized in public. But the day after the vote, Minister Kamp stressed that offensive operations would take place. He said, "the hard core of the Taliban and Al-Qaeda must be eliminated with hard action. If attacks are planned in our province, we will make sure they are not executed."[22] The artificial distinction between combat and stabilization created a tension between the mission politicians who believed they had signed up to this approach and the operational reality on the ground.

CAPABILITIES

Initially, the "Dutch approach" prescribed the military material and apparel to be used. It would also enable the Netherlands to distinguish itself from the US. The Dutch forces would ride in open jeeps if possible and "in an armoured personnel vehicle if necessary."[23] It resonated traditional counterinsurgency thinking that the more a force is protected the less secure it is, because more protection means less communication. Another seemingly trivial element was that Dutch forces would wear goggles, not the wraparound sunglasses favored by US forces. These were believed to reduce the interpersonal barrier between soldier and Afghan citizen.[24] But once they were deployed, force protection would become the priority concern. The Netherlands purchased twenty-five mine-resistant Bushmaster armored vehicles. They complemented the open jeeps, although soon the Bushmasters were the only vehicles to leave the compound, given the threat of improvised explosives. Dutch forces were prescribed to wear sunglasses instead of transparent goggles to cope with the glare. Initially Dutch forces also wore green camouflage uniforms to distinguish themselves from US desert khaki. Yet all other ISAF troops wore the same camouflage, and the

Dutch soon conformed. Besides, the military said, "[khaki] camouflages [are] better in the surrounding environment."[25] While the Netherlands had tried to be different from the US, the environment dictated rules of its own.

The Netherlands was the lead nation in Uruzgan, supported by Australia. The battalion-sized Battle Group, which would support the PRT, consisted of approximately 1,500 (later 1,700) troops. They were initially drawn from units of the 12th Air Assault Infantry battalion of the expeditionary Air Manoeuvre Brigade and the 44th Mechanized Infantry Battalion, along with a special forces task group. Six F-16 fighter aircraft and six Apache assault helicopters deployed alongside three armored panzer-howitzer artillery systems. Chinook and Cougar helicopters provided tactical lift. Military battles, such as the battle of Chora in June 2007, used the full range of these capabilities. Here, the most intensive Dutch fighting since the Korean War removed any doubt regarding the nature of the operation.[26] Slowly it became clear that the Netherlands was engaged in a high-intensity counterinsurgency operation.

EXTENDING THE MISSION

The initial two years achieved limited results. The security situation was worse than expected; suicide attacks were up, reducing the ability of the PRT to undertake reconstruction activities. In the first ten months of the deployment there were no combat casualties, but from May to November 2007 eight Dutch soldiers died. The government noted that "the circumstances are tough and the local Afghan capabilities limited."[27] Still, the Dutch government decided to extend the mission. An overarching reason was that the Netherlands had made significant investments and "now that [it] has so much knowledge and expertise," a premature Dutch withdrawal would jeopardize progress made so far.[28]

There was, however, substantial political resistance, particularly within the PvdA, which had since come to power in a coalition government with the CDA and Christenunie (CU), a small Christian party. The PvdA's initial criticism—they had supported the mission only under the assumption that it involved reconstruction, not combat activities—had hardened. In two years, combat had become very much a part of the operation. A political compromise was struck, "either way the leading role of the Netherlands in Uruzgan will end August 1, 2010."[29] The extended mission would also have different priorities: a greater emphasis on reconstruction activities and training Afghan security forces. Furthermore, operational stress meant that the mission would continue with 15 to 20 percent fewer forces and with nine instead of twelve F-16s.

WITHDRAWAL FROM URUZGAN

As 2010 approached, the government had a decision to make. In hindsight it seems straightforward that after the extension the operation would terminate. Yet it would take the collapse of the governing coalition for the mission to end. Domestic factors took precedence over military-strategic considerations. Public opinion—particularly among the PvdA's constituency—had never fully adjusted to the high-intensity nature of the mission. With the Dutch casualties in mid-2007, public opposition spiked to 50 percent; it dropped but went up again in spring 2010.

In late 2009, Verhagen signaled that he wanted to extend the mission. With local elections approaching in March 2010 and conscious of the sentiment among its constituency, the PvdA leadership were opposed. A political crisis ensued. It was made worse when NATO Secretary-General Anders Fogh Rasmussen sent a letter to The Hague formally requesting that the Netherlands continue in Uruzgan.[30] As is diplomatic custom, such letters are never sent without prior approval.[31] Since the government had not yet reached a position, there was confusion over who had requested the letter. The internal conflict led to the government's collapse on February 20, 2010. New elections would be held, but the Uruzgan mission would end in August 2010.

THE AFTERMATH OF URUZGAN: TRAINING POLICE IN KUNDUZ

In January 2011, the government decided on a small-scale police training mission. It was a compromise effort to repair the diplomatic damage in NATO. The mission was the polar opposite of the Uruzgan mission. It was in the northern Kunduz province as part of NATO's training mission and EUPOL. The Dutch contingent was embedded as part of the broader German effort. Nearly 40 police and 165 military trainers would participate in this civil-military mission totaling 500 people. Moreover, the deployment included four F-16s to provide escalation dominance and officers at various staffs in Afghanistan. The policing mission was the product of a motion adopted by parliament, sponsored by D66 and the social-green party (GroenLinks) and supported by the new minority government of CDA and the liberal-conservatives (Volkspartij voor Vrijheid en Democratie; VVD). The PvdA voted against the mission, even though it was a stabilization mission and excluded any combat role. The party remained suspicious.

Domestic political considerations, rather than a military rationale, led the Netherlands to impose a number of caveats on the training mission. Part of

NATO's evolving strategy was to train the Afghan security forces, including police, so that it could gradually withdraw. However, the Dutch mandate for the Kunduz mission explicitly prohibited deployment of its Afghan police in combat situations. They were to be trained in the spirit of modern, Western police forces, not as a paramilitary force. The trained police forces were not allowed to be deployed outside the province, further reducing the risk of combat. The Netherlands also offered the Afghan police a longer training than the NATO-wide program and emphasized cultural and gender studies. Critics denounced the mission as wholly inadequate for Afghanistan's needs.

While its allies had initially applauded the Netherlands for being a risk taker in Uruzgan, The Hague had become risk averse. The Netherlands had gone into Uruzgan among others to differentiate itself from Germany, yet the Dutch commitment to ISAF had become dependent on Germany. Since the Netherlands was the junior partner to the German Kunduz operation, it relied on its support. Germany decided to withdraw from Kunduz by mid-2013, and the Netherlands had to cut its operation short as well. By 2014, only the F-16 detachment remained. At the time of writing, the possibility remains that the Netherlands will support a small training mission to Afghanistan as part of Operation Resolute Support beyond 2015.

RESULTS ACHIEVED

The results of the Afghanistan mission fall into three categories: mission-level, military, and political-strategic. In September 2011, the government published its final evaluation of the contribution to ISAF in the period 2006–2010.[32] Its main focus was the operation in Uruzgan. The mission had achieved the following results: 3,200 Afghan military forces trained; 1,600 Afghan police forces trained; more commerce and traffic between urban centers in Uruzgan due to improved security; a better tribal balance in local representations; greater awareness of social equality and the position of women; and development projects in education, health, water, infrastructure, agriculture, and energy that led to socioeconomic improvements. The evaluation report concluded that the "mission has laid a foundation for development."[33]

But there were concerns as well: by 2010, more improvised explosive devices (IEDs) were planted, even if more were traced; local governing capability remained weak; public confidence in provincial and local governance was low; informal powerbrokers still played a substantial role in local politics; judicial capacity remained weak; and an independent report suggested that the "situation remains highly fragile."[34] In other words, the results on the ground were mixed. While the first steps had been taken to improve Uruzgan's socioeconomic conditions, progress was slow and the security environment was dangerous.

Militarily, the Netherlands became skilled in the various dimensions of counterinsurgency. The Netherlands pursued an ink-spot strategy, focusing its efforts on major populated areas first and gradually expanding the zones of relative security to accommodate reconstruction activities in a wider area. It emphasized a 3D or comprehensive approach whereby defense, diplomacy, and development go hand in hand. It implied that the political advisor, development advisors, tribal advisors, and the military senior staff worked closely together. By 2009 the Civil Representative, the highest diplomat in the mission, and the military commander were given joint responsibility for civil-military planning. Interagency cooperation in The Hague also increased. In practice, however, the major contribution remained military, as 99 percent of the personnel wore a uniform, and the threat environment meant an overwhelming effort was directed at security operations.

At the political-strategic level, participation in the Uruzgan mission contributed to Dutch attendance at various high-level meetings, including the four G-20 summits between 2008 and 2010. The Dutch role in Afghanistan ostensibly contributed to its being invited; a leaked Wikileaks cable notes that the US stressed G-20 membership when the Dutch government debated extending the Uruzgan mandate.[35] It gives credence to the argument that the Netherlands uses its military to gain international political credit.

In 2009, the Netherlands was given the opportunity to host an international conference to discuss Afghanistan's future. The conference lauded the Dutch counterinsurgency approach. By contrast, the withdrawal from Uruzgan had several negative implications. The Netherlands has not been invited to any further G-20 meetings. And in response to the diplomatic insult to the NATO Secretary-General, at the subsequent NATO summit in Lisbon the Dutch prime minister received an unpopular time slot to give his prepared remarks.

AUSTERITY STRIKES

A more material and lasting legacy from ISAF was financial. Annual expenses were much higher than anticipated. Replacement and upkeep of weapons systems put pressure on the budget. Coupled with the euro crisis and the ensuing defense austerity, the Afghanistan mission would weigh heavily on the Dutch military in subsequent years.

In late 2007, the harsh climatic and operational conditions created a number of shortfalls.[36] Helicopters and munitions were in short supply and procured expensively on the commercial market. The Dutch initially budgeted the two-year operation at 380 million euros, but it exceeded 600 million euros during the first year, almost four times as much as originally planned.[37] With 2,000 forces deployed, the operation consumed 9 percent of the annual defense budget. The financial hardship and the desire to continue in Afghanistan necessitated the sale of the military's "silverware." In 2007, substantial cuts were announced in primary weapons systems, including twenty-eight Leopard tanks (31 percent of remaining stock), twelve panzer-howitzers (33 percent of total stock), and eighteen F-16s (a 20 percent decrease in capability); withdrawal of one of two marine battalions from the Caribbean; canceled participation in NATO's Allied Ground Surveillance system; cancellation of the Dutch MALE (medium altitude, long endurance) unmanned aerial vehicle program; and no procurement of Tomahawk cruise missiles.[38]

The military was cannibalizing hardware to sustain the mission. It risked turning the Dutch armed forces into a highly experienced military force lacking the capabilities to take part in high-intensity operations. In 2007, Minister of Defense Eimert van Middelkoop said the Netherlands was close to hitting rock bottom, saying undiplomatically that "if you do not want to end up in a situation where the Dutch armed forces have the same allure as the Belgian, than you need to consider which financial measures are necessary to sustain the military."[39] Along with years of post–Cold War budget reductions, it threatened to reduce the military to a politically insignificant force.

In April 2011, a new defense policy paper—titled "Defense After the Credit Crisis: A Smaller Military in a Turbulent World"—said that while the Uruzgan mission was over, the euro crisis was biting. Austerity measures, outstanding expenses, and high maintenance costs forced twelve thousand job cuts, and the defense budget was reduced by 1 billion euros (nearly 12 percent). Major cuts were made to operational capabilities including both remaining tank battalions, along with all Leopard 2 tanks. The panzer-howitzer artillery systems were reduced from 24 to 18, F-16 aircraft from 87 to 68, mine hunters from 10 to 6, oceangoing patrol vessels from 4 to 2, and amphibious support vessels from 2 to 1.

The Netherlands drastically cut its defense capabilities. The financial crisis was partially to blame for austerity measures, but it was made worse by the legacy of Uruzgan. As a result, while the government maintained that the military was a broad expeditionary force, this ambition could no longer be met.

The high operational tempo and continued reductions in military spending had taken their toll. In 2012, Minister of Defense Hans Hillen noted that the military was incapable of contributing to any more missions aside from a frigate to the Somalia antipiracy mission and the small police training program in Kunduz. (By 2014, the Kunduz mission was finished and replaced by a special forces mission in support of the UN operation in Mali.)

CONCLUSION

As ISAF draws to a close, the Netherlands military finds itself in a difficult position. While it has operated courageously and with success, financial storm clouds hover over the military and it confronts a political climate skeptical of large-scale expeditionary operations. The Afghanistan mission—specifically Uruzgan—contributed substantially to both problems. The deployment was expensive and the defense ministry's finances were worsened by the financial crisis.

On the political front, the mission struggled with the artificial distinction between stabilization and combat. The Netherlands tried to balance being a relevant ally that can contribute to demanding military operations with a preference for stabilization operations where combat plays a marginal role, which made an accurate understanding of the needs of modern-day counterinsurgency operations difficult. The Uruzgan mission surpassed what some Dutch politicians were willing to take responsibility for. It showed the limits of the type of expeditionary operation the Dutch political establishment, and by extension the Dutch public, would support. High-intensity combat crossed that limit. The Netherlands has no appetite for, nor can it afford, a demanding mission like Uruzgan in the near future. The heated discussion over the limited and relatively risk-free training mission in Kunduz highlights how it has made policy makers and politicians wary. Together with the defense budget cuts, this means the Netherlands is no longer part of an "A-team" of expeditionary military powers.

One lesson is the need to have an accurate political understanding of the mission prior to deployment. If not, a disconnect will emerge between the political debate and the mission, which complicates giving the military the political and material support it needs and reduces public confidence in—and political support for—the military. This leads to a second lesson: the military may do a flawless job in the theater, yet the timeline for an expeditionary mission is set in the capital.

Finally, the Dutch experience in Afghanistan highlights the lack of a broader strategic debate about Afghanistan among smaller powers. When Dutch politicians and the military discussed Afghanistan, they did so almost exclusively in reference to Baghlan, Uruzgan, or Kunduz provinces. Little attention was paid to developments in other parts of the country, or beyond. This is understandable for a coalition partner with a limited military responsibility, but it made a strategic-level debate about ISAF difficult. Political decision makers, the military, and the media were interested in their piece of Afghanistan, and only while the mission lasted.

NOTES

1. Minister van Defensie, *Nederlandse Bijdrage aan ISAF in Zuid-Afghanistan*, DVB/ CV-388/05, The Hague, December 22, 2005, 3–4.

2. A. Rem Korteweg, *The Superpower, the Bridge-Builder and the Hesitant Ally: How Defense Transformation Divided NATO 1991–2008* (Leiden, Netherlands: Leiden University Press, 2011), 233–257.

3. Judy Dempsey, "Dutch Pressed over Afghanistan," *International Herald Tribune*, January 30, 2006, 1, http://www.nytimes.com/2006/01/29/world/europe/29iht-nato.html.

4. T. Koelé and M. Peeperkorn, "Tweede Kamer zwaar onder druk gezet," *De Volkskrant*, January 31, 2006, http://www.volkskrant.nl/politiek/tweede-kamer-zwaar-onder -druk-gezet~a766176/.

5. See Commandant der Strijdkrachten, *Militair Strategische Verkenning 2006*, Den Haag, Ministerie van Defensie, February 6, 2006.

6. Alfred van Staden, *Een Trouwe Bondgenoot: Nederland en het Atlantisch Bondgenootschap (1960–1971)* (Baarn, the Netherlands: In den Toren, 1974).

7. M. Verhagen, "Debat over de Nederlandse deelname aan ISAF in Zuid-Afghanistan," The Hague, February 2, 2006, *Handelingen van de Tweede Kamer*, 45/ 3013.

8. Boris Dittrich, quoted by Raoul Du Pré, "Dittrich vreest een nieuw Srebrenica," *De Volkskrant*, January 27, 2006, http://www.volkskrant.nl/politiek/dittrich-vreest-een -nieuw-srebrenica~a768726/.

9. See Nigel Aylwin-Foster, "Changing the Army for Counterinsurgency Operations," *Military Review* (November–December 2005), 2–15; Barack Obama, "State of the Union Address," Washington, DC, January 27, 2010.

10. Minister van Defensie, *Nederlandse Bijdrage aan ISAF in Zuid-Afghanistan*, December 22, 2005, 10.

11. Maxime Verhagen, "Debat over de Nederlandse deelname aan ISAF in Zuid-Afghanistan," The Hague, February 2, 2006, *Handelingen van de Tweede Kamer*, 45/ 3014.

12. Minister van Defensie, *Nederlandse Bijdrage aan ISAF in Zuid-Afghanistan*, 3–4.

13. Barbara Bedway, "Covering the 'Other' War: A Reporter in Afghanistan," *Editor & Publisher*, April 3, 2006.

14. Minister van Defensie, *Nederlandse Bijdrage aan ISAF in Zuid-Afghanistan*, 3–4.

15. Ibid., 3.

16. Norimitsu Onishi, "Dutch Soldiers Find Smiles Are a More Effective Protection," *New York Times*, October 24, 2004, http://www.nytimes.com/2004/10/24/international/middleeast/24dutch.html.

17. See T. W. Brocades Zaalberg, "The Use and Abuse of the 'Dutch Approach' to Counter-Insurgency," *Strategic Studies* 36, no. 6 (2013): 867–897.

18. General D. Berlijn, "Toespraak bij Vertrek F-16 detachment naar Afghanistan," January 9, 2006.

19. Wouter Bos, "Debat over de Nederlandse deelname aan ISAF in Zuid-Afghanistan," February 2, 2006, The Hague, *Handelingen van de Tweede Kamer*, 45/3013–3035.

20. See Eliot Cohen, Conrad Crane, John Nagl et al., "Principles, Imperatives and Paradoxes of Counterinsurgency," *Military Review* (March–April 2006): 49–53.

21. See G. R. Dimitriu and B. A. de Graaf, "De Nederlandse COIN-aanpak: drie jaar Uruzgan, 2006–2009," *Militaire Spectator* 178, no. 11: 613–635.

22. Minister of Defense Henk Kamp, quoted in *De Volkskrant*, February 3, 2006.

23. Gen. Dick Berlijn, "Toespraak bij Vertrek Deployment Task Force naar Uruzgan," March 14, 2006, Eindhoven, the Netherlands.

24. S. Ramdharie, "Uruzgan-gangers in 't nieuw," *De Volkskrant*, July 14, 2006, http://www.volkskrant.nl/binnenland/uruzgan-gangers-in-t-nieuw~a762854/.

25. Ibid.

26. Noel van Bemmel, "Infanteristen, commando's: iedereen vecht tegen Taliban," *De Volkskrant*, June 23, 2007, http://www.volkskrant.nl/binnenland/infanteristen-commandos-iedereen-vecht-tegen-taliban~a850516/; Paul Brill, "Ze schoten een magazijn op me leeg," *De Volkskrant*, June 28, 2007, http://www.volkskrant.nl/binnenland/ze-schoten-een-magazijn-op-me-leeg~a850725/.

27. Ministers van Defensie, Buitenlandse Zaken en Ontwikkelingssamenwerking, *Bestrijding Internationaal Terrorisme*, Kamerstuk 27925, no. 279, November 30, 2007, http://www.rijksbegroting.nl/algemeen/gerefereerd/1/1/3/kst113210.html.

28. Ibid.

29. Ibid.

30. Letter from NATO Secretary-General Rasmussen to Prime Minister Balkenende, February 4, 2010, http://vorige.nrc.nl/multimedia/archive/00271/brief_271598a.pdf.

31. "De Hoop Scheffer: Nederland doet afbreuk aan NAVO," *NRC Handelsblad*, February 25, 2010, http://vorige.nrc.nl/nieuwsthema/uruzgan/article2491892.ece/De_Hoop_Scheffer_Nederland_doet_afbreuk_aan_NAVO.

32. Ministerie van Defensie, "Eindevaluatie Nederlandse bijdrage aan ISAF," 2006–2010, September 23, 2011, http://www.jallc.nato.int/activities/rfoids/final_evaluat_on_netherlands_participation_in_isaf%202006-2010_tcm4-825602.pdf.

33. Ibid., 105.

34. Martine van Bijlert, "The Battle For Afghanistan—Militancy and Conflict in Zabul and Uruzgan," *New American Foundation*, September 2010, 18.

35. US Embassy, The Hague, *Ambtsbericht mbt NLD in Afghanistan en Uitnodiging G20*, September 2009, http://media.rtl.nl/media/actueel/rtlnieuws/2011/225926.pdf.

36. Ministry of Defense internal assessment document, dated March 27, 2007, in *De Telegraaf*, April 19, 2007, http://static.telegraaf.nl/mediaobjects/01969/190407_1969361a.pdf.

37. "Kosten Uruzgan 200 Miljoen Hoger," *NRC Handelsblad*, June 27, 2007, http://vorige.nrc.nl/nieuwsthema/uruzgan/article1811614.ece.

38. Ministerie van Defensie, "Het Defensiebeleid op Hoofdlijnen," HDAB200718939, The Hague, July 2, 2007.

39. "Defensie eist groter budget voor missies," *NRC Handelsblad*, July 9, 2007, http://vorige.nrc.nl/binnenland/article1816063.ece.

11 THE VISEGRAD FOUR

Achieving Long-Term Security Through Alliance
Support

Marybeth P. Ulrich

THE DAY AFTER THE SEPTEMBER 11, 2001, terrorist attacks on the US, the
North Atlantic Treaty Organization (NATO), for the first time, invoked Article 5 of the North Atlantic Treaty. This committed all parties to the treaty
to the defense of the US and helped clear the way for NATO operations in
Afghanistan. The December 2001 Bonn Agreement and United Nations Security Council Resolution (UNSCR) 1386 established the International Security
Assistance Force (ISAF) to assist the Afghan government "in the maintenance
of security in Kabul and its surrounding areas, so that the Afghan Interim
Authority as well as the personnel of the United Nations can operate in a secure environment."[1]

ISAF was envisioned as a follow-on force to the combat operations phase
known as Operation Enduring Freedom (OEF). OEF focused on the elimination of al Qaeda and the terrorist threat in Afghanistan. ISAF was to complement OEF, further developing the socioeconomic and political dimensions
needed to bring stability to the region.[2] ISAF was immediately viewed as a key
test of NATO's enduring capabilities and continued relevance to global threats.
Consequently, performance in the ISAF mission became a key indicator of
NATO's newest members' mettle and commitment to the alliance.

The focus here is specifically on the participation and contribution of the
Central European states of the Czech Republic, Slovakia, Hungary, and Poland
to the ISAF mission. What strategic interests have driven their actions? What
impact did ISAF participation have on each state's reputation in NATO and with
the US? Finally, how has participation affected each state's military capabilities

and ongoing efforts for military modernization and reform in the post-communist era?

STRATEGIC MOTIVATIONS

Although each Central European state's specific level of contribution to ISAF has varied, all four Visegrad states framed their participation in terms of overall strategic interests. Each holds an Atlanticist orientation, viewing NATO as its primary security guarantor. These leanings have also been balanced with their interest in bolstering ties to the EU for economic security. For example, Poland considers NATO its best guarantee in case of aggression from abroad but is also in favor of creating a European army to ensure the security of Europe. "Only America and NATO can give us external security, but even more pressing is domestic security, which means modernization, and nobody but the EU can give us that."[3]

Former Secretary of Defense Donald Rumsfeld dubbed these post-communist states "new Europe," to contrast their heightened sense of conventional threats in comparison to the Western European states of "old Europe." The states of "new Europe" find themselves at times navigating the competing security terrains of NATO and the European Union (EU). Each institution is critical to strategic and economic interests, and each demands that its members contribute to its initiatives in order to remain members in good standing worthy of receiving the organizations' benefits. The level of intensity of interest each state is assigned to achieve ISAF's mission of stabilizing Afghanistan, in order to attenuate threats emanating from there, has also been an issue. The intensities of interest varied from vital to important to peripheral across the coalition members. These overall foreign policy objectives, anchored in the continued viability of NATO and the EU, underpinned each of the Visegrad Four states' behavior throughout the ISAF mission in Afghanistan.

Nik Hynek and Peter Marton incorporated these strategic motivations into an analytical framework that highlighted threat balancing and alliance dependence as the key structural motives influencing all ISAF coalition members. They argue, "states are assumed to have entered Afghanistan, and stayed there over the years, either because they needed to do so themselves or because they were compelled to do so by others who did."[4] This rationale underscores the varied and mixed motivations of states weighing the direct nature of the terrorist threat in Afghanistan along with their interest in maintaining strong strategic ties with the US bilaterally and NATO collectively.

Poland's combined need to balance a significant threat to Polish interests in Afghanistan, its strong strategic interest in the efficacy of NATO, and its calculation that the US is its most valued strategic partner place it at the front of the pack. The Czechs are right behind the Poles with lower-order but still significant commitments to balancing the threat. Prague determined that it is in its "national interest to stabilize Afghanistan and that it is necessary to eliminate the possibility of Al Qaida getting this terrorist safe haven."[5] The Czechs also placed great stock in using the Afghan mission as a means of burnishing their NATO credentials. A Czech Ministry of Foreign Affairs (MFA) official noted that the engagement of the Czech military instrument put a higher priority on fulfilling membership obligations over the achievement of specific foreign policy goals for their own sake. We are "obliged to fulfill our obligations and want to be a loyal partner."[6] Such participation would prove the Czechs' reliability as a partner to the US and NATO and Czech commitment to Article 5 of the Washington Treaty.[7] As the ISAF mission progressed, the challenge became to define national success within the overall NATO mission, which was perceived to be falling short of its objectives.

The need to balance threats in Afghanistan was felt less in Bratislava and Budapest; however, Slovakia and Hungary saw the value in supporting NATO's priority global mission. Ferenc Juhasz, Hungary's Defense Minister, bluntly noted, "This is about NATO, not Afghanistan; what else would we have to do there other than taking responsibility together with our allies?"[8] Participation, even at minimal rates, still covered the "insurance premium" required for access to the security afforded to NATO members and allies of the US. It is important to note, too, that for all of the Central and East European (CEE) states, the Afghan mission was a superior choice over the Iraq mission, due to the clear United Nations Security Council (UNSC) mandate and the possibility of pitching the mission to their respective publics in humanitarian terms. The option to participate in Provincial Reconstruction Teams (PRTs) was particularly helpful, since the role of PRTs was not to impose values or a way of life as an occupying force might, but to facilitate development, construction, and modernization of infrastructure. These differences in threat perception, the need to be perceived as reliable NATO members and key strategic partners, and varied levels of public and governmental support resulted in a range of contributions and levels of commitment to the ISAF mission. These various contributions and perspectives are outlined in the following sections.

COUNTRY ROLES: POLAND, CZECH REPUBLIC, HUNGARY, SLOVAKIA

Poland

Poland is the most strategically positioned of the Visegrad Four and contributed a peak number of 2,515 troops to ISAF; 304 remained in September 2014.[9] Poland is the most populous country of the four with 38 million people and a gross domestic product (GDP) of $528 billion. Its armed forces are by far the most significant in Central Europe with over 100,000 active personnel and a defense budget of $9.28 billion.[10] Poland has pursued an Atlanticist foreign policy. The Poles' strategic orientation has been rooted in maintaining a strong US-Polish bilateral relationship. Poland is an advocate of US involvement in EU security issues to hedge against its historic suspicion of Western Europe's will and capacity to provide security. "Warsaw tends to regard NATO—and the US—as its hard security guarantor and the EU as a grouping of countries concerned with economic security."[11]

When EU and US policies diverge, the states of "new Europe" may find themselves in an awkward position. This was the case when Europe split over the George W. Bush administration's decision to invade Iraq in 2003. The Visegrad Four supported the US-led war in Iraq. Poland led one of the four military zones in Iraq, the International Zone. Such strong support for US policy despite much of the condemnation by "old Europe" of the policy stems from these states' explicit gratitude to the US for its hand in bringing about the downfall of communism.[12] These Atlanticist leanings are likely to endure and will at times be problematic in the quest for an EU Common Foreign and Security Policy (CFSP). For instance, Poland and the Baltic states were vehemently opposed to Russia's intervention in Georgia in 2008, but most other European states' responses were more muted. In 2014 Poland and the Baltic states were in favor of extracting a price from Russia for its annexation of Crimea. Germany and the UK, on the other hand, feared the economic repercussions that their economies might suffer as a result of strong sanctions.[13] However, the ongoing Russian-backed incursion in eastern Ukraine and the downing of Malaysia Airlines Flight 17 toughened EU resolve resulting in the EU tightening economic sanctions against Russia, narrowing the interest gap between "new Europe" and "old Europe."

Poland's participation in ISAF began in March 2002 with about 300 soldiers who cleared mines, protected the Kabul airport, and built infrastructure to support the mission.[14] This modest contribution grew gradually to 2,457 troops by June 2012, when Poland pledged to increase its contribution further with eight Mi-23 helicopter gunships, 400 additional troops, and 200 noncombatant aircraft support personnel. This level of participation put Poland in seventh place among participating countries.[15] In addition to its substantial overall troop contribution, Poland took on a significant development role with its assumption of responsibility for a PRT with the US in Ghazni province.[16] Poland ranked third among coalition members in terms of GDP dollars per soldier deployed.[17] These are both indicators of Poland "punching above its weight" in the coalition.

The Polish ISAF contingent deployed in five bases: Ghazni, Warrior, Giro, Vulcan, and Qarabagh, in addition to Bagram air base. As one of the Combat Groups within Regional Command–East, Poland took over responsibility for Ghazni province from US forces in 2008; their tasks included securing areas where reconstruction work was conducted within the Polish Task Force's area of responsibility, securing the Afghan Development Zone in Ghazni province, protecting the strategically important three-hundred-kilometer Kabul-Kandahar road, and training Afghan armed forces and police.[18]

To date, Poland has deployed thirteen six-month rotations of troops to Afghanistan in contingents of 2,500 soldiers. Beginning with the twelfth rotation, which served in ISAF from October 2012 to April 2013, the Polish contingent was downsized to 1,800 soldiers. This decrease in troop levels reflected the changing character of the mission from combat operations to a training-stabilization mission.[19] The mission of the Polish Military Contingent in Afghanistan (Polski Kontyngent Wojskowy Afganistanie—PKW-A) until its conclusion in 2014 was to train local police officers and prepare Afghan National Security Forces (ANSF) to take over responsibility for the Polish area of responsibility, Ghazni province. Through September 2014, 40 Poles had been killed and 21 injured in PKW-A.[20]

The Czech Republic

At its peak, the Czech Republic contributed 700 troops; 227 remained in September 2014. Ten Czech soldiers died carrying out the ISAF mission. The Czech Republic is the second most populous country of the Visegrad Four, with 10.5 million people. The Czech GDP of $206 billion supports armed forces of 21,700 and a defense budget of $2.29 billion.[21] The Army of the Czech Republic (AČR) arrived in Afghanistan in April 2002. This initial Czech participation consisted mainly of the 6th and 11th Field Hospitals. Other auxiliary support roles included a contingent of the Czech meteorological service, which operated at Kabul International Airport from September 2004 to March 2007, and a special unit of the Czech military police that operated in the south from the beginning of 2007 to the first half of 2009.

From November 2006 to March 2007, the Czechs covered the lead nation role at Kabul International Airport (KAIA) with a contingent of 68. These troops included 45 officers and a chemical detachment with the mission to evaluate the presence of radiation, chemical, and biological weapons.[22] In the realm of combat operations, in 2004 and 2006 and from November 2008 through 2009, the AČR contributed a Czech special forces team of 120 members to serve within the framework of OEF. These special forces troops served in Kandahar province under US command.

The Czech Republic's main effort in ISAF has been its participation in Provincial Reconstruction Teams (PRTs). From March 2005 until the end of 2007, Czechs contributed a few personnel to PRT Feyzabad, a Danish-German team operating in Badakhshan province. The PRT's task was to support security in the area, protect international units, and assist with reconstruction. From March 19, 2008, to January 2013, the Czech Republic was responsible for its own PRT in Logar province. PRT Logar averaged 300 personnel, 290 AČR soldiers, and 4–12 Czech civilian experts from the Ministry of Foreign Affairs (MFA).[23]

The PRT's mission was to conduct development missions consistent with the national development strategy in the province, to strengthen the role of the Afghan government in the region, and to enable the Afghan people while working closely with provincial players. The civilian PRT members' expertise included civil engineering, agriculture, veterinary medicine, security, and media.[24] The soldiers trained Afghan security forces and ensured the security of the civilian experts. By the time of its closure, PRT Logar had completed 141 projects focused on the construction of schools, hospitals, and civil service facilities in Logar. The PRT also managed a number of water projects including the building of a dam in the Khoshi district and the repair of aqueducts in the district. Civilian agricultural experts distributed seed and fertilizer, assisted with the construction of facilities to store agricultural products, and repaired traditional irrigation systems. PRT Logar also trained Afghan police, repaired five police stations along the main road from Kabul, and built a training center for Afghan police. Twenty-five hundred Czech soldiers served in PRT Logar's five-year tenure. The civilian portion of the PRT cost approximately $3.2 million annually.[25]

A military advisory team remained after the closure of the PRT in Logar province to help train an Afghan National Army (ANA) battalion. Troops in Kabul and Wardak province with the mission to train Afghan troops brought the AČR total to 500 before the 2013 drawdown. By the end of 2014 the number of Czech troops in Afghanistan will fall to 150. Those remaining will focus on logistical tasks such as repairing helicopters, training specialists, and enabling the transfer of command to Afghan leaders.

Hungary

Hungary's peak troop contribution to ISAF was 582 troops; 101 remained in September 2014. Hungary's population of 10 million produces a GDP of $130 billion. The Hungarian Defense Forces (HDF) have 28,500 troops with a defense budget of $1.7 billion.[26] On average, Hungary has 1,000 troops deployed to operations abroad. Hungarian Chief of Defense Colonel General Tibor Benko explained that these 1,000 troops have been moved "as chess pieces" across NATO operations in Afghanistan, Iraq, and Kosovo, as well as in EU and UN operations "depending on which job is more important at a given moment." Benko added that "Afghanistan is the main priority; the best prepared troops serve there and receive the most expensive equipment."[27]

Hungary deployed a handful of medical personnel and other individual officers up to company level in support of OEF operations in 2002. At this point the threat level was regarded as minimal, similar to the threat level in Balkan peace support operations, in which the Hungarians had long served. In 2003, Hungarian forces came under ISAF command and increased their participation to a company-sized contingent. In 2005 the HDF withdrew from Iraq, resulting in increased pressure from NATO to contribute to the ISAF mission. At this point the political leadership seized an opportunity to take over the Baghlan PRT from the Netherlands, which at the time was operating in the relatively safe north. "With the permissive security environment in Baghlan, it seemed that the Hungarian military would be able to continue to work with its default 'peacekeeping' posture unperturbed, while proudly flying the flag as lead nation in a relatively important province."[28]

The HDF manned its PRT with 200 to 240 personnel, depending on the level of civilian participation.[29] Thirty-four additional personnel filled individual positions across the ISAF force structure.[30] However, as the insurgency grew, Baghlan's importance as a resupply corridor for the vital Northern Distribution Network (NDN) attracted Taliban fighters, and by 2010 the area had become intensely contested territory.[31]

The PRT contributed to the stabilization of Baghlan province through humanitarian assistance and the coordination of reconstruction and development projects. Major projects included schools and roads as well as assisting the ANA and Afghan National Police (ANP). Hungary's PRT concluded in March 2013 after thirteen 180-day rotations. Twenty-five hundred Hungarian troops rotated through the PRT between October 2006 and March 2013.[32]

Besides the PRT, Hungarian special forces teamed up with Ohio National Guard troops in an Operational Mentor and Liaison Team (OMLT) under Hungarian command, which deployed to Baghlan in January 2009.[33] The same month, Hungary contributed a Special Operations Task Unit (SOTU) to eastern Afghanistan under American command. Hungary's overall contribution to the "surge" boosted its troop levels from 200 to 490. Hungary rounded out its participation by taking on the lead nation role for security at Kabul International Airport and provided a multinational helicopter unit complete with an Air Mentor Team to train Afghan pilots on the Soviet-era equipment. Hungarian forces sustained seven fatalities in Afghanistan, six in combat.[34]

Slovakia

At the end of 2012, Slovakia reached its peak troop level in Afghanistan with 344 soldiers participating in the ISAF mission.[35] In September 2014, Slovakia had 277 troops serving in ISAF and was transitioning to its follow-on mission.[36] Slovakia, with a population approximately half that of the Czech Republic and Hungary (5.4 million), has a defense budget of $1.27 billion and a GDP of $97 billion that supports the smallest of the Visegrad Four's armed forces of 16,000 personnel.

Slovakia deployed an engineer company of about forty soldiers to Bagram in August 2002 to undertake reconstruction of Bagram Airfield in support of OEF. In June 2004, seventeen members of this unit moved to Kabul to assume a demining mission and came under ISAF command. In December 2006, both engineering units unified into a Multi-Purpose Engineering Unit—SLOVCON (fifty-seven soldiers) to support ISAF operations under NATO. In May 2007, SLOVCON deployed from KAIA to Kandahar Airfield (KAF).[37]

In September 2011, Slovakia deployed 20 members of the 5th Regiment for Special Operations (Piaty Pluk Specialneho Urcenia, 5 PSU), Slovakia's premier counterterrorism and special operations unit, to Afghanistan. The participation of this heavy combat unit marked the first time Slovakia assumed such a role in ISAF and represented a significant shift in Slovak engagement in the region.[38] In 2013 the number of Slovak "special operators" in the 150-strong multinational Special Operations Training Group (SOTG) increased to 35.[39] Slovakia experienced its first fatality in Afghanistan in a July 2013 "green on blue" insider attack at the Kandahar International Airport when an Afghan citizen fired on the unit from a security tower. Six other Slovak soldiers were injured in the same attack, two seriously.[40] Three Slovak servicemen have died in support of the ISAF mission.

IMPACT OF THE VISEGRAD FOUR'S PARTICIPATION IN ISAF

Participation in ISAF operations has had a major impact on the CEE states' defense posture and performance. The Afghanistan deployment was the major military operation for each and its specific demands resulted in force restructuring, equipment purchases, and reprogramming of defense resources to meet the mission's objectives. In addition, while conducting operations in Afghanistan, the Visegrad Four were simultaneously carrying out their military reform plans, which were a condition of joining the alliance.

For example, Poland's modernization plans, which call for a smaller, more mobile force structure, reflected its gradual shift in emphasis toward building up counterterrorist response capabilities. In Poland, focus on the Afghan mission also led to the diversion of defense expenditures to paramilitary and police forces. The resultant force structure plans called for a smaller army and for the air force and navy to maintain their current sizes.

The expansion of Poland's commitment to ISAF also directly led to the development of procedures to quickly procure equipment needed for the deployments and a shift in the portion of the defense budget allocated for investment from 13.2 percent in 2001 to 24.4 percent in 2012. At the same time a series of development plans were aimed at removing obsolete equipment and the legacy military infrastructure of the Warsaw Pact. Participation in the ISAF mission also contributed to a greater emphasis on improving the quality of military personnel. All of the Visegrad Four countries either began the process of phasing out conscription or ended it completely in the decade plus of their ISAF participation.

Lieutenant Colonel Roman Nahoncik, former member of PRT Logar, observed an increase in professional skills at both the individual and unit level due to Czech participation in ISAF. He noted that the predeployment preparation and execution of the mission resulted in a growth in leadership ability and an improved capacity to cooperate multinationally.[41] With regard to the effectiveness of the Czechs' mission in Afghanistan, Nahoncik expressed concern that the infrastructure gains will not be sustained if the Afghans cannot maintain the facilities. The problem is compounded by the fact that the new structures were built according to European specifications and design with new technologies and materials uncommon to construction in Afghanistan.[42]

Hungary's Defense Minister, Csaba Hende, argued that the experience gained in ISAF has been vital to national defense. "This experience and knowledge cannot be gained in other places, only in operations during which our troops and military organizations accumulate experiences—even combat experiences—for which they would not have an opportunity in peacetime or in other places."[43] While Hungary's defense spending lagged behind the others, ISAF participation did drive the procurement process in that items needed to support the ISAF mission were prioritized.

Slovakia also sustained its armed forces overhaul while contributing to ISAF. It stayed on track with its Membership Action Plan (MAP) while increasing its participation in NATO missions and UN peacekeeping operations.[44] The deployment of the Slovak special forces unit described earlier broke the previous unwillingness of the Slovak government to deploy combat forces to Afghanistan. Indeed, the motivation to shift from purely support troops to a mix of support and combat troops came from the Slovak General Staff. The thinking was that the deployments of the combat engineering units were not having an effect on the overall transformation of the armed forces. The involvement of combat forces, however, would potentially have a more comprehensive transformative effect.[45]

CONCLUSION

The Visegrad Four's participation in ISAF, first and foremost, was rooted in the perception that it was NATO's key military operation. Consequently, their reputations as solid NATO "security providers" depended on a credible presence in Afghanistan. All four CEE states achieved their goal of being regarded as a "net security contributor" because of their efforts in the ISAF mission. In the case of Hungary, the interest of compensating for its past reputation of exploiting the benefits without adequately sharing the burdens of alliance membership was a prominent factor. Perhaps most importantly for all, NATO carried out the ISAF mission and remains intact to carry on its newfound global character. Who would have imagined in 2002 that NATO would sustain a mission twice the length of WWII, incur a large number of casualties doing so across many partner nations, and keep the coalition together in such a "horrible place"?[46] The CEE states have emerged from their ISAF missions with solid institutional reputations, armed forces conditioned to the demands of multinational operations according to NATO standards, and security strategies firmly focused on the centrality of NATO to the continued attainment of their national interests.

NOTES

1. "ISAF Mandate and PRT Mission," PRT Logar, http://www.prt-logar.cz.

2. US Central Command, "Foreign Operations in the USCENTCOM Area of Responsibility: Czech Republic," http://centcom.ahp.us.army.mil/czech-republic/.

3. Peter Ford, "New Europe's Iraq Squeeze," *Christian Science Monitor*, March 11, 2003, http://www.csmonitor.com/2003/0311/p01s04-woiq.html.

4. Nik Hynek and Peter Marton, "Introduction: What Makes Coalitions Stick?," in *Statebuilding in Afghanistan* (London: Routledge, 2012), 5.

5. Interview with Jan Eichler, analyst from the Institute of International Relations (IIR), Prague, July 2010.

6. Interview with officials in the Strategy and Analysis Office, Ministry of Foreign Affairs, Prague, July 2009.

7. Ibid.

8. Hynek and Marton, "Introduction: What Makes Coalitions Stick?," 196–197.

9. "International Security Assistance Force: Troop Numbers and Contributions," http://www.isaf.nato.int/troop-numbers-and-contributions/index.php.

10. "Poland: Executive Summary," Jane's Sentinel Security Assessment—Central Europe and the Baltic States, July 17, 2012, and September 19, 2014, https://janes.ihs .com.ezproxy.usawcpubs.org/CustomPages/Janes/DisplayPage.aspx?DocType=Refer ence&ItemId=+++1302825&Pubabbrev=CEUR. GDP data for all cases is from *Global Finance*, http://www.gfmag.com/gdp-data-country-reports.html#axzz2erhdnFIt. Dollar amounts are in US dollars unless otherwise stated.

11. "Poland: External Affairs," Jane's Sentinel Security Assessment—Central Europe and the Baltic States, July 16, 2012, https://janes.ihs.com/CustomPages/DisplayPage .aspx?DocType=Reference&ItemId.

12. Ibid.

13. "Ukraine Crisis: Europe's Leaders Respond to Russia," BBC News Europe, March 6, 2014, http://www.bbc.com/news/world-europe-26463753.

14. "Coalition Countries: Poland," US Central Command, http://www.centcom.mil/ coalition-countries.html.

15. "European Security and Transatlantic Relations," Visegrad.info, June 14, 2010, http://www.visegrad.info/european-security-transatlantic.

16. Lukasz Kulesa and Beata Gorka-Winter, "From Followers to Leaders as 'Coalition Servants,'" in *Statebuilding in Afghanistan* (London: Routledge, 2012), 212.

17. Hynek and Marton, "Introduction: What Makes Coalitions Stick?," 17.

18. US Central Command, http://www.centcom.mil/en/countries/coalition/.

19. Marek Kozubal, "Poland's Afghan Contingent Downsized by 700 Soldiers," *Rzeczpospolita*, October 27, 2012; BBC Monitoring Europe.

20. Fatality statistics for all cases come from http://icasualties.org/oef/index.aspx.

21. "International Security Assistance Force: Troop Numbers and Contributions," http://www.isaf.nato.int/troop-numbers-and-contributions/index.php.

22. US Central Command, "Foreign Operations in the USCENTCOM Area of Responsibility: Czech Republic," http://www.centcom.mil/en/about-centcom-en/coalition-countries-en/czech-republic-en.

23. Lt. Colonel Roman Nahoncik, *The Czech Provincial Reconstruction Team*, Strategy Research Project (Carlisle Barracks, PA: US Army War College, June 2013), 1.

24. PRT Logar, http://www.prt-logar.cz.

25. "Czech PRT Ends Afghanistan Mission," *Prague Daily Monitor, CTK*, February 1, 2013.

26. "International Security Assistance Force: Troop Numbers and Contributions," http://www.isaf.nato.int/troop-numbers-and-contributions/index.php.

27. Tamas Lajos Szalay, "Hungarian Army Chief Considers Downsizing Troops in International Missions," BBC Monitoring Europe, June 7, 2011.

28. Hynek and Marton, "Introduction: What Makes Coalitions Stick?," 198.

29. Szalay, "Hungarian Army Chief Considers Downsizing Troops."

30. Colonel Gabor Nagy and Lieutenant Colonel Endre Miszori, "Composition of the Liaison Team," US Central Command, http://centcom.ahp.us.army.mil/hungary/.

31. Hynek and Marton, "Introduction: What Makes Coalitions Stick?," 201.

32. "Farewell Ceremony of the Hungarian PRT team in Mazar-e Sharif," http://www.kormany.hu/en/hungary-in-afghanistan.

33. Ibid.

34. Andras Racz, "As Afghanistan Exit Looms, Let's Not Forget Hungary's Contribution," *Paprika Politik*, February 16, 2012, http://www.paprikapolitik.com/2012/02/as-afghanistan-exits-loom-let-s-not-forget-hungary-s-contribution/.

35. "Slovakia Spent €46.7 Million on Military Missions Abroad in 2012," *Slovak Spectator*, April 4, 2013, http://spectator.sme.sk/articles/view/49609/10/slovakia_spent_467_million_on_military_missions_abroad_in2012.html.

36. "International Security Assistance Force: Troop Numbers and Contributions," http://www.isaf.nato.int/troop-numbers-and-contributions/index.php.

37. Ibid.

38. "Slovakia: Security," Jane's Sentinel Security Assessment: Central Europe and the Baltic States, August 8, 2012, https://janes.ihs.com.

39. "Slovakia to Send More Troops to Afghanistan," *Slovak Spectator*, February 27, 2013, http://spectator.sme.sk/articles/view/49239/10/slovakia_to_send_more_troops_to_afghanistan.html.

40. "Afghan Soldier 'Kills NATO Colleague' at Kandahar Airport," BBC News Asia, July 9, 2013, http://www.bbc.co.uk/news/world-asia-23242444; Beata Balogova, "Afghan Suspect Escapes," *Slovak Spectator*, July 22, 2013, http://spectator.sme.sk/articles/view/50761/2/afghan_suspect_escapes.html.

41. Interview with Colonel Roman Nahoncik, Carlisle, PA, June 2013.

42. Nahoncik, *The Czech Provincial Reconstruction Team*, 17.

43. Tamas Lajos Szalay, "This Experience Cannot Be Gained in Other Places," BBC Monitoring Europe, February 11, 2013.

44. "Slovakia: External Affairs," Jane's Sentinel Security Assessment: Central Europe and the Baltic States, August 8, 2012; http://janes.ihs.com.

45. Interview with Colonel Peter Babiar, Slovak General Staff, Tartu, Estonia, September 12, 2013.

46. Interview with Dr. Karl-Heinz Kamp, Director, Research Division, NATO Defense College, Tartu, Estonia, September 10, 2013.

12 COUNTERINSURGENCY IN AFGHANISTAN

The UK, Dutch, German, and French Cases

John A. Nagl and Richard Weitz

THIS CHAPTER EXAMINES how European allies of the US applied counterinsurgency (COIN) methods in Afghanistan by examining the experiences of the UK, Germany, the Netherlands, and France. As one analyst notes, "Some European allies came to Afghanistan with the presumption that they were supposed to assure stabilization and reconstruction, while combat operations would remain a predominantly U.S.-led effort to which it would be possible to 'opt-in,' but they were quickly disabused of this perception by the reviving Taliban insurgency."[1] For several years after the North Atlantic Treaty Organization (NATO) assumed command of the International Security Assistance Force in Afghanistan (ISAF) in 2003, the UK struggled to relearn its forgotten COIN doctrine and strategy, while the Germans and French disputed how much NATO should engage in civilian reconstruction work. The Dutch kept a low-profile in this dispute while pursuing their own "Dutch approach" in their area of responsibility. Although the pressure of events often forced local commanders to adopt COIN tactics similar to those of their US colleagues, their political leaders resisted tactics that risked more military casualties by imposing various national caveats on how NATO could use their contingents and refused to provide sufficient funds or other resources to develop comprehensive national COIN capabilities even as NATO, under US leadership, was collectively developing its own COIN doctrine.

These divergences meant that ISAF was hobbled by an ad hoc patchwork of objectives without a clear consensus on a common strategy when confronted with the dual missions of nation-building and counterinsurgency. Many

NATO member states insisted that ISAF's primary mission was peacekeeping and nation-building, and not combat operations or conducting counterinsurgency. For Canada, the Netherlands, the UK, and the US, all operating in the hostile southern and eastern provinces of Afghanistan, combat was common and counterinsurgency the nominal strategy, even if it was not always properly resourced.[2] The many challenges Afghanistan posed to European military forces did eventually spur the development of national COIN capabilities and doctrines, but the failure of some European governments to provide adequate resources to their troops and accept the risks inherent in a combat environment like Afghanistan continued to stunt the full development of European COIN capabilities.

NATO'S COIN CHALLENGE

In Afghanistan, NATO has sought to apply a comprehensive approach that integrates its members' diplomatic, economic, intelligence, and military power to help the host government in Kabul provide vital services, reconstruct infrastructure, develop rural areas, and ensure population security while simultaneously defeating the insurgency. It has proven a difficult challenge, made harder by parallel chains of command among the US military and civilian commands, the NATO-led ISAF, and the Afghan government. Unity of command and purpose are critical in carrying out the comprehensive approach but are elusive when so many different groups, including governments and nongovernmental organizations (NGOs), are involved. Successful COIN depends on developing and adhering to a strategy that is not just comprehensive but also cohesive.

NATO has experienced a rough learning curve. As a collective entity, NATO had no experience before Afghanistan preparing for or waging a COIN campaign. Previous NATO combat missions in Bosnia-Herzegovina and Kosovo were initially conducted as conventional military operations that transitioned to peacekeeping missions dedicated to establishing a benign security environment in which other institutions could assume the lead role in promoting reconstruction. Many European countries' individual COIN experiences come from the post-WWII decolonization era when they struggled to maintain their overseas empires against nationalist uprisings, such as the British experience in the Malayan Emergency and the French in Algeria and Indochina. In these cases European powers usually enjoyed the support and resources of the indigenous regimes, security forces, and bureaucratic institutions they had built up over the years. Furthermore, they had considerable institutional knowledge of the culture, economy, history, and language of their colonies.[3] These colonial campaigns, while offering some tactical insights, have not been easily applicable to Afghanistan, where NATO has faced a sophisticated insurgency in a large country with a traditionally weak government. The alliance has had to contend with shortages of intelligence, lack of indigenous support, insufficient troop levels, and various political and legal restraints.[4]

NATO's fundamental structures have been ill-suited to this COIN mission. Building consensus among twenty-eight members with varying military strength, commitments elsewhere, and unique domestic political situations has been exceedingly difficult. The deployment of most European troops was qualified with national "caveats" limiting operations to certain types of missions or specific geographical areas. As a result, ISAF was divided along national lines, making specific countries responsible for particular Afghan provinces. Former NATO Secretary-General Jaap de Hoop Scheffer has acknowledged, "Multiple approaches to military operations and development assistance within one mission reduce effectiveness and can strain solidarity."[5]

THE BRITISH COUNTERINSURGENCY EXPERIENCE: LEARNING OVER TIME

In 2006, the British took over security responsibilities in Helmand province, which had been the heartland of the Taliban insurgency and a major opium production center, as part of ISAF's expansion into south Afghanistan. After an initial focus on combat operations, the British refocused the mission on supporting the local Afghan National Security Forces (ANSF) and countering narcotics trafficking.[6] The British applied a comprehensive COIN campaign initially based on the tactics they had successfully used in their Malayan ink-spot strategy. The rapid turnover in local commanders also saw some of the later ones applying COIN techniques developed by the US military. Every six months a new task force, consisting of an augmented brigade of little more than three thousand soldiers, rotated into the province.[7] After initially securing the capital of Lashkar Gah, where a British Provincial Reconstruction Team (PRT) was also stationed, the British forces then spread out and occupied small outposts throughout the province. Through this population-centered influence approach, the British sought to work with the Afghan government to expand local security, governance, and reconstruction efforts outward.[8]

The British campaign plan was audacious but underresourced, as Andrew Dorman notes in Chapter 8. The British effort was hampered by too few troops covering too much ground, shortages of helicopters and armored vehicles, and a more hostile environment than had been expected. Helmand province encompasses almost 23,000 square miles along the Pakistani border with more than 1.4 million people, many impoverished Pashtun Afghans living in villages along the Helmand River.[9] Helmand was a highway for the Taliban, foreign fighters, and arms and narcotics traffickers coming from Pakistan.[10] The area was heavily infiltrated by the Taliban, who terrorized the inhabitants. Until 2005, there had been no significant Afghan government or coalition presence in the province, while the local government barely functioned and was staffed by corrupt officials. The economy was largely agricultural and produced half of Afghanistan's opium, making it a hothouse for various insurgent and criminal groups. In addition to faulty intelligence that underestimated the Taliban threat, the British neglected to engage the local political and tribal structures that dominated the province. They placed too much faith in the weak and distant Afghan government and security forces to meet unrealistic commitments and to conduct counterinsurgency and reconstruction in a highly volatile environment.[11] Clearance operations succeeded in driving away major Taliban units, but soon after the British forces withdrew to their urban garrisons, the weak local government and security forces proved unable to prevent their return. One frustrated British commander said he felt like he was "mowing the lawn."[12]

The Taliban eventually surrounded the British units in Sangin, Musa Qala and Now Zad, forcing these garrisons to focus on defending the towns rather than expanding operations deep into rural areas.[13] The British forces inflicted heavy casualties on the insurgents in every battle, but the Taliban surprised British commanders by conducting sophisticated conventional attacks with battalion-sized units that over time killed dozens of British soldiers and wounded many more. Short on helicopters, armored vehicles, and enough troops to secure the area and push the insurgents out of population centers, the British relied heavily on bombing from the air and artillery, leading to high civilian casualties and declining popularity among local Afghans.[14] The British proved reluctant to eradicate the local poppy crop for fear of further alienating poor farmers dependent on the drug trade. British and Afghan government efforts to provide opportunities for alternative livelihood proved limited due to funding constraints as well as persistent security problems.[15] The reconstruction projects that were completed, including schools, government buildings, and roads, were often either located inside isolated "zones of development" or, if not, quickly became targets for the Taliban.[16] Their 2006 limited truce with the Taliban that led the British to withdraw from Musa Qala embarrassed London when the Taliban violated the agreement and reoccupied the town, requiring ISAF to attack the town in 2007.

Over time the British have adopted more effective COIN tactics, and their war effort benefitted from the ANSF's growing military capabilities. For example, they relied less on fixed garrisons by becoming more mobile and adopting a population-centric approach that relied on nonkinetic means of influence.[17] In this, they were recovering their early Malayan strategy of combining considerable coercion with a "hearts and minds" approach.[18] Nonetheless, it was not until the US military surge led to a major US-led military campaign in the south that the situation in Helmand finally stabilized.

GERMANY AND "NETWORKED SECURITY" IN AFGHANISTAN

Although Germany has been the third largest troop contributor to ISAF, Germans did not anticipate fighting a major insurgency and were politically challenged to accept the daily operational realities their forces faced on the ground. The expansion of the Taliban insurgency into the once-peaceful northern provinces where German troops operated sparked a decade-long debate over Germany's proper military role and tactics in Afghanistan, as well as its future role in NATO combat operations.[19] In October 2003, the German Bundestag approved the deployment of a contingent of troops and civilians to conduct peacekeeping and reconstruction work in the northern province of Kunduz and in late 2003 took over a PRT.[20] German politicians sold their presence in Afghanistan to a skeptical domestic audience as a noncombat operation that would provide support for a multinational stability and reconstruction operation resembling NATO's 1990s efforts in the Balkans. Few Germans expected their troops to engage in dangerous combat operations given the public consensus since WWII that the Bundeswehr existed solely for territorial defense. Although the Bundeswehr had expanded its mandate since 1994 and assumed an increasingly important role in multinational operations abroad, these have generally been in the areas of crisis management, conflict prevention, peacekeeping, or humanitarian, relief as Gale Mattox discusses in Chapter 7.[21]

In Afghanistan, the Bundeswehr employed the concept of "networked security," an all-encompassing multilateral approach to civilian-military reconstruction efforts, development projects, and indigenous security force training. Some aspects of networked security can be seen as integral parts of counterinsurgency, particularly interagency and civilian-military cooperation on reconstruction projects and security forces training. Networked security, however, lacks emphasis on the war fighting aspects of counterinsurgency, particularly at the operational and tactical levels.[22] Arguing that ISAF's mandate in Afghanistan was restricted to stability and reconstruction, German politicians and military commanders refused to allow their troops to be used in COIN, counternarcotics, or counterterrorism operations, which were seen as combat and therefore the responsibility of the US and coalition forces operating under separate OEF command. The German government placed extensive national caveats on their troops' use for combat and limited their deployment to the north and Kabul, areas with little Taliban activity.[23] Even there, the focus on force protection limited Germans' contribution to local security. The large fortified compound at Mazar-e Sharif that served as the Bundeswehr's headquarters sealed the Germans off from the local population. To limit casualties, the troops only patrolled initially in the daytime from inside armored vehicles, depriving them of interaction with locals and their intelligence. If under fire, the troops were required to disengage, leaving locals to fend for themselves.[24]

It was not until the May 2007 Operation Harekate Yolo campaign to stabilize the Badakshan, Badghis, and Faryab provinces by suppressing Taliban strongholds and criminal gangs in order to allow UN reconstruction work to resume in those areas that the Bundeswehr conducted its first large offensive since WWII. Although the Norwegians made up the bulk of the operation's combat force, the Germans provided leadership, planning, and logistical support.[25] It was an important first step in the Bundeswehr's reorienting its mission from simple force protection to counterinsurgency and population defense. Unfortunately, the initial tactical successes of Operation Harekate Yolo were not exploited and the second stage of the operation was cut short. Senior commanders had set ambitious goals to disperse the insurgents and provide security for civilian reconstruction work, but political and strategic support to continue the operation was not forthcoming. Political nervousness about the risks and poor coordination between the civilian and the military contingents eventually allowed the Taliban to return.[26]

The Bundeswehr was not properly structured or equipped for a sustained COIN campaign. The typical rotation for a German unit in Afghanistan lasted three to four months, which is not enough time for units to gain familiarity with their area or build lasting relationships with locals. According to Seth Jones, the Bundeswehr "lacked trained personnel, combat equipment, and supporting communications and intelligence gear necessary to perform offensive attacks, raids and reconnaissance patrols."[27] They also suffered from serious shortages of tactical airlift helicopters, mine-resistant vehicles, and combat multipliers such as artillery and attack helicopters. Even German units that were fully equipped were not effectively employed, in part due to restrictive caveats. In October 2008, the German foreign minister revealed that 100 commandos from the elite German Kommando Spezialkrafte (KSK) unit had been in Afghanistan for three years without being deployed for a single mission and hence were being withdrawn.[28]

On September 4, 2009, a German commander called in a US airstrike on two hijacked fuel trucks believed to be surrounded by Taliban insurgents outside Kunduz province. The airstrike killed approximately 142 people, primarily civilians. The German public was shocked that its forces were responsible for such an incident. Defense Minister Franz Josef Jung resigned over the controversy, and the event triggered investigations in the Bundeswehr and the German Parliament. The airstrike also raised questions over the expanded use of force by German troops.[29] ISAF had to redeploy 2,500 US troops to northern Afghanistan to stabilize the region's security situation and protect vital ISAF supply lines. The US deployment to the north was seen as a vote of no confidence in the capabilities of German forces to control the situation. Unlike German troops, the US forces integrated Afghans into joint combat operations against insurgents.[30]

THE DUTCH APPROACH: "REBUILD WHERE POSSIBLE, FIGHT WHERE NECESSARY"

Despite considerable opposition in the national legislature and among the Dutch public, the Netherlands decided in December 2005 to support NATO's expanding mission in Afghanistan by sending combat forces to the southern province of Uruzgan to provide security and to support the region's political and economic development. The Dutch government justified its participation in NATO's first out-of-Europe operation and the first combat deployment by the Royal Netherlands Army since the Korean War by citing alliance and transatlantic solidarity, as discussed by Rem Korteweg in Chapter 10.[31] The Dutch considered their eight-year troop deployment in the former Yugoslavia as primarily a peacekeeping mission; they read the failure of the Dutch troops to prevent the Srebrenica massacre in 1995 as a lesson on the need for a more robust protection of a threatened population.[32]

From the spring of 2006 until August 2010, the Netherlands deployed approximately 2,000 troops in Afghanistan. Some 1,400 of these Dutch soldiers, along with a smaller number of Australians, were in Uruzgan, a small mountainous province north of Helmand and Kandahar that had long had a strong Taliban presence with substantial opium production. The Dutch order of battle included Task Force Uruzgan (TFU), a battalion-sized battle group of airmobile and mechanized infantry, and a battalion-sized PRT in the provincial capital of Tarin Kowt. These formations were accompanied by various fire support units, headquarters staff, medical personnel, and several aircraft crews.[33]

The Dutch employed what they called a 3D strategy of "defense, development, and diplomacy," though in practice their forces emphasized reconstruction over security and governance. The Dutch stressed support for Afghan-led economic initiatives through engaging community leaders in developing and implementing local projects. The defense dimension focused on protecting population centers in a modified version of the British "ink-blot" COIN strategy rather than aggressively seeking out fights with the Taliban. Dutch forces were generally reluctant to engage in combat operations against the Taliban and instead operated under rules of engagement that typically required them to use force only if attacked and to maneuver out of enemy fire instead of staying in contact. They did not regularly patrol into Taliban-controlled territory but focused on building relationships with the local population, which provided useful intelligence and some degree of force protection.[34] The Dutch approach was to limit force protection measures and allow their soldiers to patrol on foot and in open vehicles with a minimum brandishing of weapons.[35] The Dutch also managed to keep civilian deaths and physical destruction relatively low and established a compensation system for local property damaged by combat or otherwise.[36] The motto of TFU was "Rebuild Where Possible, Fight Where Necessary," which demonstrated the primacy of reconstruction in the Dutch strategy and highlighted a reluctance to use force.[37]

The Dutch enjoyed some degree of success. The number of NGOs in Uruzgan province increased from six to fifty during the years of the Dutch deployment.[38] According to the Dutch Foreign Ministry, while Uruzgan province had no Afghan police officers in 2006, it had 1,600 by summer of 2010. In addition, the number of schools in the province doubled and local health services improved considerably.[39] Unlike in Helmand province, the Taliban in Uruzgan appeared unwilling or unable to challenge the Dutch directly for control of urban areas. Despite these successes, critics complained that the Dutch troops spent excessive time in secured areas working on reconstruction projects rather than fighting insurgents. Furthermore, the Dutch approach, while minimizing casualties, failed to contest the Taliban's control over most rural areas or over the narcotics trade, which remained robust despite the development projects generated by the Dutch soldiers and the NGO community.[40] The Dutch strategy was politically motivated to avoid fighting in order to appease the casualty-averse Dutch public, though the Netherlands was hardly unique in this regard.

The Dutch troops were originally scheduled to leave by the end of 2008, but in November 2007 the new Dutch coalition government, elected the previous year, extended their Uruzgan deployment until August 2010, when the attempt to secure another extension failed. One factor strengthening the Dutch desire to withdraw was popular resentment of other NATO member state governments that refused to rotate their forces into more dangerous southern Afghanistan, which would have allowed Dutch troops to relocate to more secure regions. On August 1, 2010, the Netherlands was the first NATO country to remove all its combat forces from Afghanistan.

THE FRENCH APPROACH: EMBRACING COIN AND NATO

France contributed the fourth largest number of troops to ISAF, with some 1,400 troops in Kabul and, after 2008, approximately 1,200 soldiers in the small northeast province of Kapisa. Several hundred additional French troops deployed to Kandahar Airbase in southern Afghanistan, where they supported several French combat aircraft.[41] Despite having a long history fighting insurgencies in Indochina and Algeria, France did not fully embrace counterinsurgency as its strategy in Afghanistan.[42] For many years, the French saw their role in ISAF as engaging in limited combat operations but mostly as training the Afghanistan National Police (ANP) and the Afghanistan National Army (ANA). French troops served under national caveats that barred them from combat in the southern provinces; the strict rules of engagement minimized risk and casualties.[43] In practice, some French units adopted elements of a COIN campaign while avoiding overt military-sponsored nation-building.

The situation changed after Colonel Francis Chanson assumed command in Kapisa province in June 2009. He implemented a strategy to deter Taliban attacks by seeking to "protect, seduce, and convince" the population.[44] This new approach provided help to build local government capacity and encouraged NGO-led economic development. Later that year, some other French commanders followed suit. In addition to training ANF units, French forces began to construct combat outposts within populated areas while employing political officers to partner with local leaders.[45] Under President Nicolas Sarkozy, France's troop deployments gradually increased and French soldiers took on a larger role in conducting joint operations alongside ANSF personnel in Kabul and Kapisa provinces. The joint US-French operations in eastern Afghanistan won praise from US commanders.

French officials sought to keep NATO focused on military operations in Afghanistan and to have ISAF, the UN, and the EU assume the lead role on diplomatic and reconstruction efforts, which worked against the integrated COIN strategy that the US favored.[46] When the new socialist government led by President François Hollande took office in May 2012, it fulfilled a campaign pledge to end French combat operations in Afghanistan several years ahead of most other major NATO allies. (See Chapter 9.) The Hollande government also cut back on defense spending and did not support proposals to build greater counterinsurgency capabilities within the French armed forces.

COIN IN COMPARATIVE PERSPECTIVE

The British have placed great emphasis on learning lessons from their COIN campaign in southern Afghanistan that augment the lessons of previous COIN campaigns. British Army Colonel Alex Alderson, who later led the newly established British Army Counterinsurgency Centre, summed up the strategic lessons as "Presence matters, numbers are required, and plans need resources. Without them, in counterinsurgency, securing the population is an unachievable aspiration."[47] Two important innovations were the Non-Kinetic Effects Teams (NKETs) that helped develop, deliver, and evaluate nonkinetic effects and influence operations and the new Tactical Conflict Assessment Framework (TCAF), which used multiple and iterative questionnaires to identity local sources of instability.[48] But in the end, the British proved unable to compensate for shortages in military personnel and other kinetic capabilities.

Modern Germany has never fought a COIN war on a distant battlefield. Germany had no institutional experience with counterinsurgency on which to formulate its approach, and the Bundeswehr has no comprehensive COIN doctrine. German field commanders came to realize the need to relax force protection requirements and accept a greater risk of their own casualties in order to achieve the greater operational flexibility demanded in counterinsurgency, but this understanding was not mirrored at home. The 2009 Kunduz airstrike that killed 142 Afghans revealed a credibility gap. German officials had long insisted that they were participating in a stabilization operation, not COIN, in Afghanistan. The government responded to the outcry by raising the Bundeswehr's force protection requirements, thereby reversing the process of ground-up reforms that were developing a German COIN capability.[49] The Germans have since begun undertaking COIN training at the officer level, but the German public remains highly averse to this form of warfare.

Unlike the Germans and other Europeans who perceived the core of ISAF's mission to be stabilization and reconstruction, the French rejected the PRT model and military participation in reconstruction efforts, which they believe are best carried out by civilian institutions. French officials also rejected US efforts aimed at using NATO and ISAF to promote Afghan democratization and nation-building. They believe these goals were not authorized under ISAF's mission and best pursued by the European Union, the United Nations, or other bodies.[50] Although French field commanders moved away from this position and French troops started to achieve good results with a COIN strategy, the French government failed to resource a robust COIN capability beyond that required for France's fleeting military operations in Africa. The French are suffering from the same capability shortages as other NATO governments—a problem likely to deepen in coming years.

NOTES

1. Henrik B. L. Larsen, *NATO in Afghanistan: Democratization Warfare, National Narratives, and Budgetary Austerity* (Cambridge, UK: Belfer Center for Science and International Affairs, December 2013), 6.

2. Christopher J. Lamb and Martin Cinnamond, "Unity of Effort: Key to Success in Afghanistan," *Strategic Forum*, no. 248 (October 2009): 3, http://www.ndu.edu/inss/docUploaded/SF248_Lamb.pdf.

3. Warren Chin, "British Counter-Insurgency in Afghanistan," *Defense and Security Analysis* 23, no. 2 (June 2007): 202; John A. Nagl, *Learning to Eat Soup with a Knife: Counterinsurgency Lessons from Malaya and Vietnam* (Chicago: University of Chicago Press, 2005).

4. Seth G. Jones, *In the Graveyard of Empires: America's War in Afghanistan* (New York: Norton, 2009), 301.

5. Christopher M. Schnaubelt, "The Counterinsurgency Challenge for NATO," in *Counterinsurgency: The Challenge for NATO Strategy and Operations*, ed. Christopher Schnaubelt (Rome: NATO Defense College, 2009), 8.

6. Jeffrey Dressler, "Securing Helmand: Understanding and Responding to the Enemy," *Afghanistan Report*, no. 2 (September 28, 2009): 33, http://www.understanding war.org/report/securing-helmand-understanding-and-responding-enemy.

7. Theo Farrell, "Improving in War: Military Adaptation and the British in Helmand Province, Afghanistan, 2006–2009," *Journal of Strategic Studies* 33, no. 4 (2010): 584–585.

8. Ibid., 575–576.

9. "Helmand," Naval Postgraduate School Program for Culture and Conflict Studies, February 12, 2009, http://www.nps.edu/programs/CCS/Docs/Executive Summaries/Helmand_Executive_Summary.pdf.

10. "Regional Command South," Institute for the Study of War, http://www.under standingwar.org/region/regional-command-south-0.

11. Theo Farrell and Stuart Gordon, "COIN Machine: The British Military in Afghanistan," *RUSI Journal* 154, no. 3 (June 2009): 20–21.

12. Farrell, "Improving in War," 578.

13. Ahmed Rashid, *Descent into Chaos: The United States and the Failure of Nation Building in Pakistan, Afghanistan, and Central Asia* (New York City: Viking, 2008), 360.

14. Farrell, "Improving in War," 575–576.

15. Farrell and Gordon, "COIN Machine," 2.

16. Dressler, "Securing Helmand," 34.

17. Farrell, "Improving in War," 589–590.

18. Paul Dixon, "'Hearts and Minds'? British Counter-Insurgency from Malaya to Iraq," *Journal of Strategic Studies* 32, no. 3 (2009): 355.

19. Timo Noetzel and Benjamin Schreer, "Counter-What? Germany and Counter-Insurgency in Afghanistan," *RUSI Journal* 153, no. 1 (February 2008): 42–46.

20. Timo Noetzel and Martin Zapfe, "NATO and Counterinsurgency: The Case of Germany," in *Counterinsurgency: The Challenge for NATO Strategy and Operations*, ed. Christopher M. Schnaubelt (Rome: NATO Defense College, 2009), 131.

21. Timo Noetzel and Benjamin Schreer, "Missing Links: The Evolution of German Counter-Insurgency Thinking," *RUSI Journal* 154, no. 1 (February 2009): 16–21.

22. Ibid., 18.

23. Noetzel and Zapfe, "NATO and Counterinsurgency," 132.

24. Rashid, *Descent into Chaos*, 354.

25. Timo Noetzel and Benjamin Schreer, *The German Army and Counterinsurgency in Afghanistan: The Need for Strategy* (Berlin: German Institute for International and Security Affairs, 2008), 3.

26. Noetzel and Zapfe, "NATO and Counterinsurgency," 146–147.

27. Jones, *In the Graveyard of Empires*, 251.

28. Jerome Starkey, "They Came, They Saw, Then Left the Afghan War Without a Single Mission," *The Scotsman*, October 9, 2008, http://news.scotsman.com/world/They-came-they-saw-.4573584.jp.

29. Holger Stark, "German Colonel Wanted to 'Destroy' Insurgents," *Der Spiegel*, December 29, 2009, http://www.spiegel.de/international/germany/0,1518,669444,00 .html.

30. Matthias Gebauer, "US to Send 2,500 Soldiers to German-Controlled Area," *Der Spiegel*, January 4, 2010, http://www.spiegel.de/international/world/0,1518,670085,00 .html.

31. Vincent Morelli and Paul Belkin, "NATO in Afghanistan: A Test of the Transatlantic Alliance," Congressional Research Service, RL33627, December 3, 2009, 24, http://www.fas.org/sgp/crs/row/RL33627.pdf.

32. Thijs Brocades Zaalberg and Arthur ten Cate, "A Gentle Occupation: Unravelling the Dutch Approach in Iraq, 2003–2005," *Small Wars and Insurgencies* 23, no. 1 (2012): 118.

33. "Coalition Countries—Netherlands," US Central Command, http://www.cent com.mil/en/netherlands/.

34. C. J. Chivers, "Dutch Soldiers Stress Restraint in Afghanistan," *New York Times*, April 6, 2007, http://www.nytimes.com/2007/04/06/world/asia/06afghan.html? pagewanted=1&_r=3.

35. Zaalberg and ten Cate, "A Gentle Occupation," 117.

36. C. J. Chivers, "An Ambush in the Taliban Heartland," *New York Times*, April 10, 2007, http://www.nytimes.com/2007/04/10/world/asia/10afghan.html?pagewanted=2.

37. "Coalition Countries—Netherlands."

38. "Netherlands Begins Afghan Troop Withdrawal," UPI.com, August 1, 2010, http://www.upi.com/Top_News/US/2010/08/01/Netherlands-begins-Afghan-troop -withdrawal/UPI-74941280670601/.

39. "Dutch Troops Begin to Withdraw from Afghanistan," *Earth Times*, August 1, 2010, http://www.earthtimes.org/articles/news/337478,dutch-troops-withdraw-afghani stan.html.

40. "Regional Command South—Uruzgan," Institute for the Study of War, http:// www.understandingwar.org/region/regional-command-south-0#Uruzgan.

41. Morelli and Belkin, "NATO in Afghanistan," 28; "Troop Contributing Nations— France," ISAF, http://www.isaf.nato.int/en/troop-contributing-nations/france/index .php.

42. Etienne de Durand, "France," in *Understanding Counterinsurgency: Doctrine, Operations, Challenges*, ed. Thomas Rid and Thomas A. Keaney (London: Routledge, 2010); Minister of Defence, "Doctrine for Counterinsurgency at the Tactical Level" Forces Employment Doctrine Center, April 2010, http://smallwarsjournal.com/docu ments/frenchcoindoctrine.pdf.

43. Morelli and Belkin, "NATO in Afghanistan," 28.

44. Stéphane Taillat, "National Traditions and International Context: French Adaptation to Counterinsurgency in the 21st Century," *Security Challenges* 6, no. 1 (Autumn 2010): 93, http://www.securitychallenges.org.au/ArticlePDFs/vol6no1Taillat.pdf.

45. Taillat, "National Traditions and International Context," 94–95.

46. Larsen, *NATO in Afghanistan*, 42.

47. Alex Alderson, "Britain," in *Understanding Counterinsurgency: Doctrine, Operations, Challenges*, ed. Thomas Rid and Thomas A. Keaney (London: Routledge, 2010): 40.

48. Farrell, "Improving in War," 579–580.

49. Noetzel and Zapfe, "NATO and Counterinsurgency," 151.

50. Morelli and Belkin, "NATO in Afghanistan," 29.

13 NORTH ATLANTIC TREATY ORGANIZATION
Transformation Under Fire

Jack J. Porter

THE ONGOING CONFLICT in Afghanistan remains the preeminent challenge for the North Atlantic Treaty Organization (NATO). Depending on the source, the stakes associated with the outcome are potentially monumental not only for the citizens of Afghanistan and the prospects of broader regional stability but even the very credibility and possibly the survival of the alliance itself. This chapter will examine NATO's decade-plus involvement in the war. Particular attention will be placed on key strategic and tactical adjustments made by leaders in Brussels as well as lingering problems and persistent complications in managing stabilization, combat, and transition operations. Before turning to the analysis, a number of clarifications are warranted. With the US so actively engaged in Afghanistan since September 11, 2001, and understandably so committed to a successful outcome, it is important (and often difficult) to disentangle US decisions and actions from those of the alliance. Although US and NATO policy share many characteristics, this chapter will focus on the collective perspective of the alliance.

NATO AND SEPTEMBER 11, 2001

Article 5 (Collective Defense) of the North Atlantic Treaty was invoked for the first time by the alliance after the terrorist attacks on the US on September 11, 2001. As stated in the 1949 treaty, Article 5 pledges that "an armed attack on one or more of them [official member states of the North Atlantic Treaty Organization] in Europe or North America shall be considered an attack against them all and consequently they agree that, if such an armed attack occurs, each of them ... will assist the party or parties so attacked."[1] On September 12, 2011, alliance members responded to the attack with anticipated enthusiasm and solidarity, declaring that the alliance was "ready to provide the assistance that may be required as a consequence of these acts of barbarism."[2] Although the Bush administration was initially reluctant to take up the offer and directly involve Brussels, the basis for subsequent collective action was established.

Initially, NATO's contribution was somewhat limited as the US preferred to organize Operation Enduring Freedom (OEF) more on the basis of an American-led "coalition of the willing" rather than as a truly NATO multinational operation like the 1999 Kosovo campaign Operation Allied Force.[3] In practical terms, NATO's direct involvement in Afghanistan began in December 2001 with its authority outlined in United Nations Security Council Resolution (UNSCR) 1386, which called for the establishment of an "international security assistance force" to provide security for the new Afghan Interim Authority (AIA) basically in and around Kabul. The resulting entity, the International Security Assistance Force (ISAF), was led by individual NATO members on a rotating six-month basis. For the next two years, ISAF filled a predominantly secondary role to the US-led Special Operations Forces combat operations in eastern and southern Afghanistan. In 2002, 4,500 ISAF soldiers guarded the Kabul area in support of the newly installed Afghan Transition Authority. According to one analyst, the limited number of troops by both the US and ISAF reflected a conscious decision to avoid a "heavy footprint" and accompanying perceptions of foreign occupation that had characterized the Soviet experience of the 1980s.[4] During this time, US Special Forces and Afghan militias hunted down members of the Taliban and al Qaeda.

NATO's presence and operations in Afghanistan remained relatively limited in 2002–2004. Initial plans to rebuild the Afghan security forces and address other areas of state-building were based on the "lead nation" concept. At a conference held in early December 2002 at the Petersberg Hotel in Bonn, Germany, Afghanistan and donor nations agreed to a five-pillar plan. The UK would take charge of counternarcotics efforts; Germany would assist in the reorganization and retraining of the Afghan National Police (ANP); Italy would concentrate on judicial reform; Japan would lead efforts at disarming, demobilizing, and reintegrating Afghan militias; and the US was responsible for the rebuilding of the Afghan National Army (ANA). The original plan called for an Afghan army numbering seventy thousand soldiers, but the size of the ANA would be a recurring topic of discussion as the conflict progressed.

Washington's decision to adopt a light footprint in Afghanistan provided Brussels with the rationale for a restrained role in operations during the first two years of the conflict. Most NATO members had little capacity to conduct sustained combat operations against Taliban and al Qaeda members. The end of the Cold War, changing demographics, and the transition from a conscripted army to an all-volunteer force put considerable pressures on the armed forces of many European countries. NATO's focus on peace operations and political efforts extending NATO membership to other European nations distracted Brussels from transforming NATO's actual capabilities. This led to a transatlantic "transformation gap" that limited European NATO members' combat capabilities.[5] Although "the September 2001 terrorist attacks in the United States jolted the Atlantic Alliance into action," it would clearly take considerable time and resources to correct this imbalance.[6] Recognizing the importance of improving NATO's capability to respond to an increasingly diverse set of security threats and challenges, the alliance made transformation its priority at the November 2002 Prague summit. It established a new Allied Command Transformation and a new NATO Reaction Force, which improved expeditionary capabilities and better alliance responses to terrorism and missile attacks. Despite these efforts, the transatlantic gap continued to impede the alliance's performance throughout the next decade. These weaknesses and differences in military capabilities would become increasingly evident as NATO assumed full operational command of ISAF and assumed countrywide combat responsibilities in August 2003.

NATO AND ISAF, 2003–2006

NATO formally assumed command responsibilities for ISAF on August 11, 2003, and immediately began to explore the possibility of expanding its mission beyond Kabul. The UN Security Council provided the necessary authorization on October 13, 2003, in UNSCR 1510, which allowed ISAF to operate beyond Kabul to maintain security for those engaged in reconstruction and humanitarian efforts. While the new mandate suggested a more extensive role for NATO, its activities remained limited to stabilization operations. Germany's subsequent decision to assume responsibility of a US Provincial Reconstruction Team (PRT) in December 2003 coupled with a new set of "concepts of operations" outlined by NATO military authorities in early 2004 established the strategic blueprint for ISAF.[7]

In practical terms, ISAF's plan centered on the PRT concept (which was first implemented in Afghanistan in 2002 by the US) which offered a way for NATO members to increase their contributions yet avoid any real commitment to combat. Each PRT has a lead nation and is composed of a diverse mix of civilian and military personnel and in some cases, representatives from humanitarian NGOs. There is no standard organizational blueprint for a PRT, and its exact makeup depends considerably on the perspectives and resources of the lead nation. One early evaluation points out that in addition to the lack of overarching common strategy, common metrics of success, or common organizational structure, "(t)he importance of personalities, donor countries' political caveats, and imbalances in program funding have also negatively affected PRT performance."[8] While many efforts would be made over the years to address some of these shortcomings, NATO/ISAF's increased involvement in Afghanistan was manifested through the intermittent and often haphazard expansion of NATO member and US-led PRTs.

As violence and insurgent activity began to increase significantly in 2003, most NATO members were still reluctant to conduct activities in the more problematic areas of the country. Instead, many NATO countries deployed their troops to the much more stable areas of the north and west. At the time, Afghanistan was divided into five regional commands (RC): RC–Capital in Kabul; RC–North, headquartered in Mazar-e Sharif; RC–West, headquartered in Herat; RC–South, headquartered in Kandahar; and RC–East, headquartered in Bagram. Between December 2003 and February 2006, NATO established twenty-six PRTs throughout the country.

As NATO's responsibilities and missions expanded, the alliance augmented its command structure to improve intra-alliance military coordination. As noted, Washington's initial preference for a "coalition of the willing" as opposed to a genuinely multilateral/NATO approach meant that Operation Enduring Freedom–Afghanistan (OEF-A) forces and ISAF forces would operate under different commands.[9] When NATO assumed command of ISAF in August 2003 it began coordinating the mission through the Allied Joint Forces Command (JFC) based in Brunssum, the Netherlands. ISAF Joint Command Headquarters (located in Kabul) is responsible for all operations in Afghanistan and oversees a number of subordinate commands, including the various regional commands and NATO Training Mission–Afghanistan (NTM-A). Up until February 2007, ISAF was under the command of non-American generals from the

UK, Turkey, Germany, Canada, and Italy. The "Americanization" of ISAF in late 2006 and the 2009 "surge" of US troops into the theater meant that all subsequent ISAF commanders would be four-star US generals.[10]

NATO/ISAF: STATE- AND NATION-BUILDING, 2006–2008

As NATO assumed full operational control of ISAF by the end of 2006, it focused yet again on defining its strategy. The increase in insurgent activity forced previously reluctant nations to undertake combat operations. ISAF fatalities tripled from 60 in 2004 to 191 in 2006 as insurgents began to engage coalition forces with improvised explosive devices.[11] NATO's authority to undertake these increasingly dangerous activities was addressed in 2007 with UNSCR 1776 and in 2008 with UNSCR 1833, which identified the threats to the security situation in Afghanistan posed by "the Taliban, Al-Qaida, illegally armed groups and those involved in the narcotics trade" and "stressed" the need to address these threats. Obtaining the UN authority to act was a relatively easy matter. Overcoming the vast differences in combat capabilities and political will among alliance members was a much more formidable challenge.

Many governments were adamant that their soldiers could only be deployed to the relatively safe and secure areas to the north and west. The exceptions to this general pattern were the UK, Canada, the Netherlands, and Denmark. Politically, NATO officials made every effort to convey alliance solidarity and a unified vision for Afghanistan as well as address concerns surrounding NATO capabilities. For example, in November 2006 the alliance adopted the Comprehensive Political Guidance (CPG) with the goal of improving NATO military capabilities in terms of both reducing disparities between members and improving interoperability of their armed forces. In addition to reiterating the importance of Article 5 (Collective Defense), the CPG identified a broader range of security threats, such as global terrorism, the spread of weapons of mass destruction (WMDs), and instability due to failed and failing states. The CPG stressed the need for NATO members to commit adequate resources to conduct non–Article 5 crisis response missions, stabilization operations, and low-intensity conflicts. In practical terms, the CPG called on all members to continue transforming their military forces so that each could address unanticipated contingencies such as multinational expeditionary operations "far from home" with little or no host country support for extended periods of time.

With relevance to the war, Brussels had also been active in adjusting its strategy toward Afghanistan, and at the Riga November 2006 summit it had adopted a "comprehensive approach" (CA) to its overall mission. On the surface, NATO's comprehensive approach seemed to be well suited for subsequent COIN operations. Among other things, the aforementioned CPG called on NATO to prepare capabilities for a range of combat scenarios, including high-intensity conflict and counterterrorism, as well as the ability to engage in crisis response, stabilization, and reconstruction efforts.[12] Perhaps most significantly, the CPG specifically acknowledged that "peace, security, and development are more interconnected than ever." Thus, at the strategic level Brussels apparently understood that success in Afghanistan would require sustained and coordinated combat/kinetic operations in combination with reconstruction and development projects. The alliance's and more importantly the member states' actual capacity, in terms of both political will and institutional competence, to execute this overall CA would prove elusive for all but a few.

At the April 2008 Bucharest summit, NATO leaders issued an ISAF "Strategic Vision." The ISAF Strategic Vision referred to Afghanistan as the alliance's key priority and reaffirmed its "determination to help the people and the elected Government of Afghanistan build an enduring stable, secure, prosperous and democratic state, respectful of human rights and free from the threat of terrorism."[13] Four broad sets of objectives were identified: a long-term commitment by NATO in terms of troops, tools, and other necessary resources; construction of capable Afghan security forces and political/military leadership; coordination between Afghan and international actors in pursuit of both development and security (with PRTs remaining an essential component); and concerted and sustained diplomatic efforts to promote regional security and constructive relations with neighbors.[14] By April 2008, NATO had clearly assumed a leadership role in Afghanistan with a comprehensive strategy designed to promote good governance, security, and economic development. Unfortunately, despite committing considerable energy and resources to developing Afghanistan's political institutions and economic development, the security environment would continue to deteriorate.

NATO/ISAF AND COIN, 2008–2009

By 2006, NATO/ISAF had extended its footprint into all five Regional Commands. In doing so, Brussels signaled an increased willingness to commit necessary political capital and material resources to the monumental goal of reconstructing Afghan political, security, and economic institutions. However, while the alliance had demonstrated political and strategic flexibility in its adaptations since its involvement in the country, the growing violence and concomitant demands on the allies in terms of resources and operations would represent the most significant test for NATO to date. Unfortunately, the performance of member state armed forces and subsequent results would be mixed at best.

In 2008 NATO/ISAF undertook its most serious military challenge since the beginning of the war—COIN operations against an insurgency made up of a heterogeneous mix of increasingly hostile and opportunistic actors. The growing insurgency coupled with 2008 election year dynamics in the US contributed to a renewed focus on Afghanistan and NATO/ISAF capacity to restore stability, maintain security, and ultimately help the Afghan government rebuild the country. It became increasingly apparent that progress toward this goal was foundering in large part because of the rising levels of insurgent activity and the coalition's inability to address three key issues. First, NATO members lacked the training, equipment, or will to conduct combat operations to secure local areas. Without an existential threat like the Soviet Union, military budgets, training, and political will all suffered; limiting allies' ability to effectively engage in combat missions. Second, ISAF failed to effectively coordinate its activities under the "unity of effort" principle. Not only did NATO forces have difficulty coordinating operations with one another, efforts to synchronize operations and objectives with a host of civilian agencies and international organizations and NGOs were a formidable (and often insurmountable) obstacle. Third, NATO did not commit adequate resources such as trainers, supplies, and money to adequately train and advise Afghan security forces. Despite repeated public pledges, this low-visibility but essential component of successful counterinsurgency (COIN) operations remained hostage to the same budgetary constraints and political ambivalence as other aspects of the war. While each of these areas will be briefly addressed in the following discussion of the implementation of NATO/ISAF COIN operations from 2008 to present, they also constitute an important aspect of the alliance's chronic struggle with burden-sharing.

The most significant obstacle to NATO/ISAF's ability to execute COIN operations in Afghanistan was the numerous national caveats that each ally imposed on its forces and their potential use.[15] The reluctance of some nations to permit their troops to conduct combat operations was evident in the earlier expansion of NATO/ISAF outside Kabul. Germany, Spain, and Italy, for example, initially preferred to station their forces in the more secure northern and western provinces. In addition to public opinion, this hesitancy was also a function of limits in military training and equipment, as indicated earlier with reference to gaps in "transformation." Many NATO members had significantly reduced their defense budgets during the 1990s as they struggled to redefine their military strategy away from the Cold War conventional-style combat scenarios to the post–Cold War strategic environment, which until the September 2001 terrorist attacks was associated with peacekeeping and stabilization operations. Absent a well-defined, existential threat, allies differed in their progress toward restructuring their armed forces and concomitant willingness to undertake a range of combat operations. NATO officials in Brussels adopted a new Strategic Concept in April 1999 that attempted to provide unified guidance on future missions and necessary capabilities and force structures. However, the 1999 Strategic Concept did not go much beyond the extremely broad commitment that "Allies' military forces have a credible ability to fulfill the full range of Alliance missions." For practical purposes, there was a wide gap in how allies approached this obligation. By late 2010 conditions in Afghanistan suggested that "(f)or the Europeans, Afghanistan reveals the gaps within NATO between those that are truly committed to transforming and employing their forces for current operations, and those that are not."[16]

Coordination of various missions and activities was a second profound challenge for the alliance's ability to engage in COIN operations after 2008. ISAF's complex structure and heterogeneous mix of governmental and nongovernmental actors in Afghanistan all but guaranteed that the alliance would have difficulty synchronizing military, economic, and political efforts. In terms of command, efforts were initially frustrated by the separation of NATO-led ISAF troops from US-led OEF forces, but these problems were largely resolved by February 2007 when US Army General Dan McNeill became the first American general to command ISAF. However, since NATO's Joint Force Command HQ Brunssum was still formally in charge of ISAF, problems persisted. Characteristic of other multilateral military operations, "(t)he drivers of this process were not efficiency and simplicity but Alliance diplomacy."[17]

Similar obstacles in multinational coordination were also evident at the operational and tactical level. PRTs, for example, often reported directly to their respective governments rather than through the ISAF chain of command. This command arrangement is not surprising since the PRT's sponsoring government usually dictated how the PRT was organized and where it would operate, and often approved the funding for civic and humanitarian projects.[18]

The third element in successful COIN operations hinges on developing effective and relatively legitimate security forces, broadly defined. In addition to the armed forces, counterinsurgents must assist the host nation as they restructure and retrain the police, border guards, and other institutions necessary for restoring and maintaining security. NATO and other actors appreciated the significance of this task almost from the establishment of the ISAF mission. In April 2002, the US assumed responsibility for creating the Afghan National Army (ANA), and Germany took the lead in creating the new Afghan National Police (ANP). By 2006, both efforts had largely failed because of a lack of strategic vision, competent trainers, and adequate weapons and equipment.[19] NATO, with the assistance of the European Union, redoubled its efforts to the development of effective Afghan security forces by establishing two new organizations focused on training the ANA and ANP. The Combined Security Transition Command–Afghanistan (CSTC-A) was created to train the ANA, and the European Police Mission (EUPOL) was formed to expand the fledgling ANP into an effective and legitimate institution.

Before turning to the next (post-2008) phase of NATO's involvement in the Afghan campaign, it is important to note efforts by Brussels to coordinate its activities with those of the United Nations. Originally created through UN Security Council Resolution 1401 in March 2002, the United Nations Assistance Mission in Afghanistan (UNAMA) was given a mandate to coordinate all UN activities in the country. When the US took command of ISAF in early 2007 and NATO found itself increasingly involved in COIN operations, leaders in Washington, D.C., and Brussels sought to better synchronize the activities of the two organizations.[20] In 2008, the UN Security Council passed Resolution 1806, which not only extended the mandate of UNAMA but also stressed in direct terms the "need for strengthened cooperation, coordination, and mutual support" with ISAF.[21] Despite continued resistance in Kabul and minimal organizational change, the commitment represented an important shift to a new type of "comprehensive approach whereby civil-military cooperation was sought anchored in the UNAMA-ISAF-Afghanistan triangle."[22]

NATO/ISAF AND THE US "SURGE," 2009–2011

As the security situation continued to deteriorate, NATO allies struggled to counter increased insurgent activity by increasing the number of coalition troops serving in Afghanistan from almost twenty thousand troops in September 2006 to over fifty-six thousand in February 2009.[23] These additional troops enabled ISAF to field additional Operational Mentor and Liaison Teams (OMLTs), small groups of advisors that focused on training and mentoring Afghan military units. By mid-March 2009, there were fifty-two OMLTs, and while an acute awareness remained that more trainers were required, Brussels seemed to be making a sincere effort to correct identified deficiencies.[24] Despite these efforts, however, it became more apparent that drastic changes were necessary if the operation in Afghanistan was to be salvaged.

Both the degenerating situation in Afghanistan and domestic politics in the US were the primary driving force behind the refocused attention to the country. Then candidate Barack Obama strongly criticized outgoing president George W. Bush's failure to properly resource the "right" war in Afghanistan. After taking office in January 2009, President Obama came under increased pressure to reevaluate and correct the situation, in terms of both strategy and resources. The public release of Commander of International Security Assistance Force (COMISAF) General Stanley McChrystal's classified reassessment of the Afghan campaign later that year only added to the urgency. While strongly asserting that the war would be won, General McChrystal nonetheless emphasized the critical importance of more troops and that ISAF must adopt a new strategy and do a more adequate job of implementing existing COIN doctrine.[25] In practical terms, this recognition of NATO/ISAF inadequacies in Afghanistan resulted in the late 2009 decision by Washington to "surge" an additional thirty thousand US troops.[26]

Beyond a commitment to increased resources, NATO made more pronounced efforts at incorporating an alliance-wide COIN strategy into its ISAF Operations Plan (OPLAN) 38302 based on the recently developed US COIN doctrine. The strategy placed primary focus on the protection of the local population as an initial step toward enhanced legitimacy of the Kabul government. NATO allies formally adopted this "clear-hold-build" approach into their national strategies with the hopes of providing the essential (and illusive) "unity of effort" on behalf of the alliance. With national caveats, resource shortfalls, and overlapping chains of command continuing to frustrate ISAF COIN operations, the alliance had at least formally articulated a strategic guidance based on its earlier comprehensive approach and US experience.[27] According to some assessments, ISAF began to see some gains in the war against the insurgents, and while much was still needed, "[t]he International Security Assistance Force (ISAF) is seeing some early indications that comprehensive COIN operations are having localized positive effects and are producing initial signs of progress."[28] This guarded optimism was not consensual and would give way to a more bleak reality in the ensuing years.

In addition to addressing the preeminent challenges related to the war in Afghanistan in 2008–2009, Brussels was drafting its new strategic concept. Even though the NATO 2010 Strategic Concept was to be about much more than Afghanistan, the concept provided the fundamental logic for NATO involvement in missions in theaters outside NATO national borders, so called out-of-area operations, and beyond Article 5 contingencies associated with collective defense. In an extraordinary departure from its earlier, more restrictive strategies of prior decades, NATO recognized that the Euro-Atlantic area is at peace and explicitly acknowledged the enhanced probability that alliance security is increasingly a function of crises and instability in regions beyond NATO territory; "instability and conflict beyond NATO borders can directly threaten Alliance security, including by fostering extremism, terrorism, trans-national illegal activities such as trafficking in arms, narcotics, and people."[29] With Afghanistan clearly at the forefront, the 2010 Strategic Concept articulated an updated and more nuanced vision of the post-9/11 strategic environment and stressed the critical significance of alliance solidarity and the necessity of sustained actions in distant theaters.

NATO/ISAF TRANSITION AND EXIT, 2011–PRESENT

As the war in Afghanistan entered its second decade, individual NATO allies found it significantly more difficult to sustain their commitments to ISAF. Although remarkable progress had been accomplished in terms of political and strategic adjustments from early stabilization efforts to more recent COIN operations, conditions on the ground remained problematic at best. Insurgent violence continued to increase so that by 2010 the number of insurgent initiated attacks averaged approximately 4,000 during the summer months.[30] Subsequently the numbers subsided, yet there were still an average of 3,000 attacks per month in the summer of 2011. NATO casualties also reflected the increasingly violent and deadly environment. By summer 2011, approximately 132,000 combined NATO/ISAF troops were deployed throughout Afghanistan, about 90,000 of which were US troops committed to ISAF. ISAF casualties were also mounting—711 deaths in 2010 and 566 deaths in 2011—reflecting the increase in both troop strength and insurgency-related violence.[31] Even though the overwhelming number of the casualties was from the US, non-US NATO contributors also suffered. Combined with the escalating financial costs, the violence suggested to a growing number of NATO allies that progress was a great deal more illusive than hoped. For many, this meant that the time had come for NATO to begin transitioning out of combat operations, with the eventual goal of concluding the ISAF mission.

NATO formally agreed to its transition strategy at the November 2010 Lisbon summit. Officially called the Inteqal Framework, the plan provides a formal, integrated decision-making structure to help the Afghan government assume full "ownership and leadership across all the functions of government and throughout the territory of Afghanistan."[32] The Joint Afghan–NATO In-teqal Board (JANIB) was created in 2010 to provide technical assessments and advice to local government officials. While insisting that the scope and pace of the transition is still a function of the actual progress on the ground and not a formal timetable for withdrawal, for Brussels the Inteqal Framework clearly represents a concerted effort by the alliance to shift responsibility for the three pillars of security, governance, and development to the host nation. Acknowl-edging the ongoing necessity of ISAF troops and mentoring, the framework allows for the gradual reduction of ISAF assets as progress dictates. PRTs re-main the operational backbone for ISAF during the transition process but are scheduled to "evolve" from the direct providers of security and development assistance to a more advisory role. Ultimately PRTs will be replaced by Afghan government officials as they develop the capacity to effectively carry out their necessary responsibilities.[33]

The construction of effective and legitimate Afghan security forces is the cornerstone of NATO's transition strategy. To support this effort, NATO es-tablished NTM-A at the Strasbourg-Kehl Summit in April 2009 and formally activated it in November 2009. In addition to the armed forces under the authority of the Ministry of Defense, NTM-A has been involved in training, equipping, and funding a variety of personnel that fall under the Ministry of the Interior. Consistent with other training efforts, NATO has suffered from a chronic shortfall in terms of trainers from member countries. For example, according to a 2012 US Department of Defense report on Afghanistan, only 1,752 of the 2,612 required trainers have been placed.[34] Even with the additional 524 "pledged" to NTM-A, a significant gap remains.

CONCLUSION: NATO AFTER AFGHANISTAN

At the NATO Chicago summit in May 2012, NATO members reaffirmed their commitment to turn over full security responsibilities to the government of

Afghanistan by the end of 2014.[35] In spring and summer 2014, Brussels maintained its optimistic outlook in the wake of Afghanistan's "successful" presidential elections with repeated expressions of congratulations to the Afghan people. The alliance remains steadfast in its aspiration for a secure, stable, prosperous, and democratic Afghanistan and insists that this end of ISAF does not signal an end of the broader international community's involvement with the country. For example, numerous pledges have been made to provide ongoing financial support and assistance for the maturing Afghan National Security Forces. Thus, 2014 represent the potential for a new and perhaps freer Afghanistan. For NATO, the end of 2014 also suggests a new chapter. Thirteen years of stabilization and combat operations in one of the world's most hostile terrains has certainly taken its toll on the alliance. The cracks and strains that have emerged in terms of capabilities and commitments will take time to heal, particularly in a time of profound financial strain. Yet NATO has survived numerous crises throughout its history, and with a potentially resurgent Russia, continued instability in North Africa and the Middle East, and the ongoing threats of terrorism, the alliance is certain to remain an essential contributor to global security and stability.

NOTES

1. NATO, http://www.nato.int/cps/en/natolive/official_texts_17120.htm.

2. NATO, http://www.nato.int/docu/pr/2001/p01-124e.htm.

3. See James Sperling and Mark Webber, "NATO: from Kosovo to Kabul," *International Affairs* 85, no. 3 (2009): 491–511.

4. Astri Suhrke, "A Contradictory Mission? NATO from Stabilization to Combat," *International Peacekeeping* 15, no. 2 (April 2008): 214–236.

5. Theo Farrell and Sten Rynning, "NATO's Transformation Gaps: Transatlantic Differences and the War in Afghanistan," *Journal of Strategic Studies* 33, no. 5 (October 2010): 673–699.

6. Ibid., 678–679.

7. Sten Rynning, *NATO in Afghanistan: The Liberal Disconnect*, (Stanford, CA: Stanford University Press, 2012), 48–49.

8. *Provincial Reconstruction Teams: Lessons and Recommendations*, Princeton University, Woodrow Wilson School of Public and International Affairs, January 2008, 5.

9. Operation Enduring Freedom–Afghanistan (OEF-A) is the official term for the US-led war in Afghanistan. OEF-A operations were the primary mechanism for US combat operations in the country until February 2007, when ISAF took over most US operations, particularly in the south.

10. There was one exception to this arrangement when Lieutenant General Sir Nick Parker, Deputy Commander ISAF, was appointed interim commander from June 23 to July 4, 2010, after the resignation of General McChrystal. NATO, http://www.isaf.nato.int/history.html.

11. http://www.icasualties.org.

12. NATO, http://www.nato.int/cps/en/SID-852D14D1-2290B8BF/natolive/official_texts_56425.htm?selectedLocale=en.

13. NATO, http://www.nato.int/cps/en/natolive/official_texts_8444.htm. See Rynning, *NATO in Afghanistan*, 57.

14. *NATO Strategic Vision*, April 3, 2008, http://www.nato.int/cps/en/natolive/official_texts_8444.htm.

15. Stephen M. Saideman and David P. Auerswald, "Comparing Caveats: Understanding the Sources of National Restrictions upon NATO's Mission in Afghanistan," *International Studies Quarterly* 56 (2012): 67–84.

16. Theo Farrell and Sten Rynning, "NATO's Transformation Gaps: Transatlantic Differences and the War in Afghanistan," *Journal of Strategic Studies* 33, no. 5 (October 2010): 688.

17. Rynning, *NATO in Afghanistan*, 137.

18. Jens Ringsmose and Peter Dahl Thruelsen, "NATO's Counterinsurgency Campaign in Afghanistan: Are Classical Doctrines Suitable for Alliances?" *UNISCI Discussion Papers*, no. 22 (January 2010): 68–69.

19. Among the many assessments, see Mark Sedra, "Security Sector Reform in Afghanistan: The Slide Towards Expediency," *International Peacekeeping* 13, no. 1 (2007), 94–110, and *A Force in Fragments: Reconstituting the Afghan National Army*, International Crisis Group, Asian Report No. 190, May 12, 2010. On the ANA, see Robert M. Perito, "Afghanistan's Police: The Weak Link in Security Sector Reform," Special Report 227, United States Institute of Peace, August 2009.

20. Rynning, *NATO in Afghanistan*, 138–140.

21. UNSCR 1806, http://www.un.org/ga/search/view_doc.asp?symbol=S/RES/1806 (2008).

22. Rynning, *NATO in Afghanistan*, 141.

23. *Afghanistan Report 2009*, Brussels: NATO Public Diplomacy Division, 7. See also http://www.isaf.nato.int/isaf-placemat-archives.html/.

24. See John Nagl and Richard Weitz, "Counterinsurgency and the Future of NATO," Transatlantic Paper Series #1, October 2010, 16.

25. For a redacted version of the assessment, see http://media.washingtonpost.com/wp-srv/politics/documents/Assessment_Redacted_092109.pdf?hpid=topnews.

26. See also Chapter 4 of this volume.

27. David E. Johnson, "What Are You Prepared to Do? NATO and the Strategic Mismatch Between Ends, Ways, and Means in Afghanistan—and in the Future," *Studies in Conflict and Terrorism*, 34 (2011): 383–401.

28. *Report on Progress Toward Security and Stability in Afghanistan*, U.S. Department of Defense, November 2010, 8, http://www.defense.gov/pubs/November_1230_Report_FINAL.pdf.

29. *NATO Strategic Concept 2010*, NATO Public Diplomacy Division, 11. Accessed through NATO website, http://www.nato.int/nato_static_fl2014/assets/pdf/pdf_publications/20120214_strategic-concept-2010-eng.pdf.

30. See Ian S. Livingston and Michael O'Hanlon, eds., *Afghanistan Index*, Brookings, May 16, 2012, http://www.brookings.edu/~/media/Programs/foreign-policy/afghanistan-index/index20120516.pdf.

31. http://icasualties.org/OEF/Index.aspx.

32. http://www.isaf.nato.int/images/stories/File/factsheets/1667-10_Inteqal_LR_en.pdf.

33. For details of NATO's Transition plan, see http://www.nato.int/nato_static/assets/pdf/pdf_2012_10/20121008_media-backgrounder_inteqal_en.pdf.

34. *Report on Progress Toward Security and Stability in Afghanistan*, U.S. Department of Defense, December 2012, 58, http://www.defense.gov/news/1230_Report_final.pdf.

35. http://www.nato.int/cps/en/SID-078317A5-3FDE6609/natolive/official_texts_87595.htm.

Part IV
The Middle East and Asia

14 JORDAN AND THE UNITED ARAB EMIRATES
Arab Partners in Afghanistan

Daniel P. Brown and Ariel I. Ahram

MOST ACCOUNTS OF the international campaign in Afghanistan would overlook the role of Jordan or the United Arab Emirates (UAE). In official tallies and military terms their contributions have been minuscule, and analysts who even bother to mention them would dismiss their contribution as "symbolic" at best. But the fact that these two Arab Muslim countries publicly joined the US and its allies after September 11, 2001, in a campaign against a Muslim terrorist group is noteworthy, highlighting the complex ways and reasons countries contributed to the campaign.

Why did the UAE and Jordan join the international coalition? Unlike fellow Muslim countries like Pakistan, Iran, Turkey, and Saudi Arabia, neither has historically significant strategic interests in Central Asia. Even if the UAE and Jordan had committed the maximum possible support to the mission, their individual contributions were unlikely to have determined success or failure in defeating al Qaeda and the Taliban. Thus, it would have been logical to free-ride, allowing the US and its more powerful allies to assume the risk and cost and waiting to enjoy the benefits.[1] The role of the UAE and Jordan in the coalition must be considered in the context of their security environment and their long-standing relationship with the US. Afghanistan was, in a sense, incidental, and their participation in the campaign was never solely—or even primarily—about defeating al Qaeda. Their role in the coalition was part of the larger pursuit of securing their interests against what was seen as the multifaceted threat of radical Islamism by deepening ties with the last remaining superpower. For Jordan, the stability of the regime in large part depends on subduing the internal forces of Islamist factions, which they feared had and would continue to gravitate toward al Qaeda. For the UAE, the primary threat was Iran exporting the Islamic revolution abroad, and participation in the coalition was largely a means to ensure continued US involvement in the Persian Gulf.

Though international relations theory tends to draw a stark contrast between interests and identity, representing respectively the competing research paradigms of realism and constructivism, most studies of Jordanian and UAE foreign policy avoid such a blunt dichotomy and instead highlight the interaction between these two fields. As Marc Lynch observes of Jordan, discourse about national strategic interest often depends on the presumption of national identity, and vice versa.[2] In joining the coalition, the UAE and Jordan made an ideational pivot, constructing a national identity that was premised on a more moderate and peaceful interpretation of Islam.[3] This notion of Islam provided an important diplomatic and strategic asset to the coalition. This chapter examines first the origins and dynamics of the US-Jordan and US-UAE alliance to explain what brought them into the Afghanistan coalition, then examines the operational role that these countries had in the campaign. Despite their limited scale, the chapter shows how Jordan and the UAE each made unique and valuable contributions.

THE ORIGINS AND EVOLUTION OF THE STRATEGIC PARTNERSHIP WITH THE US

The strategic partnerships between the US and Jordan and the UAE are long-standing. These origins stem from what Malcolm Kerr called the Arab Cold War of the 1950s to the 1970s, in which nominally socialist and secular pan-Arab-oriented radical republican regimes, typically aligned with the Soviet Union, competed against conservative, mainly monarchial and Western-aligned regimes.[4] In this struggle, both the UAE and Jordan were considered minor states, vulnerable to internal subversion and external aggression. For both, partnership with the US seemed a way to ensure stability domestically and internationally.

The Hashemite Kingdom of Transjordan (later Jordan) was established under Great Britain's colonial protection in 1921 and became independent in 1946. Control over the kingdom was placed in the hand of Abdullah bin Hussein, the second son of Sharif Hussein bin Ali al-Hashemi, as a reward for the Hashemites' support of the British war effort in the First World War. The Hashemites were the traditional rulers of the Hejaz in eastern Arabia and protectors of the holy shrines at Mecca and Medina. Virtually landlocked, with a sparse population, and devoid of natural resources, Jordan was an obvious consolation prize. Jordan's population was nearly evenly split between so-called East Bankers, mainly Bedouin tribes who lived east of the Jordan River, and the Palestinians of the West Bank, who were generally more urban and better educated and preferred to pursue self-determination under an independent Palestinian state rather than be subsumed under Hashemite rule. Embattled from the outset by this internal cleavage, the monarchy tended to rely heavily on the East Bankers, whom it favored with appointment in the civil service and the military, to the exclusion of those of Palestinian origins. Despite adopting the trappings of a constitutional monarchy, including a parliament, the Jordanian political system was always dominated by the crown and was never democratic in any substantive sense. For its defense, Jordan initially relied heavily on British military aid and advisors, such as Sir John "Pasha" Glubb, who oversaw the Jordanian Arab Legion.

Jordan became a pivotal US ally in the 1950s as British power began to recede. Jordan was a bulwark of anti-communism during the Cold War and instrumental in US-backed peace negotiations with Israel, often to the dismay of Jordan's Palestinian citizenry. The current King, Abdullah II, attended preparatory schools in England and the US before studying at Sandhurst, Oxford, and Georgetown. Abdullah was commissioned in the Jordanian army and rose to the rank of major general and commander of the Jordanian special forces. But the legacy of this relationship goes much deeper than the top echelons. Between 2006 and 2011, around three thousand Jordanian officers per year participated in the US's International Military Education and Training (IMET) program, making it by far the largest contingent hailing from the Middle East.[5] Overall, the Jordanian army is considered among the most effective fighting forces in the region. To make up for its meager size compared to Egypt and Syria, the Jordanian army has historically emphasized professionalism and military skill. From 1990 to 2010, over 20 percent of Jordan's national budget (and in some years over a third) has been devoted to defense. The Jordanian military has also been dispatched in several humanitarian missions under UN auspices.

Similar to Jordan, the UAE turned to the US with the abeyance of British regional influence. In 1971 the treaties that placed the emirates of the Trucial Coast under British protection for over a century was allowed to expire. Individually, the security outlook for each of these tiny states was grim. Neighboring Oman, another traditional British dependency, faced a protracted insurgency supported by the Soviet-backed South Yemen. Moreover, Iran under the shah appeared at the apex of its military power and sought to establish its hegemony on both sides of the gulf. In fact, in the midst of the decolonization, Iran seized the Tunbs and Abu Musa islands, which both sides claimed as their historical territory. In response to these challenges, Sheikh Zayed bin Sultan an-Nahyran (1918–2004), the Emir of Abu Dhabi, led the drive for the creation of the UAE as federation of the former Trucial States, subsidizing the poorer emirates in return for their pooling their combined financial and military resources.

Despite its agglomeration, the UAE has always been more an economic than a military powerhouse. Thanks to ample oil wealth, the rulers of the UAE have been able to lavish their populace with economic benefits, turning the country into a prototypical rentier state in which the transfer of economic largesse is used to satiate the public and deflect any demands for popular representation.[6] This reliance on financial largesse extends also the military sphere. At the eve of independence, Sheikh Zayed even offered to offset the cost of continued British military commitment in the region.[7] Rebuffed by the British, the UAE quickly positioned itself beneath the US security umbrella. Since the late 1980s the US used a variety of bases within the UAE to conduct air, naval, and ground operations throughout the Persian Gulf. In 1994 the UAE and US signed a bilateral defense pact, the text of which remains classified. Besides access to the bases, the UAE "paid" for this protection in a number of ways, the most important and obvious being by ensuring a steady supply of cheap oil and gas for the global market. Ironically, the UAE's often outsized purchases of advanced weaponry from the US and other Western manufacturers often accomplishes the same thing, even though it has had little impact in enhancing the UAE's overall military capacity.[8]

In the context of the Arab Cold War, monarchical regimes like Jordan, the UAE, and Saudi Arabia claimed to carry the mantle of protecting Islam from the secularism and atheism of socialism. However, the presumption that Islam would be a force favoring conservatism and stability began to weaken with Iran's Islamic revolution and the overthrow of the shah and then the seizure of the Grand Mosque of Mecca by an anti-Saudi Islamic millenarian group in 1979. By the 1980s, Islamic movements appeared at the forefront of dissent throughout the region, challenging their governments' legitimacy and claiming to offer Islamic solutions to a range of problems, from the economic to the geopolitical. While many Islamic groups tried to work within the confines of acceptable opposition in the authoritarian Arab regimes, a fraction turned to violence against what they deemed apostate (*kafir*) regimes.

In response to these challenges, the leaders of both countries began to make more explicit claims to legitimacy derived from Islam. In an effort to counter the reformist and revolutionary nature of many of the Islamic challengers, both regimes sought to highlight different facets of Islamic legitimacy claims, thereby attempting to disarm the challengers' contestation of authenticity. In 1980, for instance, Jordan's monarchy established the Royal Ahl al-Bayt Institute for Islamic Thought, a kind of international think tank devoted to cultivating a "modern integrated Islamic conception of the values and systems of society."[9] The choice of names of the institute—Ahl al-Bayt (Family of the House of the Prophet Muhammed)—emphasized the Hashemites' venerable lineage, a quality commanding almost automatic respect in the Islamic world. King Abdullah also worked with leading clerics to craft his *Risalaat 'Amman* (Amman Message) articulating his moderate vision of Islam.[10] Similarly, the UAE began to put its more substantial financial influence to reach out primarily (but not exclusively) to the Muslim world. From 1974 to 2000 Abu Dhabi alone distributed $6 billion US dollars in loans to fellow Arab states. In addition to formal state-to-state aid, charities closely tied to the emirates' royal families are also involved in distribution of billions.[11]

Yet Jordan and the UAE perceived the threat posed by radical Islam differently. For the UAE, the primary challenge was again the Islamic Republic of Iran, which sought to export its version of Islamic revolution abroad. Though tensions decreased by the 1990s, Iran remained the biggest security threat to the UAE. Many in the UAE perceived Iran in sectarian terms of Sunni versus Shi'a Islam. In addition to its effort to maintain US commitments within the Persian Gulf as a security umbrella, the UAE also pursued an encirclement strategy against Iran, joining Saudi Arabia and Pakistan as the only countries to extend diplomatic recognition to the Taliban government.

In contrast, Islamic radicalism was primarily an internal matter in Jordan. Unlike the UAE, Jordan did not have the economic largesse capable of placating society and thus had to maintain at least the pretense of mass political participation through parliamentary elections. With the limited political opening of the late 1980s, the Jordanian branch of the Muslim Brotherhood (MB) emerged as a significant political and social force. The MB has historically been especially popular among Jordan's Palestinian population, who had long felt marginalized and discriminated against by the East Bank–dominated government and the monarchy. The MB-backed slate has consistently won large blocs in the parliament, despite obvious rigging of the electoral system to favor candidates backed by the monarchy. Within the Jordanian political system, the brotherhood and its party arm, the Islamic Action Front, has generally sought to position itself as loyal opposition and to work within the authoritarian regime, while keeping up pressure on the government regarding corruption and its relationship with Israel and the US. Still, other more strident Islamist groups, such as Hizb al-Tahrir, the Army of Muhammad, and Youth of the Islamic Trumpet, have refused to play by the rules set by the regime. The ranks of these groups were often filled with veterans of the Afghan civil war in the 1980s, the so-called Afghan Arabs, and they advocated violence against the Jordanian regime to remove what they saw as an un-Islamic regime, lending credence to the regime's fears of an internal Islamist threat. In 1999, Jordan's security services uncovered an apparent al Qaeda cell operating in the country that had planned attacks against foreigners, Christians, and Jews.[12]

Yet the relationship between the US as a superpower patron, the regimes as local agents, and the proverbial "Arab Street" was always fragile. While it is clear that the rulers of both countries saw their interests bound up with the US campaign in Afghanistan, these positions put the regimes at odds with their own populations, who regarded the US with skepticism if not antipathy. In Jordan in 2002, according to the Pew Research Center, 75 percent expressed an unfavorable view of the US, a number that would climb to 99 percent with the beginning of the war in Iraq in 2003. In all the years surveyed to 2012, well over 70 percent of Jordanians expressed unfavorable opinions of the US.[13] In the UAE, the Arab American Institute/Zogby International Poll found that 87 percent viewed the US unfavorably in 2002, a number that also increased with the Iraq war.[14] Though perhaps necessary for regime survival, then, partnership with the US had its costs. Beyond public displeasure with their cooperation, the regimes themselves became targets. Throughout the 2000s Jordan was a target for al Qaeda–backed terrorist groups, most famously the coordinated suicide bombing against three Amman hotels that killed sixty people on November 9, 2005. Terrorists did not strike the UAE, but Iran remained a menace to its international security.

OPERATIONAL CONTRIBUTIONS

The complexity and contentiousness of the partnership between the US and these regimes is also reflected in the diverse and often unacknowledged operational contributions they made. It is useful to think about their role in terms of two dimensions. The first is between direct contributions to combat and indirect support. The second is between overt and publicly acknowledged contributions, which the regime wanted to broadcast to audiences internally or abroad, and covert and secret contributions, that either the regime or the US wished to downplay or conceal. Obviously, it is difficult to ascertain much about covert activities; however, the release of the classified US State Department documents from WikiLeaks provides at least a glimpse into this.

Publicly, Jordanian operational support began with American use of Jordanian bases for staging, support, and training. In 2001, Jordanian opened a field hospital in Mazar-e Sharif, which was described as part of a "strictly humanitarian mission."[15] In 2003 the Jordanian army opened an additional field hospital in Qalat, which in seven years treated over 750,000 people.[16] Yet leaked diplomatic cables show that Jordan requested that its involvement be kept secret, supported by media reports that Jordanian forces "have been carrying out some basic security duties," suggesting that there is perhaps more to Jordanian involvement than the establishment and staffing of field hospitals in both Afghanistan and Iraq.[17] Likewise, in 2003, Jordan was one of the first countries to commit de-mining teams to Afghanistan.[18]

Jordan's military ties to the US have been particularly strong at the level of special operations forces (SOF). In addition to military hardware sales, programs like IMET introduce Jordanian officers to US military education programs and English-language training.[19] Forty-seven Jordanians completed courses at the US Army John F. Kennedy Special Warfare Center at Fort Bragg, including the Special Forces Qualification Course, between 2002 and 2012.[20] As early as 2007 Jordan committed a 90-man SOF detachment to assist ISAF forces.[21] According to WikiLeaks sources, in 2009 two Jordanian SOF battalions were deployed. Task Force 222, numbering 720 men and two helicopters, contributed supporting actions for the elections in Logar province, and was later redeployed with US Task Force Spartan.[22] The second was the 110-man Task Force 111, which served near Qalat.[23] Since their initial deployment, Jordanian forces have been repeatedly cycled back to Afghanistan.

Besides their direct combat role, Jordan's SOF have also been involved in helping to train Afghanistan's burgeoning special forces units. Though they spoke different languages and were of different ethnicities, Afghan soldiers were presumed to respond better to instruction and direction from fellow Muslims. Some 2,500 members of the Afghan SOF trained at Jordan's King Abdullah II Special Operations Training Center (KASOTC).[24] This facility was partially financed by the US and served as a regional headquarters for counterterrorism training, including hosting competitions for SOF units from across the region and the world.[25]

Jordanian intelligence agencies—particularly the General Intelligence Directorate (GID/Dairat al-Mukhabarat al-'Aamma)—have been extensively, although even more covertly, involved in the Afghanistan campaign.[26] Jordan is a major destination for the US program for the rendition and interrogation of suspected terrorists from throughout the globe.[27] The depth of Jordanian intelligence cooperation in the Afghanistan campaign surfaced in 2010 with the suicide bombing of the Central Intelligence Agency (CIA) operations center in Khost. The bomber was a Palestinian Jordanian, Humam Khalil Abu Mulal al-Balawi, an apparent triple agent, whom Jordanian intelligence had tasked with penetrating al Qaeda's inner circle. The bombing killed his GID handler, Captain Ali Bin Zeid, a member of the Hashemite royal family, along with seven American operatives.[28] In addition to the Khost incident, Jordanian First Lieutenant Majid Amir Abu Qdairi was killed and three of his Jordanian compatriots injured by an improvised explosive device (IED) attack on a humanitarian convoy the unit was escorting in May 2011, bringing Jordan's casualties to date to at least three.[29]

Until the Khost bombing, the Jordanian regime largely maintained that its Afghanistan mission was confined to the provision of medical support. The bombing understandably embarrassed Jordanian officials, who tried to suggest that the attacker was not actually the same man who had been recruited in Amman or otherwise deny the extent of their covert cooperation with US intelligence.[30] Even in the wake of the incident, the Hashemite regime maintained that Bin Zeid was involved only as part of a humanitarian mission.[31] The opposition (both inside and outside parliament) called on the government to cease cooperation and security operations with US forces.[32] The Muslim Brotherhood went so far as to issue a *fatwa*, an opinion in Islamic law, against Jordanians participating in operations in Afghanistan. In response, the religious affairs ministry issued a statement of its own, claiming that it alone had authority to issue such opinions and questioning why there would be such opposition to the Jordanian government's providing humanitarian assistance to a fellow Muslim country. Deputy Prime Minister Ayman Safadi went further in publicly defending the kingdom's military role, claiming that Jordan's primary function in Afghanistan was aiding co-religionists and linking the success of operations in Afghanistan to Jordan's internal security and stability.[33] WikiLeaks documents reveal that behind the scenes Jordan also sought to have the US (as well as the UAE) offset the costs of its military commitment in Afghanistan. Of particular importance was the $1,600-per-month combat bonus due to Jordanian troops serving abroad. While the US refused to subsidize the salaries directly, it did provide essential predeployment training, airlifting, equipment, and billeting for the Jordanian forces.[34] In compensation, Jordan committed to provide a set number of helicopter flight hours and other forms of in-kind transfers.

In comparison to Jordan, the UAE's role has been relatively public but also less directly oriented to combat, at least on its face. The UAE likewise contributed funding and personnel to field hospitals, with a special focus on maternal and child health services.[35] An official report from the UAE government highlights UAE forces' role in establishing or building eleven schools, six medical clinics, a public library, and 160 water wells. They have focused a great deal of effort on Khost, where they paid for accommodation for two hundred displaced families, as well as a university campus, dubbed Zayed University after the founder of the UAE. In addition, private donations from UAE citizens have totaled $22 million "for food, medicine and basic relief projects providing housing and shelter" while "the UAE Red Crescent has invested $19 million in local projects, and the UAE Government has dedicated US$30 million to international reconstruction efforts in the country."[36] More directly, UAE forces have been deployed, albeit in smaller numbers, to Helmand province to assist in mine- and IED-clearing operations, similarly to Jordanian forces. In 2010, British officials heartily praised the UAE's role in IED-clearing operations, its use of unmanned aerial surveillance vehicles, and its participation in various joint naval and air exercises.[37]

Militarily, UAE SOF forces have been deployed in smaller numbers. The UAE embassy in Washington states that its forces on the ground in Afghanistan are for purely defensive purposes and downplays military involvement as providing support for humanitarian and cultural assistance projects.[38] UAE Major Ghanem al-Mazroui, commanding UAE troops in Afghanistan, with some element of irony, described the UAE mission as follows: "if you are asking back in the UAE or in the Gulf, or you [are] asking here, we have the same answer . . . We make a contract with the US Army to help the people down here, not to fight."[39] Emirati casualties are either nonexistent or deliberately unreported. In both the media and a documentary film, *Mission: Winds of Goodness*, the role of UAE forces is likewise framed as an Islamic humanitarian and cultural mission.[40] Indeed, the UAE financed the construction of mosques in the installations of the Afghan National Army (ANA), a role that the US cannot take.[41] Given the real risk of domestic backlash, the UAE, like Jordan, has a strong incentive to conceal its involvement in riskier combat operations.

CONCLUSION

Before September 11, 2001, neither Jordan nor the UAE had an intrinsic interest in the fate of Afghanistan. Yet the assembly of the coalition to oust the Taliban and al Qaeda provided an opportunity for these regimes both to cement their credentials as moderate Muslim governments and to strengthen their long-standing security relationship with the US. In doing so, though, both these regimes went against the overwhelming popular sentiment of hostility to the US. By joining ISAF, both regimes in a sense proved their critics correct, acting more in the interest of self-preservation than in enacting the will of their people.[42]

The secrecy of these country's involvement makes it difficult to gauge their role in combat. In the case of Jordan, at least, revelations about their contribution of SOF and intelligence operatives do indicate significant commitment. Yet secrecy also mitigated one of their most important, albeit symbolic, assets within the coalition. Though both Jordan and the UAE at times touted their role in Afghanistan as a humanitarian mission to aid fellow Muslims, concern about offending domestic opinion prevented broadcasting too much about their cooperation with the US. There was some advantage to having Muslim troops interact with the Muslim Afghan population. But these tactical gains in the campaign to win hearts and minds could not be translated to the more strategic level of public diplomacy. Given that Jordan's and the UAE's populations overall disapproved of their rulers' decisions to join the coalition, it was impossible to point to Jordan's and the UAE's contributions to deflect the widespread belief that ISAF was truly a Christian crusader force bent merely on subjugating the Muslim world.

Overall, Jordan and the UAE illustrate remarkable flexibility in the form and substance of coalition burden sharing. When viewed comparatively, there is a kind of symmetry in these two Arab partners. On one hand, Jordan was cash-poor but was willing (and seemingly able) to fight al Qaeda. As the WikiLeaks documents show, it sought financial sponsorship to enable it to carry out its combat contributions. On the other hand, the UAE had ample economic resources but seemed averse and ill-suited to combat. As evident from its pre-9/11 stance, the UAE's interests were primarily oriented toward countering Iran, not necessarily al Qaeda and the Taliban. It therefore positioned itself as a source of capital for the coalition's campaign, while seeming to minimize its direct combat role. In joining the coalition, both states sought to accomplish an ideational pivot against perceived internal and external Islamist threats and ensuring their place in a regional order defined by American power.

NOTES

1. On the notion of burden-sharing and free-riders in the Afghanistan coalition, see S. M. Ali Ashraf, *The Politics of Coalition Burden-Sharing: The Case of the War in Afghanistan*, Ph.D. diss., University of Pittsburgh, 2011; Sarah Kreps, "When does the mission determine the coalition? The logic of multilateral intervention and the case of Afghanistan," *Security Studies* 17, no. 3 (2008): 531–567.

2. Marc Lynch, *State Interests and Public Spheres: The International Politics of Jordan's Identity* (New York: Columbia University Press, 1999).

3. For a critical discussion of the distinction between "moderate" and "radical" Islam, see Mahmoud Mamdani, *Good Muslim, Bad Muslim: America, the Cold War, and the Roots of Terror* (New York: Random House, 2005).

4. Malcolm Kerr, *The Arab Cold War: Gamal 'Abd al-Nasir and His Rivals, 1958–1970* (London: Oxford University Press, 1971).

5. Department of State, Office of Electronic Information, Bureau of Public Affairs. "International Military Education and Training Account Summary," http://www.state .gov/t/pm/ppa/sat/c14562.htm.

6. For discussion of rentierism in the UAE and the political system, see F. Gregory Gause, *Oil Monarchies* (New York: Council on Foreign Relations, 1994); Michael Herb, "A Nation of Bureaucrats: Political Participation and Economic Diversification in Kuwait and the United Arab Emirates," *International Journal of Middle East Studies* 41, no. 3 (2009), 375–395.

7. F. Gregory Gause III, *The International Relations of the Persian Gulf* (New York: Cambridge University Press, 2010), 19.

8. Sean Foley, "The UAE: Political Issues and Security Dilemmas," *Middle East Review of International Affairs* 3, no. 1 (1999); Kenneth Katzman, *The United Arab Emirates (UAE): Issues for US Policy*, Congressional Research Service Report, June 23, 2010.

9. "Law of the Institute," Royal Aal al-Bayt Institute for Islamic Thought, http:// aalalbayt.org/en/law.html, 2007.

10. Abdallah bin al-Hussein II, "The Amman Message," Royal Aal al-Bayt Institute for Islamic Thought, 2004, http://ammanmessage.com/index.php?option=com_content& task=view&id=121&Itemid=41&lang=en.

11. Khalid S. Almeziani, *The UAE and Foreign Policy: Foreign Aid, Identities, and Interests* (New York: Routledge, 2012), 60.

12. Nachum Tal, *Radical Islam in Egypt and Jordan* (London: Sussex Academic Press, 2005), 168–178, 198.

13. Pew Research Center, *Opinion of the United States: Middle East/N. Africa: Percent Responding Unfavorable*. Pew Global Attitudes Project, 2002. http://www.pewglobal.org/database/indicator/1/group/6/.

14. Arab American Institute/Zogby International, *Arabs: What They Believe and What They Value Most*, 2002, http://www.aaiusa.org/reports/arabs-what-they-believe-and -what-they-value-most-2002.

15. Saad G. Hattar, "Abul Ragheb Says Jordan to Set Up Afghan Field Hospital," *Jordan Times*, Amman, December 4, 2001, http://www.albawaba.com/news/abul -ragheb-jordan-send-troops-afghanistan.

16. *10AMMAN91: Jordan: Regional Security Support—Afghanistan*, Diplomatic Cable, January 7, 2010, https://cablegatesearch.wikileaks.org/cable.php?id=10AMMAN91.

17. Media Operations Centre (MOC), *NATO in Afghanistan: Master Narrative as at 6 October 2008*, https://wikileaks.org/wiki/NATO_Media_Operations_Centre:_NATO_ in_Afghanistan:_Master_Narrative,_6_Oct_2008; See also Frank Gardner, "Muslim Troops Help Win Afghan Minds," BBC News, March 28, 2008, http://news.bbc.co.uk/2/ hi/south_asia/7318731.stm.

18. *10AMMAN91*.

19. Jeremy M. Sharp, *Jordan: Background and US Relations* (Washington, D.C.: Congressional Research Service, May 3, 2012), 12.

20. Email correspondence, Office of Strategic Communication, US Army John F. Kennedy Special Warfare Center and School, Fort Bragg, N.C., January 16, 2013.

21. "Jordan Commits Troops, Poland Helicopters to Afghanistan," *Conflict Monitor: Human Security Reports Project: Afghanistan Conflict Monitor*, December 7, 2007.

22. *10AMMAN91*.

23. *10AMMAN91*.

24. Sharp, *Jordan: Background*, 12.

25. "Annual Warrior Competition: Registered Teams for the 5th Annual Warrior Competition as of March 7, 2013," http://www.warriorcompetition.com/home/index .php.

26. Ian Black and Middle East editor, "Jordan Embarrassed as Bombing Reveals CIA Link," *The Guardian*, January 6, 2010, http://www.theguardian.com/world/2010/jan/06/ jordan-embarrassed-cia-link.

27. Jane Mayer, "Outsourcing Torture: The secret history of America's 'extraordinary rendition' program," *New Yorker*, February 14, 2005.

28. Tom A. Peter, "CIA Killings in Afghanistan Spotlight Jordan as Key US Intelligence Partner," *Christian Science Monitor*, January 6, 2010, http://www.csmonitor.com/ World/Middle-East/2010/0106/CIA-killings-in-Afghanistan-spotlight-Jordan-as-key

-US-intelligence-partner; for general discussion, see Joby Warrick, *The Triple Agent* (New York: Doubleday, 2011).

29. "Coalition Deaths by Nationality," *iCasualties*, n.d, http://icasualties.org/oef/.

30. F. Gardner, "Afghanistan CIA killings a major blow to US and Jordan," BBC News. January 5, 2010; http://news.bbc.co.uk/2/hi/americas/8442473.stm. See also Black, "Jordan Embarrassed."

31. Black, "Jordan Embarrassed."

32. *AMMAN 000329*, Diplomatic Cable, n.d., WikiLeaks.org.

33. Suda Phillip Ma'ayeh, "Jordan Denounces Brotherhood's Fatwa Against Afghan Role," *The National*, December 18, 2010, http://www.thenational.ae/news/world/middle -east/jordan-denounces-brotherhoods-fatwa-against-afghan-role.

34. *10AMMAN91*.

35. *UAE Policy for the Provision of Direct Support to Afghanistan*, Government/ Embassy of the United Arab Emirates, n.d., http://www.uae-embassy.org/sites/ default/files/UAE_Policy_for_provision_of_direct_support_to_Afghanistan_English .pdf; Shehab A. Makahleh, "UAE Troops Spare No Effort to Bring Peace to Afghani- stan," *Gulf News*, August 24, 2011, http://gulfnews.com/news/uae/general/uae-troops -spare-no-effort-to-bring-peace-to-afghanistan-1.856240.

36. *UAE Policy*.

37. "UK Attaché Says UAE Plays Crucial Role in Afghanistan," *The National*, January 20, 2010, http://www.thenational.ae/news/uae-news/uk-attach-says-uae-plays-crucial-role -in-afghanistan.

38. "The UAE: Foreign Policy," UAE Embassy, Washington, D.C., June 12, 2012, http://www.uaeinteract.com/government/foreign_policy.asp.

39. Gardner, "Muslim Troops"; Alex Gardiner, "On the Frontline with UAE Forces in Helmand," *The National*, Abu Dhabi, n.d., http://www.thenational.ae/news/uae-news/ on-the-frontline-with-uae-forces-in-helmand.

40. Gardner, "Muslim Troops"; *Mission: Winds of Goodness*, dir. David Eberts and Khaled bin Lahej Al Falas, http://www.uaeafghanistan.ae/en/filmmakers.php.

41. Makaleh, "UAE Troops"; Gardiner, "On the Frontline."

42. UAE and Jordan were not alone, though, in ignoring public opinion in the Afghanistan campaign. See Sarah Kreps, "Elite Consensus as a Determinant of Alliance Cohesion: Why Public Opinion Hardly Matters for NATO Led Operations in Afghanistan," *Foreign Policy Analysis*, 6, no. 3 (2010), 191–215.

15 JAPAN

A New Self-Defense Force Role . . . or Not?

Takamichi Takahashi

WHILE JAPAN DID NOT deploy its Self-Defense Force (SDF) to Afghanistan, it has assisted the country in various ways. Overall, Japan has expended more than $4 billion since 2001 in various forms of assistance.[1] Despite the fact that there is no SDF footprint in Afghanistan, Japan's tanker fleet provided the logistical support for Operation Enduring Freedom (OEF) from November 2001 to January 2010. Furthermore, the Government of Japan (GOJ) has considered SDF deployment to support Afghanistan at least twice from 2008 to 2011 but has always decided not to deploy its force.

This chapter reviews the logistical support that has been rendered for Afghanistan and analyzes the two cases in which the GOJ decided not to provide support. This will permit a comparison of cases in which support was approved and those in which it was not, thereby permitting a discussion of the lessons learned for past and future deployments by Japan outside its waters.

LOGISTICAL SUPPORT FOR OEF AND ITS BACKGROUND

Immediately after the tragic events of September 11, 2001, Prime Minister Junichiro Koizumi stated that "Japan strongly supports the United States"[2] and announced "specific measures" including "dispatching SDF for providing support . . . to the US forces."[3] That was surprising news because at that time, the GOJ could deploy the SDF overseas only for peacekeeping operations (PKO), humanitarian assistance/disaster relief (HA/DR) and exercises. Even for PKO, strict conditions are applied.[4] Therefore, the prime minister's statement was not a sufficient basis for SDF deployment and a new law would be required.

To that end, the Parliament enacted the Anti-Terrorism Special Measures Law,[5] which went into effect on November 2, 2001. It authorized the GOJ to use the SDF for "Cooperation and Support Activities, Search and Rescue, Assistance to Affected People and other necessary measures" for OEF.[6] The law was subsequently extended three times in 2003, 2005, and 2006. On November 9, the Maritime Self-Defense Force (MSDF) squadron left Japan for the Indian Ocean to provide a fuel supply to the US force. Never before had a law for SDF overseas deployment been enacted within such an astonishingly short period of time.

There were four reasons for the swift decision. First, the government leadership strongly thought that Japan should not repeat the same mistake it had made during the Gulf War of 1990–1991. In that case, the GOJ did not dispatch the SDF. Instead, Japan made a financial contribution of $13 billion to assist the coalition forces, and was criticized by the international community for exercising "checkbook diplomacy." As a result, Japan felt it had lost prestige internationally and had even threatened the US-Japan alliance. In the end, Japan dispatched minesweepers after the war in an effort to save face, but it was clearly too little, too late.

The case of 9/11 was more serious, because the US itself was attacked. If Japan had again assisted with "checkbook diplomacy," the alliance could have been undermined and Japanese national security threatened. This concern was widely shared by Japanese politicians, including the opposition parties.[7] The fear was that such action again could be "a final exam for the alliance," while "Japan had failed its first exam."[8]

The second reason was that the domestic political situation was stable on several points. The coalition government of the Liberal Democratic Party (LDP) and the New Komei held a majority in both the House of Council (the Upper House) and the House of Representatives (the Lower House). So Prime Minister Koizumi's administration could enact the new law even without the opposition party's cooperation. Probably even more important than this fact, Koizumi had a very high approval rating of 84.5 percent just before 9/11.[9] This record rating provided the prime minister with enough political capital to assure a positive, possibly otherwise difficult vote.

The third reason was strong national support for assisting the US. The Japanese public believed in the legitimacy of the US military action. For example, just after the US assault on the Taliban, 82.7 percent of respondents to a national poll stated that it was legitimate; 57.1 percent stated that Japan should conduct "logistic support for the US force."[10]

The fourth reason for the swift decision was that the controversial issues to enact the new law had been previously debated, discussed, and legally resolved. Japan already had a law in place enabling SDF support to the US military in the regional contingency. That law permitted the SDF to conduct rear-area logistic support, rear-area search and rescue, and other related activities. While "rear area" is defined by Japanese law, the term *integration with other countries' use of force* cannot be found in any Japanese law. This concept was established through the National Diet discussion on the constitutionality of the SDF's overseas activities. It was introduced as a measure to ensure the constitutionality of the SDF's activities to support the US force. The logic is as follows.

Article 9 of the constitution states that Japan renounces "war . . . and the threat of use of force as a *means of settling international disputes*." If the SDF's activity is integrated with another country's use of force for international disputes, the activity itself might be regarded as a part of the other's armed action, and that would violate Article 9. By limiting the operation to the rear area, or an area where it is unlikely a battle will occur, the other country's use of force and SDF activities would be separate. A similar idea was applied to the Anti-Terrorism Special Measure Law. Thus, the controversial points had been resolved before the 9/11 attack on the US.

SUSPENSION AND RESUMPTION OF LOGISTICAL SUPPORT FOR THE COALITION FORCE

In the summer of 2007 the ruling parties, the LDP and the New Komei, lost the majority in the Upper House. In November 2007 Japanese logistical support was suspended as the Anti-Terrorism Special Measure Law expired. Support resumed in January 2008 when another law was enacted. But even with losing the majority, theoretically the original law could have been extended. According to the constitution, a bill rejected by the Upper House can be approved by a two-thirds majority of the Lower House. At that point the governing parties had a supermajority. However, the administration had to convince the public to use the supermajority, because a supermajority had not been reached in the latest election for the Upper House in 2007 but rather by the election for the Lower House in 2005.

In the midst of the discussions, suspicion arose over the lawfulness of the fuel provision. A Member of Parliament, Rep. Eda Kenji, found a statement of appreciation from the US Fifth Fleet for allied contributions to Operation Iraqi Freedom (OIF). It thanked the GOJ for contributing "in excess of 86,629,675 gallons of F76 Fuel."[11] According to the agreement between Japan and the US, the fuel provided by the MSDF was to be used for the US operation responding to 9/11 or for Operation Enduring Freedom (OEF). If the fuel had been diverted to OIF, as the statement appeared to indicate, then it was illegal.

As the GOJ worked to convince its citizens of the legitimacy of the deployments, the time to extend the original law expired. The government turned to the New Anti-Terrorism Special Measure Law, enacted in January 2008, to resume the operation through the supermajority. But this new law was somewhat more restrictive and approved action by the SDF to replenish the coalition force by conducting maritime intervention with fuel and water, while the original law had authorized wider logistical support. The resumed refueling again terminated in January 2010 as the law expired under the administration of the Democratic Party Japan (DPJ), which had had a landslide victory in the election for the Lower House in the summer of 2009.

When we examine the suspension, resumption, and then termination of SDF logistical support for OEF, the influence of the public's perception of OIF cannot be ignored. Although Prime Minister Koizumi immediately stated Japan's support for the US decision to invade Iraq in March 2003,[12] public opinion strongly opposed the US action. For example, according to a poll that month by *Sankei Shinbun*, a major conservative newspaper, 63.6 percent of respondents opposed the invasion.[13] Furthermore, public opinion with respect to the SDF deployment to Iraq for reconstruction was also divided. According to polls on November 29 and 30, 2003,[14] 43 percent of respondents did not approve of this use of the SDF, while 40 percent approved albeit with conditions. The major reason for the support of the SDF deployment was the importance of international cooperation and Iraqi reconstruction rather than the previous support for the US-Japan alliance. In other words, the Japanese were doubtful of the legitimacy of OIF. In the prevailing political climate, the possible misappropriation of fuel for OIF from OEF forced the Japanese government to expend unnecessary political capital to convince its people.

Thus, the political turmoil on suspension and resumption of SDF logistical support made politicians more cautious and prudent. Additionally, this turmoil undermined the credibility of the GOJ led by the Liberal Democratic Party and the New Komei, which was an indirect cause of the administration's fall.

THE UNREALIZED SDF'S DEPLOYMENT

As mentioned earlier, there were two additional cases where the GOJ considered deploying SDF personnel or troops as a contribution to Afghanistan or as part of ISAF but failed in its efforts. The first case occurred from May to July 2008. The idea was introduced by Chief Cabinet Secretary Machimura Nobutaka on May 31 in a public speech. He commented before an audience that the GOJ was studying additional options including deployment of Ground Self-Defense Force (GSDF) troops to Afghanistan.[15] There were three reasons that the GOJ initiated the study.

The first reason was the US-Japan alliance. Japan had deployed the GSDF logistic support battalion and an Air Self-Defense Force (ASDF) C-130 aircraft for Iraqi reconstruction, but the GSDF troops had redeployed in 2006 and the airlift support could have been terminated by the end of 2008, because of the legal deadline.

The deadline to extend the refueling operation for OEF was also January 2009. To maintain its good relationship with the US, the GOJ felt that the SDF footprint in the region should be maintained. There were two ways for the administration to ensure that: either enact a new law or extend operations through a supermajority. Enacting a new law looked like the better course of action for two reasons. One, using the supermajority would appear to ignore the views of the public. Two, prominent leaders of the LDP thought that taking the major opposition party, the DPJ, into the discussion of a new approach to contributing to Afghanistan would be better than using the supermajority option that the DPJ had opposed. The leaders might have thought it was even possible that the DPJ would agree to their proposal. The DPJ had actually submitted a bill to deploy the SDF as a counterproposal to the New Anti-Terrorism Special Measure Law. In the end, when the GOJ decided on the second option in order to include the DPJ, the party opted not to get involved in the discussion, allowing the new approach to be enacted.

The second reason to initiate a study was the upcoming July G8 summit in Japan. As the host country, Japan wanted to announce its contribution to the Afghanistan operation to the international community. Japanese leaders considered the new SDF operation to be the best approach to ensure that option.[16] As a result, Japan sent a study team to Afghanistan and Tajikistan in June. The team's task was to research whether an airlift by GSDF helicopter and/or ASDF plane would be most appropriate for the operation.

In the end the administration abandoned the plan because the LDP's coalition partner, the New Komei, opposed it. The New Komei argued that just six months previously, the original Anti-Terrorism Law, theoretically allowing the SDF's operation for transportation, had expired and the new law approving refueling at sea had been passed by the Diet with a supermajority. It was too early for the coalition government to propose another law to reauthorize SDF transportation that mirrored the original law.[17]

The second case where SDF deployment was considered occurred from 2010 to 2011. After the election in August 2009, the DPJ and the People's New Party had assumed the reins of power in Tokyo. Just after the regime change, the coalition took up the issue of the Afghanistan refueling operation. The government could not reach a consensus on whether they should continue refueling operations by the Maritime Self-Defense Force. The coalition did study a possible substitute for the refueling operation, but the option to use the SDF was shelved at an early stage. Finally, the cabinet decided to terminate the operation entirely.

Given this result, the DPJ administration considered an option to send SDF medical staff—doctors or nurses—to Afghanistan in early November 2010. To decide whether the option would be feasible, a research team led by the former Chairman of the Joint Staff Council, retired General Tetsuya Nishimoto, was sent to Afghanistan in December.[18] The reason for the DPJ's change in position was President Obama's planned visit to Japan to attend the Asian Pacific Economic Cooperation (APEC) meeting to be held in November. After the DPJ had assumed power, the credibility of the US-Japan alliance had been weakened by the debate over the US Marine Corps Air Station Futenma. The Japanese administration thought that it could reinstate its credibility with the US through an additional contribution that would not be just financial, as in the Gulf War. Indeed, Prime Minister Naoto Kan proposed the idea to President Obama on November 13.[19]

At that time, the GOJ did not intend to propose a new legal scheme. Instead, its concept was to send the medical staff under the pretext of training and education. If the idea had been implemented, the program could have been legally regarded as a mere business trip, and the personnel would not have been paid a special allowance and could not have carried any personal weapons for self-defense. Compensation also would not have been allowed in the event of casualties. It was natural that not only the opposition party but the media criticized this approach. The administration, led by PM Kan and later Prime Minister Yoshihiko Noda, suspended the study because the GOJ had to concentrate on the response to the Great East Japan Earthquake in March 2011. Finally, the administration decided to give up the study officially in September 2011.[20]

THE FACTORS IN JAPAN'S DECISION TO USE THE SDF IN AFGHANISTAN

Reviewing the cases discussed earlier, three factors in Japan's decision to use the SDF in its contribution in Afghanistan should be noted.

First and foremost, Japanese leaders considered the US-Japan alliance in their decision making on potential SDF deployments to Afghanistan. In the preceding two cases under the different administrations, the former was put on the table as an alternative to an SDF retreat from Iraq. The latter case was started at the time of President Obama's visit.

It took a long time for the US and its allies to stabilize Afghanistan. Under the difficult situation the US was facing, unless Japan had shown a visible contribution, the US-Japan alliance might have been damaged. For Japan, relations with the US are critical for diplomacy and national security, so maintaining those relations is always imperative. In this context, it was natural that the US-Japanese alliance was an incentive to initiate a high-level study on the feasibility of an SDF deployment.

The importance of the alliance was also key in the decision to deploy the MSDF fleet for OEF. However, there was a big difference between that case and the two cases when the SDF did *not* deploy: the issue of public support. As already mentioned, the public supported MSDF deployment. Moreover, the attack on the Taliban by the US, the main recipient of the Japanese logistical support, was also widely supported by the public. While there was no public opinion poll in the two cases that did not result in deployment, according to a poll in January 2009, six months after the study on the first unrealized case, 70.4 percent of the Japanese public supported the refueling operation. Asked the reason for this support, just 24.5 percent answered "to strengthen US-Japan relations," while 65.2 percent answered "to fulfill Japan's duty for the international community."[21] This poll suggests that the public was influenced by the legitimacy of the operation rather than by the US-Japanese alliance, which influenced the GOJ. This gap between the public and the leaders will make it difficult to reach a national consensus for a deployment of the SDF to Afghanistan in the future.

The third factor is that the issue of an SDF deployment tends to be transformed from decisions strictly in line with its national security agenda to more of a political power game. The two cases occurred under different ruling parties. Since both administrations—led by the LDP or the DPJ—studied the potential for an SDF deployment, they should have reached the same conclusion and been able to find agreement with each other. The reality was not so simple.

When the DPJ and its coalition rejected the New Anti-Terrorism Special Measure Law to resume the refueling operation, they submitted a bill to permit deployment to Afghanistan. Just six months later, the DPJ did not involve itself in the discussion about the LDP's proposal to dispatch SDF forces. In turn, the DPJ's idea to send SDF medical staff was not agreed to by the LDP. In other words, each party's proposal was opposed by its opposition party and vice versa. As a result, consensus could not be reached. This fact shows that Japanese politicians have tended to deal with an SDF deployment, unintentionally, as a power game. The real question is why the issue of the SDF became a power game. The answer appears to lie with the political climate built up over time.

Although the constitutionality of the SDF is not in question, it had been a significant political issue since its establishment. While the LDP administration introduced a discussion over the interpretation of SDF constitutionality, it tried to avoid any potential chaos in the Diet and appeased its opponents by introducing a series of pacifist policy language such as "exclusively defense-oriented policy." In this context, SDF deployments have proved to be a challenge. As a result, Japan has been very prudent in its use of the SDF. On this point, Andrew Oros, who analyzes Japan's national security practice through a constructivist lens, argues that there is "security identity of domestic antimilitarism" in Japan, which has three central tenets: (1) no traditional armed forces involved in domestic policy making; (2) no use of force by Japan to resolve international disputes, except in self-defense; and (3) no Japanese participation in foreign wars.[22] It is unclear whether the Japanese attitude can be defined as identity, but there is no question that the Japanese generally hesitate to deploy the SDF overseas, especially into conflict. Therefore, every time an SDF issue is discussed in the Diet, it is possible for the opponent to weaken the government by opposing any deployments. This has become a structural factor, and any efforts encounter difficulty in deploying the SDF.

CONCLUSION: LESSONS LEARNED

The lessons learned from the Japanese participation in Afghanistan—and lack of participation—are as follows: (1) Japanese leaders tend to decide on SDF deployment in the context of US-Japan relations, including any Afghanistan deployment; (2) the leaders' attitude appears to diverge from the views of the public, who tend to view SDF deployments as legitimate; and (3) SDF deployment tends to become a power game because the Japanese public hesitates to deploy the SDF for international disputes.

If Japan wants to play a role as a major stakeholder in the international system, it cannot continue to avoid using the SDF. Therefore, there is work ahead for Japan to overcome the difficulties mentioned earlier.

To overcome the first and second difficulties, two approaches are required for Japanese leaders. The first is that they need to make an effort to convince the people of the necessity and significance of the US-Japan alliance. Some leaders have attempted to do this, but sometimes the explanation has been abstract or ambiguous. This approach is required not only for potential SDF deployments but also to solve contentious issues like that of the US Marine Corps Air Station Futenma. The second approach is to convince the public of the legitimacy of SDF deployments in the international system.

The third point is closely related to the political and social culture discussed earlier, and it may be more difficult to overcome. If leaders continuously try to convince their people that there are legitimate reasons to use the SDF and take on an international role, a public willingness to candidly discuss national security issues would be gradually established. Last, but not least, if the US as an alliance partner wants to mobilize Japan, it is important to ensure the legitimacy of any involvement in a conflict and operate under a UN resolution. In Afghanistan, the US presence was clearly legitimate on the basis of a UN Security Council mandate. But because military action in Afghanistan and the Iraq invasion were conducted simultaneously by the US, the Japanese public often questioned the legitimacy of both operations. If Operation Iraqi Freedom had been conducted under a UN mandate or with multinational support, the landscape over the issue of SDF deployment to Afghanistan might have been different.

On July 1, 2014, the GOJ, led by Prime Minister Shinzo Abe, who came back into office in December 2012, presented the "Cabinet Decision on Development of Seamless Security Legislation to Ensure Japan's Survival and Protect Its People." Considering the national security environment, the decision aims at securing "the lives and peaceful livelihood of its people" and contributing "even more proactively to the peace and stability of the international community under the policy of 'Proactive Contribution to Peace.'" A series of bills for the decision were to be decided by the cabinet on May 14, 2015, and start being discussed in the Diet beginning on May 26, 2015. One of the notable focal points is that the legislation may allow Japan to exercise collective self-defense under very strict conditions. That will be the first challenge to the Japanese: to discuss the legal framework expanding the SDF's activities since the termination of the fuel supply operation for OEF in Afghanistan. The process may be the first test for how the Japanese realize the lessons learned that were discussed in this chapter.

NOTES

1. Ministry of Foreign Affairs, "Japan's Assistance in Afghanistan: Towards Self-Reliance," September 2012, http://www.mofa.go.jp/region/middle_e/afghanistan/pdfs/japan_assistance.pdf.

2. Prime Minister of Japan and His Cabinet, "Statement by Prime Minister Junichiro Koizumi at the Press Conference," September 12, 2001, http://www.kantei.go.jp/foreign/koizumispeech/2001/0912kaiken_e.html.

3. Prime Minister of Japan and His Cabinet, "Opening Statement by Prime Minister Junichiro Koizumi at the Press Conference," September 19, 2001, http://www.kantei.go.jp/foreign/koizumispeech/2001/0919sourikaiken_e.html.

4. Ministry of Foreign Affairs, "Current Issues Surrounding UN Peace-keeping Operations and Japanese Perspective," January 1997, http://www.mofa.go.jp/policy/un/pko/issues.html.

5. Tero Taisaku Tokubetsu Sochi Ho (The Anti-Terrorism Special Measures Law), http://www.cas.go.jp/jp/hourei/houritu/tero_h.html; "The Anti-Terrorism Special Measures Law," http://www.kantei.go.jp/foreign/policy/2001/anti-terrorism/1029terohougaiyou_e.html.

6. The Anti-Terrorism Special Measures Law, Article 2, supra note 5.

7. Shotaro Yauchi, "*9.11 Tero Kougeki No Keii To Nihon No Taio*" (September 11 attacks and Japanese response), *Kokusai Mondai* (February 2002): 8.

8. Richard J. Samuels, *Securing Japan: Tokyo's Grand Strategy and the Future of East Asia* (London: Cornell University Press, 2007), 95.

9. *Yomiuri*, July 3, 2001, 1.

10. *Yomiuri*, October 23, 2001, 2.

11. After Eda's statement, the original article on the home page was deleted, but it is preserved at the Internet Archive at http://web.archive.org/web/20050425080024/.

12. Prime Minister of Japan and His Cabinet, "Press Conference by Prime Minister Junichiro Koizumi on the Issue of Iraq," March 20, 2003, http://www.kantei.go.jp/foreign/koizumispeech/2003/03/20kaiken_e.html.

13. *Sankei*, March 24, 2003, 6.

14. *Mainichi*, December 1, 2003, 1.

15. *Yomiuri*, June 1, 2008, 2.

16. *Asahi*, June 18, 2008, 4.

17. *Asahi*, July 13, 2008, 2. On August 26, 2008, a Japanese NGO member was abducted and killed in Afghanistan (*Yomiuri*, August 26, 2008, evening edition, 1; August 28, 2008, 1). This incident itself did not influence the GOJ decision to give up SDF deployment because the decision had already been made. If the incident had occurred before the decision was made, it might have played a large role.

18. *Mainichi*, December 7, 2010, 5.

19. *Yomiuri*, November 13, 2010, evening edition, 1.

20. *Mainichi*, September 18, 2011, 1.

21. Cabinet Office, "*Jieitai no Hoyu Shien Katudo ni Kansuru Tokubetu Yoron Chosa*" (Special public opinion poll on SDF's logistic support activities), March 5, 2009, http://www8.cao.go.jp/survey/tokubetu/h20/h20-hokyu.pdf.

22. Andrew L. Oros, *Normalizing Japan: Politics, Identity, and the Evolution of Security Practice* (Stanford, CA: Stanford University Press, 2008), 45–48.

16 AUSTRALIA

Terrorism, Regional Security, and the US Alliance

Maryanne Kelton and Aaron P. Jackson

AT THE DAWN OF THE NEW millennium it would have required a stretch to imagine that the Australian Defence Force (ADF) would shortly be deployed to Afghanistan. But by December 2001 approximately 200 Special Forces (SF) members were deployed to Afghanistan, and a decade later 1,550 troops were in theater. Australia's commitment was supported on a bipartisan basis and strategically and politically motivated to counter the rise of terrorism, enhance regional security, support the US, and, by doing so, augment its alliance relationship.

Australia's deployment to Afghanistan occurred in four stages that marked part of a revived expeditionary approach to confront a threat distant from Australian shores and in conjunction with its US ally. The first stage, with the initial SF contribution, was designed to disable Taliban support for terrorist attacks on the West. The second stage was population focused, with SF and conventional forces and incorporated engineers assigned to reconstruction roles in Uruzgan province. In the third stage, as Australia hesitantly assumed control from the Dutch in Uruzgan, capacity building was designed to progressively transfer responsibility to the local population. Finally, in the fourth stage, following withdrawal from Uruzgan, a relatively smaller force remained in Afghanistan to continue to provide limited training and advice to Afghan security forces.

Complementary to analysis of these stages is an examination of the lack of public debate in Australia that would question the mission and Australia's role within it. Though a more robust debate took place in other coalition countries about the effectiveness of the counterinsurgency strategy, this debate was largely bypassed in Australia. For the most part too, despite rippling concerns over the unilateralism of the Bush administration's foreign policy, Australians exhibited wariness that any critique of the war could be interpreted as disrespect for the ADF. Ultimately, however, while Australia significantly increased its expenditures to upgrade intelligence agencies and coordinate national security responses to the terrorist threat, counterterrorism eventually subsided as a priority in national strategy documents, being replaced by a focus on shifting regional power dynamics.

WHY AFGHANISTAN? AUSTRALIAN MOTIVES FOR PARTICIPATION

Since it became evident that al Qaeda was responsible for the 9/11 terrorist attacks on the US in 2001, Australian prime ministers, regardless of political affiliation, cited three primary motivations for Australia's participation: to remove al Qaeda and its affiliates from their bases in Afghanistan; by doing so, to deny threats to Western targets and regional stability; and importantly, to bolster the strength of Australia's US alliance by supporting the US in its pursuit of al Qaeda. This section explores these and additional political motivations.

First, Australia supported the US action as a response to the 9/11 attacks, in which nearly three thousand people perished, including eleven Australian nationals. Both at the time and since, Australian governments have justified the action in Afghanistan as necessary to remove the al Qaeda threat and to deny that transnational organization and its affiliated networks sanctuary to plan, arm, and train in Afghanistan. The military response directed toward Afghanistan understood that the Afghan Taliban and elements of the Pakistani Directorate of Inter-Service Intelligence (ISI) with interests in Afghanistan had provided al Qaeda with safe haven to develop its international terrorist network since 1996.[1] The Australian government was thus motivated to work in coalition to eliminate the threat of continued strikes by al Qaeda and affiliated militant groups against international targets, as it threatened international order.

Second, the Australian government was concerned about al Qaeda's impact on Australia's regional security. In Afghanistan itself, al Qaeda may have provided "strategic depth" for Pakistan in the latter's ongoing rivalry with India (any inflation of tension between these two nuclear armed states remains of strategic concern for Australia).[2] More broadly but in the same ilk, Australia was also motivated to participate in the deployment to eliminate al Qaeda, as its reach was believed to extend to Southeast Asia, proximal to Australian shores. Australia harbored particular concerns about the development of affiliated terrorist groups.[3] Three of these groups—Jemaah Islamiyah in Indonesia (believed to be the perpetrator of the 2004 bombing of the Australian embassy in Jakarta, and the 2002 and 2005 Bali bombings where ninety-two Australians were killed), and Abu Sayyaf and the Moro Islamic Liberation Front in the Philippines—contained central command members who had trained in Afghanistan in the late 1980s and 1990s.[4] Al Qaeda was considered to be supporting militant Islamic interests in autonomy for Indonesia's Aceh and Maluku provinces, and in Mindanao in the Philippines. Specifically, Australia was concerned to disrupt al Qaeda's provision of finance and training to these groups.

Australia was also concerned about preventing direct attacks on Australian nationals and its interests, but it was also aware of the transnational consequences of intrastate hostilities. Any consequent escalation of aggression could result in the destabilization of states within the region, inflate refugee movements, and threaten Australia's extensive maritime trade. As to the charge that Australia's participation in the war in Afghanistan sparked attacks against Australians in Jakarta, such as the bombing of the Australian embassy, Sidney Jones has argued both that the war was cited by some of the perpetrators as the reason for the targeting and that many of these bombers had been recruited into the Salafi jihadist network prior to the war.[5]

Third, Australia has historically been both an attentive and a prompt supporter of US military deployments. It has done so either as its interests have directly converged with those of the US, or because Australian policy makers have sought to maintain US regional presence, bolster Australia's alliance stocks, and enhance the possibility of reciprocity from the larger power in alliance relations. Two years before the Afghanistan deployment, conservative Prime Minister John Howard witnessed the valuable US provision of diplomatic and logistical support for Australia to lead the United Nations (UN) mission to East Timor during the 1999 sovereignty crisis. Consequently, Howard was inclined to provide immediate support for the US in 2001, and on September 14, 2001, Howard invoked Article IV of the ANZUS Treaty to respond to the attacks.

Remarkably, Howard was present in Washington, D.C., on September 11, 2001. Feeling a personal connection to the surprise attack on the US homeland, Howard demonstrated solidarity with the US by attending the first joint session of Congress held after 9/11. Politically too, the government's subsequent promotion of its security credentials, which was quickly interlinked with a tough approach to asylum seekers, contributed to Howard's reelection in November 2001.

This tripartite rationale for Australia's participation in Afghanistan evolved by 2005–2006. To justify the redeployment of the ADF and its upgraded role in "nation-building" and provincial reconstruction, Howard articulated that Australia's challenge was to rebuild a safe Afghan society and strengthen democracy and economic growth in response to a resurgent Taliban and al Qaeda.

Supplementary to this objective, in 2007 Labor Prime Minister Kevin Rudd homed in on Australia's goal of contributing to a stable and self-sufficient Afghanistan and to training Afghan National Army (ANA) personnel to eventually enable a withdrawal of the ADF. Specifically, he argued that through a comprehensive military-political-civil approach in Uruzgan province, Australia would enable the transition of the province through its administrative and capacity-building endeavors.[6] Labor Prime Minister Julia Gillard, who replaced Rudd in 2010, immediately adopted this theme.[7]

By the latter stages of the decade the difficulties of "nation-building" were becoming increasingly apparent, and the facilitation of transition, at least on paper, became necessary to enable an exit strategy to be implemented. This process began under Gillard and was continued by Rudd (who briefly returned to the prime minister role in June 2013) and then by conservative Prime Minister Tony Abbott, whose government was elected in September 2013. Abbott immediately aligned his support, citing broad-based but unspecified benefits for Australia, Afghanistan, and the world.

AUSTRALIAN PUBLIC SUPPORT FOR THE ADF, IF NOT THE WAR

Both the bipartisan consensus on the deployment, and a post–Vietnam War legacy to ensure that Australian soldiers were duly honored for their sacrifice, explained the relatively constrained debate in Australia regarding the appropriateness of the war and its conduct. In part it also explained the limited polling completed relative to Australia's US, British, and Canadian equivalents.[8] Moreover, that polling revealed reasonable levels of support for the war despite the lack of demonstrable military success and "nation-building" achievements over the decade. Nevertheless, public support declined in proportion to the increasing number of battlefield casualties—41 fatalities and 261 major injuries at the time of writing[9]—the majority of which occurred from 2010 onward as Australia reluctantly assumed a greater (and more dangerous) responsibility for the International Security Assistance Force (ISAF) mission in Uruzgan province. On the question of whether Australia should continue to be involved militarily in Afghanistan, a Lowy Institute for International Policy poll recorded that in 2007 support for the deployment was evenly divided (46 percent in favor and 46 percent opposed). By 2012, however, nearly two thirds of Australians opposed continuing involvement.[10]

AUSTRALIA'S MILITARY CONTRIBUTION TO AFGHANISTAN

Australia's military contribution cannot be accurately assessed in isolation from the broader context of Australia's military strategy and concurrent deployments. In the ADF (particularly the Australian Army), the years between Australia's withdrawal from Vietnam in 1972 and the deployment of the International Force in East Timor (INTERFET) in 1999 are colloquially known as "the long peace." A smattering of peacekeeping operations aside (the largest being the deployment of a battalion group to Somalia in 1992), the ADF did not deploy on operations during this period. A national security strategy dubbed the "Defence of Australia" gave priority to the Royal Australian Navy (RAN) and Royal Australian Air Force (RAAF) in preparing to defend the Australian continental landmass from an ill-defined threat. The result was the utter degradation of the army, which by 2000 was described as a "phantom" force, plagued by equipment, personnel, and funding shortages.[11]

The INTERFET deployment stretched the ADF almost to the breaking point. In the longer term, however, it and the subsequent UN peacekeeping missions in East Timor appear to have been blessings in disguise. As Paul Kelly observed (citing an anonymous interviewee): "When Howard came to power [in 1996] the Defence Department regarded the deployment of 100 personnel to Bougainville as a major operation yet a decade later Australia had nearly 4000 personnel abroad in about 10 operational missions."[12] The INTERFET operation, which peaked at the deployment of 5,521 personnel in late 1999, allowed shortfalls in Australia's military capabilities to be identified and addressed in a forgiving environment, relative to Afghanistan and Iraq. As a result the ADF was able to avoid having to learn these lessons a few years later and at what would almost certainly have been a much higher cost.

Australia's subsequent military commitment to Afghanistan, which began in October 2001, has been complicated. The deployment has frequently involved SF and conventional force elements concurrently conducting different missions, often in different parts of the country. It has been characterized by changing titles, frequently varying force numbers, and several changes to military strategy and operational priorities, which have in turn placed emphasis on different tactical tasks at different times. It has been further complicated by the concurrent deployment of forces to other parts of the Middle East, most notably to the Iraq War (2003–2009). To simplify this complication, it is useful to break Australia's military commitment to Afghanistan into four distinct stages, noting that this is for explanatory purposes only (neither the Australian government nor the ADF has referred to any such stages).

The first stage of Australia's military commitment to Afghanistan was from October 2001 to November 2002. This stage involved the commitment of a SF Task Force of approximately two hundred personnel to assist in overthrowing the Taliban. Toward the end of 2002, when the coalition focus shifted from combat operations to post-Taliban reconstruction, the minister for defense announced: "As the focus of operations has moved towards supporting the reconstruction of Afghanistan, the particular skills of our Special Forces are in less demand." As a result, the SF Task Force was withdrawn.[13] From this withdrawal until August 2005, Australia effectively ceased its military commitment to Afghanistan, with only an observer attached to the UN Assistance Mission in Afghanistan remaining in the country.

The second stage of Australia's military commitment to Afghanistan commenced in August 2005 with the deployment of another SF Task Force. During this period the SF Task Force numbered 150 to 190 personnel and performed "a variety of roles similar to those performed in 2001 including combat patrols of remote regions, reconnaissance and surveillance operations working closely with our Coalition partners."[14] Although Howard linked the deployment to coalition activity in the lead-up to the December 2005 Afghan national elections, the deployment was always publicly acknowledged as twelve months in duration and was withdrawn from Afghanistan in November 2006, a few months behind the original schedule and almost a year after the 2005 elections.

Unlike the first stage, the second stage also involved the deployment of conventional force elements. A Reconstruction Task Force (RTF) of four hundred personnel was deployed in August 2006. This title was changed in October 2008 to the Mentoring and Reconstruction Task Force (MRTF), following a change in operational focus from reconstruction to a more even balance between reconstruction and mentoring the fledgling ANA. The RTF deployed to Uruzgan province, where it formed part of a Dutch Provincial Reconstruction Team (PRT) that had also deployed in 2006 and that maintained overall command within the province. The bulk of the initial Australian conventional force deployment consisted of engineers (accompanied by other arms corps soldiers to provide their "close protection"), and the RTF was primarily geared toward conducting reconstruction tasks.[15]

A third SF Task Force, this time approximately 300 in strength, deployed in April 2007. The mission of this task force was provision of SF support to conventional forces deployed in Uruzgan, primarily by seeking to deny the Taliban sanctuaries and freedom of movement within the province. Australia also deployed up to 200 personnel in various roles in Kabul and Kandahar during 2007–2010 and gradually expanded the MRTF to 600 personnel by mid-2009.[16] By the end of that year, Australia's military deployment to Afghanistan numbered 1,080 personnel.

The third stage of Australia's military commitment to Afghanistan commenced in January 2010 with the symbolic name change of the MRTF to the Mentoring Task Force (MTF). In reality, reconstruction activities continued with little change; the important change that defined the new stage was Australia's preparations for the Dutch withdrawal from Afghanistan in August 2010. Subsequent to this withdrawal the US led a combined ISAF team in Uruzgan, and Australia provided a civilian PRT leader. Australia's troop contribution rose to a peak of 1,550, including both the MTF and the SF Task Force, and Australia assumed greater (but not total) responsibility for security within Uruzgan. Australia's troop numbers in Afghanistan began to decline as a gradual withdrawal commenced in late 2012. In November it was announced that the MTF had withdrawn from several forward operating bases in Uruzgan, handing these over to the ANA, which had assumed primary responsibility for security in the province.[17]

The fourth stage of Australia's military commitment to Afghanistan commenced in December 2013 when the largest Australian base in Uruzgan, at Tarin Kot, was closed and the MTF withdrawn.[18] From January 2014, approximately four hundred Australian personnel remained in Afghanistan to provide ongoing training and advice to Afghan security forces.[19] Australian development assistance also continued, although the PRT mission in Uruzgan officially ended on October 31, 2013, and assistance thereafter focused on "the national level." Other government agencies seemed to be providing this assistance in preference to the military.[20] At the time of writing the nature and duration of any possible Australian commitment to Afghanistan after 2014 has not been announced; however, Australia will likely withdraw within a similar time frame to that of the US.[21]

Concurrent to its Afghanistan deployment, Australia's other military commitments included major operations in East Timor (1999–2005 and 2006–2013), Iraq (2003–2009), and the Solomon Islands (2003–2013), as well as several minor operations. Notably, Afghanistan greatly increased in significance over time relative to Australia's other military deployments. This increase is summarized in Table 16.1, which shows the number of Australian troops deployed to

Table 16.1 Australian personnel deployed to Afghanistan and elsewhere, 1998–2013

| Year | Number of Australian Defence Force personnel deployed to . . . | | | | | Total personnel deployed | Afghanistan deployment (% of total) |
	East Timor	Solomon Islands	Iraq	Afghanistan	Other overseas operations		
1998	—	—	—	—	138	138	0.0
1999	5,521	—	—	—	188	5,709	0.0
2000	1,620	—	—	—	187	1,807	0.0
2001	1,474	—	—	~200	189	1,863	10.7
2002	1,315	—	—	~200	73	1,588	12.6
2003	824	1,500	~1,000	1	38	3,363	< 0.1
2004	259	530	850	1	38	1,678	< 0.1
2005	2	530	850	~151	~45	1,578	9.6
2006	3	140	1,350	400	~52	1,945	20.6
2007	925	140	1,400	400	~52	2,917	13.7
2008	850	140	1,575	907	~60	3,532	25.7
2009	750	140	350	1,080	~385	2,705	39.9
2010	650	80	80	1,350	~360	2,520	53.6
2011	404	80	35	1,550	~365	2,434	63.7
2012	380	80	35	1,550	~362	2,407	64.4
2013	390	80	2	1,550	348	2,370	65.4

NOTES

1. Figures given are based on publicly available data found in International Institute of Strategic Studies, *The Military Balance*, vols. 98–113 (published annually from 1998 to 2013), supplemented by publicly available Australian government data (sources of this data are cited elsewhere in this chapter).

2. Approximate figures are included in cases where exact numbers of personnel deployed are not available. Approximate figures are denoted by the symbol ~.

3. Where approximate figures are given, the possible variance between them and the actual number of personnel deployed is unlikely to be greater than plus or minus 10 percent.

4. Figures in the "Other overseas operations" column include the deployment of up to approximately one hundred personnel to Bougainville (Papua New Guinea) from 1998 to 2003.

5. Figures in the "Other overseas operations" column also include troops deployed to the Middle East Area of Operations (MEAO) (313 personnel) from 2009 onward. Personnel deployed to the MEAO provided support to operations in both Iraq and Afghanistan. Note that personnel deployed to the MEAO from 2003 to 2008 were considered rear elements of the Iraq deployment, and so they are included in the figures given in the Iraq column.

Afghanistan as a percentage of the total number deployed on all overseas operations from 1998 to 2013. During the first stage of the Afghanistan deployment, Australian personnel there numbered 10 to 13 percent of the total number deployed on all operations. During the second stage this increased to almost 40 percent, and during the third and fourth stages it was consistently 50 to 65 percent.[22]

MILITARY REFORMS

For the ADF, major reforms undertaken during the period of the Afghanistan deployment have resulted as much from other operations as from Afghanistan. These reforms began with changes to Australia's national strategy, which progressively moved away from "Defence of Australia" and toward an expeditionary paradigm with a less explicit policy supporting it. This paradigm is characterized by a dual willingness to deploy the ADF to support Pacific countries during periods of instability and to make force contributions, alongside allies, to other locations to support global security and the international community.

The relationship between this strategic shift and the Afghanistan commitment was indirect at best. As Michael Evans observed, since federation in 1901, Australian defense strategy has oscillated between continentally focused defense strategies and expeditionary defense strategies. The former tend to prioritize the RAN and RAAF as the first line of continental defense, while the latter tend to focus on the army as an instrument to pursue Australian security interests overseas.[23] At the end of the 1990s, Australia was reaching the end of a quarter century of continentally focused strategic policy. The deployment to East Timor in 1999, and the confidence Howard gained from its success, signaled the end of this strategy and the commencement of a period of expeditionary operations.[24] Australia's deployment to Afghanistan can be seen as part of this broader shift, rather than a trigger for it.

Although it did not directly shape national strategy, the Afghanistan deployment (as well as deployments to East Timor and Iraq) nevertheless shaped military strategy, operations, and tactics. Beginning in 2004, the combined experiences of these deployments led to major reforms to ADF joint command and control arrangements. These included the establishment of a Joint Operations Command (JOC), which can be viewed as the most recent step in a series of ADF joint reforms that began in the 1970s. Since the establishment of JOC there has been "only one operational headquarters in Australia, with one operations room."[25] The three services (RAN, the Australian Army, and

RAAF) are today responsible for raising, training and sustaining forces, which are transferred to the authority of the commander of JOC for deployment on operations. This has greatly streamlined the process for command and control of all ADF deployed forces, not just those in Afghanistan.

Another Australian command structure change was the establishment of a Special Operations Command (SOCOMD) in 2003. Modeled along the lines of its British and American counterparts, SOCOMD has equal status to Australia's traditional commands; however, its constituent units are all drawn from the army.[26] Like its allies' SF, Australian SF constitute a "niche" capability that is ideally suited to counterinsurgency operations of the type conducted in Afghanistan. This conflict, together with East Timor and Iraq, has since 1999 generated an almost constant demand for Australia's SF, in turn necessitating the enhanced command arrangements provided by SOCOMD.

Beyond their operational capabilities, the deployment of SF yields another important benefit to Australia. Because of their strategic visibility, SF operations can have a relatively high impact within a coalition context. Given the alliance motives underlying Australia's participation in Afghanistan, it is unsurprising that the government would seek to maximize the visibility of its military contribution. This additional benefit of SF was particularly strong during the early 2000s, but it has now diminished somewhat. Since 2007 the SF Task Force deployed to Uruzgan has primarily provided SF support to the Australian conventional forces in the province. This role, while greatly important, has primarily an operational rather than a strategic impact.

Afghanistan and Australia's concurrent deployments have also influenced the development of operating concepts, particularly within the army, which in 2005 was credited by *The Military Balance* as being "the first to publish a comprehensive analysis of the new conflict environment and its implications."[27] This was manifest in two documents, *Complex Warfighting*, released in 2004, and *Adaptive Campaigning*, released in 2006. The timing of the release of these documents suggests that East Timor and Iraq were more pertinent to their development than Afghanistan, but they nonetheless warrant mentioning as they have since affected ADF operations and tactics in Afghanistan.

Complex Warfighting addressed the contemporary operating environment in detail before making the (then novel but now clichéd) observation that it was becoming increasingly complex. In response, it called for forces that were "optimized for versatility, agility and orchestration."[28] *Adaptive Campaigning* elaborated on this idea considerably, establishing five "lines of operation" that focused on either the host nation population, capacity building, or fighting the enemy. It then declared that "the key to the Land Force's success will be its ability to effectively orchestrate effort across the five lines of operation."[29] The first of these documents seems to have influenced conceptual developments in the US, with *The Military Balance* also observing that "large portions of the new US future land warfighting concept appear to have been drawn directly from the Australian Complex Warfighting doctrine."[30] This is opposite to the usual Australia-US relationship, in which warfighting concepts have traditionally flowed from the US military to Australia.[31]

The Australian influence on US conceptual development was short-lived, and less than a year after the preceding observation was made, the US Army and Marine Corps published their famous 2006 *Counterinsurgency* doctrine without any noteworthy reference to Australian developments. Furthermore, the extensive debate in the US in the lead-up to the publication of this doctrine had no parallel in Australia. In fact, despite a strong tradition of "irregular warfare" that dates to the anti-Japanese campaigns of WWII,[32] the ADF as an institution seems to have all but missed the contemporary debate on counterinsurgency. Addressing why this may be the case, Albert Palazzo offered three explanations. First, a culture of anti-intellectualism, which also pervades Australian society, has led to the preeminence of pragmatism and empiricism within the ADF. Second, bureaucratic processes within the Australian Department of Defence impede and deter members of the ADF who might otherwise seek to engage in public debate. Third, the operational roles of the ADF as a junior coalition partner have averted the need to think about warfare above the realm of tactics—as a junior coalition partner, the ADF is able instead to simply follow the intellectual trends of its American and British allies (a pragmatic approach that has the benefit of enhancing interoperability).[33]

In light of this, it is unsurprising that the Australian Army's concept papers discussed earlier were published during the mid-2000s, when allied intellectual developments were failing to keep pace with events. Even then the Australian response was through institutional publications, with debate seldom spilling over into the public realm. Since its allies, the US in particular, began to engage in their own debates about contemporary conflict, the pace of Australian conceptual development has greatly slowed.

NATIONAL STRATEGIC REFOCUS TO THE IMMEDIATE REGION

Certainly the Australian government made significant investments in its Afghanistan campaign as part of its wider "war on terror" strategy. As regards financial costs, since 2001 (and with the two-year hiatus in 2003–2005) Australia allocated in the order of AUD 8 billion to the campaign, with AUD 1.4 billion allocated in the 2012–2013 budget alone.[34] Between 2001 and 2012, Australia allocated an additional AUD 916 million in aid funding for Afghanistan. Domestically, Australia reformed its national security apparatus and endeavored to coordinate a more comprehensive approach. Australia's first National Security Statement, delivered in 2008, formalized the attempted integration. Adding capacity to human intelligence gathering and analysis, three key Australian intelligence agencies also experienced per annum budgetary growth between 11.4 and 14.4 percent between 2001–2002 and 2012–2013.[35]

As Australia prepared to withdraw troops from Uruzgan province in December 2013, questions arose about the impact of the Afghanistan campaign on national strategy. History reveals that Australian governments have reduced defense expenditure after every war since WWII. So it may be anticipated that expenditure on operations will decline. Yet there are two factors that may militate against the cessation of the expeditionary approach or dramatic reductions in defense expenditure. For the peaceful society that is Australia, a surprising history of expeditionary militarism endures. This incongruity can be understood historically as Australia has assiduously supported both the British Empire and, after WWII, its US ally in conducting military operations globally. The maintenance of an alliance with a larger power has been integral to Australian strategic policy. Though the lessons of Afghanistan demonstrate the problematic nature of missions demanding nation-building in complex, messy wars of the typology described by Mary Kaldor and Rupert Smith,[36] the US alliance remains a constant in Australian strategic calculations.

Additionally, for all of the extraordinary focus and expenditure on countering terrorism and the key place of the Afghanistan mission within it, Australia's strategic attention has now been diverted to the shifting power dynamics of the East Asian and Indo-Pacific regions. Despite the antiterrorist campaign of the 2000s, traditional interstate concerns are now being increasingly identified within Australian policy documents. Australian White Papers and Defence Updates have accentuated the state-based threat and response. For example, the *Defence Update 2007* specified that "despite the security challenges posed by terrorism—as serious as they are—nation-states are still the key players shaping our security environment."[37] Responsive to this mixed set of challenges, Australia's defense expenditure increased from AUD 13.1 billion in 2001 to AUD 23.6 billion in 2010, and with 1.92 percent GDP allocated, Australia ranked as the world's twelfth largest military in terms of defense expenditure.[38] From 2010 to 2013, however, with increasing pressures on the Australian economy and rising budgetary restraint, the Australian government cut the ADF's day-to-day operating budget substantially, although costs directly relating to Afghanistan were quarantined from these cuts.

With its exit from Afghanistan imminent, Australian strategic cooperation with the US is now attuned to the demands of the strategic rebalance to the East Asian region. Up to 2,500 US Marines will be based in Darwin in Australia's Northern Territory, while a series of Australia-US communiqués articulated increasing cooperation in the maritime, space, and cyber domains.[39] This cooperation is intended to bolster Australian security and enhance US regional primacy in response to emerging Chinese power in the region.

The cooperation also facilitates increased collaboration regarding surveillance of Indian Ocean sea lines of communication and energy transport routes, as well as helping Australia to access surveillance of the Central Asian and Middle Eastern regions. In this respect, with the increasing prominence of the Indo-Pacific in alliance consciousness, Australia's convergence of interests with NATO in Central Asia and the western Indian Ocean may also become more germane. Though Australia's primary strategic concerns are geographically separate from those of NATO,[40] its links may be of consequence if future US-led coalition deployments require cooperation. The recent Australia-NATO joint declaration to strengthen the partnership remains a rhetorical acknowledgement, at least, of both ongoing counterterrorism and increasing interests in a partnership to respond to transnational energy, cyber, piracy, and disaster relief concerns.[41]

PROGNOSIS: LIKELY IMPACT INTO THE FUTURE

Where Australia's commitment to Afghanistan is likely to have an enduring impact is at the operational level (i.e., within the military). In particular, the standing up of JOC has fundamentally changed the way the ADF plans and executes military operations, and this is likely to have an enduring impact well into the twenty-first century. Another likely future impact, albeit not immediately obvious, is the ongoing effect that Australia's military operations in Afghanistan are likely to have on training, particularly within the army. Australia's major military operations, the longest of which had been ongoing since 1999, had all ceased by 2013 with the exception of Afghanistan, where the majority of forces were withdrawn at the end of 2013 (although a greatly reduced force remained deployed thereafter). As a result the ADF faces the possibility of a situation similar to "the long peace" of the last quarter of the twentieth century. Given the growing prominence of Afghanistan relative to Australia's other military commitments (see Table 16.1), it may well become the template for tactical-level (and perhaps operational-level) training well into the future, in the same way that operations in Vietnam had an ongoing impact on training well into the 1990s.

Regarding Australian strategic policy, Afghanistan is likely to have a minimal impact, even in the very near future. Instead, Australia is undergoing a strategic refocus on the East Asian and Indo-Pacific regions. Although this may in the midterm result in a full-scale revival of the "Defence of Australia" policy of the late 1980s and early 1990s, such a revival will be costly given the changing strategic dynamics of these regions.[42] It is more realistic, therefore, to expect that Australia will continue to deploy forces abroad but will seek to limit its deployments to these regions and to lower-intensity operations, such as humanitarian or peacekeeping-type operations. Following its election in September 2013, the Abbott government announced that it would release a new Defence White Paper within eighteen months, meaning that the exact direction of the current government's strategic policy is unlikely to be officially published until mid-2015.[43]

Regardless of its stated strategic policy, Australia has a very strong strategic tradition of being the "first follower" of its great power ally. In 2001, Australia very quickly modified its national strategy in response to the terrorist attacks against the US, a modification that was accompanied by a rapid deployment of SF to Afghanistan. Should the US, which is itself shifting strategic focus to East Asia and the Indo-Pacific, quickly change its focus back to another region, then Australia is likely to be there with the US in some capacity.

NOTES

1. Amin Saikal, "Afghanistan, Terrorism, and American and Australian Responses," *Australian Journal of International Affairs* 56, no. 1 (2002): 23–30.

2. Ibid., 24.

3. Joseph M. Siracusa, "John Howard, Australia, and the Coalition of the Willing," *Yale Journal of International Affairs* 1, no. 2 (2006): 43; Prime Minister John Howard, "Philippines Counter-terrorism Assistance Initiative," media release, Canberra, July 14, 2003.

4. International Crisis Group, "Jemaah Islamiyah in South East Asia: Damaged but Still Dangerous," *Asia Report* 63 (August 26, 2003), 7–10, 16–18, http://www.crisisgroup

.org/~/media/Files/asia/south-east-asia/indonesia/063-jemaah-islamiyah-in-south-east-asia.pdf.

5. Sidney Jones, "The Changing Face of Terrorism in Indonesia: Weaker, More Diffuse, and Still a Threat," speech at the Australian Strategic Policy Institute, September 15, 2005.

6. Prime Minister Kevin Rudd, "Transcript of Press Conference," April 29, 2009.

7. Prime Minister Julia Gillard, "Our Security Is at Stake in Afghanistan," *Sydney Morning Herald*, July 12, 2010, http://www.smh.com.au/federal-politics/our-security-is-at-stake-in-afghanistan-20100711-105jz.html.

8. Kevin Foster (ed.), *What Are We Doing in Afghanistan: The Military and the Media at War* (Melbourne: Australian Scholarly Publishing, 2009).

9. Statistics correct as of August 1, 2014. Nathan Church, *Australia at War in Afghanistan: Updated Facts and Figures*, Parliament of Australia, December 13, 2013, http://www.aph.gov.au/About_Parliament/Parliamentary_Departments/Parliamentary_Library/pubs/rp/rp1314/AfghanistanFactsUpdated; Australian Special Broadcasting Service, "Timeline: ADF Deaths in Afghanistan," July 2, 2014, http://www.sbs.com.au/news/article/2014/07/02/timeline-adf-deaths-afghanistan.

10. Fergus Hanson, "Australia and New Zealand in the World: Public Opinion and Foreign Policy," in *The Lowy Institute Poll 2012* (Sydney: Lowy Institute for International Policy, 2012), 7.

11. Joint Standing Committee on Foreign Affairs and Trade, *From Phantom to Force: Towards a More Efficient and Effective Army* (Canberra: Parliament of the Commonwealth of Australia, August 2000).

12. Paul Kelly, *Howard's Decade: An Australian Foreign Policy Reappraisal*, Lowy Institute Paper No. 15 (Double Bay: Lowy Institute for International Policy, 2006), 39.

13. Senator Robert Hill, Minister for Defence, "Media Release: Australian Special Forces to Return from Afghanistan," MIN 664/02, November 20, 2002.

14. Senator Robert Hill, "Media Release: Special Forces Task Group Deploy to Afghanistan," 135/2005, August 24, 2005.

15. Lieutenant Colonel Mick Ryan, "The Other Side of the COIN: Reconstruction Operations in Southern Afghanistan," *Australian Army Journal* 4, no. 2 (Winter 2007), 125–143.

16. Nicole Brangwin, *Australia's Military Involvement in Afghanistan Since 2001: A Chronology*, Parliament of Australia: Parliamentary Library Background Note 2010-11, July 16, 2010, 18–19.

17. Ben Doherty and David Wroe, "Australia Pulls Back in Afghanistan, Timor," *Sydney Morning Herald*, November 22, 2012, http://www.smh.com.au/federal-politics/political-news/australia-pulls-back-in-afghanistan-timor-20121121-29qgw.html.

18. Prime Minister Tony Abbott and Defence Minister David Johnston, "Joint Press Conference," December 16, 2013.

19. Australian Department of Defence, "Operation SLIPPER," current as of August 2014, http://www.defence.gov.au/operations/afghanistan/home.asp.

20. Australian Department of Foreign Affairs and Trade, *Conclusion of the Provincial Reconstruction Team mission in Uruzgan*, n.d., http://dfat.gov.au/geo/afghanistan/pages/afghanistan.aspx.

21. David Wroe, "Australia Expected to Follow US Timetable and Withdraw from Afghanistan by End of 2016," *Sydney Morning Herald*, May 28, 2014, http://www.smh.com.au/federal-politics/political-news/australia-expected-to-follow-us-timetable-and-withdraw-from-afghanistan-by-end-of-2016-20140528-39402.html.

22. Percentages based on publicly available statistics in International Institute of Strategic Studies, *The Military Balance*, Vols. 98–113 (published annually 1998–2013).

23. Michael Evans, "Overcoming the Creswell-Foster Divide in Australian Strategy: The Challenge for Twenty-first Century Policy-makers," *Australian Journal of International Affairs* 61, no. 2 (June 2007), 193–195.

24. Kelly, *Howard's Decade*, 39–46.

25. David Horner, "The Higher Command Structure for Joint ADF Operations," in *History as Policy: Framing the Debate on the Future of Australia's Defence Policy*, ed. Ron Huisken and Meredith Thatcher, Canberra Papers on Strategy and Defence No. 167 (Canberra: Australian National University Press, 2007), 159.

26. Australian Army, *Special Operations Command*, n.d., http://www.army.gov.au/Who-we-are/Divisions-and-Brigades/Special-Operations-Command.

27. International Institute for Strategic Studies (IISS), *Military Balance* 105 (2005): 418.

28. Australian Army, *Complex Warfighting*, May 7, 2004, 19.

29. Australian Army, *Adaptive Campaigning: The Land Force Response to Complex Warfighting*, Version 4.18, reproduced as Appendix 2 to Scott Hopkins (ed.), *Chief of Army's Exercise Proceedings 2006* (Duntroon, Australia: Land Warfare Studies Centre, 2006), 7.

30. IISS, *Military Balance* 105 (2005): 419.

31. Aaron P. Jackson, "Moving Beyond Manoeuvre: A Conceptual Coming-of-age for the Australian and Canadian Armies," *Australian Defence Force Journal* 177 (November/December 2008): 85–100.

32. Russell Parkin, "The Sources of the Australian Tradition in Irregular Warfare, 1942–1974," *Small Wars and Insurgencies* 20, no. 1 (March 2009), 118–140.

33. Albert Palazzo, *The Future of War Debate in Australia: Why Has There Not Been One? Has the Need for One Now Arrived?* Working Paper No. 140 (Canberra: Australian Army Land Warfare Studies Centre, August 2012).

34. Mark Thompson, *The Cost of Defence: ASPI Defence Budget Brief 2012–2013* (Canberra, Australian Strategic Policy Institute, May 2012), 178.

35. Ibid., 17.

36. Mary Kaldor, *New and Old Wars: Organised Violence in a Global Era*, 2nd ed. (Cambridge: Polity Press, 2006); Rupert Smith, *The Utility of Force: The Art of War in the Modern World* (London: Allen Lane, 2005).

37. Australian Department of Defence, *Australia's National Security: Defence Update 2007*, Canberra, 2007.

38. Thompson, *The Cost of Defence*, 167.

39. Australia-US Ministerial Meeting, "Joint Communiqué," Melbourne, November 8, 2010.

40. Benjamin Schreer, *Beyond Afghanistan: NATO's Global Partnerships in the Asia Pacific*, Research Paper No. 75 (Rome: NATO Defense College, April 2012), 4.

41. Prime Minister Julia Gillard and Anders Fogh Rasmussen, "Transcript of Joint Press Conference with the NATO Secretary General," June 14, 2012.

42. Hugh White, "A Middling Power," *The Monthly* 82 (September 2012), https://www.themonthly.com.au/issue/2012/september/1346903463/hugh-white/middling-power.

43. Peter Jennings, "Not Dead Yet: 2013 White Paper Clings On," *The Strategist: Australian Strategic Policy Institute Blog*, October 2013, http://www.aspistrategist.org.au/not-dead-yet-white-paper-2013-clings-on.

17 NEW ZEALAND

Fostering the US–New Zealand Relationship

Robert Ayson

AS NEW ZEALAND'S FLAG was lowered in Bamyan province in April 2013, some of the media reporting suggested that the ten-year deployment of a Kiwi Provincial Reconstruction Team (PRT) represented the start and finish of the contribution by the New Zealand Defence Force (NZDF) in Afghanistan. The PRT's continuous presence in Bamyan on a seemingly endless stream of six-month rotations had provided most of the ongoing news about New Zealand's presence in Afghanistan. It had also been the focus of much of the grief and concern about the loss of New Zealand personnel, with the majority of the NZDF's ten fatalities in theater occurring in the increasingly hazardous northeast sector of Bamyan in the last two years of the decade-long commitment. New Zealand's effort in Bamyan also reflected elements of a wider governmental approach, with police, aid personnel, and diplomats deployed to the province. And, attracting support from the major political parties, both the center-right National Party and the center-left Labour Party, who alternated in leading coalition governments over the period, the Bamyan element of New Zealand's contribution in Afghanistan also enjoyed a good deal of favorable political coverage.

But New Zealand's commitment in Afghanistan did not begin or end in Bamyan. It did not *end* because New Zealand's ministers of defense and foreign affairs and trade announced in early 2013 that "a small but proportionate military commitment to the international mission in Afghanistan"[1] (consisting of about two dozen NZDF personnel) would be stationed in Kabul, a deployment that was then extended a year later. This was New Zealand's recognition that clean and clear exits are rare in the long and complex missions that run the spectrum from peace-building and nation-building to counterinsurgency and conventional military operations. New Zealand thereby remained connected to the NATO effort in its closing months and will also continue after that time as a provider of development assistance to Afghanistan. Moreover, New Zealand's commitment in Afghanistan did not *begin* in Bamyan either. Two years before-hand, as part of the strong international response to the terrorist attacks of September 11, 2001, on the US, the NZDF was an early contributor to the combined international military effort that, at least in its initial phase, helped drive the Taliban from power and degrade al Qaeda in Afghanistan.

As this chapter will demonstrate, New Zealand's involvement in Afghanistan from late 2001 is as much about the wider diplomatic context in which military affairs take place as it is about what happened in theater. The small NZDF (which at the time of writing numbers less than ten thousand regular personnel) was never going to play a quantitatively significant role in the external military presence in Afghanistan. Even during the periods when New Zealand's Special Forces (the Special Air Service or SAS) were deployed concurrently with the Bamyan PRT and the headquarters contingent in Kabul, the NZDF's numbers in Afghanistan rarely exceeded two hundred. This is not to question the quality of the New Zealanders' role. Few other PRTs appear to have worked as effectively and readily with the provincial population. In fact, the repeated interest from Washington and elsewhere for the retention and redeployment of the New Zealand SAS is a sign of the high esteem in which this particular component of the NZDF is held. But the most long-standing implications for New Zealand of its commitment in Afghanistan have come in the kick-start that this commitment has given to New Zealand's international relationships. This was particularly the case for New Zealand–US relations, which were still in a fairly modest state of repair when the first NZDF elements deployed in Afghanistan. A decade later, the two countries were enjoying a new security partnership. New Zealand did not join the mission in Afghanistan to achieve a closer relationship with the US. But thanks to its Afghanistan commitment, such a relationship became possible.

GETTING AND STAYING INVOLVED

As is the case in many other parts of the world, New Zealanders can still recall the moment they first learned of the devastating terrorist attacks on the US in 2001. Television channels immediately switched to live coverage from New York and Washington. The New Zealand government, led by Labour Prime Minster Helen Clark, was quick to join the international condemnation of the attacks, supported by parties across the political spectrum in New Zealand's single-chamber parliament. Unlike her Australian counterpart John Howard, Prime Minister Clark was not visiting the US when the attacks occurred. Nor did New Zealand join Australia by symbolically invoking the 1951 Australia–New Zealand–US (ANZUS) Security Treaty to signal its decision to come to America's assistance.[2] In New Zealand's case this would have been politically awkward; the US had suspended its ANZUS security relationship with New Zealand in the mid-1980s after an earlier Labour government (in which Prime Minister Clark also served) had applied its nuclear free policy to the potential visits of US naval vessels.[3] But in its own clear way New Zealand did join the conflict in Afghanistan with special forces personnel, long-range maritime patrol and Hercules transport aircraft, and a frigate deployed to a Persian Gulf interception force, all part of its role in Operation Enduring Freedom. This seems to set up a very clear cause-and-effect relationship in New Zealand's decision making toward Afghanistan. The independent variable consisted of the outrageous acts of terrorism organized from within Afghanistan that were perpetrated on the US. The dependent variable was New Zealand's participation in an international coalition designed to dislodge and defeat the organization responsible for these attacks and the unsavory Taliban regime in Kabul that was hosting al Qaeda. While New Zealand did not join the George W. Bush administration in referring to this multinational action as part of a "war on terror," it was certainly part of the team.

Yet this was more than a simple cause-and-effect relationship. There was a significant intervening variable, the full significance of which was only to become clear in 2003 when the US sought international support for a much more controversial military operation in Iraq. This intervening variable, which made New Zealand's involvement in Afghanistan possible, came at the United Nations, where the Security Council (UNSC) approved resolutions paving the way for states to take action against the perpetrators of the terrorist acts in accordance with their rights of self-defense under the UN Charter.[4] This suited New Zealand's preference for internationally legitimized military commitments, a philosophy that runs especially deep in the foreign policy of Labour-led governments. Eighteen months later, as the Bush administration was looking for partners in the invasion of Iraq, the lack of specific UNSC authorization for this controversial action was a central reason for New Zealand's absence from the rather select coalition of the willing. To put it bluntly, the Clark government regarded international military action in Afghanistan in late 2001 as both necessary and legitimate. In its view, the situation in Iraq in 2003 satisfied neither of these criteria.[5]

As anyone with a map can see, Afghanistan and Iraq are not in completely different parts of the world, and because New Zealand became part of a maritime interception force, the potential for overlap with the maritime isolation of Iraq became a challenging question. A polarizing study of New Zealand's involvement in Afghanistan made this gray zone a point of some public controversy years afterward.[6] But during the course of New Zealand's commitment in Afghanistan, it was the presence of special forces that were the most politically and publicly controversial. This may have in part been a result of the levels of secrecy that are normally attached to the activities of the SAS. But it is also because of perceptions in New Zealand that the special forces were most likely, of any of the military components sent to Afghanistan, to be involved in assertive combat roles. These concerns grew as New Zealand's participation in Afghanistan went on, and by the time their party was in opposition after losing the 2009 general election to a center-right National Party coalition, Labour politicians themselves were publicly asking questions about the roles and justification of the SAS commitment.

By comparison, questions were rarely raised about the successive deployment of New Zealand forces to the PRT that began operating in Bamyan in 2003.[7] This less controversial part of the NZDF's presence in Afghanistan was clearly supported more widely because of the reconstruction and nation-building purposes with which it was closely associated. It was as if in the minds of many New Zealanders, the PRT forces were on a peacekeeping mission. These feelings may have been encouraged by the government's announcement at the time of the 2003 deployment that "A PRT is not a combat unit. It provides a strengthened military observer capacity, which also acts as a center for the facilitation of NGO and other civilian contributions to reconstruction."[8] To the extent that this belief existed, it was relatively untested in the early years of New Zealand's involvement in Bamyan, with few reports of hostile encounters to greet the NZDF. The same could not be said of the experience of the special forces, whose combat role was recognized by the Bush administration in 2004 by the award of the US Presidential Unit Citation to those in the first rotation that had served in Afghanistan in 2001 and 2002.

This was the most obvious sign of Washington's growing awareness of New Zealand's contribution in Afghanistan, and of an improvement in the security relationship between the two countries. Before long NZDF officers were stationed in Tampa, Florida, at US Central Command (USCENTCOM), a development that would have been hard to imagine not so many years earlier. New Zealand's PRT in Bamyan, which quickly became the main representation of NZ's commitment in Afghanistan, had an American connection as well: the NZDF had taken over responsibility for the security of this mountainous province from the US. It had done so in 2003 when most Americans were focused on the evolving Iraqi conflict. This was the start of a period (which some still regard as having been decisive for the evolution of the conflict in Afghanistan) where Washington's attention was distracted from the growing Afghan insurgency being fed from across the nebulous Pakistani border. As a key partner for the US and the UK in the initial assault on Saddam Hussein's Iraq, New Zealand's main security partner, Australia, also focused its own efforts farther west and took rather longer than New Zealand to step up its involvement in Afghanistan. In that sense at least, New Zealand was unencumbered (and undistracted) by a simultaneous commitment to two wars in Central Asia and the Middle East. However, New Zealand was involved at the same time in stabilization missions in Timor Leste and the Solomon Islands (which had been initiated by Australian-led coalitions in 1999 and 2003 respectively). Indeed, even without an Iraq commitment, this period was notable for the high operational tempo at which the NZDF found itself.

In Bamyan, New Zealand inherited responsibility for the security and reconstruction of a province that had been visibly scarred by the Taliban, who were despised by the local Hazari people. That disfigurement was evident in the destruction of the famous Buddhas in a site long regarded as an international United Nations Educational, Scientific and Cultural Organization (UNESCO) treasure. But in part because of those local attitudes, and perhaps because of the relative inaccessibility, Bamyan was never a hotbed of what became known as the Afghan insurgency. This offered a relatively permissive environment for the NZDF approach, which was also on display in Timor Leste and the Solomon Islands and which emphasized close engagement between the defense force and local populations and the development of medical, transport, and educational infrastructure attuned to local capacities. The New Zealanders also had the advantage of working with one of the most exceptional provincial governors in Afghanistan in Habiba Sarabi.

But the NZDF encountered difficult terrain, and Bamyan's neighboring provinces across the border conducted menacing attacks that would eventually take the lives of both New Zealand and provincial personnel. This required patrols to be made some distance from the provincial capital, accentuating the asymmetry between the modest size of New Zealand's contingent and the scale of the province. These same challenges put a premium on training local security forces for the transition that would eventually come, a task on which considerable New Zealand efforts were concentrated. Part of that training also came from a detachment of New Zealand police officers who worked as part of the multiagency aspect of the PRT. Again, this mirrored to some extent the placement of New Zealand police in the Timor Leste and Solomon Islands stabilization missions.

The training needs of Afghan forces were also one of the main reasons used by John Key's government for justifying the redeployment of New Zealand SAS personnel in 2009. This explanation was designed in part to address concerns in the public debate about the combat role of the SAS. But in a series of incidents in which New Zealand forces had come to the assistance of the Afghan troops they were training, it was clear that the Kiwis were getting caught up in combat. The contrast between the later deployment and the earlier roles of the SAS (between 2001 and 2004) was less clear than the government would have wanted in the minds of New Zealanders. Indeed, as international media reporting often broke the news of the engagement of New Zealand Special Forces in exchanges of fire with insurgents, including in the capital, Kabul, pressure grew on the government to be more forthcoming about its role. As a result, the Afghanistan conflict probably did more than any other in recent years to increase the transparency of the government over the roles of the Special Forces, not least as one of their number had been awarded the very rare Victoria Cross.

At the same time the New Zealand government was acutely aware that it was taking more political flak in Wellington over the deployment and role of the Special Forces than over any other part of its contribution in Afghanistan. It is very likely that New Zealand's partners, including the US, the North Atlantic Treaty Organization (NATO), and Afghanistan itself, would have welcomed the continuation of their deployment. But as international coverage grew of the likelihood that the overall external military role in Afghanistan was to end, it was the SAS who were the first New Zealand force to have left that rank; in 2011 the Key government announced that the Special Forces would return home early the following year and showed little signs of any enthusiasm for their return in substantial numbers.

In the meantime, the human costs of New Zealand's contribution in Afghanistan were becoming more evident. Somewhat ironically, this was occurring more in Bamyan itself (often thought to be relatively peaceful) than in provinces closer to much of the action. Moreover, most of the New Zealand deaths in Afghanistan occurred in the later years of 2011 and especially 2012, including from improvised explosive device (IED) attacks. These casualties did not generate national protests. The casualty aversion among modern liberal democracies has on the whole been grossly exaggerated as observers have extrapolated from the Vietnam experience and the disastrous turn of events in the early 1990s in Mogadishu. In New Zealand's case, the highest loss of life among its forces since the war in Vietnam[9] did not create an immediate groundswell for full and immediate withdrawal. If a public generally believes the cause to be legitimate, the tolerance of casualties may be higher than expected.

But it was inevitable that the cost of lives would generate a wider national conversation about why New Zealand was in Afghanistan and how long that commitment would last. Over ten years after 9/11, it had become harder to argue that the New Zealand forces that remained in Afghanistan had very much to do with the battle against terrorism that had precipitated the original deployment. Moreover, the widespread impression that Karzai's government was corrupt and that the Taliban was far from defeated made it hard for the government to convince New Zealanders that the troops were there to help support a more stable Afghanistan. The media debate increasingly threw up questions about what had been achieved, a result partly of the fact that most deaths had occurred toward the later stages of the Bamyan mission.

In response to the initial upsurge in these attacks, the New Zealand government had increased the protection offered to its forces there by deploying light armored vehicles in 2011. But the unwelcome news of an increase in the violence in parts of the province in 2012 did not change the schedule in which Bamyan was listed as one of the first provinces for transition. As other countries, including Australia, were focusing on 2014 as the exit date for combat forces, it was therefore possible for New Zealand to consider an earlier departure. With the Special Forces already coming home, the National Party–led government announced in 2012 that the PRT would return in early 2013. While that would not be the end of New Zealand's involvement (especially in light of the NZDF personnel deployed to Kabul in headquarters roles), this represented the return of the main NZDF presence in Afghanistan. And as the flag came down, there did appear to be reasons to think that progress had been achieved. Among the metrics to be cited were the thousands of security personnel trained, the miles of roads built, and the number of Bamyan students enrolled in the province's schools and university.

THE DIPLOMATIC GAINS

Only time will tell how locally sustainable these gains will be without the presence of the New Zealand forces in Bamyan. Neither is it clear how Afghanistan as a whole will fare politically, economically, and socially in the post-Karzai era. Even after many years of training, the readiness of Afghanistan's national security forces has been challenged by insurgent attacks, including in Kabul. It makes sense, then, for countries that have participated in Afghanistan over a long period of time and at some cost to be able to point to gains that will be safe from whatever happens in Afghanistan itself. In New Zealand's case at least, there are a wider set of diplomatic and security relationships that have benefited from the twelve-year involvement.

Perhaps the least such impact has been on NZ's relationship with Australia, which was already its main defense partner; it is a relationship that developed in part as a result of the split between New Zealand and the US in the mid-1980s. While New Zealand and Australia were both deployed in Afghanistan, the bulk of their forces were in different places, with Australia having a major role in the more hazardous Uruzgan province. These were parallel but not combined deployments. In this regard they were similar to the "forward defense" commitments in Asia that both countries had made with leading allies in the 1950s and 1960s (Korea and Vietnam with the US, Malaya with the UK), where New Zealand and Australian forces plugged separately into a wider coalition structure.[10] Their Afghanistan commitments were less similar to recent missions in the South Pacific (including Bougainville, the Solomon Islands, and Tonga), where as leading contributors the two countries have worked very closely together. The parallel Australian and New Zealand contributions in Afghanistan have certainly given the two trans-Tasman neighbors notes to compare, but have not been a basis for a new Australia–New Zealand (or ANZAC) force. Indeed, after Australia had suggested as much in 2009, inviting New Zealand to send forces to Uruzgan on an ANZAC basis, New Zealand eventually declined the offer,[11] preferring to signal that the South Pacific was where this type of cooperation should be happening. Somewhat ironically by comparison,

New Zealand's Afghanistan experience provided for elements of cooperation with its traditional security partners in Southeast Asia, with both Malaysia and Singapore sending noncombat detachments to work with the Bamyan PRT.

CLOSER TIES TO NATO: CAN THEY PERSIST?

Rather more has come from New Zealand's Afghanistan role for the relationship with NATO (and the same might be said for Australia's NATO connections). New Zealand's main links with NATO in the post–Cold War period had been founded on the NZDF's earlier role in Bosnia-Herzegovina. But participation in the International Security Assistance Force (ISAF, which was itself approved by a UNSC Resolution 1386 in December 2001) in Afghanistan has brought links with NATO to a level that they have not seen in any corresponding overseas commitment. Like their Australian counterparts, successive New Zealand ministers of defense sought to involve themselves in NATO consultations, partly out of a concern to ensure that contributing countries had a say in the future course of the wider deployment. At least in a formal sense, these connections are likely to live on, as New Zealand and NATO signed a partnership agreement in 2012. But despite the commitment in that agreement to "maintaining a strategic and inclusive approach to New Zealand's participation in future NATO-led operations,"[12] and the similar military and political cultures with a number of NATO members that have helped this relationship to flourish, it is not clear what will sustain this relationship after Afghanistan.

This limitation seems unlikely to apply to New Zealand's burgeoning relationship with the US, which showed the greatest development of all such connections during the Afghanistan era. The security relationship between the two, who were formal allies from the early 1950s until the mid-1980s, had not been completely frozen by the time New Zealand committed itself to a role in Afghanistan in late 2001. There had been limited, one-off cooperation not least because of common interests in similar missions. Wider diplomatic and economic relations had remained in good heart, and New Zealand had come to take advantage of the relative autonomy that a severed alliance relationship offered. Despite US stronger opposition and subsequent suspension of ANZUS (Australia–New Zealand–United States), the US was coming to acknowledge the nuclear-free legislation as a rather permanent fixture. But in Afghanistan, as it had earlier in Bosnia, Somalia, and Timor Leste, New Zealand was demonstrating that it was willing to endure military risks for causes shared with Washington. The longer the NZDF's participation went on, the more absurd it seemed that the US continued to shut New Zealand out from a more active security relationship.

Efforts to recognize that absurdity were made during the Bush administration and were publicly raised by then Assistant Secretary of State for East Asian and Pacific Affairs Christopher Hill. At the same time, Helen Clark's government (1999–2008), as it took an increasingly pragmatic approach to national security issues, also showed interest in a closer relationship. Ironically, the foundations for those closer links were laid by the governments of Bush and Clark, whose political philosophies could not have been more different. But it was the 2008 elections of the National Party coalition government under John Key, and of President Obama, that set the stage for the full flowering of the US relationship. Within a few short years, the two countries had signed the Wellington Declaration on closer security cooperation in the South Pacific and the Washington Declaration on closer maritime defense cooperation in the wider Asia-Pacific.[13]

No one could deny the fact that for the Obama administration, a closer security partnership with New Zealand was suitable in a period where its main concern was China's rise in Asia. And in part because of its good relationship with China, New Zealand has found it useful to be able to develop a security partnership but not return to a full military alliance relationship with the US.[14] But the improvement in New Zealand–US relations was occurring well before President Obama and his first-term Secretary of State Hillary Clinton (and Hill's successor, Kurt Campbell) were laying out the principles of America's diplomatic, military, and economic pivot toward Asia. And that was primarily because of the value that New Zealand had shown in Afghanistan. The China factor may have meant that in Washington's eyes a closer relationship with New Zealand became especially desirable (among closer links with almost every Asia-Pacific country). But it was involvement in Afghanistan that really made that closer relationship fully possible.

CONCLUSION

The desire for lessons to be learned from any individual conflict is complicated by the more pressing demands of the next contingency, which is always likely to be different in significant ways. But if we treat New Zealand's military involvement in Afghanistan as a case study of a national deployment, there are at least two interesting findings.

The first finding is that what may appear to much larger countries to be a relatively modest contribution in numerical terms can have more significant effects than might otherwise be expected. As a small but disciplined force, the NZDF was able to offer contributions that were fit for type, although it was probably significant that Bamyan and not a more violent, insurgent-ridden province was selected for the New Zealanders. That said, while New Zealand's expertise in interagency stabilization and reconstruction missions came in handy, so too did the fact that it was able to deploy combat-trained components, including the SAS, in Afghanistan. Yet the modest scale of what New Zealand could offer always meant that it was dependent on the bigger contributions from the leading players.

The second finding is that it is quite possible to advance national goals as a contributing country even when the overall course of the conflict is unclear. None of us can say definitively whether historians will look back on the post-9/11 multinational military commitment in Afghanistan as a success, a disappointment, or something in between. If one is a betting person, the last of these seems a safe refuge. But as the main parts of NZDF commitment to Afghanistan returned home, it was possible to conclude with some vigor that New Zealand's security and diplomatic relationships, and especially the once-strained relationship with Washington, had been significantly enhanced. I am not sure that Carl von Clausewitz quite had foreign policy goals in mind when he said that war is diplomacy by other means. But in the case of New Zealand's long-standing commitment in Afghanistan, war has generated some diplomatic advances. That still leaves the question open as to whether in future years New Zealanders will feel that it was all worth it.

NOTES

1. Hon. Jonathan Coleman and Hon. Murray McCully, "New Zealand Continues Commitment to Afghanistan," media release, February 18, 2013, http://www.beehive .govt.nz/release/nz-continues-commitment-afghanistan.

2. On Australia's approach, see Robert Garran, *True Believer: John Howard, George Bush, and the American Alliance* (Crows Nest, NSW: Allen and Unwin, 2004).

3. See Malcolm McKinnon, *Independence and Foreign Policy: New Zealand and the World since 1935* (Auckland: Auckland University Press, 1993), 278–301.

4. UNSC Resolution 1373, September 28, 2001, and Resolution 1368, September 12, 2001.

5. On this period, see Robert Ayson, "New Zealand Defence and Security Policy, 1990–2005," in *New Zealand in World Affairs, IV, 1990–2005*, ed. Roderic Alley (Wellington: Victoria University Press), 131–151.

6. Nicky Hagar, *Other People's Wars: New Zealand in Iraq, Afghanistan, and the War on Terror* (Nelson, New Zealand: Craig Potton, 2011).

7. For more, see Stephen Hoadley, "The New Zealand PRT Experience in Bamyan Province: Assessing Political Legitimacy and Operational Achievements," in *Statebuilding in Afghanistan: Multinational Contributions to Reconstruction*, ed. Nik Hynek and Peter Marton (New York: Routledge, 2011), 139–156.

8. Prime Minister Helen Clark, "Government Assistance to Operation Enduring Freedom and Iraq," media statement, June 9, 2003, http://medals.nzdf.mil.nz/news/articles/2003/0609-oef.html.

9. On New Zealand's experience in Vietnam, see Roberto Rabel, *New Zealand and the Vietnam War: Politics and Diplomacy* (Auckland: Auckland University Press, 2005), and Ian McGibbon, *New Zealand's Vietnam War: A History of Combat, Commitment, and Controversy* (Auckland: Exisle, 2010).

10. Ian McGibbon, "Forward Defence: The Southeast Asian Commitment," in *New Zealand in World Affairs II, 1957–1972*, ed. Malcolm McKinnon (Wellington: New Zealand Institute of International Affairs), 9–39.

11. For an example of subsequent Australian reporting of this decision, see Gerard Henderson, "New Zealand Puts Nation First, War Second," *Sydney Morning Herald*, July 6, 2010, http://www.smh.com.au/opinion/politics/nz-puts-nation-first-war-second-20100705-zxiq.html. ANZAC stands for Australian and New Zealand Army Corps, established in 1915 during the First World War and deployed at Gallipoli during the fateful Dardanelles campaign.

12. "Individual Partnership and Cooperation Programme Between New Zealand and NATO," 2012, 2, http://www.beehive.govt.nz/sites/all/files/New_Zealand_-_NATO_Partnership_and_Cooperation_Programme.pdf.

13. "Wellington Declaration on a New Strategic Partnership Between New Zealand and the United States of America," November 4, 2010, http://www.mfat.govt.nz/Media-and-publications/Features/665-Wellington-declaration-on-new-NZ-US-partnership.php, and "Washington Declaration on Defense Cooperation Between the Department of Defense of the United States of America and the Ministry of Defence of NZ and the NZ Defence Force," June 19, 2012, http://www.beehive.govt.nz/sites/all/files/Washington Declaration.pdf.

14. Robert Ayson, "Choosing Ahead of Time? Australia, New Zealand and the US-China Contest in Asia," *Contemporary Southeast Asia* 34, no. 3 (December 2012): 338–364.

18 PAKISTAN

A Tale of Two Allies

Timothy D. Hoyt

THE ROLE OF PAKISTAN as an ally in the war on terror is unique. Unlike other allies discussed in this volume, Pakistan has not contributed military forces or other resources to support coalition operations *inside* Afghanistan. Pakistani military forces play roles that affect coalition operation in Afghanistan in several ways, both positive and negative. First, Pakistani military (the two-division XI Corps) and paramilitary forces (the Frontier Corps) man the border outposts on the Durand Line, monitoring and at least theoretically constraining movement by militants across the border. This mission has been supported by US training missions and technology and facilitated by US bilateral military assistance and Coalition Support Funds. At times, tactical cooperation between coalition forces and their Pakistani counterparts has been close and effective. At other times, Pakistani border forces have been accused of actually supporting either infiltration or exfiltration of militant groups—most infamously in a firefight in November 2011 that led to a diplomatic crisis between the US and Pakistan.

Second, Pakistan's intelligence services have monitored and arrested members of certain militant groups that threaten the coalition in Afghanistan, and that potentially threaten the homelands of Coalition partners. Major al Qaeda figures, including Khalid Sheikh Muhammed, Ramzi Binalshibh, and Abu Faraj al-Libi have been arrested in Pakistan and handed over to the coalition for interrogation.[1] According to press reports, Pakistan's intelligence agencies have also facilitated targeting and other intelligence for US air strikes—carried out by unmanned aircraft or "drones"—against militant targets in the Federally

Administered Tribal Areas (FATA) of Pakistan.[2] Cooperation between Western intelligence and Pakistan's Directorate for Inter-Service Intelligence (ISI) has been close on counterterrorism issues. That cooperation, however, is marred by contradiction, suspicion, and outright failure, spectacularly demonstrated by the May 2011 US raid that killed Osama bin Laden in a compound in Abbottabad less than a mile from one of Pakistan's military academies.[3]

Third, and much more controversially, Pakistan's military and intelligence agencies provide sanctuary, shelter, and support for militant groups that actively fight the coalition. This support—both tacit and direct—dates back to the beginning of Operation Enduring Freedom (OEF), when nine thousand Pashtun volunteers from the Tehreek-e-Nafaz-e-Shariat-e-Mohammadi movement (Movement for the Enforcement of Islamic Law—TNSM) crossed the Durand Line to fight American and Northern Alliance forces, and when the Pakistani military reportedly staged an airlift out of Kunduz in November 2001 to exfiltrate Pakistani military advisors and possibly some members of Taliban leadership.[4] Pakistan's active support for the Afghan Taliban, the Haqqani network, and Gulbuddin Hekmatyar was specifically identified in congressional testimony by US chairman of the Joint Chiefs of Staff Admiral Michael Mullen in September 2011.[5]

THE PAKISTANI STATE AND REGIONAL SECURITY PERSPECTIVES

Pakistan maintains one of the largest armies in the world—over 550,000 active duty members of the military, with 500,000 reserves. In addition, Pakistan fields a series of government-controlled paramilitary forces, including the Rangers (based in the provinces of Punhab and Sindh) and the Frontier Corps (in Khyber Pakhtunkhwa and Baluchistan), that perform important roles in border and internal security. Finally, Pakistan also permits the existence of dozens of armed religious militant groups—a 2004 book identified 125 separate groups—that can be used for defense in depth, for supporting domestic policy, or to support Pakistan's foreign policy aims against its neighbors.[6]

Pakistan's armed forces focus specifically—some might say obsessively—on India. The reasons for this are deep-rooted and historical. The Pakistani state emerged from the partition of the Indian empire, envisioned by its leaders as a home for all Muslims in the subcontinent. But partition created an East and West Pakistan separated by a thousand miles, with an Indian state in between that still contained a large Muslim population. The population shifts and brutal violence that accompanied partition created hostility between the new states that was exacerbated by two wars over the disputed territory of Kashmir in 1947 and 1965. Pakistan's inability to assimilate the Bengali population of East Pakistan, and its incompetent and genocidal response to democratic elections in 1970–1971, led to another war that created the independent state of Bangladesh.[7] India's intervention exploited ethnic divisions in the Pakistani state and effectively cut Pakistan in half. The sense of humiliation and vulnerability that remains, and its impact on Pakistan's decision making and national psyche, cannot be overstated. Since 1971, India and Pakistan have experienced at least six separate crises since 1984 that risked military and possibly even nuclear conflict.[8]

As a matter of policy, Pakistan seeks to exploit potential internal vulnerabilities in neighboring India and Afghanistan to gain leverage in regional security disputes. The Line of Control in Kashmir remains contested territory on Pakistan's eastern borders, and Afghanistan still does not recognize the Durand Line as an international border. As a result, Pakistan has used "deniable" militant proxies to advance its claims, backing separatist movements in Punjab (Sikh) and Kashmir (Muslim) against India, and Islamist groups including the Taliban in Afghanistan. The use of these groups dates back to 1947 and the first Kashmir War, but use of terrorist proxies became a staple of Pakistani regional policy in the 1980s during the Afghan War against the Soviet Union. Militant training camps in the FATA—a marginally governed space with political deniability—are run by ISI, the army, and sometimes even the Frontier Corps.[9] Thus the organizations tasked with fighting terrorism and militancy (as part of the US relationship) have supported many of these groups, creating an environment conducive to misunderstanding and distrust.

Finally, Pakistan suffers from extraordinarily problematic governance. The army dominates the political sphere, having ruled the country for more than half of its history. The two major political parties are based on leading families—the Bhutto family for the Sindh-based Pakistan People's Party (PPP), and the Sharif clan for the Punjab-based Pakistan Muslim League Nawaz (PML-N). Both parties condemn the army when out of power but quickly choose to allow the army to maintain its traditional dominance of foreign policy and national security when in power.[10] As a result, elections only minimally affect Pakistan's foreign policy.

This can be seen by events during OEF. In 2001, General Musharraf still ruled the country by virtue of a 1999 military coup. Elections held in 2002 were far from free, as the government disqualified large numbers of candidates from the traditional parties and the heads of both major parties were in exile abroad.[11] A political crisis and elections in 2008 removed Musharraf from power, but the new PPP government was unable to exert authority over the military or ISI.[12] 2013 elections put the PML-N in power and saw the emergence of a new party named Pakistan Tehreek-e-Insaf (PTI), which actively campaigned to negotiate a cease-fire with the Pakistani Taliban. There is no indication that the new government will attempt to increase its influence over the military's traditional areas of dominance.

PAKISTAN'S ROLE IN THE COALITION

Pakistan became a US partner almost immediately after the 9/11 terrorist attack. The Director General of ISI (DGISI), then Lieutenant General Mahmoud Ahmed, was visiting Washington for talks on September 11, 2001. The next day, in conference with Pakistan's ambassador to the US, Maleeha Lodi, Ahmed engaged in a heated discussion with Deputy Secretary of State Richard Armitage regarding US intentions and possible Pakistani support.[13] The US presented a list of seven demands, and Armitage and Secretary of State Colin Powell were reportedly shocked when, after telephone consultation with General Musharraf, the Pakistanis agreed to all the demands, including intelligence support and use of Pakistani airbases and air space.[14]

Pakistan's internal discussions on this issue were probably complex and testy. At the time, US-Pakistan relations were at an extraordinarily low point due to long-standing disagreements on Pakistan's nuclear program, Pakistan's invasion of Indian-held areas of Kashmir in 1999, the military coup that put Musharraf in power, and Pakistan's recognition of the Taliban regime and support for Islamist militancy.[15] The opportunity to recast the US-Pakistan relationship, end economic sanctions, and restore American military and economic assistance was a powerful lure. Nevertheless, in consultation with Pakistan's army corps commanders and other key leaders, General Musharraf faced strong opposition from supporters of the Taliban connection—opposition that probably influenced the decision to replace DGISI Ahmed and other high-ranking generals later that year.[16] An additional factor influencing Pakistan's thinking was India's offer of air bases and support facilities to the US. Finally, Pakistan was in a unique but dangerous position—its intelligence services were remarkably well informed about al Qaeda and the Taliban, but this intelligence was the result of close links and decades of cooperation with Islamist extremists.[17]

Pakistan's policies throughout OEF mirror this ambiguous commitment. From 2001 to 2004, Pakistan provided important counterterrorism support to the US, capturing important al Qaeda leaders and providing valuable bases and access during the early stages of OEF. This cooperation, unfortunately, was marred by evidence of ongoing support to terrorist groups, including the murder of American reporter Daniel Pearl by an ISI-backed group and a terrorist assault on India's parliament in December 2001 that nearly led to regional war.[18] This period also saw the establishment of sanctuaries and support for a Taliban regime in exile known as the Quetta *shura* and headed by Mullah Omar.[19]

US policy attention shifted after 2003 to the Iraqi theater, and during this period Pakistan's military reportedly concluded that the US would withdraw from Afghanistan. Pakistan's support for the Quetta *shura* therefore increased, in an effort to acquire leverage over the Afghan government in the future. A Pakistani army intervention in the FATA led to an embarrassing peace deal with local Islamist militias—the first indication that the policy of official support for Islamist groups might create "blowback" against the state and the military. This resulted in another "first"—an air strike attributed to US drones against Nek Muhammad, the leader of the offending group.[20]

Pakistani policy and US-Pakistan cooperation shifted dramatically in 2007–2009.[21] Musharraf's regime came under threat from two separate vectors. A loose Islamist alliance that eventually became Tehrik-e Taliban Pakistan (TTP, or Pakistan Taliban) emerged after the suppression of a radical mosque in the center of Islamabad and began to seize control of districts throughout the northwest. At the same time, the economic and judicial policies of the Musharraf regime created a broad rejectionist movement known as "the Lawyers' Revolt" throughout metropolitan Pakistan.[22] American policy makers became alarmed at Pakistani instability, fearing the possibility of an Islamist takeover or loss of physical control of Pakistan's nuclear arsenal.[23] The US increased training missions and dialogues with Pakistan on counterinsurgency (COIN) and counterterrorism, created new economic aid programs including the Kerry-Lugar-Berman bill, provided new equipment to the Pakistani military, and pressured Musharraf to hold elections (elections that eventually sent Musharraf into exile).[24] US-Pakistan military cooperation also increased on the border, and its aid workers multiplied inside Pakistan, facilitating both economic assistance programs and disaster relief (an influx of personnel that Pakistan eventually suspected included covert intelligence operatives).[25]

The Obama administration's declaration of an "AFPAK" strategy introduced new variables into the relationship.[26] Aid flows increased, as did drone
strikes. As American and coalition forces flowed into Afghanistan, friction increased between the US and Pakistan. The US military demanded cooperation
that Pakistan was reluctant to provide. Intelligence cooperation deteriorated
after ISI-backed terrorists launched a bloody raid on Mumbai in 2008, and
an American citizen was implicated as an ISI asset.[27] By 2010 DGISI Ahmad
Shuja Pasha was determined to downgrade the relationship—a step easily implemented in the aftermath of the Raymond Davis affair in January 2011. The
Abbottabad raid that killed Osama bin Laden caused another crisis, and the
November 2011 border firefight between coalition and Pakistani troops resulted
in the death of two dozen Pakistanis and a near-total breakdown in relations,
including the temporary closure of the Karachi-Afghanistan supply route that
provided for most of the Coalition's logistics.[28]

PAKISTAN'S INTERNATIONAL RELATIONS

Pakistan's key bilateral relationships revolve around three countries—the US,
India, and China. All three impact Pakistan's policy and actions in Afghanistan.
These relationships create pressures on Pakistani behavior that contribute to
the apparent contradictions in its Afghan policy. As noted earlier, Pakistan's relationship with the US dominates and complicates policy. On the one hand, the
US remains Pakistan's most important partner in terms of security assistance,
economic aid, and support through international lending institutions. The
US connection also bolsters Pakistan's reputation and standing in the international community. On the other hand, the history of the US-Pakistan relationship is marked by high peaks and low troughs based around particular (and
sometimes short-lived) US security concerns. Pakistani leaders are justifiably
concerned over the fickle nature of US policy and the possibility of an abrupt
reversal with little or no consultation.[29]

Viewed from this perspective, the US intervention in Afghanistan after
9/11 posed a series of challenges for Pakistani decision makers. First, they were
forced to choose between the Taliban and the US. Having made this choice,
they received an apparent "blank check" from the Bush administration for a
number of years in terms of economic and military aid, including large Coalition Support Fund payments with little or no supervision or oversight. This
assistance occurred as the US shifted its strategic focus from Afghanistan to
Iraq, apparently verifying Pakistan's expectations that the US commitment in

the region remained marginal. At the same time the Bush administration vigorously pursued improved relations with India. This alarmed Pakistan's leaders and emphasized the need for a continuing relationship to prevent a US-Indian alliance.[30]

The late Bush administration shifted policy in Afghanistan as a response to the rise in Taliban attacks in 2006–2007. In addition, the US leadership interpreted the political crisis in Pakistan—the Lawyers' Revolt and the rise in domestic terrorism after the Lal Masjid incident—as evidence of an imminent state collapse.[31] While the risk of state failure was exaggerated, the possibility that the Musharraf regime would fall was very real. Efforts to simultaneously bolster Pakistan's institutions and wage war against the Taliban and other militants in western Pakistan continued under the new Obama administration.

American course shifts complicate Pakistan's decision making and contribute to the continuing cycle of peaks and troughs in the US-Pakistan relationship. Pakistan conceived its current strategy—supporting the coalition but maintaining the Quetta *shura* and other groups as effective political and military forces—after the Bush administration shift to Iraq. This policy appears to be based on logical assumptions—that the US lacked the commitment and staying power to maintain a presence in Afghanistan indefinitely. Pakistan was unable to adapt and correct course, however, when the Obama administration announced a change in focus back to Afghanistan. This inflexibility contributed to a downward spiral in relations, with Pakistan blaming American involvement in Afghanistan for its terrorism problems, and the coalition recognizing that the threat to Afghanistan was receiving significant Pakistani support.[32] The unpleasant facts that Pakistan's proxies have killed hundreds of American and coalition soldiers, that Osama bin Laden was discovered living in comfort in a military garrison city, and that Pakistan has refused to play a constructive role in negotiating an Afghan settlement that would allow the coalition to consider withdrawal all suggest that US-Pakistan relations are headed, once again, toward a protracted trough.

The bilateral relationship—bordering on obsession—with India continues to contribute to Pakistani policy as well. India is not generally considered a major provider of economic assistance, but Afghanistan has traditionally been a major recipient of Indian aid. In the aftermath of OEF, it is therefore not surprising that a more prosperous India provided significant economic assistance to the Karzai government. Pakistan perceives this as a security threat and an encirclement effort by New Delhi. As a result, ISI has supported attacks on Indian diplomatic facilities in Afghanistan.[33] Supporting the Taliban and other groups also maintains a cadre of trained potential future terrorists for use against India, and the Taliban's historical willingness to let Pakistan use Afghan territory for training in the past provides a powerful incentive for continued Pakistan-Taliban cooperation.

Pakistan's sensitivity to separatist movements and support for militant groups contributes to ongoing regional tensions. Pakistan's poor treatment of its Baluch population perpetuates an ongoing insurgency, which Pakistan blames on the enhanced Indian presence in Afghanistan.[34] Pakistani-backed terrorist groups—Lashkar e Taiba and Jaish e Muhammad—provoked two regional crises during OEF.[35] Attacks on the Indian Parliament in December 2001 disrupted combined US and Pakistani efforts to monitor the Durand Line and the Afghanistan-Pakistan border. A terrorist attack on Mumbai in November 2008 effectively ended promising back-channel talks between Indian and Pakistani civilian leaders.[36] The Pakistani public and media continue to blame India, and sometimes the US and even Israel, for terrorism and insurgency inside Pakistan. As a result, Indo-Pakistani relations inevitably constrain Pakistani support for the coalition—but there is no indication that *any* series of concessions by India could change Pakistan's revanchist policies.

Pakistan's relationship with China is frequently referred to in flowery terms, like "all-weather friendship."[37] China's interests in Afghanistan revolve around two simple priorities—economic access and safety for Chinese citizens. China places little importance on what regime rules Afghanistan—it is only concerned about the behavior of that regime. The safety of Chinese citizens impacts Pakistani policy more significantly. Attacks on Chinese inside Pakistan are met with rapid and harsh responses. Attacks on Chinese citizens by militants from the Lal Masjid complex apparently constituted a key element in the decision to isolate and storm the complex, which in turn played a major role in the formation of Tehrik-e Taliban Pakistan and the surge in terrorism since 2007.[38] In addition, although Pakistan has a long record of supporting virtually every ethnic separatist or Islamist militant group in the region, potential Chinese separatists pose a unique problem.[39] As a result, Uighurs with ties to western China are monitored, are treated with suspicion, and receive little or no state support. Baluchistan, site of the Chinese-funded Gwadar port complex, remains a major concern because of the insurgency, the growing TTP presence in Baluchistan, and potential threats to Chinese economic interests.

These bilateral relationships affect the manner in which Pakistan juggles the three major national interests that are at the heart of its Afghan policy. First, Pakistan desires to maintain leverage and, if possible, exercise control over the Afghan government and its foreign policy. This desire is similar to, and inherited from, British imperial policy in the era of the raj. Afghanistan does not recognize the Durand Line—the boundary between Afghanistan and Pakistan that is accepted by most other states as the official border. In addition, the Pashtun population of Pakistan is larger than the Pashtun population of Afghanistan, and some Afghan governments have attempted to appeal to Pashtun nationalist and/or separatist sympathies. As a result, a strong unfriendly Afghan regime poses a potential security threat to Islamabad.

Second, Pakistan views Afghan policy through the lens of its concerns about India. Pakistan cannot afford a hostile Afghanistan in its rear. Nor can it afford one that is overtly supportive of India. A friendly Afghanistan can serve and has served as a training ground for anti-Indian militant groups and as a general asset to Pakistan's foreign policy.

Since the overthrow of the Afghan monarchy, Pakistan has employed irregular warfare and the support of friendly Afghan factions to weaken Afghanistan and maximize its leverage. In the mid-1970s, the Pakistani army and intelligence services established links with a number of Islamist groups to oppose the modernizing influences of pro-Soviet regimes, and the "Peshawar Seven" received the bulk of all covert funding for *mujahideen* operations against the Soviets in the 1980s.[40] In the early 1990s, ISI backed Gulbuddin Hekmatyar's faction.[41] After the Taliban defeated Hekmatyar's forces, the ISI switched sides, and Pakistan became one of three states to recognize the Taliban regime.[42] Since Mullah Omar has not expressed strong interest in unifying the Pashtun community, Pakistan continues to support and sustain the Quetta *shura* despite its odious international reputation.

The third, and in this case contradictory, national interest Pakistan must reconcile in its Afghan policy is maximizing the benefit from US involvement in the region. This leads to policies that appear two-faced and encompass significant risk. Pakistan supports US efforts in the short term, and particularly those that create some tangible benefit for Pakistan. This includes supporting the movement of supplies from Karachi into Afghanistan, coordinating counterterrorism efforts with the US and other partners, permitting drone strikes into the FATA, and sometimes cooperating with International Security

Assistance Force (ISAF) forces on the other side of the Durand Line and the border.

At the same time, Pakistan also limits its cooperation with the coalition and attempts to draw hard boundaries in its relationship with the US. Hunting al Qaeda is acceptable, but certain other militant groups are considered strictly out of bounds (Lashkar e-Taiba is considered particularly favored by ISI, and Pakistan resists US efforts to target the Haqqani network). Coalition operations in Pakistan are limited, and the areas in which drone strikes can be carried out are strictly circumscribed—regardless of the nature of the target.[43] Although the locations of the Quetta *shura* are widely known, Pakistan strongly opposes leadership strikes against its favored proxies. Preference is given to groups that actively attack the Pakistani state and military—but this does not include even all the constituent groups of the TTP, as some are considered potential future assets.[44] Both civilian and military leaders condemn the drone campaign and stir up public resentment of the US role in the region, even when US strikes target enemies of Pakistan.[45]

PAKISTAN'S DILEMMA

Ultimately, Pakistan's interests drive it to a double game in Afghanistan. It does everything it can to delegitimize the Karzai government. It actively supports groups that are opposed to Karzai in hopes of outlasting the coalition support for Karzai's regime, including the Quetta *shura*, the Hizb-i Islami Gulbuddin (Gulbuddin Hekmatyar's group), and the Haqqani network.[46] These groups are responsible for the deaths of hundreds of coalition soldiers and thousands of Afghans. In the past, Islamabad has been successful at co-opting and controlling Islamists throughout the region.[47] More recently it has found itself faced with "blowback," as groups and individuals radicalized in Afghanistan attempt to impose their politics on the FATA and areas in the northwest and in some of the major cities. The "Janus strategy," therefore, is creating demonstrable costs for Pakistan—it remains to be seen whether Pakistan will be able to rein in its proxies as the coalition reduces its presence post-2014, or whether these armed militants will try to establish or expand their control in Pakistan itself.

Pakistan has relied on tried-and-true methods to carry out two missions in support of its interests: fomenting and maintaining armed opposition to the Karzai regime and combating internal threats including local insurgencies, terrorism, and separatist movements. Pakistan's support for the Taliban and other groups is widely reported and acknowledged in the West. A formal policy of obfuscation and denial, however, simply replicates Pakistan's actions during the Soviet Afghan War in the 1980s. Although the Taliban leadership is known as the Quetta *shura*, the bulk of activities are carried out across the Durand Line from the FATA. FATA's reputation as a less than fully governed space and tradition of lawless independence provides political deniability that has been useful in providing support for terrorist and irregular campaigns since the 1970s.[48]

Pakistan's proxy war with the Karzai regime and its coalition support is more limited and less destructive than it might be. The annual number of deaths to political violence in Afghanistan is lower than in Iraq (which has a smaller population), and perhaps even lower than in Pakistan (where terrorism and political violence has claimed thousands of lives in the last decade). Pakistan has followed a strategy of exhaustion—raising costs and outwaiting the coalition—that again replicates past efforts in Afghanistan (successful against the Soviets) and Kashmir. The weapons available to the Taliban have been controlled—shoulder-fired anti-aircraft missiles, which proved so effective in the 1980s, have not been widely used by the Taliban forces. This suggests a deliberate calibration of ends and means and a willingness to accept decreased tactical effectiveness in return for minimizing the political and military risks of a negative US or international response to escalation.

Relying on tried-and-true methods also introduced a new set of problems. Paramilitary organizations, including the Frontier Corps, the Frontier Scouts, and the Northern Light Infantry (now integrated into the Pakistani army) were used in the past for training militants.[49] This provided an additional layer of deniability between the army and the militants, and these paramilitaries were commanded by regular army officers. In the western provinces these units are also responsible for patrolling the border and were recruited heavily from the local (Pashtun or Baluch) population. Furthermore, they were poorly funded, were viewed as weak cousins by the regulars, and lacked training and capability. Using these forces to train militants created significant unintended consequences.

First, the paramilitaries did a good job of training militants. As a result, when militant groups began slipping the leash and operating against the state, paramilitaries and local militias (*lashkars*) in the FATA were inadequate to control them. From 2003 to 2006, tribal leaders in the FATA were systematically suborned or eliminated.[50] Second, because of the inefficiency of the paramilitaries, the army decided to take the initiative beginning in 2004—but without significantly reinforcing forces on the Western border (because of the Indian focus of the military). It did not, apparently, provide regular forces with adequate training or doctrine, and the predominantly Punjabi forces employed lacked local knowledge of terrain, culture, and networks. The result was a series of embarrassing defeats by and humiliating negotiations with local militants.[51]

By 2007, events in Pakistan created a "perfect storm" for the creation of an anti-government insurgency. The military government had lost the confidence of key social elites, a harsh military assault on Islamist radicals at the Red Mosque in Islamabad provided a unifying theme for disaffected militants, and the military had demonstrated a lack of competence and capability in dealing with internal threats. Further, as the political crisis evolved, the new army leadership backed away from a leadership role, preferring the civilians to take the blame for the emerging situation and responsibility for authorizing any military action.

The period from 2007 to 2010 was marked by significant cooperation between Pakistan and the US. Pakistan requested greater cooperation on COIN and counterterrorism training, even as Pakistani support for the Afghan militants continued.[52] US forces provided advice on COIN doctrine and strategy, training for paramilitary forces that substantially enhanced their effectiveness, new equipment for the Pakistani army and air force, and robust intelligence support and later kinetic strikes in the FATA through a fleet of unmanned aircraft.

Pakistan's counterinsurgency practice differed significantly from US doctrine, primarily because Pakistan had little interest in "state-building" in the west, but only in reasserting authority and punishing wayward militants.[53] Pakistani COIN efforts in practice were slow and methodical, involving the deliberate relocation of hundreds of thousands of local civilians before military operations commenced. Once those operations began, the operating theater was treated as a free-fire zone, with any remaining population assumed to be hostile. When resistance ceased, the civilian population was restored into their former homes. These tactics are being used in the current 2014 offensive in North Waziristan. Unlike Western practices, sometimes summed up as "Clear, Hold, Build," Pakistani efforts focused on clearing and provided minimal support postoperation (despite the availability of funding from US and other sources).[54]

Today Pakistan faces an unpleasant regional future. Pakistani leaders argue that they must play a key role in determining an Afghan settlement because of the potential Indian threat—and have manipulated efforts to promote high-level talks between the Taliban and the Afghan government.[55] What they perhaps fail to realize is that no other state in the world supports their preferred outcome in Afghanistan. Additionally, militants once supported by Pakistan for foreign policy purposes now cooperate against the Pakistani state and have even infiltrated the military and intelligence services. In 2012–2013, Pakistan experienced significant attacks by TTP elements using Afghan territory as sanctuary.[56] As a result, Pakistan faces a future where international support will be harder to come by, where even a Taliban victory in Afghanistan may not provide significant security, and where traditional proxies may become more and more threatening. The "victory" that the Pakistani military and some elites see just around the corner, with the 2014 withdrawal of US and international forces, may prove short-lived and intensely problematic.

NOTES

1. Ron Suskind, *The One Percent Doctrine* (New York: Simon and Schuster, 2006).

2. "Pakistan CIA Informant: 'Drone Attacks Are the Right Thing to Do,'" *Der Spiegel*, December 4, 2013, http://www.spiegel.de/international/zeitgeist/interview-pakistani -cia-informant-on-drone-warfare-and-taliban-a-937045.html.

3. A controversial but compelling early account of the raid is Nicholas Schmidle, "Getting Bin Laden," *Atlantic Monthly*, August 8, 2011, http://www.newyorker.com/reporting/2011/08/08/110808fa_fact_schmidle.

4. Ahmed Rashid, *Descent into Chaos* (New York: Viking, 2008), 91.

5. *Statement of Admiral Michael Mullen, US Navy, Chairman Joint Chiefs of Staff Before the Senate Armed Services Committee on Afghanistan and Iraq, September 22, 2011.*

6. Muhammad Amir Rana, *A to Z of Jehadi Organizations in Pakistan*, trans. Saba Ansari (Lahore: Mashal Books, 2004).

7. Richard Sisson and Leo E. Rose, *War and Secession: Pakistan, India, and the Creation of Bangladesh* (Berkeley: University of California Press, 1990).

8. Sumit Ganguly and Devin T. Hagerty, *Fearful Symmetry: India-Pakistan Crises in the Shadow of Nuclear Weapons* (Seattle: University of Washington Press, 2005); Rajesh Basrur, Timothy Hoyt, Rifaat Hussain, and Sujoyini Mandel, *The 2008 Mumbai Terrorist Attacks: Strategic Fallout*, RSIS Monograph No. 17 (Singapore: S. Rajaratnam School of International Studies, 2009).

9. For reports of US identification of forty-two separate militant training camps in Pakistan, see "Pakistan Hesitates to Eradicate US-Mapped Militant Camps," *Washington Times*, July 11, 2011, http://www.washingtontimes.com/news/2011/jul/11/pakistan-hesi tates-to-eradicate-us-mapped-militant/?page=all. See also Rizwan Hussain, *Pakistan and the Emergence of Islamist Militancy in Afghanistan* (London: Ashgate, 2005).

10. Stephen Philip Cohen, *The Idea of Pakistan* (Washington, DC: Brookings Institution Press, 2004), 131.

11. Hussain Haqqani, *Pakistan: Between Mosque and Military* (Washington, DC: Carnegie Endowment for International Peace, 2005), 259–260.

12. Pamela Constable, *Playing with Fire: Pakistan at War with Itself* (New York: Random House, 2011), 109.

13. Shuja Nawaz, *Crossed Swords* (Oxford: Oxford University Press, 2008), 538–542; Pervez Musharraf, *In the Line of Fire* (New York: Free Press, 2006), 199–207.

14. Bob Woodward, *Bush at War* (New York: Simon and Schuster, 2002), 47, 58–59.

15. Dennis Kux, *Disenchanted Allies: The United States and Pakistan, 1947–2000* (Washington, DC: Woodrow Wilson Center Press, 2001), 351–359.

16. Rashid, *Descent into Chaos*, 78–79; Hassan Abbas, *Pakistan's Drift into Extremism* (London: Sharpe, 2005), 217–221; Owen Bennett Jones, *Pakistan: Eye of the Storm* (New Haven, CT: Yale University Press, 2002), 25.

17. Mary Anne Weaver, *Pakistan: In the Shadow of Jihad and Afghanistan* (New York: Farrar, Straus and Giroux, 2002), 33, notes that in the cruise missile strikes on bin Laden camps in Paktia province, five ISI officers and twenty trainees were killed. See also Jones, *Pakistan: Eye of the Storm*, 27–28.

18. Polly Nayak and Michael Krepon, *US Crisis Management in South Asia's Twin Peaks Crisis* (Washington, DC: Stimson Center, September 2006), http://www.stimson.org/images/uploads/research-pdfs/USCrisisManagement.pdf.

19. Antonio Giustozzi, *Koran, Kalashnikov, and Laptop: The NeoTaliban Insurgency in Afghanistan, 2002–2007* (New York: Columbia University Press, 2008).

20. Mark Mazzetti, "A Secret Deal on Drones, Sealed in Blood," *New York Times*, April 6, 2013, http://www.nytimes.com/2013/04/07/world/asia/origins-of-cias-not-so-secret-drone-war-in-pakistan.html?pagewanted=all&_r=0.

21. Daniel S. Markey, *No Exit from Pakistan* (Cambridge: Cambridge University Press, 2013), 129–168.

22. Constable, *Playing with Fire*, 107–108.

23. Timothy Hoyt, *Pakistan and the U.S.—Rebalancing the Relationship* (Washington, DC: American Security Project, January 29, 2008), http://americansecurityproject.org/perspectives/2008/pakistan-and-the-united-states-rebalancing-the-relationship/.

24. Markey, *No Exit from Pakistan*, 140–145.

25. Jeremy Scahill, *Dirty Wars: The World Is a Battlefield* (New York: Nation Books, 2013), 215–219; Mark Mazzetti, *The Way of the Knife* (New York: Penguin, 2013).

26. Bob Woodward, *Obama's Wars* (New York: Simon and Schuster, 2010); Robert M. Gates, *Duty* (New York: Knopf, 2014), 335–385.

27. Ahmed Rashid, *Pakistan on the Brink* (New York: Viking, 2012), 156.

28. "Pakistan Cuts Off NATO Supply Lines after 25 Killed," *The Independent*, November 27, 2011, http://www.independent.co.uk/news/world/asia/pakistan-cuts-off-natos-supply-line-after-25-troops-killed-6268682.html.

29. Kux, *Disenchanted Allies*; Hussain Haqqani, *Magnificent Delusion* (New York: Public Affairs, 2013).

30. See Markey, *No Exit From Pakistan*.

31. John R. Schmidt, *The Unraveling: Pakistan in the Age of Jihad* (New York: Farrar, Straus and Giroux, 2011).

32. Bruce Riedel, *Deadly Embrace: Pakistan, America and the Future of the Global Jihad* (Washington, DC: Brookings Institution Press, 2011), 81–82.

33. Mark Mazzetti and Eric Schmitt, "Pakistanis Aided Attack in Kabul, U.S. Officials Say," *New York Times*, August 1, 2008, http://www.nytimes.com/2008/08/01/world/asia/01pstan.html.

34. Frederic Grare, *Baluchistan: The State Versus the Nation* (New York: Carnegie Endowment for International Peace, April 11, 2013), http://m.ceip.org/2013/04/11/balochistan-state-versus-nation/fz4k&lang=en.

35. Stephen Tankel, *Storming The World Stage: The Story of Lashkar-e-Taiba* (New York: Columbia University Press, 2011).

36. Steve Coll, "The Back Channel: India and Pakistan's Secret Kashmir Talks," *The New Yorker*, March 2, 2009, http://www.newyorker.com/reporting/2009/03/02/090302fa_fact_coll.

37. Paul J. Smith, "The China-Pakistan-U.S. Triangle: From Cold War to the 'War on Terrorism,'" *Asian Age: An American Review* 38, no. 4 (2011): 197–220.

38. Nicholas Schmidle, *To Live or to Perish Forever* (New York: Holt, 2009), 130–155.

39. Michael Wines, "China Blames Foreign-Trained Separatists for Attacks in Xinjiang," *New York Times*, August 1, 2011, http://www.nytimes.com/2011/08/02/world/asia/02china.html.

40. Steve Coll, *Ghost Wars* (New York: Penguin, 2005), 53–169.

41. Ibid., 67.

42. Ahmed Rashid, *Taliban* (New Haven, CT: Yale University Press, 2000).

43. Greg Miller and Bob Woodward, "Secret Memos Reveal Explicit Nature of U.S., Pakistan Agreement on Drones," *Washington Post*, October 23, 2013.

44. Christine C. Fair, "The Militant Challenge in Pakistan," *Asia Policy* 11, no. 1 (2011): 105–137.

45. The drone debate is extremely controversial. A starting place for considering the available data is Rikita Singh, "A Meta-Study of Drone Strike Casualties," http://www.lawfareblog.com/2013/07/a-meta-study-of-drone-strike-casualties/. The author's views are briefly summarized in Timothy D. Hoyt, "Striking Back on the Drone Debate: 3 Questions," http://warontherocks.com/2013/10/striking-back-on-the-drone-debate-3-questions/.

46. See *Statement of Admiral Michael Mullen*.

47. Ryan Clarke, *Lashkar-I-Taiba: The Fallacy of Subservient Proxies and the Future of Islamist Terrorism in India* (Carlisle, PA: Strategic Studies Institute, n.d.).

48. Imtiaz Gul, *The Most Dangerous Place: Pakistan's Lawless Frontier* (New York: Viking, 2011).

49. Rashid, *Descent into Chaos*, 9, 17, 78, 91; Gul, *The Most Dangerous Place*, 3.

50. The South Asia Terrorism Portal—an Indian source—has a list of "Attacks on Tribal Elders in Pakistan" at http://www.satp.org/satporgtp/countries/pakistan/data base/Tribalelders.htm.

51. Zahid Hussain, "Pakistan's Most Dangerous Place," *Wilson Quarterly* (Winter 2012), http://www.wilsonquarterly.com/essays/pakistans-most-dangerous-place.

52. Haider A. H. Mullick, *Pakistan's Security Paradox: Countering and Fomenting Insurgencies*, JSOU Report 9-09 (Hurlbert Field, FL: Joint Special Operations University, December 2009).

53. Rashid, *Pakistan on the Brink*, 173–175.

54. Shuja Nawaz, *Learning by Doing: The Pakistani Army's Experience with Counterinsurgency* (Washington, DC: Atlantic Council, February 2011).

55. "Shaky Afghan-Taliban Peace Talks Run into Pakistani Obstruction," *Christian Science Monitor*, February 19, 2014, http://www.csmonitor.com/World/Security -Watch/2014/0219/Shaky-Afghan-Taliban-peace-talks-run-into-Pakistani-obstruction -video.

56. "TTP Admits to Having Safe Haven in Afghanistan," *Tribune Express*, June 26, 2012, http://tribune.com.pk/story/399205/ttp-admits-to-having-safe-haven-in-afghanistan/.

19 RUSSIA

Friend or Foe on Afghanistan?

Renanah Miles

THE FIRST SOVIET TANKS rolled into Afghanistan in 1979, determined to crush the *mujahideen* whose insurgency threatened the pro-Soviet government there. When the last Red Army soldiers withdrew ten years later, the Russians had discovered the "power of militant Islam," and the defeat left a long-lasting impression on their national consciousness.[1] When US and North Atlantic Treaty Organization (NATO) troops entered Afghanistan in 2001, Moscow quickly provided political and intelligence support—empathy over shared experiences with terrorism (and Afghanistan) carried the day. Although difficult to believe now, President Vladimir Putin's call to President George Bush was the first from a foreign leader after the 9/11 attacks. Yet as the conflict lengthened and NATO presence expanded in Central Asia, Russian enthusiasm waned and Moscow moved to contain the Western presence. During the war, Russia chose to cooperate with NATO on practical initiatives, but support was often lukewarm.

When the NATO drawdown began, Russia simultaneously took measures to expedite the withdrawal, urge against precipitous departure, and challenge a post-2016 Western presence. On one hand, Russia wants NATO to succeed in Afghanistan because the alternative—a destabilized region beset with drug trafficking and rising extremism spilling across Russian borders—is worse. On the other hand, Moscow wants NATO success without a NATO presence; attempts to counter Western influence in the region frequently rendered Russia's objectives and actions inconsistent. The result was a transactional approach that allowed tactical cooperation to continue despite dissonant views. Yet practical cooperation will only go so far.

Much of the NATO-Russian interaction has focused on logistics, a critical consideration for operations in a landlocked country in a difficult and distant neighborhood. Both the surge and drawdown efforts hinged on logistics, as did the broader US vision for Central Asia—though this has waned in the face of difficult implementation. This chapter traces the history of NATO-Russia logistics cooperation vis-à-vis Afghanistan, concluding that practical cooperation can persist but is of limited use when strategic interests diverge. It identifies the key considerations that have shaped the relationship to date and argues that Russia's influence and interests in Central Asia make its objectives a necessary consideration for any long-term strategy.

The following section reviews the logistical considerations that led NATO to develop alternate transportation corridors through Central Asia, Russia, and the Caucasus. Next, the chapter turns to the costs of doing business in Central Asia and analyzes Russia's incentives to support or thwart the NATO mission, finding Russia's goals ultimately incongruent. The final section discusses future implications for cooperation.

THE NORTHERN DISTRIBUTION NETWORK

Over the course of operations in Afghanistan, NATO's reasons to engage Russia pivoted on logistics. Solving what one senior military officer called "the logistics challenge of our generation"[2] became a multiyear effort with geostrategic implications. Each coalition member in the International Security Assistance Force (ISAF) mission was responsible for supplying its own forces; however, the US handled the bulk of logistical support including for US troops, smaller coalition partners, and the Afghan National Security Forces (ANSF).[3]

Initially, the US relied heavily on Pakistan for supply routes into landlocked Afghanistan. Insurgent strikes and pilferage coupled with capacity and political problems rendered these routes insecure. Pakistan's ground routes were shut down between November 2011 and July 2012 after a strike killed twenty-four Pakistani soldiers, and other border crossings were at times blocked, such as Khyber Pakhtunkhwa. The Pentagon's unease with this vulnerability and its anticipated need for a surge capacity led to exploration of alternatives beginning in 2008. The ensuing military and diplomatic effort included the Department of Defense (DOD) Transportation Command, Central Command, Europe Command, Defense Logistics Agency, and Department of State and created the Northern Distribution Network (NDN). By the end of 2011, nearly 75 percent of ground sustainment cargo (approximately 40 percent of all cargo) flowed through this network.[4] Subsequent years brought a flurry of diplomacy aimed at Central Asia, with the result in 2012 of most states approving the reverse transit of supplies, equipment, and other nonlethal cargo out of Afghanistan.[5] However, the NDN's anticipated potential for retrograde diminished because of high costs and regional diplomatic and bureaucratic impasses.

The NDN is a web of ground lines that relies on commercial transportation providers and local infrastructure across Latvia, Azerbaijan, Georgia, Kazakhstan, Russia, Tajikistan, and Uzbekistan. Kyrgyzstan was a critical part of the system, with Manas Air Force Base serving as a personnel and air-refueling hub until 2014. Ports and rail lines composing the NDN followed three routes: NDN South, which traverses the Caucasus and bypasses Russia; NDN North, which runs through Russia; and the KKT (Kazakhstan, Kyrgyzstan, and Tajikistan), which bypassed the Uzbek border into Afghanistan.[6] Of the participating NDN countries, only Latvia is a NATO member. Georgia is a NATO partner but membership prospects are currently frozen, and Azerbaijan, the other Caucasus NDN country, is historically wary of aligning with either the West or Russia.[7] The remaining countries are members of the Collective Security Treaty Organization (CSTO), with the exception of Uzbekistan.

The southern and northern NDN routes traverse Kazakhstan and Uzbekistan, both weak states emblematic of the balancing act between US and Russian interests that has defined the regional security dynamic. Kazakhstan kept a foot in both camps as a CSTO member and a participant in the NATO Partnership for Peace program. Uzbekistan also chartered an uneven course, rapidly inviting a US presence after September 11, when its Karshi-Khanabad base became a major staging point for US forces. After a tepid yet unexpected US rebuke to an Uzbek crackdown on anti-government demonstrators, Tashkent ousted US forces and rejoined the CSTO. When Uzbekistan left the CSTO again in 2012, some analysts suggested that the decision was driven by a desire for a better position in the NDN and acquisition of US excess defense articles (EDAs). Likewise, Tajikistan's delay in signing a basing agreement with Russia may have been fueled by a desire to benefit from the NDN.[8]

The KKT route relied on Kyrgyzstan. The US fought a losing battle to retain access to Manas Air Force Base, a critical hub for which Bishkek's various governments exacted a heavy price. In 2006 and 2009, then-president Kurmanbek Bakiyev threatened to close the base—reportedly under Russian pressure—until Washington agreed to a rent jump from $17.4 million annually to $60 million. After taking office in 2011, pro-Moscow Kyrgyz President Almazbek

Atambayev pledged to close the base; US forces vacated Manas in June 2014, shifting operations to Romania's MK Air Base. Meanwhile, Russia has enjoyed rent-free use of a military base and continues to provide Kyrgyzstan with generous military assistance.

THE CENTRAL ASIAN NEIGHBORHOOD

Although the NDN's initial results were impressive, they came with a hefty price tag. The most obvious cost was transportation via the circuitous NDN routes. Initially, it cost nearly three times per container compared to Pakistan, down to 2.5 times the cost per container by 2012. As Karimjan Akhmedov and Evgeniya Usmanova note, "The added expense is what might be described as the price of enhancing the US and NATO role in Central Asia."[9] Former ISAF commander General Stanley McChrystal observed in his initial assessment that the NDN is "dependent on support from Russia and Central Asian states, giving them the potential to act either as spoilers or positive influences."[10]

The Central Asian states are marked by varying degrees of authoritarianism, instability, and malleability to Russian influence, making them weak and potentially difficult partners. Moreover, they face serious threats, two of which are Islamist extremism and drug trafficking. Although the threat of Central Asian jihad is, in the view of some, "the dog that didn't bark,"[11] groups like the Islamic Movement of Uzbekistan and the Islamic Jihad Union are based out of Pakistan and active in Afghanistan. As military action in Afghanistan winds down, they may return to their *raison d'être*—overthrowing Central Asian governments.[12] In 2012, the World Health Organization announced that Eastern Europe and Central Asia suffer the world's fastest-growing HIV/AIDS epidemic, with most new infections linked to intravenous drug use. Up to one fifth of opium and heroin produced in Afghanistan transits Central Asia, and addiction and criminality follow. A UN report warns that without measures to counter the deadly nexus of drugs, crime, and insurgency, "a big chunk of Eurasia could be lost."[13]

In this context, the NDN extends beyond the necessities of supply and retrograde as part of a broader calculus of economic development. As part of the NDN incentive package, the 2010 US National Defense Authorization Act provided temporary procurement authorities for Operation Enduring Freedom requirements in Georgia, Kyrgyzstan, Pakistan, Armenia, Azerbaijan, Kazakhstan, Tajikistan, Uzbekistan, and Turkmenistan.[14] DoD policy further scoped this to the five Central Asian states (CAS), launching its "CAS-First" policy. These procurement authorities encouraged local sourcing from the Central Asian states in an effort to support economic growth and enhance regional stability.

In 2011, then-Secretary of State Hillary Clinton announced the "New Silk Road" initiative, a vision of regional webs of trade/transit routes connecting South and Central Asia via Afghanistan, promoting stability and growth. Critics argued that it was a regional approach in a region where cooperation is elusive. George Gavrilis notes, "There is no chance that you can get anything resembling a regional free trade system where goods flow across its borders through these nice new silk roads."[15] Regional rivalries and distrust run high. One incident highlights the perverse incentives at stake: in late 2011, an explosion damaged a southern Uzbek railway bridge, part of the NDN and a critical rail connection for Tajikistan. Uzbek state-controlled media claimed it was a terrorist act, but Tajik observers argued that it was an attempt to sideline Dushanbe from NDN action. Hundreds of freight cars piled up waiting while Tajikistan's offers to help repair the bridge were reportedly ignored.[16] It took two months and World Food Program warnings of an emergent food shortage for Tashkent to initiate repairs in what Tajik officials claimed should have been a twenty-four-hour job.[17]

Regional rivalries tend to cultivate zero-sum thinking, as does Russia's tendency to view its neighborhood jealously.[18] Although the Central Asian states have taken pains to appear independent, the NDN's success has largely been predicated on Russian support. Yet the US is not the only major power sharing the neighborhood with Russia. Dmitri Trenin and Alexei Malashenko suggest, "The rise of China has challenged Russia's position in Central Asia even more massively, fundamentally, and permanently than America's insertion into the region."[19] The two powers pursue influence in Central Asia in parallel—China pours loans, investments, and infrastructure development into the region while Russia extends its military presence and business relationships.[20] Although Russia appears less threatened by China's focus on economic influence, the Moscow-Beijing partnership, of which the Shanghai Cooperation Organization forms the capstone, is tenuous. The two countries did not share a common position on Afghanistan; in fact, Russia supported NATO over Chinese objections.[21] In the long term, China is the only regional actor with the power to pose a direct threat to Russian supremacy, and competition over Central Asian energy resources may prove a catalyst for conflict.[22]

India, Iran, and Pakistan would also benefit from revived commerce and trade along the silk roads. Russia has long enjoyed close Iranian and Indian relationships, while historically viewing Pakistan—to an extent—as its "principal adversary's accomplice."[23] Nonetheless, as the Pakistani-American relationship came under strain, Russia took steps toward rapprochement with Islamabad—including groundbreaking visits by state officials to each country. Multiple factors may be at play, including stemming Chinese influence, exploiting the rift with America to marginalize US influence, and a desire to improve ties in anticipation that Russia and Pakistan will bear the brunt of future instability in Afghanistan.

RUSSIA'S SUPPORT TO ISAF

When Putin reached out to Bush after the 2001 attacks to offer support, the common ground each saw in combating terrorism represented a high-water mark in goodwill. By the end of the Bush administration, relations were cooling, although stabilizing Afghanistan remained a driver of and opportunity for US/NATO-Russian cooperation. The Obama administration seized the opportunity, calling for a "reset" with Russia. Yet expectations fell rapidly after Putin resumed the presidency in 2012. Instead, Russian domestic politics and resurgent Great Power politics drove relations to a new low.

Despite Russia's 2012 accession to the World Trade Organization with US support, Andrew Kuchins notes that Putin used anti-US propaganda to consolidate domestic support.[24] Among anti-US measures was the expulsion of the US Agency for International Development (USAID) from Russia; Putin alleged that US-funded nongovernmental organizations (NGOs) organized protests around his reelection, a charge likely contributing to the move. There was an effort in 2012 to launch a "reset 2," with some speculation that unchecked Russian influence in the post-Soviet space would be part of the deal, if one occurred at all.[25] No reset was to happen. The Arab Spring became another source of division, with Syria's civil war at the center of dispute. Moscow's position against forced regime change underscores its skepticism over the viability of democratic transitions in the Middle East or elsewhere—Russia openly suggests to Central Asian dictators that the US would be happy to see them deposed in the name of democracy.[26] Although an agreement on Syrian chemical weapon disposal eased tensions in 2013, the crisis in Ukraine and Russia's annexation of Crimea in 2014 has put the strategic relationship on an unclear and unpromising future trajectory.

Nonetheless, practical cooperation largely prevailed when it came to Afghanistan. Efforts clustered around Russia's concern with Afghanistan drug production and NATO's need for logistics support. Narcotics cooperation began in 2005, when the NATO-Russia Council (NRC) initiated a pilot project for counternarcotics training for Afghan and Central Asian personnel in conjunction with the UN Office on Drugs and Crime. Russia's support for land transit began in the spring of 2008, with Putin's offer at the NATO Bucharest Summit to allow nonlethal cargo from NATO and other ISAF contributors to transit Russian territory to Afghanistan.[27] This was a significant green light for the NDN, as was the 2012 decision to host a NATO transit hub in Ulyanovsk, Russia, for supplies. Despite the perceived significance of the hub, it had been used only once as of 2014—another instance of the NDN's unrealized potential. Other efforts included an NRC Helicopter Maintenance Trust Fund and a 2011 deal to upgrade the ANSF helicopter fleet through the US purchase of Russian Mi-17 helicopters.

NATO-Russian military cooperation was officially suspended in April 2014 as the Ukraine conflict deepened. Yet unofficial coordination continued, following the precedent set during the 2008 conflict in Georgia. One ameliorating factor is that commercial providers carry out most of the logistics activity along the NDN. Future sanctions targeting those providers could jeopardize the status quo, yet both sides would have reasons to make exceptions; the US for continued access and Russia for the estimated $1 billion it receives annually through NDN-affiliated transactions.[28]

Given Russia's primary aims in Afghanistan—to curb the drug flow and prevent the country from becoming an extremist safe haven—these cooperative measures make sense. Yet the different modalities of Russia's multilateral relationship with NATO and its US bilateral relationship further complicate the view from Moscow. Resurgent US-Russian tensions contribute to conflicting attitudes. Trenin and Malashenko describe a continuum of Russian thought on Afghanistan that has ranged from a desire to see NATO bogged down indefinitely to the view that Russia would benefit from a Western victory in Afghanistan regardless of other considerations.[29] The resulting "interplay" of these positions, they suggest, resulted in nominal support. Given that a transactional, albeit complex, approach toward the NATO mission in Afghanistan prevailed, it is worth examining the incentives Russia has perceived to support or undermine the effort.

INCENTIVES TO SUPPORT

The most compelling incentive for support was Russia's fear of an unstable Afghanistan post-2016. Any scenario in which NATO retreats without restoring, in Prime Minister Dmitry Medvedev's words, "the functioning of an effective state,"[30] is a bad scenario for Russia. As then-permanent representative to NATO Dmitry Rogozin warned several years ago, NATO failure in Afghanistan would leave Russia with "a strengthened enemy, emboldened by success, standing on the threshold of our home."[31] Putin himself noted that it was in Russia's interest to have "peace on our southern borders," adding grimly, "if [Western forces] have made the commitment, let them follow through on it."[32] Although these comments implicitly suggested a view of Central Asia as part of Russia,[33] they highlighted fears that battle-tested fighters with jihadist bona fides earned in Afghanistan would eventually leave their Pakistan bases and join the fight in the North Caucasus or Central Asia.

Drug trafficking is another major threat that fueled Russian cooperation with NATO. Russia faces an escalating drug crisis linked to conditions in Afghanistan, which produces 90 percent of the world's opium. Russia pays a bitter price, with users consuming a fifth of the world's heroin every year— Viktor Ivanov, head of Russia's Federal Drug Control Service, cited the number of Russian drug addicts at roughly 9 million. Of these, 90 percent use heroin, consuming as much as eighty tons of Afghan heroin a year.[34] More than twice as many Russians die from these drugs annually (most counts estimate thirty to forty thousand) as the number of Red Army soldiers killed during the decade-long war in Afghanistan (estimated to be fifteen thousand). The problem continues to metastasize despite intensive counternarcotics efforts. In 2013, Russian authorities seized 106 tons of illegal drugs, mostly originating from Afghanistan (at least one product transits the Silk Road with ease). Like Central Asia, Russia suffers a drug-related HIV epidemic. Despite some animosity over NATO's role in the problem—Russian politicians are quick to observe that opium production in Afghanistan is forty times higher since the "notorious resolutions"[35] in 2001—Moscow recognized that "neither Afghanistan, nor Russia, nor the US can deal with this problem alone."[36] Interests converged on counternarcotics efforts, and NRC efforts to build counternarcotics capabilities proved a relatively bright spot.

Russia also derives economic and political benefits from the NDN. At its peak, roughly three quarters of supplies transiting the network moved through Russia, generating business opportunities for local commercial carriers. DOD awarded hundreds of millions of dollars in fuel contracts to a joint Russian-Kyrgyz gas venture in which Russia's state-owned Gazprom owns the majority share.[37] In addition to the financial benefits, Russia perceives opportunities for leverage over NATO and its neighbors. Encouraging reliance on the northern route may discourage or reduce use of the southern route running through Georgia. By fostering NATO reliance on Russian supply routes, "Moscow is in a stronger position to put the 'squeeze' on if and when it believes its interests are being encroached."[38] Indeed, Russian policy makers frequently observe, "NATO needs Russia more than Russia needs NATO."[39]

INCENTIVES TO THWART

Despite the incentives to support a successful mission in Afghanistan, Russia's predilection toward a geopolitical view of the world creates negative incentives. Russian determination to check perceived expansion of US influence resulted in a contradictory stance that undermined as many activities as it allowed. The focal point of cooperation—the NDN—was itself viewed with suspicion that the intent was "soft conquest." Both the NDN and the modern Silk Road were suspect in a region where Moscow wants to control energy resources and new oil and gas pipelines.[40] In one Russian view, "the US and NATO are now buying their way into target countries," calling economic incentives "NATO bribes (that) are . . . as addictive as narcotics."[41] Security cooperation is even more competitive. Oksana Antonenko and Bastian Giegerich note, "It is telling that Russia and NATO have been engaged separately in security cooperation with different Central Asian states for over a decade, but have never really cooperated in addressing regional security challenges."[42]

Central Asian posturing for NDN business has fueled Russian competition despite the relatively anemic use of the network for retrograde given constraints caused, in part, by intraregional wrangling. In 2012, Russia prepared a multi-year, $1.3 billion military aid package to Kyrgyzstan and Tajikistan coupled with waivers on fuel and lubricant custom duties. This was ostensibly intended to counter US support to Uzbekistan after the Uzbek departure from the CSTO, a move some suggest was designed to gain a monopoly on EDA from ISAF. Both Moscow and Tashkent appeared to accept this view. An Uzbek paper reported that NATO is planning to leave "most of the NATO weapons used in Afghanistan" in Uzbekistan, while a Russian paper cited an official saying, "It was only recently after all that Bishkek and Dushanbe flirted with Washington in the hope to lay hands on the weapons and military hardware withdrawn from Afghanistan . . . American influence with the region would have grown."[43] By 2014 this EDA arrangement seemed increasingly unlikely to materialize, with the State Department claiming, "We have not and do not intend to transfer this equipment to the governments neighboring Afghanistan."[44] Moscow's aid to Uzbekistan's neighbors may well further destabilize the region—especially if they do not get the anticipated EDA.

Russia's historic view of NATO as the "primary threat to its international aspirations"[45] and its opposition to NATO out-of-area operations contributes to its ambivalence. As Russia's ambassador to Afghanistan Zamir Kabulov said, "It's not in Russia's interests for NATO to be defeated and leave behind all these problems . . . We'd prefer NATO to complete its job and then leave this unnatural geography."[46] Yet as operations end in Afghanistan, Russia's dismay over the length of the war has been tempered by fear that it is ending too soon and Moscow will be left holding the bag.[47] If Russia believes an alternate strategy or force (such as the CSTO rapid reaction force) is viable, incentives to cooperate may disappear even sooner.

Lastly, while Russia's drug problem provides incentive to support NATO in Afghanistan, it paradoxically seeds doubt as to NATO's true intentions. The ISAF decision not to focus on poppy eradication was a major source of contention: if the US eradicated coca crops in Colombia, why not in Afghanistan?[48] When Russia promulgated a "Rainbow Strategy" to make eradication part of the ISAF mandate, ISAF refused to adopt the tenets, putting the two approaches in conflict. Viktor Ivanov warned in 2012 that NATO could be sued in international courts over failure to curb drug production and trafficking in Afghanistan.[49] Others have argued that targeting drug trafficking requires targeting trafficking routes—where better to start than by shutting down the NDN routes?[50]

IMPLICATIONS

One of the ironies in this discussion of incentives is that no irreconcilable differences have existed between NATO and Russian interests in Afghanistan. Yet shared interest in Afghan stability was undermined by divergent interests elsewhere, including immediately outside Afghan borders. While all benefit from a secure and stable Afghanistan, both parties' interests are jeopardized by conflicting incentives. NATO success cannot be achieved without a NATO presence, nor can stability be achieved without a regional approach that includes Russia.

As ISAF ends conflict operations in Afghanistan, a key lesson from the NDN effort is that practical cooperation can persist in the face of strategic differences but is unlikely to achieve much unless they are reconciled. The current

trajectory in Central Asia puts these differences on a competitive course resulting in a bidding war for influence, inadvertent contribution to local arms races,
and encouragement of Russian-Chinese cooperation to counter Western influence. This raises several implications for decision makers considering future policies in the region. First, it is unclear who has leverage and how much it is worth.

Leverage has been a driving force in NATO's pursuit of the NDN and in
Russia's support for it. The US wanted leverage over Pakistan to guarantee open
transit routes, and Russia has sought leverage over NATO and its neighbors by
exercising influence over the network. Both sides have gained and lost in the
battle for influence writ large—the US lost access to Manas while the CSTO
lost Uzbekistan, one of only a few members with any noteworthy military capabilities. Yet the network itself remained underutilized, and over the course of
the conflict neither side sought to use it as leverage even as other aspects of the
relationship deteriorated. Moreover, the network led to divergent expectations;
Central Asian partners viewed it as a means of income, prestige, and access to
security cooperation, while US military planners viewed it as extra capacity to
be kept "warm" in case of need.[51]

Second, a better understanding of Russian incentives and Central Asian
regional security dynamics must inform any strategy for Central Asia post-
operations in Afghanistan. The expansive vision of a new Silk Road running
through what H. J. Mackinder famously called "the pivot region of the world's
politics"[52] also requires clarifying US interests and moving past the current
transactional approach. Although stated US objectives are, among others, to
move past "limited transactional-based relationships into more constructive
cooperative exchanges,"[53] the fact that security cooperation spending is dropping as the mission winds down suggests that the Silk Road may become some-
one else's—for instance, China's twenty-first-century Silk Road strategy.[54]

The US must define its own interests to determine the opportunities (and
limits) for engagement. In a region marked by poor human rights records and
poor progress toward democracy, the US must ensure that security objectives
are not pursued at the expense of universal principles of governance. The US
Senate Committee on Foreign Relations notes, "Achieving our security goals
and promoting good governance and human rights are not mutually exclusive.
In fact, security and political engagement are complementary strategies that are
more likely to be effective when pursued together."[55]

As the end of operations in Afghanistan nears, the future for the country and the region remain uncertain. If the US and Russia continue to vie for

influence in Central Asia with competing visions for regional stability, the result will likely be instability, egging on local power struggles and detracting from a coherent strategic approach. Yet the outbreak of conflict in the Ukraine in 2014 and the multiyear civil war in Syria increasingly constrain the limits of even practical cooperation with Russia. It is too early to tell whether opportunities to integrate Russia into economic strategies like the New Silk Road will exist, but it is apparent that US policies are unlikely to persist in the face of resistance or limited results. The current crises could yet prove a boon to certain NDN partners like Georgia and Uzbekistan even while a regional approach remains elusive. Logistical dependencies will continue through the final drawdown and could yet become a driver of geostrategy if connected to long-term considerations. Following from Mackinder's heartland theory, Central Asia may yet emerge as a prosperous region, with Afghanistan as a conduit for resources to reach markets in South Asia. But such visions are unlikely to materialize if Russia's view of Central Asian security persists.

NOTES

1. Dmitri Trenin and Alexei Malashenko, *Afghanistan: A view from Moscow* (Washington, DC: Carnegie Endowment for International Peace, April 2010), 7.

2. Vice Admiral Mark Harnitchek, quoted in Tom Gjelten, "U.S. Now Relies on Alternate Afghan Supply Routes," NPR, September 16, 2011, http://www.npr.org/2011/09/16/140510790/u-s-now-relies-on-alternate-afghan-supply-routes.

3. Andrew C. Kuchins, Thomas M. Sanderson, and David A. Gordon, *The Northern Distribution Network and the Modern Silk Road* (Center for International and Strategic Studies, December 2009), 5.

4. US Senate Committee on Foreign Relations, *Central Asia and the Transition in Afghanistan: A Majority Staff Report Prepared for the Use of the Committee on Foreign Relations*, 112th Cong., 1st Sess., 2011, 5.

5. See Jim Nichol, *Central Asia: Regional Developments and Implications for U.S. Interests*, US Congressional Research Service (Washington, DC: Government Printing Office, 2012).

6. Kuchins, Sanderson, and Gordon, *The Northern Distribution Network*, 9–11.

7. Andrew C. Kuchins and Thomas M. Sanderson, *The Northern Distribution Network and Afghanistan* (Center for International and Strategic Studies, January 2010), 14–16.

8. Karimjan Akhmedov and Evgeniya Usmanova, "Afghanistan Withdrawal: The Pros and Cons of Using the Northern Distribution Network," EurasiaNet, September 12, 2012, http://www.eurasianet.org/node/65904.

9. Ibid.

10. International Security Assistance Force, "Commander's Initial Assessment," *Washington Post*, August 30, 2009, http://media.washingtonpost.com/wp-srv/politics/documents/Assessment_Redacted_092109.pdf.

11. Kuchins and Sanderson, *The Northern Distribution Network and Afghanistan*, 11.

12. US Senate Committee, *Central Asia*, 1.

13. United Nations Office on Drugs and Crime, *Addiction, Crime and Insurgency: The Transnational Threat of Afghan Opium* (Vienna: UNODC, 2009), 3–7.

14. *National Defense Authorization Act for Fiscal Year 2010*, HR 2647, 111th Cong., 1st sess., *Congressional Record* 155, no. 104 (July 13, 2009), § 801.

15. George Gavrilis, quoted in David Trilling, "Northern Distribution Nightmare," *Foreign Policy*, December 6, 2011, http://www.foreignpolicy.com/articles/2011/12/06/afghanistan_resupply_nato_ndn?page=0,1&wp_login_redirect=0.

16. Matthew Stourbridge, "Uzbekistan: Eyewitness Observation of Rail Blast Site Discounts Terrorism Claim," EurasiaNet, January 5, 2012, http://www.eurasianet.org/node/64795.

17. Aleksandr Shustov, "Uzbek-Tajik Relations at a New Low," Strategic Culture Foundation, January 31, 2012, http://www.strategic-culture.org/pview/2012/01/31/uzbek-tajik-relations-at-a-new-low.html.

18. U.S. Senate Committee, *Central Asia*, 4.

19. Ibid., 21.

20. Ibid., 4.

21. Jeffrey Mankoff, *Russian Foreign Policy: The Return of Great Power Politics* (Lanham, MD: Rowman and Littlefield, 2009), 207.

22. See Marlene Laruelle, "Russia in Central Asia: Old History, New Challenges?" EUCAM Working Paper no. 3, Centre for European Policy Studies, 2009), 5–8, http://www.ceps.eu/system/files/book/2009/12/WP3-EN.pdf.

23. Trenin and Malashenko, *Afghanistan*, 23.

24. Andrew Kuchins, "The Demise of the US-Russia Reset: What's Next?" REP meeting summary, 2012, http://www.chathamhouse.org/sites/files/chathamhouse/public/Research/Russia%20and%20Eurasia/181012summary.pdf.

25. Konstantin von Eggert, "Due West: Why Russia's Leaders Don't Respect the US Anymore," RIA Novosti, January 12, 2013, http://en.rian.ru/columnists/20130112/178730583/Due_West_Why_Russias_Leaders_Dont.html.

26. Nichol, *Central Asia*, 10.

27. Oksana Antonenko and Bastian Giegerich, "Rebooting NATO-Russia Relations," *Survival* 51, no. 2 (2009): 17.

28. Anna Mulrine, "Punish Russia? Why Some Pentagon Officials Would Prefer Restraint," *Christian Science Monitor*, March 4, 2014, http://www.csmonitor.com/

World/Security-Watch/2014/0304/Punish-Russia-Why-some-Pentagon-officials
-would-prefer-restraint.-video.

29. Trenin and Malashenko, *Afghanistan*, 17–18.

30. White House, "Remarks by President Obama and President Medvedev of Russia at Joint Press Conference," Office of the Press Secretary, June 24, 2010, http://www.whitehouse.gov/the-press-office/remarks-president-obama-and-president-medvedev-russia-joint-press-conference.

31. Dmitry Rogozin, quoted in Roger McDermott, "Russia's Views on Afghanistan: Does 'Size Matter'?" *Eurasia Daily Monitor* 5, no. 129 (July 8, 2008), http://www.jamestown.org/single/?no_cache=1&tx_ttnews%5Btt_news%5D=33781.

32. "Putin Reiterates Support for NATO Afghan Operation," RIA Novosti, August 1, 2012, http://en.rian.ru/russia/20120801/174911173.html.

33. Jim Nichol, *Russian Political, Economic, and Security Issues and U.S. Interests*, US Congressional Research Service (Washington, DC: Government Printing Office, 2012), 50.

34. "Number of Drug Addicts in Russia Nears 9 Million," RIA Novosti, December 27, 2012, http://en.rian.ru/crime/20121227/178441734/Number_of_Drug_Addicts_in_Russia_Nears.html. Other government statistics estimate about 2.5 million addicts.

35. Victor Ivanov, "Proposals for the Elimination of Afghan Drug Production," remarks as delivered at the international forum "Drug Production in Afghanistan: A Challenge to the International Community," June 10, 2010, http://www.unodc.org/documents/afghanistan/Events/Ivanov_speech.pdf.

36. Dmitry Medvedev, remarks as delivered at the international forum "Drug Production in Afghanistan: A Challenge to the International Community," June 9, 2010, http://eng.special.kremlin.ru/news/398.

37. Nichol, *Russian Political, Economic, and Security Issues*, 50.

38. Kuchins and Sanderson, *The Northern Distribution Network and Afghanistan*, 7.

39. Antonenko and Giegerich, "Rebooting NATO-Russia Relations," 14.

40. Mankoff, *Russian Foreign Policy*, 113.

41. Veronika Krasheninnikova, "NATO's Business Strategy: No Need to Attack, Just Buy Them Up," *RT*, August 1, 2012, http://rt.com/news/first-nato-military-facility-russia-539/.

42. Antonenko and Giegerich, "Rebooting NATO-Russia Relations," 16.

43. Joshua Kucera, "Report: Russia Spending $1.3 Billion to Arm Kyrgyzstan, Tajikistan," Bug Pit Blog, November 7, 2012, http://www.eurasianet.org/node/66152; "Russia to Arm Kyrgyzstan, Tajikistan," Uznews.net, http://www.uznews.net/news_single.php?lng=en&sub=top&cid=32&nid=21229.

44. US Department of State, "Excess Defense Articles in Afghanistan," Office of the Spokesperson, March 31, 2014, http://www.state.gov/r/pa/prs/ps/2014/03/224223.htm.

45. Arthur R. Rachwald, "A 'Reset' of NATO-Russia Relations: Real or Imaginary?" *European Security* 20, no. 1 (March 2011): 117.

46. Zamir Kabulov, quoted in Kuchins and Sanderson, *The Northern Distribution Network and Afghanistan*, 4.

47. Akhmedov and Usmanova, "Afghanistan Withdrawal."

48. Ivanov, "Proposals for the Elimination of Afghan Drug Production."

49. "NATO Could be Sued over Afghan Drug Epidemic—FSDC Director," RIA Novosti, April 5, 2012, http://en.rian.ru/russia/20120405/172629207.html.

50. Arkady Dziuba, "NATO Leaving Afghanistan: Have Transit Routes Going Through Russia Become Redundant?" Strategic Culture Foundation, May 20, 2014, http://m.strategic-culture.org/news/2014/05/20/nato-leaving-afghanistan-have-transit -routes-going-through-russia-become-redundant.html.

51. Donna Miles, "Centcom Undertakes Massive Logistical Drawdown in Afghanistan," Armed Forces Press Service, June 21, 2013, http://www.defense.gov/news/news article.aspx?id=120348.

52. H. J. Mackinder, "The Geographical Pivot of History," *Geographical Journal* 23, no. 4 (April 1904): 434.

53. US Central Command, *Commander's Posture Statement*, March 5, 2014, http:// www.centcom.mil/en/about-centcom-en/commanders-posture-statement-en.

54. John Wong, "Reviving the Ancient Silk Road: China's New Economic Diplomacy," *Straits Times*, July 9, 2014, http://www.straitstimes.com/news/opinion/invitation/ story/reviving-the-ancient-silk-road-chinas-new-economic-diplomacy-20140709.

55. US Senate Committee, *Central Asia*, 7.

20 GOING FORWARD

Lessons Learned

Gale A. Mattox

THE CONFLICT IN AFGHANISTAN required close collaboration for North Atlantic Treaty Organization (NATO) allies and coalition members for an extended period of over thirteen years, the longest war in US history. The end result has proved broadly positive in terms of cooperation but produced mixed results for the alliance generally and particularly the future of Afghanistan. The shifting mission and overall strategy of the coalition made "success" illusive and prospects for post-2014 Afghanistan unclear. Moreover, the definition of "success" varied over time and International Security Assistance Force (ISAF) coalition members—particularly smaller coalition members—did not always feel they were sufficiently considered and consulted on critical strategic issues. Addressing identified challenges for its first conflict outside Europe has strengthened NATO in many respects. Less certain is NATO's preparedness for future conflicts.

There is no question that the experience in Afghanistan should not be viewed as the end of NATO, as many scholars and policy makers warned when the conflict failed to meet initial expectations.[1] Whether there is success or failure in Afghanistan, the crisis in Ukraine has shown the need for a continued strong alliance. The collaboration of politically and culturally diverse nations (NATO members as well as nonmembers) that evolved during operations—at times bumpy, at times surprisingly smooth—set a new standard for alliance operations within a coalition from which much can be learned. However, the post-2014 road ahead will be difficult for Afghanistan, and incorporating lessons learned for NATO and its coalition allies will be challenging.

In the first-ever invocation of Article 5 following the 9/11 attacks on the US, the NATO allies offered assistance to the US. While initially the US chose not to involve the NATO alliance directly in Afghanistan and looked primarily to the UK and Afghan Northern Alliance, the allies sent a clear signal of their support with the mobilization of AWACS sent to fly the US East and West Coasts for eight months. This commitment is seldom referenced but provided a sign of allegiance with the US, their transatlantic ally. By the end of 2001 and the beginning of 2002, the NATO allies and other coalition members had responded to US requests for assistance in Afghanistan. That assistance—with only a few exceptions—remained remarkably steady from deployments initially to Kabul and then into commands outside the city with ISAF—a force that eventually numbered up to fifty nations and included NATO nonmembers/partners. (See Appendix A.)

One of the most striking challenges was the difference in national cultures, differences not only between the Afghan society and its government, but also between ISAF coalition members. Particularly in the early days, these differences were a source of friction and outright contention. The refusal, for instance, of the Germans to move south into the contested areas of Afghanistan where the Dutch, Canadians, British, and Americans were encountering heavy resistance caused considerable strain within the alliance. The friction subsided over time as the Germans moved to adjust—albeit not to move into the south—and the troops in the south were able to suppress large-scale organized resistance in the region. In other areas as well, initial lack of cooperation due to different troop deployment configurations as related by the Dutch, lack of equipment interoperability, approaches to reconstruction and development as experienced by the Canadians, and other initial incompatibilities gradually found resolution and improved overall operations. The differences in national cultures proved both a strength and a vulnerability for the alliance as the conflict persisted far longer than anticipated—or perhaps should have persisted. But the cooperation within NATO and particularly with allied coalition members has reinforced and strengthened the strategic culture and operations of the mission's effort with impact on future cooperation.

In reviewing the Afghan geopolitical framework within which the individual countries had to operate and case studies of selected countries, there were clearly areas of overlap as well as striking differences in approach, particularly given the sense of a shifting overall strategy. The enormity of challenges presented by the Afghanistan conflict was often daunting (widespread corruption; illegal drugs; lack of basic shelter, food, and overall good governance; schools limited to boys as a result of religious beliefs; and others). Ethnic-based tension made army and police training difficult. For many of the challenges, corrections were immediate and successful, while for others the differences confounded the most agile and bright minds. There are a number of general areas where the country and institutional studies revealed similarities and differences that contribute to our understanding of the coalition presence in Afghanistan and the challenges encountered. The following commentary is not a comprehensive account but rather an attempt to highlight issues and, finally, lessons from the preceding chapters critical to future conflicts.

COMMITMENTS AND CAPABILITIES

United Nations Mandate

An issue important to recognize for the future is the determining role of the United Nations. Not only was a UN Security Council Resolution in support of the Afghanistan coalition a factor in the decision to participate in Afghanistan, several allies specifically mentioned the absence of a clear UNSC (UN Security Council) resolution for the Iraq incursion to be a determining factor in the decision *not* to join the Iraq coalition in March 2003. For those coalition allies that were not members of the Atlantic Alliance, UNSC Resolution 1386 (and others on Afghanistan) laid an important legal foundation that legitimized the conflict in ways that Kosovo in retrospect had not created for a necessary broad international consensus. For some countries, such as New Zealand and Japan, the UN mandate was critical to participation.

NATO's Global Role

For NATO in 2001, the Afghanistan experience was de facto its first international operational role outside Europe. For an alliance that rejected out-of-area ops during the Cold War and debated vigorously the concept of Global NATO proposed by Ivo Daalder, later NATO Ambassador, and James Goldgeier this foray into South Asia presented a challenge.[2] The eventual coalition of NATO members and nonmembers in Afghanistan without a change to the North Atlantic Treaty Organization has moved NATO clearly into a new role that is more international, if not global.

Motivation to Join the Coalition

A striking similarity across coalition members was the allied allegiance to the US in the wake of attacks on its territory. Sentiments such as expressed by the

French newspaper *Le Monde* declaration that "We are all Americans" published September 12, 2001, coupled with a sense of the need by long-time NATO members to demonstrate support and by the newer (Baltic states) or expectant members (Georgia, Moldova, Montenegro) to demonstrate their willingness and ability to not only "consume, but produce security" as well represented the primary motivation for joining the Afghanistan coalition.[3] But the public support so strongly in favor initially to stand with the US against the terrorist threat in almost all cases diminished as the conflict dragged on, a situation that occurred as well in the US.

This was particularly true with the election of President Obama, for whom Afghanistan was a "war of necessity" and not a war of choice, as he declared at the Phoenix Convention of the Veterans of Foreign Wars in 2009.[4] For the US the Afghanistan conflict was to assure that al Qaeda was not permitted to launch an attack against the US or other countries in the future. With the disappointing long-term outcome of the 2009 surge of forces later that year, the death of Osama bin Laden in 2011, and the rise in casualties (see Appendix B), the public and allied governments' support began to wane across countries.

Threat

The primacy of allegiance to the US did not diminish the sense of threat from nonstate actors. But with the exception of the US, whose territory had come under attack in 2001, and potentially the UK as well as Spain (both of which experienced deadly terrorist attacks to their territory thereafter), overwhelmingly country studies indicated a greater motivation to demonstrate support for the US than a conviction that the presence of their forces would prohibit a national terrorist attack. For most allies, the terrorist threat was secondary and a domestic threat to be handled by domestic means. And even while the United Kingdom appeared prompted by the terrorist threat, it also expressed its allegiance to the "special relationship with the US."

ISAF Mission

The UN-mandated ISAF mission was an essential legitimizing factor in the initial stages of the national deployments and throughout the conflict. Marrying security to assistance, particularly the education of women and girls, human rights, good governance, and rule of law was a critical aspect in the decision to join and remain a part of the effort in Afghanistan, in terms of public support. The convening of the Bonn Conference in December 2001 appealed to the allied publics in a way that a call to arms without a development component would not have. Even as most of the partner nations became disillusioned with the cost and length of the deployment and public support waned, as the development aspect came under close and critical scrutiny, development remained an essential element in retaining public support and broadly the coalition.

Division of Responsibilities

The decisions at the Bonn Conference 2001 and the subsequent London Conference assigned countries responsibilities that crossed the national commands/deployments, but regretfully did not achieve the anticipated results. They included UK oversight to prevent drug cultivation, Italy to oversee judicial reform, Japan to tackle demining, Germany to train police, and the US to train the army. The failure of the European Union to assume responsibilities at that point is not addressed here but was viewed a significant shortfall in the eyes of many who had envisioned a potentially lead role for the EU and did eventually include the police. Domestic issues or budgetary concerns impeded success by and large. For the most part, this division of labor failed nationally for a wide range of reasons and in the ability to coordinate cross-nationally as well. The US decision to adopt counterinsurgency encountered similar obstacles. Each country adopted its own approach, with the result that there were nearly as many versions in approach as there were countries involved in the effort, not to mention varying expectations and execution.

Provincial Reconstruction Teams (PRTs)

The initial reaction to the concept of PRTs was positive. As envisioned, PRTs held tremendous promise. They could create that necessary link between the military who provided security; the civil servants/nongovernmental experts; the local population who were to be the beneficiary of the concept through opportunities for new schools, roads, business, and agricultural innovations; and a range of other development projects for towns/villages without their own resources to undertake such improvements. This reconstruction could be done with the knowledge that workers and the local populations were secure. In short, the PRTs could lead the way in the development and reconstruction of Afghanistan. The reality fell short of the expectations.

First, the security situation proved to be more difficult than anticipated. It required greater effort than initially expected to secure villages to the extent necessary for civilian workers and stationed forces. A thorough assessment of the shortfalls needed close review and practices adopted across countries accordingly, a practice that did not occur successfully.

Second, filling out the civilian ranks with professionals from home ministries was an unanticipated challenge. Professionals did not jump to volunteer for duty in volatile Afghanistan. For many countries such as the US, the legal terms under which civilian experts could be "ordered" to serve were unclear. While making such deployments attractive by promising high value in the promotion process helped, it did not always address the reluctance, particularly to go to a volatile area. In a number of countries, the national government simply lacked the legal competences to require state and municipalities to provide the necessary personnel.

Third, volunteers sent to PRTs were often not trained for the task. A highly educated expert in US education policy was not necessarily aware of the special needs of a Muslim student body. This training took time and the PRTs generally lacked the civilian expertise for years, depending in their absence on military personnel (also often not with specialized training).

Finally, each country took charge of its own PRT staffing that permitted cohesive national approaches and language within the team. While the multilateral PRTs prompted positive collaboration cross-nationally and with success in this respect, generally the final assessment of their impact fell short of expectations both from a civilian-military and a development perspective. Unfortunately, there appear to be few attempts to develop the effort further within the alliance for future conflicts. This is not to say that there were not successes by development initiatives within the regional commands, but the lack of metrics across coalition commands of success and the differing political expectations of capitals made it difficult to measure and learn from those successes by coalition members. Scrutiny must be given to reconcile PRT objectives and the reality on the ground. If nation-building is to be a major objective for future coalitions, greater attention is needed in this area and agreements on metrics and standards across countries established.

ISAF Coordination

ISAF coordination between the allied forces left much to be desired in many cases. On the one hand, coordination significantly improved from the earliest days to the end of the conflict. On the other hand, smaller powers felt that the division of Afghanistan deployments to specific regions made cooperation at points difficult. This was less the case for the US as command, but for the smaller countries, the potential for cross-national interaction was limited.

Beyond the difficult operational conditions, the sense of mission and common purpose reinforced the Transatlantic Alliance and forged closer relations between coalition members not part of NATO. In the meantime, several of the latter have become more closely aligned with NATO. A case in point is New Zealand, which over the deployment felt more integrated into alliance operations and identifies more recently as a "partner," strengthening the support for the 2012 NATO Chicago Summit development of a "partner" structure. This is also the case for several other participating countries in Afghanistan, such as Finland and Sweden. The underlying sense of threat in the wake of the 9/11attacks against the US promoted a sense of common mission on which the Atlantic Alliance and its partners were able to build. Unfortunately this sense of mission did not translate to all countries or persist over the thirteen-year duration of the conflict across coalition members.

The failure of countries to contribute sufficiently to the Afghanistan mission was often charged to limitations dictated by national constraints or often self-imposed limitations. While a number of countries had caveats, such as the Dutch, the Germans came under direct criticism in this respect, particularly in their refusal to contribute to the effort in the south as allied casualties mounted in the region. As a "parliamentary" army, the Bundeswehr had little room to maneuver because of self-imposed limits to meet the Bundestag constraints on military missions. Other restrictions varied from country to country, often imposed by long-standing legislation but also often by political and domestic considerations. Simple lack of equipment and training also restricted countries in their ability to contribute, as in the case of smaller countries such as the Baltic states, El Salvador, and Belgium. For others such as Jordan and Indonesia who played important roles bridging cultural divides, those cultural and religious differences also dictated limitations. Conversely, over the period of deployment, equipment and material acquisition and improvements led to more involvement by national forces.

GOING FORWARD

What lessons can be learned from the Afghanistan commitment since 2001? What pitfalls can be avoided, and where can the alliance enhance its capabilities and build on its successful efforts? What are the lessons for the alliance and for the members of the ISAF force for the future?

First, both a clear objective and an exit strategy were never well articulated. If the removal of Osama bin Laden was the objective, the Afghanistan effort cannot be termed a resounding success in terms of the continued challenge of al Qaeda and its spin-offs in Mali, Syria, Yemen, and elsewhere. But the effort was eventually able to rout Osama bin Laden and his hierarchy, the ostensible objective of the initial mission until December 2011. And a concerted persistence focused on this objective may have allowed the effort to be declared a success and permitted ISAF members to depart for home after removing the threat of al Qaeda. This was not the case as NATO objectives became moving targets and shifted over time. An exit strategy, moreover, was also difficult to discern. A recognition and clear articulation from the outset of both a counterterrorism and development/reconstruction mission may have been more controversial initially but more palatable in the longer term, particularly for the operational end phase. In any case, there must be a clear articulation of the mission and its objectives, and an exit strategy acceptable to all parties of the coalition.

Second, the issue of the shifting overall strategy for Afghanistan proved problematic and was addressed in the US chapter most pointedly. The changing strategy from a counterterrorism focus initially to reconstruction to counterinsurgency challenged policy makers and military command alike. Add to the challenge the differing national approaches to each and the difficulties are evident. Future strategy should not exclude "niche" considerations for smaller countries, but such considerations must be a part of the overall planning as well as differing country-specific national expectations. There is no easy answer except targeted allied broader collaboration.[5] The Ukraine crisis has demonstrated that even "contingency planning" rejected just a few years ago can provide a excellent tool for long-range strategy.

Moreover, whereas there appeared to be agreement that a broader regional strategy to include regional actors Pakistan, India, Iran, and the Central Asian states as well as Russia and China was necessary, cross-border issues as well as bilateral tensions hindered easy resolution to complex disputes, particularly with Pakistan. Possibly most successful in ameliorating tensions was an institutional framework for the NATO-Russia Council (NRC) together with areas of overlapping interest with the coalition, such as the reduction of drug transport into Russia and Europe. The Northern Distribution Network (NDN) also evolved out of the collaboration when the US and allies needed transportation routes in and out of country, particularly as troop withdrawals began. The Russians benefited from the fees and, even more, a sense of longer-term stability in the region and a mutual interest with NATO. Even as the Ukraine crisis evolved, discussions in these areas initially continued.

Third, while coordination with other participating organizations was not a major consideration of this volume, supporting organizations played an important role and will be increasingly significant in future operations. Not only was the UN mandate in 2001 and those thereafter critical to the legitimacy of the operation, its continuing role cannot be underemphasized, particularly the UN role during the Afghan presidential elections so vital to the future of Afghanistan. But its role on the ground in development could have been more robust and encouraged through inclusion in overall planning. Likewise, heightened cross-national collaboration by NGOs would have benefited from closer overall coordination, an across-the-board lesson learned from the Balkans as well as from Afghanistan.

Similarly, the Organization for Security and Cooperation in Europe (OSCE) set out broad areas for assistance both in 2002 and later in 2011, but its largest impact may have been in electoral and legislative improvements that it undertook beginning primarily in 2004.[6] Its monitoring of general and local elections played a legitimizing role, particularly in the contentious and critical 2014 election. Discussions for the post-2014 phase include facilitation of regional cooperation with Central Asian neighbors through confidence-building measures such as water and resource management and cross-border private sector collaboration.[7] OSCE border security training has also occurred, and there are calls for enhanced funding of its Border Management Staff College in Dushanbe.

In contrast, the European Union proved less involved than initially anticipated, to the dismay of many who expected far more. Its promises for police training and other assistance came up short as the European Policing Mission (EUPOL) only launched in 2007 with police, law enforcement, and justice experts being sent to Kabul and provincial and local levels. Other areas of assistance included rural development, governance, and health. From 2007 to 2013, the EU gave 225 million euros to the Law and Order Trust Fund. Overall aid was estimated in 2010 at 610 million euros through 2013 (not including the trust fund). In 2012 at one point aid was partially deferred subject to the implementation of promised reforms. The bottom line was, to say the least, disappointing. Coordination for a more active role will be necessary in the future if the Common Foreign and Security Policy promised at the 1992 Maastricht Summit and its subsequent Common Security and Defense Policy are to have any impact. In total, the inclusion of these organizations—the UN, OSCE, and the EU—broadly in their areas of expertise played important legitimizing roles but in many cases fell short of their potential. It is an area that needs review for the future.

Fourth, the decision of the UNSC to pass Resolution 1386 on December 20, 2001 established the International Security Assistance Force (ISAF) to reinforce the Afghan Interim Administration around Kabul. Encouraged at the Bonn Conference, it was important for the Atlantic Alliance and coalition members. It replaced a reliance on the US-led Operation Enduring Freedom with a multilateral force in which other countries felt invested.

Fifth, special operations forces played a pivotal role in Afghanistan from the outset. During the initial invasion, the combination of special forces operators, Northern Alliance militia, and coalition aircraft armed with precision guided munitions quickly overwhelmed Taliban forces and forced al Qaeda leaders into hiding. By December 2001, all major Afghan cities—Kabul, Herat, Gardez, Jalalabad, Mazar-e Sharif, and Kandahar—were under Northern Alliance control. The use of elite forces did not cease with the fall of the Taliban. Several coalition governments elected to deploy special operations troops in lieu of—or in addition to—conventional forces. Small special operations teams were often better trained and equipped and required less logistical support than larger conventional units.

This enabled political leaders to contribute military forces while maintaining a "light footprint" in Afghanistan, reducing the likelihood that they would face unwanted political criticism back home. However, this strategy did not always work. In New Zealand, the lack of transparency surrounding the deployment of its special operations forces generated a political firestorm as suspicions arose about what roles and missions their commandos were performing. The collective special operations experience of NATO member countries in Afghanistan also led to the creation of the NATO Special Operations Headquarters (NSHQ) in 2010. Located in Belgium, NSHQ was charged with developing and coordinating all NATO special operations activities, to include predeployment training of NATO special operations forces to Afghanistan and the sharing of lessons learned.

Unfortunately, not all special operations initiatives positively contributed to coalition efforts and should receive closer scrutiny. In 2002, senior US leaders initially touted the unique capability of special operations forces to build the new Afghanistan National Army (ANA), but instead of developing a long-term relationship with newly formed ANA battalions, special operations commanders lobbied Washington to transfer the responsibility of training the ANA to

US Army National Guard units that had little or no experience training foreign military forces. Even worse, while the ANA struggled to recruit enough soldiers to fill the ranks, special operations forces continued to expand numerous local militia units. ANA recruiting officers could not match the higher wages that coalition forces were paying local fighters. Potential recruits saw little incentive in joining the ANA. When President Hamid Karzai and senior coalition leaders mandated that all coalition forces work only with legitimate Afghan National Security Forces (ANSF) a few years later, US special operations forces responded by creating specialized, niche ANA units such as the ANA Commando battalions. Although these units did achieve some intermittent tactical successes, they ultimately eroded the ANA's overall combat effectiveness by sparking unnecessary bureaucratic infighting among ANA leaders and by diverting promising junior officers and sergeants from the ranks of regular units that were in desperate need of competent leadership.

Sixth, a number of countries reported lessons for their domestic decision making where the need for greater institutional coordination was sharply felt. This was particularly the case between the defense/foreign/development ministries as each nation attempted to fashion reconstruction efforts through the PRTs and private contractors and with NGOs. In the US, other than defense, there is no precedent to require government employees to be sent internationally into conflict. In a number of countries, the police are state or local workers and also not subject to deployment out of the country. Furthermore, the training had not caught up with the demand of the efforts in Afghanistan for schools, roads, new judicial instruments, good governance, and many other structures needed in the country. Consequently, civilian assistance for the PRTs often lagged behind for either lack of "volunteers" or the necessary military-civilian coordination at home or in country. The nature of the PRTs differed from region to region, some with civilian leadership, others with military. The different emphasis on mission rendered very different results. This is clearly an area for NATO introspection and further work, both between allied countries within NATO and with partners outside NATO. Domestic coordination between home ministries within coalition member states also proved a challenge.

Seventh, a positive aspect of operations was highly increased use of multilateral forces, particularly in concert with smaller nations. The US/UK/Jordanian collaboration proved successful, as did the Norwegian/German and Baltic states' air control and intelligence expertise. Mongolian and El Salvadoran forces garnered high marks despite their small numbers for their effectiveness. The multinational crew who flew AWACS along the East and West Coasts after 9/11 until spring 2002 were highly effective and a potential model in future scenarios.

Eighth, a factor mentioned for a number of countries was the conflict in Iraq. The UK public conflated Iraq and Afghanistan with a negative impact for the Afghan mission, particularly in terms of public opinion. For the Germans who did not participate in Iraq, the need to show support for the US at the time of the Iraq conflict meant an increase in troops in Afghanistan as well as a larger role in Bosnia.[8] For Japan, the suspected diversion of fuel to Iraq challenged the government's tanker support in Afghanistan. For the US, Iraq clearly diverted resources and the most highly trained troops as well as political capital and focus. It diverted US attention away from South Asia to the Middle East with repercussions for a broader, much-needed South Asian regional strategy and comprehensive vision.

Ninth, a major issue mentioned in a number of interviews but interestingly a peripheral issue at best in the chapters may prove to be a longer-term legacy for Afghanistan—the corruption and deficit of accountability for the resources expended over thirteen-plus years. While the global financial situation in 2001 was stable to very good across countries, it was followed by an economic nose-dive by many of the countries participating in Afghanistan in 2008–2009. In the midst of a conflict in a less developed country, accountability for cash doled out was difficult from the Afghan side but even less forgiving on the side of the coalition members. While recognized earlier in the conflict, more attention appears to have been directed at the issue of corruption with the assignment of Major General H. R. McMaster to the 2010 Joint Anti-Corruption Task Force (CJIATF-Shafafiyat) at ISAF Headquarters as the issue reached a disturbing magnitude.

In 2012 the appointment of US Special Inspector General for Afghanistan Reconstruction (SIGAR) John Sopko brought the degree of the corruption and particularly accountability into greater focus for the US.[9] While some of the projects demonstrated the lack of any comprehensive long-term planning (e.g., a $34 million office building that will never be used and will possibly be torn down because the Afghans will not have the resources to maintain it), other expenditures undermined the very mission of ISAF; for example, bringing literacy to the Afghan army to improve their effectiveness. As ISAF troops departed, only 50 percent of the army had become literate after a $200 million expenditure.[10] In another instance a $600,000 hospital with no well and not enough electricity for four lightbulbs remained without funding.[11] There was no lack of green-shaded accountants overseeing the budgets of individual coalition countries, but an important lesson for future NATO deployments should be a SIGAR-like approach on the part of NATO to ensure greater effective use of public funds.

Tenth is the shortfall in the capabilities issue, which is arguably the most important as year after year the NATO allies fall short of promised increases in defense budgets. This presents a tremendous challenge not just for Afghanistan but for the ability of the alliance to respond to threats in a number of theaters. In fact, with the participation of non-NATO countries, the shortfall in capabilities moves an ever-greater responsibility to the US, one that the US public may not continue to support into the future unless redressed. In fact, the issue of diminishing NATO member defense budgets was the focus of Defense Secretary Robert Gates' final speech in Brussels as he left office in 2011.[12] The issue dates as far back as the earliest days of the alliance, where in 1979 NATO set a desired 3 percent increase of GDP target for defense spending with scant success; today's 2 percent target agreed at the 2014 Wales summit is still unlikely to be met, not to mention the 20 percent target over ten years for major programs.[13] Afghanistan should have demonstrated the importance of high-value capabilities for deployment to protect European security as posed by the unexpected 9/11 attacks, as well as the involvement in Libya and in other contingencies. In 2012, the US spent 4.4 percent of GDP compared to 2.5 percent by the UK and 2.3 percent by France, with all other countries dropping below the goal (Germany 1.4 percent, Italy 1.7 percent, and even less for many other countries). While this data does not weigh quality, in the face of the Ukrainian crisis, Russia's defense budget share of GDP equaled that of the US in 2012 at 4.4 percent (and increasing).[14] The need to demonstrate commitment to Alliance defense may be expected to increase, not decrease, as the mission in Afghanistan comes to an end and the shortfall in meeting this NATO objective of 2 percent GDP by every member remains critical.

Finally, attention to good governance will need to be addressed in the future. The inertia for change in the widespread corruption and cronyism of a Karzai government permitted to govern far longer than prudent should provide a lesson—especially in light of his refusal to sign a Bilateral Security Agreement and Status of Forces Agreement (SOFA). The replacement of the Karzai regime by the new Ghani government should resolve some of the obstacles to governance. But the potential hurdles cannot be overestimated. The lack of clear distinctions at this point between the role of President Ashraf Ghani and Chief Executive Abdullah Abdullah poses potentially huge hurdles to be surmounted. The role of Vice President Abdul Rashid Dostum in light of the warlords chapter also may create a challenge. The divisions between their supporters over the 2014 election have created substantial tensions that will require sustained efforts to reconcile, not to mention the necessary continued training of the ANA and ANP that will be crucial to any long-term stability. While all this is not impossible, it will require determined policies by the remaining Resolute Support coalition members—in both political, on-the-ground, and visible presence and financial contributions.

In sum, participation in Afghanistan and ISAF was an opportunity for fifty countries to rally around the US following the tragic terrorist attack in 2001. It offered expanded cooperation between NATO members and nonmembers in a coalition that demonstrated a commitment to the US, the first time Article 5 has been invoked by NATO since its founding. Overwhelmingly, it was this allegiance to the US that prompted broad participation and held countries' commitment for over a decade. For most of the ISAF nations, the objective to counter and defeat al Qaeda took second place to this allegiance, a factor particularly evidenced by the smaller countries. Also true for many of the countries was the conviction that terrorism is best countered domestically rather than by the military and that the distant involvement potentially encouraged terrorist attacks on the homeland; for example, Spanish and UK sentiment reflected this concern after attacks on their territory, causing, in the case of Spain, the fall of the government.

In addition, a number of countries deployed with ISAF primarily to assist Afghanistan in development—building schools, educating women, constructing roads, promoting good governance, and other development projects. This mission was vital to continued domestic support for ISAF deployments projects but is not one with which NATO is particularly comfortable or even well-prepared to take on. A review of lessons learned for the future will be important. While there was not a comprehensive single-focused objective and strategy for the deployment in Afghanistan, the multifaceted objectives of counterterrorism, counterinsurgency, and development each had its appeal for government elites and/or the public and strikingly avoided large public demonstrations in coalition countries that have accompanied other conflicts, despite lack of support on the part of the public for military operations per se in South Asia.

The capabilities the member countries brought to the effort varied widely—from Baltic air traffic controllers and intelligence experts to more internationally experienced troops such as the French, with training and equipment appropriate to the terrain and operations. More often, though, adjustments had to be made and/or assistance had to be rendered, usually in the form of partnering smaller forces with larger ones, as in the case of the Norwegians with the Germans, New Zealand with the Australians, or El Salvador with the US. The participation of the UAE, Jordan, and Malaysia played a critical role in the building of mosques and other institutions that crossed the cultural/religious divide. These pairings in the longer term may be expected to reinforce countries' capabilities and effectiveness. The innovations necessary for ground operations have been substantial, not only in terms of force capabilities, even uniforms and night equipment, but also in medical advances on the field and in the processing of the wounded. The lessons of the latter in the face of post-traumatic stress disorder (PTSD) in most of the participating states continued to need close collaboration on appropriate approaches. Many of these advances have already become incorporated into medical procedures in home countries.

The longest conflict in US history, Afghanistan represented for most coalition nations a more demanding responsibility than had been encountered since WWII. The security situation required skills not previously developed and engaged many of the post-Soviet emerging democracies in challenges not envisioned when they had begun the road to NATO membership, which many achieved in 2004 and attributed to their contribution, such as Romania and Bulgaria. Even for longer-term members, there was a substantial increase in operational experience. Restrictions or caveats by participating countries abated over the time of deployments by and large, but will not disappear and continue to need addressing. For the historically reluctant Germans, a discussion has begun on a greater international role, and it has assumed Deputy Command for the post-2014 Resolute Support. The presence of a Japanese tanker and its withdrawal precipitated an ongoing national debate over the Japanese self-defense force. Afghanistan followed by the even more directly challenging Ukraine crisis has led to discussions in Sweden and Finland about the benefits of NATO membership. More broadly, a number of ISAF coalition members outside Europe have become part of the NATO "partners across the globe" initiative.

As the Afghanistan deployments wound down and moved at the end of 2014 to a post-conflict phase where the focus of the final mission Resolute Support became training, advice, and assistance, collaboration among participating coalition members has continued to be critical in this end phase of the conflict. With attention turned to the Ukrainian crisis, the "end of NATO" debate has abated, and the alliance continues to be the focus of this next crisis. The hope is that with the pressure of that crisis, the Transatlantic Alliance will not neglect its need to absorb and act on the lessons from the 2001–2014 Afghanistan commitment and the coalition it built.

The end result of NATO's presence in Afghanistan for the country itself remains unclear as the Afghans assume primary responsibility for security of their territory and populations. Ethnic tensions and geopolitical divisions remain a major challenge for the country, and the ability of the ANSF to counter internal and external forces may become overwhelming as they have many times in the past. The lessons of coalition suggest a strengthened NATO alliance if its lessons are learned and absorbed operationally as well as politically. This is true for the patterns of cooperation and collaboration developed between NATO members, as well as between and among coalition nonmembers of NATO.

NOTES

This chapter reflects solely the views of the author and does not reflect any institutional or government affiliation of the author. The Institute for National Security Studies graciously provided the travel support to undertake the research for this chapter.

1. As Andrew Bacevich commented, "To think of NATO as a great alliance makes about as much sense as thinking of Pittsburgh as the Steel City or of Detroit as the car capital of the world. It's sheer nostalgia. It's time to jettison the capital letters: NATO has become nato." *Los Angeles Times*, February 11, 2008, http://articles.latimes.com/2008/feb/11/opinion/oe-bacevich11. See also discussions of this debate in David Auerswald and Stephen Saideman, *NATO in Afghanistan: Fighting Together, Fighting Alone* (Princeton, NJ: Princeton University Press, 2014), and Sten Rynning, *NATO in Afghanistan: The Liberal Disconnect* (Stanford, CA: Stanford University Press, 2012). See Chapter 1 on the debate.

2. Ivo Daalder and James Goldgeier, "Global NATO?" *Foreign Affairs* (September 2006): 105–113.

3. The concept that aspirants for NATO membership be both "consumers and producers of security" was often voiced in the 1990s in discussions with the emerging democracies desiring NATO admittance.

4. President Barack Obama, Remarks to Veterans of Foreign Wars Convention, Phoenix, Arizona, August 17, 2009, http://www.whitehouse.gov/the-press-office/remarks -president-veterans-foreign-wars-convention.

5. The debate with respect to the Baltics several years ago should no longer deter such long-term planning after the Ukrainian crisis.

6. Organization for Security and Co-operation in Europe, Ministerial Council, Decision No. 4/11: Strengthening OSCE Engagement with Afghanistan, MC(18) Journal No. 2, Agenda item 8, Vilnius, December 7, 2011.

7. OSCE, "Challenges Linked to Afghanistan after 2014 Is Focus of OSCE Meeting in Vienna," October 9, 2013, http://www.osce.org/pc/106844.

8. Dieter Dettke, *Germany Says No: The Iraq War and the Future of German Foreign and Security Policy* (Baltimore: Johns Hopkins University Press, 2009). See his discussion of the range of activities undertaken by the Germans to assist the US while refusing boots on the ground or other participation, including frigate deployments to the Horn of Africa and CW units in Kuwait ready to disarm potential chemical weapons (not used).

9. Rajiv Chandrasekaran, "A Brand-New Military Headquarters in Afghanistan. And Nobody to Use It," *Washington Post*, July 9, 2013, http://www.washingtonpost.com/ world/national-security/a-brand-new-us-military-headquarters-in-afghanistan-and -nobody-to-use-it/2013/07/09/2bb73728-e8cd-11e2-a301-ea5a8116d211_story.html.

10. Josh Rogin, "After $200 Million, Afghan Soldiers Still Can't Read, *Daily Beast*, January 28, 2014, http://www.thedailybeast.com/articles/2014/01/28/after-200-million -afghan-soldiers-still-can-t-read.html.

11. Hayes Brown. "US Paid Contractor in Full for Afghan Hospital in Danger of Collapse," *Think Progress*, January 29, 2014, http://thinkprogress.org/world/2014/01/ 29/3220191/report-paid-contractor-afghan-hospital-danger-collapse/. Further incidents may be found on the SIGAR web site, https://www.sigar.mil/.

12. Robert Gates, "The Security and Defense Agenda (Future of NATO)," June 10, 2011, Brussels, http://www.defense.gov/speeches/speech.aspx?speechid=1581.

13. NATO Wales Summit Declaration, para. 14, September 5, 2014, http://www.nato .int/cps/en/natohq/official_texts_112964.htm.

14. Patterson Clark, "Spending on the Military, 1988–2012," *Washington Post*, March 28, 2014, 8. Statistics are drawn from the Stockholm International Peace Research Institute.

Appendixes

APPENDIX A

International Security Assistance Force Contributing Nations, 2001–2014

Albania	Republic of Korea
Armenia	Latvia
Australia	Lithuania
Austria	Luxembourg
Azerbaijan	Macedonia (Former Yugoslav Republic of)
Bahrain	Malaysia
Belgium	Mongolia
Bosnia-Herzegovina	Montenegro
Bulgaria	Netherlands
Canada	New Zealand
Croatia	Norway
Czech Republic	Poland
Denmark	Portugal
El Salvador	Romania
Estonia	Singapore
Finland	Slovakia
France	Slovenia
Georgia	Spain
Germany	Sweden
Greece	Tonga
Hungary	Turkey
Iceland	Ukraine
Ireland	United Arab Emirates
Italy	United Kingdom
Jordan	United States

NOTE: Current as of September 15, 2014.

APPENDIX B
Coalition Fatalities in Afghanistan, 2001–2014

Country	Size of population[a]	Size of active armed forces[b]	Number of fatalities[c]	Number of active military troops per fatality	Number of residents per fatality
Albania	3,002,859	14,250	1	14,250	3,002,859
Australia	22,015,576	57,050	41	1,391	536,965
Belgium	10,438,353	32,650	1	32,650	10,438,353
Canada	34,300,083	66,000	162	407	211,728
Czech Republic	10,177,300	23,650	10	2,365	1,017,730
Denmark	5,543,453	16,450	43	383	128,918
Estonia	1,274,709	5,750	9	639	141,634
Finland	5,262,930	22,200	2	11,100	2,631,465
France	65,630,692	228,850	89	2,571	737,424
Georgia	4,570,934	20,650	27	765	169,294
Germany	81,305,856	196,000	54	3,630	1,505,664
Hungary	9,958,453	26,500	7	3,786	1,422,636
Italy	61,261,254	181,450	48	3,780	1,276,276
Jordan	6,508,887	100,500	3	33,500	2,169,629
Latvia	2,191,580	5,350	3	1,783	730,527
Lithuania	3,525,761	11,800	1	11,800	3,525,761
Netherlands	16,730,632	37,400	25	1,496	669,225
New Zealand	4,327,944	8,550	11	777	393,449
Norway	4,707,270	24,450	10	2,445	470,727
Poland	38,415,284	96,000	40	2,400	960,382
Portugal	10,781,459	42,600	2	21,300	5,390,730

Country	Size of population[a]	Size of active armed forces[b]	Number of fatalities[c]	Number of active military troops per fatality	Number of residents per fatality
Romania	21,848,504	71,400	21	3,400	1,040,405
Slovakia	5,483,088	15,850	3	5,283	1,827,696
South Korea	48,860,500	655,000	1	655,000	48,860,500
Spain	47,042,984	135,500	34	3,985	1,383,617
Sweden	9,103,788	20,500	5	4,100	1,820,758
Turkey	79,749,461	510,600	14	36,471	5,696,390
United Kingdom	63,047,162	165,650	453	381	139,177
United States	313,847,465	1,520,100	2,349	647	133,609

NOTE: Current as of September 15, 2014.

[a]*The Military Balance 2013* (London: Routledge, 2013).

[b]Ibid.

[c]Data concerning the number of coalition troops killed or wounded in action were compiled from multiple government, nongovernment, and media sources.

CONTRIBUTORS

Ariel I. Ahram is an Assistant Professor at Virginia Tech's School of Public and International Affairs, Alexandria, Virginia. He was previously an assistant professor and Middle East studies coordinator at the University of Oklahoma. He is the author of *Proxy Warriors: The Rise and Fall of State Sponsored Militias* (2011) and has written widely on issues of international and human security in the Middle East. He earned a Ph.D. in government and an M.A. in Arab studies from Georgetown University.

Robert Ayson is Professor of Strategic Studies at Victoria University, Wellington, New Zealand. He has also held academic positions with the Australian National University, Massey University, and the University of Waikato and official positions in New Zealand with what is now the National Assessments Bureau and the Foreign Affairs, Defence and Trade select committee. Ayson completed his Ph.D. in war studies at King's College London as a Commonwealth Scholar and his M.A. at ANU as a New Zealand Defence Freyberg Scholar. He is Honorary Professor at New Zealand Defence Force Command and Staff College and author of *Thomas Schelling and the Nuclear Age* (2004) and *Hedley Bull and the Accommodation of Power* (2012).

Daniel P. Brown is a Visiting Assistant Professor of Political Science at the University of Arkansas, studying comparative politics and international relations, with a specialization in the Middle East and North Africa. He holds an M.A. in political science and Middle East studies from the University of Arkansas and is completing his Ph.D. at the University of Oklahoma. His dissertation focuses on the "monarchical advantage" and the effects of regime type on popular mobilization in the Arab Spring, comparing Tunisia and Jordan. Other projects examine the effects of international norms and international law compliance in the Israeli-Palestinian conflict. His other research interests include Levantine politics, the Israeli-Palestinian conflict, authoritarian regimes and regime dynamics, revolution, contentious politics, nationalism and ethnic politics, international law, norms, and regimes.

Rebecca Bill Chavez is Professor of Political Science at the US Naval Academy. She spent 2009 at the Pentagon, where she served as Principal Strategic Advisor on Western Hemisphere Affairs for OSD Policy, and she has served on the US Southern Command Advisory Board since 2007. Professor Chavez received her Ph.D. in political science from Stanford University and her A.B. in international and public policy from Princeton University. She is the author of *The Rule of Law in Nascent Democracies: Judicial Politics in Argentina* (2004). Her work has appeared in *Joint Forces Quarterly*, *Comparative Politics*, *The Journal of Latin American Studies*, and *Latin American Politics and Society*.

Howard G. Coombs is an Assistant Professor at the Royal Military College of Canada as well as a Canadian Army Reserve Officer. He received his Ph.D. in military history from Queen's University in Kingston, Ontario, and is a graduate of the US Army Command and General Staff College in addition to the US Army School of Advanced Military Studies. Coombs first served in Kabul in 2004 as an Army Reservist and a strategic planner for the Commander International Security Assistance Forces. During 2010–2011 he deployed to Kandahar with Canada's Joint Task Force Afghanistan as a civilian advisor to the Task Force Commander.

Andrew M. Dorman is Professor of International Security at King's College, London, and an Associate Fellow at the Royal Institute of International Affairs, Chatham House. His research focuses on the interaction of strategy and policy utilizing the case studies of British defense and security policy and European security. His recent books include co-editing (with J. Kaufman) *Providing for National Security: A Comparative Analysis & The Future of Transatlantic Relations: Perceptions, Policy and Practice* (2011, 2014) and *Blair's Successful War: British Military Intervention in Sierra Leone* (2009).

Nicolas Fescharek is with APPRO (Afghanistan Public Policy Research Organization) in Kabul, Afghanistan. He is a Ph.D. candidate at CERI (Centre d'études et de recherches internationales de Sciences Po) in Paris. He studied at the universities of Tübingen and Aix-en-Provence, and graduated from the master's program in international security at Sciences Po Paris. His Ph.D. thesis focuses on European contributions to security sector reform in Afghanistan and contributes to the debate around a "European strategy."

Stephen M. Grenier is a career active-duty US Army Special Forces officer currently serving as the Director for Canadian Affairs in the Office of the Under Secretary of Defense for Policy. He has participated in operations in thirty-two countries throughout Africa, Europe, and Asia, including eight combat tours to Afghanistan. Grenier is an Adjunct Professor of International Security at Johns Hopkins University, an Adjunct Professor of American Politics at George Washington University, and the current president of the Committee for the Analysis of Military Operations and Strategy (CAMOS), an affiliated group of both the American Political Science Association and the International Studies Association. He is a member of the International Institute for Strategic Studies and a life member of the Council on Foreign Relations.

Timothy D. Hoyt is Professor of Strategy and Policy and John Nicholas Brown Chair of Counterterrorism Studies at the US Naval War College, where he co-founded the Indian Ocean Studies Group. Prior to NWC, Hoyt taught at the Security Studies Program at Georgetown University, specializing in strategy, war in the developing world, and South Asian security. He has authored *Military Industries and Regional Defense Policy: India, Iraq and Israel* (2006) and over forty articles and chapters on topics including the war on terrorism in South Asia, the impact of culture on military doctrine and strategy, military innovation and warfare in the developing world, US-Pakistan relations, the impact of nuclear weapons on South Asia crises, and the strategic effectiveness of terrorism.

Aaron P. Jackson is Doctrine Desk Officer at the Australian Defence Force Joint Doctrine Centre. In addition to this civilian appointment he has served over twelve years in the Australian Army Reserve, including on operations in Timor Leste. He is the author of several publications about military strategy, doctrine and operational art, including *The Roots of Military Doctrine: Change and Continuity in Understanding the Practise of Warfare* (2013) and *Doctrine, Strategy and Military Culture: Military-Strategic Doctrine Development in Australia, Canada and New Zealand, 1987–2007* (2013).

Maryanne Kelton is a Senior Lecturer in International Relations and Deputy Director of the Centre for United States and Asia Policy Studies at Flinders University in South Australia. Her research interests include alliance relations specializing in security and economy, Australian foreign policy, and regional maritime security and cooperation. She is author of *More Than an Ally? Contemporary Australia-US Relations* (2008) and *New Depths: The Collins Class Submarine Project* (2005). She is also author of in-person simulations for the tertiary and not-for-profit sector.

Rem Korteweg is a senior research fellow at the Centre for European Reform (CER), London, focusing on European diplomatic, defense, and security issues. Previously he worked at The Hague Center for Strategic Studies (HCSS). He has written on the future of the transatlantic alliance, military transformation, East Asian security, and economic diplomacy. His Ph.D. research focused on the influence of strategic cultures on defense transformation in Germany, the Netherlands, and the US. In 2006–2007 he was a Fulbright scholar at the Johns Hopkins–SAIS Center for Transatlantic Relations. Korteweg has a Ph.D. in international relations from Leiden University, and an M.A. in the history of international relations from Utrecht University.

Romain Malejacq is an Assistant Professor at Radboud University Nijmegen, Centre for International Conflict Analysis and Management. He obtained a dual Ph.D. in political science from Sciences Po, Paris, and Northwestern University and was a visiting scholar at the Harriman Institute, Columbia University. His fieldwork in Afghanistan has been supported by the French Ministry of Foreign Affairs and the Institut des Hautes Etudes de Défense Nationale, among others. His research interests lie in state-building, violence, and nonstate armed actors. He also maintains a blog on Afghan politics (www .afghanopoly.com).

Gale A. Mattox is a Professor of Political Science, US Naval Academy; Adjunct Professor, Graduate Security Studies Georgetown University; former Chair of the International Security and Arms Control Section, American Political Science Association; Director, Foreign/Domestic Policies, American Institute for Contemporary German Studies, Johns Hopkins University. She was a Distinguished Fulbright Research Chair in the Netherlands and Bosch Fellow in Germany. She served on the US State Department Policy Planning Staff as well as in the Office of Strategic and Theater Nuclear Policy; as President of Women in International Security; as Vice President of the International Studies Association; and as a NATO Research Fellow. She has served on boards including Marshall Center, Germany, and Forum for Security Studies, Swedish National Defense University. Publications include seven books and over twenty-five chapters/articles on national security policy, European security, Germany, arms control, and women and security policy.

Renanah Miles served as a program analyst in the Office of the Deputy Chief Management Officer, US Department of Defense, and worked to optimize defense business operations with a focus on identifying and addressing combatant command logistics requirements. Miles worked for a strategic communications firm, The Rendon Group, as an Arabic media analyst. From 2007 to 2008, she deployed to Iraq providing communications support to the Multi-National Division–Center headquarters in Baghdad. Her work has been featured in *Political Science Quarterly*, *The National Interest*, and *PRISM*, among others. She holds an M.A. in security studies from Georgetown University and is now a Ph.D. student in political science at Columbia University.

John A. Nagl is the ninth Headmaster of The Haverford School in Haverford, Pennsylvania, member of the Board of Advisors at the Center for a New American Security, and previously President of CNAS. He was the Minerva Research Fellow at the US Naval Academy; a member of the Defense Policy Board; and a Visiting Professor in the War Studies Department at Kings College in London. A West Point graduate, he served in both wars in Iraq. Nagl taught national security studies at West Point and Georgetown University. He earned his Master of the Military Arts and Sciences Degree from the US Army Command and General Staff College and his doctorate from Oxford University as a Rhodes Scholar. Nagl is the author of *Learning to Eat Soup with a Knife:*

Counterinsurgency Lessons from Malaya and Vietnam (2002) and was on the writing team that produced the US Army/Marine Corps Counterinsurgency Field Manual.

Jack J. Porter is Associate Professor in the Department of Political Science at The Citadel, where he teaches courses on international relations and US national security policy. His current research interests include civil-military relations in the transition to democracy in Afghanistan, counterinsurgency strategies and power, and the diffusion of Western civil-military relations. He received a master's degree in international affairs from Columbia University and an M.A. and Ph.D. from the University of California, Berkeley. Dr. Porter was a Presidential Management Intern in the Office of the Secretary of Defense.

Takamichi Takahashi, CAPT JMSDF, is Dean of the Operational Art and Design Studies Department at JMSDF Command and Staff College. He graduated from the National Defense Academy in 1982; earned his M.A. in area studies at Tsukuba University in 1995; attended the Naval Command College at the US Naval War College in Newport, Rhode Island; researched as a visiting fellow for the Stimson Center in Washington, D.C.; and taught in the Political Science Department of the US Naval Academy from 2008 to 2011. As a naval officer, he served as the commanding officer of JS *Shimayuki* (DD133); as Chief of Plans and Policy Section of the Plans and Programs Division, Maritime Staff Office; as Director of Plans and Operation and Commander in Chief of the Self-Defense Fleet; and as Dean of the Strategic Studies Department, Maritime Command and Staff College.

Marybeth P. Ulrich is a Professor of Government in the Department of National Security and Strategy at the US Army War College. Her research is focused on strategic studies, especially civil-military relations, European security, and national security democratization. Her publications include *Democratizing Communist Militaries: The Cases of the Czech and Russian Armed Forces* (1999). She retired from the Air Force Reserve as a colonel and served as the reserve air attaché to the Russian Federation, the Czech Republic, and Greece. She received her Ph.D. in political science from the University of Illinois and her B.S. degree from the US Air Force Academy, where she was a Distinguished Graduate in the Class of 1984.

Richard Weitz is Senior Fellow and Director of the Center for Political-Military Analysis at Hudson Institute. His current research includes regional security developments relating to Europe, Eurasia, and East Asia as well as US foreign, defense, and homeland security policies. Dr. Weitz is also an expert at Wikistrat and a nonresident Senior Fellow at the Center for a New American Security, where he contributes to various defense projects. Dr. Weitz has published or edited several books and monographs and written numerous articles.

S. Rebecca Zimmerman is a doctoral candidate in strategic studies at Johns Hopkins University School of Advanced International Studies (SAIS), writing on US military institutions in Afghanistan, and is adjunct staff at RAND. She is a specialist in field research, and her work focuses on Afghanistan/Southeast Asia, researching issues of governance, rule of law, and security force development. In numerous deployments to Afghanistan she has conducted extensive interviews of Afghan National Police and Army, assisted with implementation of the Special Forces Village Stability Operations (VSO) program, and studied security force assistance programs.

INDEX

Page numbers followed by "f" or "t" indicate material in figures or tables.